WAR AND TECHNOLOGY

WAR
AND
TECHNOLOGY

JEREMY BLACK

INDIANA UNIVERSITY PRESS   *Bloomington & Indianapolis*

This book is a publication of

Indiana University Press
Office of Scholarly Publishing
Herman B Wells Library 350
1320 East 10th Street
Bloomington, Indiana 47405 USA

iupress.indiana.edu

Telephone orders   800-842-6796
Fax orders   812-855-7931

☉ The paper used in this publication
meets the minimum requirements of
the American National Standard for
Information Sciences—Permanence
of Paper for Printed Library Materials,
ANSI Z39.48-1992.

Manufactured in the
United States of America

Library of Congress Cataloging-in-
Publication Data

Black, Jeremy, [date-]
    War and technology / Jeremy Black.
       pages cm
    Includes bibliographical references and
index.
    ISBN 978-0-253-00984-5 (cloth : alk.
paper) — ISBN 978-0-253-00989-0
(e-book) 1. Military weapons—History.
2. Military art and science—History. 3.
Military art and science—Technological
innovations—History. I. Title.
    U800.B573 2013
    355'.07—dc23

                                    2013005851

1 2 3 4 5 18 17 16 15 14 13

FOR

Janice & Peter Kay

Contents

Preface

The plans of the Bruce-Partington submarine. . . . Its importance can
hardly be exaggerated. It has been the most jealously guarded of all
government secrets. You may take it from me that naval warfare becomes
impossible within the radius of a Bruce-Partington operation. . . . The plans
are exceedingly intricate, comprising some thirty separate patents, each
essential to the working of the whole.

—*Mycroft Holmes to his brother Sherlock Holmes in*
  The Bruce-Partington Plans

The Martian tripods that stalked the New Jersey flatlands in 1938 seemed
all too deadly to American radio audiences in Orson Welles's gripping,
doom-laden production of H. G. Wells's novel *The War of the Worlds*
(1898). With their death rays, the tripods slaughtered troops on the
ground and brought down attacking aircraft. These tripods also testified to the strong grasp of technology on the modern imagination and
its ability to link power and the future. The mechanization of war was
a topic discussed since at least the 1870s, although at that time, little of
the technology of "modern" war had been invented. While there were
iron warships, the diesel engine (and turbine crucial to the *Dreadnought*
battleships) had yet to be invented, as had the petrol engine.

As a reminder of the pace of technological innovation, the situation
was very different by 1913, a century ago. Manned, powered flight, which
had begun in 1903, was now a reality converted to military purposes.
In 1913, in a series of articles for the *Daily Mail,* London's most popular
daily newspaper, Wells predicted that science and engineering would
be crucial in winning the next war, which he claimed would be more
mechanized than any conflict hitherto, putting a premium on "the best
brains." A focus on how the new and the soon-to-be-new would trans-

form the present into a very different future became powerful in Western culture and also with modernizers elsewhere,[1] and it has since been a dominant theme in the discussion of war and technology.

Despite the searing experience for the United States of the Vietnam War and other more recent conflicts, it still appears self-evident to many today that the side with the best weapons is likely to triumph, and that it has always been so. The widespread conviction of the relationship between technology and fighting abilities ensures that technology frequently becomes the explanation for battlefield success and thus victory in war. This account, however, is flawed. Not only does victory not necessarily flow from battlefield success but there are many elements involved in victory.

Moreover, linked to the latter, there has long been a cultural predisposition, in Western as well as non-Western societies, to believe that other factors, notably fighting quality and morale, are more important, and this view is well founded. While advanced weaponry may provide the recipe for success, and in both symmetrical and asymmetrical warfare—conflict between similar and dissimilar military forces, respectively—this weaponry does not automatically confer success. The fighting quality and determination of fighters play an opposite role, while technology can be countered with tactics.

Technology is, and has been, variously defined and glossed, but it is most appropriate to see it as a relationship between materials and human ingenuity. As such, technology is the application of a process (using science knowingly or otherwise) to a raw material or materials so as to fabricate an object that could not otherwise be made from those materials. By extension, it is the product of that process. The word tends to be used in the associated form rather than in the first sense, especially when the product is a device that does something when energy is supplied to it. Thus, "technology" becomes such a device. This sort of definition applies equally well to swords as to tanks.

Technological advance is closely tied to innovation and invention, the process as well as the event. Technology, moreover, is almost everything we touch, from bread to televisions, being very much a part of the evolution of humankind. Thus, technology does not necessarily lead to a perfect solution to a problem; rather it is another step along. As such, the location of technology in industrial culture, which was so important to the effectiveness of both, depended (and depends) in part on broader patterns of social, economic, and technological development, as well as on the character of particular conjunctures.

In addition, technology is not an independent variable, and assessments of its potency must be contextualized in terms of the practicalities and ideas of the period, contexts that are related but also different. In particular, alongside the assumption of clear-cut advances in effectiveness, and thus potential, through scientific development and technological change, come issues of application and cost. These issues are linked to the possibility of implementing technological advances and to the use to which they are put. Moreover, it is important to consider the multi-faceted, even ambiguous, nature of effectiveness and the varied limitations of technology. The latter arise through the circumstances of conflict but also reflect the technical constraints affecting technological change. Furthermore, related to such constraints, the lack of technical understanding of such change is a major issue.

The understanding and use of the term "technology" varies. Engineers and historians are apt to give different answers: part of the problem is perspective, part is perception, but part is also understanding.[2] There is a misleading tendency to treat technology as simple or to regard a technical understanding of weapons and other machines as unnecessary. Instead, it is important to understand precisely how weapons function.[3]

The preference among users and commentators for a "magic bullet" technology ensures that the generally incremental character of technological advances and applications is underrated. This preference leads to and stems from a tendency to focus on one technology or weapon. This tendency is at the expense, first, of the cumulative nature of advances and application, and, secondly, of the related extent to which weapons systems bring these advances and applications together and need to be considered from tactical, operational, and strategic perspectives.

For example, the Indian Ocean saw Western naval power do well in large part due to cumulative advantages. This was true of the Portuguese in the sixteenth century and, subsequently, of the English in the seventeenth to twentieth centuries. Western ships in the sixteenth to eighteenth centuries had a superior armament but also benefited from their use of information technology, notably the telescope and the compass, which were rarely used on Indian vessels, as well as better maps and cartographic techniques, for example, measurement by degrees. As a result, the Portuguese and English ships were able to sail new routes that were generally not followed by Indian vessels.[4]

This book is designed as a sequel and natural follow-up to my *War and the Cultural Turn* (2011). As such, I seek to complement that book by considering the place of technology in the analysis of military capability and warfare, notably given the cultural direction of much recent discussion. The two books are designed to be read separately but can also be profitably read together. Sections of this new book also develop passages from my *Rethinking Military History* (2004) and *Tools of War* (2007).

This book also represents an attempt to reexamine the issue of technology in light of the crisis for theories of the RMA (Revolution in Military Affairs) and Military Transformation created by the conflicts of the 2000s and early 2010s. As this book will show, technology still has a major part to play but is scarcely either an independent variable or a factor operating without major limitations. These limitations include the contrast between output in the form of military activity, in which technology, indeed, plays a key role, and, on the other hand, outcome in the shape of obtaining end results. The latter is not controlled by the output, and technological proficiency does not determine end results. As a consequence, the ability of technology to ensure strategic outcomes is limited.[5]

Complicating the situation, this book will follow my cultural study in indicating the malleability and porosity of the term "technology" and the number of potential uses that are relevant. Technology is so pervasive that it makes it harder to focus the discussion than with such "angles" on warfare as command or logistics. As with the use of the term "culture," this range of usage may be frustrating in analytical terms but is also an aspect of the significance of the issue while, simultaneously, underlining its importance for public discussion of warfare. Moreover, the extent to which there are very few things to say on this topic that hold up across time and space helps explain the lack of strong and broad arguments about the subject. As a result, there is the danger of being caught between crippling particularization and banal generalization. I have sought to avoid simplistic generalizations and to convey a clear and accessible message, but each of these lies in the eye of the beholder.

After a lengthy introduction, in which I consider key conceptual points, I will examine important technological advances in weaponry and power projection. In each case, I will indicate the changes arising from these advances as well as their limitations, so as to consider what difference these advances made. The advances chosen will indicate the range of issues that can be addressed in terms of technological impact. In particular, the emphasis will not consistently be on firepower, important as that is and notably, but not only, in the Western tradition. Instead, there will also be a consideration of power projection and of technologies of logistics, command, and control. The intention is to offer a series of themes or episodes in order to reevaluate military technologies in their historical contexts. Important as case studies, these themes contribute, alongside the introduction, to a general history of technology and war, especially over the last half millennium.

The impact of technology is far from simple. Nuclear weaponry, considered in chapter 5, remains the apotheosis and nemesis combined of technological triumphalism, and this weaponry continues, to a degree, to condition everything else by not being used. The prospect of nuclear war was fundamental to the Cold War, but as a reminder of the need to locate technology in its multiple contexts, this prospect and the Cold War itself were an ideological and cultural phenomenon as well as a military confrontation.

I will then offer a discussion of the present centered on the RMA and the ideas and practices for which it acted as a focus. There will then be consideration of possible future trends before a conclusion.

Throughout, the stress will be on a less clear-cut pattern of change and effectiveness than is generally offered and popularly believed. Alongside recognition of technology's limitations, there is the demonstration that technology's pathways are by no means clear. "Fog and friction" apply in this area as much as in any aspect of war making, and perhaps even more intensely because of the three-way interactions of designers, the military, and politicians. Focusing on weapons as end results can lead to an underplaying of the complex processes by which they are developed and used.

I know, from recent work as a consultant for a television series, that it is necessary to address the view that history has to be portrayed in terms of dramatic changes. And weapons, "the cannon that brought down castle walls" and so on, provide key instances of this portrayal. In fact, relatively few castles fell simply as a result of gunpowder weapons, at least initially.[6]

In this book, I have doubtless at times fallen into the same trap, but I have tried to bring out the problematic characteristics of technological change and weapons effectiveness. For example, the problem with possessing up-to-date weapons is knowing how to exploit their strengths and minimize their deficiencies, as well as understanding the appropriate tactics. Mere possession of a weapon is no guarantee of success in battle. I hope to return us to the complexities and difficulties of those preparing, making, implementing, and experiencing the decisions in the past, and thus to undermine the misleading clarity of accounts of technological transformation, accounts, moreover, that are often triumphalist or Whiggish in character.

This book is also an invitation to a debate, and one that discussion of present and future indicates is very much an ongoing debate. As I have indicated, in this and other books, history is not only the account of what happened in the past but also of how we shape the past with our analysis. Warfare is particularly prone to this process. It might sometimes appear that soldiers have only limited interest in military history but, in fact, ideas and images of the past play an important role, both subliminally and, more explicitly, in current training and planning. Thus, ideas about what air power, or the use of tanks, or a resort to terrorism, achieved in the past are highly significant for a consideration of present options. In Britain, much of the discussion of the future of naval air power has taken place with reference to discussion of its past. Consideration of the failed experience of "dual control" in the 1920s and 1930s serves, implicitly or explicitly, as a critique of "jointery" today, specifically air force control of naval air assets.[7] Meanwhile, the focus on new carriers as the latest iteration of a noble tradition leads to an underrating of the potential for unmanned aerial vehicles. Debate about the past, therefore, is not simply an academic exercise, interesting and educational as that can be, but, instead, part of the process by which the present is understood and the future shaped.

Note: As a key point of nomenclature, the Ottoman (Turkish) conquest of southeast Europe in the fourteenth and fifteenth centuries, and Ottoman rule there until the 1910s, ensures that "the West" is used within to denote Christian European culture and societies, both in the continent of Europe and more generally.

Acknowledgments

I have profited greatly from the opportunity to teach military history since 1980, and would like to thank the students, both undergraduates and postgraduates, who have proved valuable sounding boards. I have benefited more recently, while working on this book, from being appointed to a visiting lectureship at Keio University and from lecturing at the Japanese National Institute for Defense Studies, the American Naval War College, Assumption University, Glasgow University, the University of North Carolina at Chapel Hill, the University of Southern Mississippi, and Waseda University, as well as at the Citadel, the Bologna Center of the Paul Nitze School of Advanced International Studies, the Global History Seminar of the Institute of Historical Research, and the University of Notre Dame's London Program. Conversations over many years with Anthony Saunders, a friend and former student, have proved very fruitful. I would like to thank him, Colin Baxter, Brian Davies, Kelly DeVries, David Gates, Alexander Johnson, Tim May, Ran Mei, Alex Roland, Cliff Rogers, Rick Schneid, Gary Sheffield, Dennis Showalter, and Spencer Tucker for their helpful comments on all or part of an earlier draft, and Roger Burt, Mike Dobson, John France, and Richard Wylde for reflections on particular points. I would like to thank Colin Gray for showing me an unpublished chapter. The advice of three readers on the original proposal proved most stimulating.

History as an intellectual practice is truly a group activity in that individual work is informed and shaped by that of colleagues and predecessors. The mistake is to imagine that any work can be definitive. Instead, there is a common chord to which many contribute and from which we all benefit. This book is dedicated to Janice and Peter Kay, two good friends, with thanks for many years of friendship.

Abbreviations

Add	Additional Manuscripts
AWM	Canberra, Australian War Memorial
BL	London, British Library, Department of Western Manuscripts
CAB	Cabinet Office papers
FO	Foreign Office papers
LH	London, King's College, Liddell Hart Archive
MM	Montgomery Massingberd papers
NA	London, National Archives (formerly Public Record Office)
NMM	London, National Maritime Museum
RMA	Revolution in Military Affairs

WAR AND TECHNOLOGY

INTRODUCTION

The Key Themes

The nature of modern weapons and scientific armament development renders surprise attack on a considerable scale and with weapons of great destructive power more possible than in the past. The old idea that a nation can "muddle through" possesses inherent dangers in the light of the speed with which aggressive action can be initiated in these days.

—*British Chiefs of Staff Sub-Committee, Annual Review, October 12, 1933*

The wars of the 2000s and early 2010s in Iraq and Afghanistan have caused a strong reaction against what has been presented as technological triumphalism, a term generally employed in order to suggest guilt by association. Any use of triumphalism, by its very nature, is intended to discredit; but it is also instructive to see how technology is itself employed by many today in a critical tone. This usage draws on a pronounced anti-modernist strand in both intellectual and popular thought, one enhanced by environmentalist arguments as well, differently, as drawing on a long-standing predisposition to prefer individual bravery to machines when responding to conflict. The last, of course, is generally the spectator's view but is also the theme in much "face-of-battle" literature written from the perspective of individual soldiers.

More particularly, much of the recent criticism focused on the Revolution in Military Affairs (RMA), a term that was widely used, notably within the Pentagon, in particular to describe the interaction between the acquisition of information and the rapid application of force, the two creating precision violence.[1] The RMA is discussed in greater detail in chapter 6. Significant for broader questions of military capability and history, this criticism was not a free-floating intellectual exercise but, rather, an aspect of the apparent crisis of American power that followed the chaos in Iraq after the successful American-led invasion of 2003 rapidly overthrew the government of Saddam Hussein. Moreover, the criticism was both an objective discussion of a flawed military-political analysis (in the shape both of the RMA and of postconquest policy in Iraq) and a more pointedly political critique directed at the United States. The role of technological optimism, both in American military planning and in the supporting civilian and political context,[2] help place this critical discussion.

Returning to triumphalism, some of the scholarly literature also goes surprisingly far. For instance, in 2005, Bruce Seely wrote baldly of the Second World War (1939–1945): "Car makers produced much of the dizzying array of equipment and weapons, ranging from machine guns and aircraft, to tanks, ships, and artillery . . . the assembly lines of the auto industry largely explained the Allied victory."[3] So much, in this account of resource determinism, for improvements in fighting quality or the Red (Soviet) Army or the Battle of the Atlantic and so forth.[4] To emphasize that the war was a war of attrition, and consequently of industrial production, which it was, is potentially to underplay other factors unless they also receive due recognition. In the case of the Battle of the Atlantic against German submarines, Allied shipbuilding was a key factor as was technology in the shape of signals interception and decryption, but so also was the development of effective techniques for antisubmarine warfare.

In practice, alongside triumphalism, technological interpretations have generally been handled, both by writers on technology and by the military, with considerably more sophistication than in much public and military discussion. In short, a dynamic analytical matrix is established by contrasting understandings and uses of technology, as well as by changes across time. This book will consider a number of crucial developments and related key episodes and will discuss them in order to assess the general themes of the subject, war and technology. In turn, these themes will be considered in order to discuss the developments and episodes. The length and complexity of this introduction reflect the number of these aspects and, thus, the range of the subject.

The issue of technology in conflict interests most modern commentators on war and plays a major role in accounts of military change, past, present, and future. This is especially true of developments in weaponry, and notably, but not only, at the popular level. For example, and this is but an instance of a trend, Chris McNab's *A History of the World in 100 Weapons* (2011) was advertised on the back cover of the June 2011 issue of the London monthly magazine *Standpoint* as "a lavish guide to the armaments that have shaped history."[5]

In practice, some of the arguments made for changes in weaponry are pushed too far, while weapons themselves are only a part of the question of the role of technology. The steam engine, the internal combustion engine, and electronics have had a greater impact than any weapon. In addition, the popular focus on the "bigger, better, faster" approach takes little account of handling techniques, training, or tactics, nor indeed of the will to win or of the multiple environmental contexts, human and natural, of operations.

Moreover, no weapon is derived from a single technology but, rather, from many, especially complex systems, such as aircraft and warships. Such systems are made effective by how the diversity of technologies were brought together to work cooperatively, a process that requires analysis, thought, and implementation. And while technologies have never advanced in smooth developmental steps but usually in an incremental process of learning from experience and, less commonly, in sudden leaps, the advances do not exist in a cultural or political vacuum. In fact, other factors play a role in the adoption of the technologies, and by those responsible for fighting wars, not only the commanders and procurers but also the men who have to use the technologies. The relationships are complex.

DEFINING TECHNOLOGY

Discussion of the role of technology commonly proceeds from considering particular military contexts or epochs, as in the weaponry of the

Age of "Total War," but, more generally, this discussion can be seen as an aspect of the problem of assessing changes in military culture, resource utilization, and economic capability. This point is valid for the long periods delimited in terms of a particular material culture, notably the Stone, Bronze, and Iron Ages, as of more recent centuries. Some of the latter, in turn, may be described in such terms, for example, the Age of Steam.

It has been argued, notably by Leo Marx, that the term "technology" is inappropriate before the nineteenth century. From the sixteenth to the eighteenth centuries, this argument accepts, there were significant changes in the invention and use of machines in the West, and this process of change would extend in the military sphere to new types of warships and gunpowder weaponry, the subjects of the next two chapters. However, Marx claimed that technology, in the sense of the full integration of the invention, development, and use of machines into society and the economy, was conditional upon a prior social revolution, one in which earlier social divisions had been blurred, rapid social ascent was possible, financial capital was readily available, and mobility of labor was established. At that point, Marx argued, "technology" can be discerned; in other words, it is to be seen as part of an entire socioeconomic system and of the relevant permissive changes.[6]

This approach, however, goes too far, not least because it takes one definition of technology and one account of society and seeks to apply them more generally. In practice, while Leo Marx's argument correctly locates individual machines—for example, specific weapons—in a wider context, there is no reason to believe that this context is only relevant if it relates to a particular type of socio-economic system.

Instead, it is best to employ a working definition of technology, in terms of functional value across time, and to rate technology as a thread running through the history of warfare. The technological perspective entails study of how weapons actually worked[7] and were produced and improved. The perspective also involves assessing the impact of weapons within the context of a situation in which human beings develop and use technology for some purpose. This usage is related both to the organization of resources for war and to how innovations in organization are achieved but also to the purposes under consideration.

It is also necessary to consider the values apparently represented by technological facets and choices. For example, Admiral Sir John Fisher's support for the development of the *Dreadnought,* the first all-big-gun battleship and the first powered by marine turbines, which was launched by the British in 1906, starting a naval race with Germany, rested in part on his conviction of the moral as well as practical worth of efficiency. Fisher's strong Protestant faith, Liberal Unionist political commitment to a rational and mighty British Empire, and interest in electrical equipment combined in his interest in and understanding of efficiency. For Fisher, warships were efficient machines for concentrated firepower.[8]

Technology was often very important in human efforts to organize resources more efficiently, but the driving force behind these efforts was not technology appearing from nowhere but, rather, human needs and desires that focused minds on some kind of change where technology was a part and could be an enabler. Yet, the contexts of change are not simply political, cultural, and social. Instead, inventiveness and application are themselves important variables and, as such, have varied greatly across time and space, not least due to important contrasts between cultures. At the same time, material culture has played a role as the availability of the necessary equipment, energy sources, and measuring tools are all important for experimentation.

Most notably, the role of technology in helping to create capability gaps between powers in force projection and battlefield effectiveness is greater in naval[9] and air than in land warfare. Man does not naturally fight while swimming and does not naturally fly. Indeed, the possibilities offered by the latter appeared genuinely revolutionary, although initial hopes were to be disabused. In 1784, Jon Ingenhousz, a Dutch-born scientist who lived in Britain, suggested that the new use of balloons for manned flight might lead to perpetual peace:

> If they can conduct the balloons in the same way as they do ships how could an army subsist when the enemy can throw force and destruction upon their stores and magazines at any time? How can an armed fleet attack any seacoast town, when the people of the country can swarm in the clouds and then fire upon it in the middle of the night? Do not you think that this discovery will put an end to all wars and thus force monarchs to perpetual peace or to fight their own quarrels among themselves in a duel?[10]

More prosaically, due in large part to balloons' dependence on the wind and the difficulties of transporting the apparatus for inflating them, as well as to the time taken to prepare them, balloons proved a disappointment when used by the French as a military tool in the 1790s, and Napoleon disbanded the force.[11]

Sentiments similar to that of Ingenhousz concerning the longed-for prophylactic nature of technology could also be found on other occasions. The Gatling and Maxim guns elicited similar sentiments during the nineteenth century, while, in the twentieth, some hoped that air power would exercise a restraining influence similar to Ingenhousz's balloons.

Many problems are faced when discussing technology and its role in warfare, not least that we have been "educated" since the 1960s to expect technological solutions to be definitive. Prior to the 1960s, despite remarks similar to that by Ingenhousz, technology seems to have been viewed more pragmatically by most commentators and users.

THE PROBLEMS OF INVENTION

Assessment is also complicated by the issue of novelty. There is a tendency in considering technology to devote particular attention to the first use of a weapon and to the factors involved in this innovation. This approach can exaggerate the impact, and thus importance, of first usage. In practice, some changes are hardly noticeable, not because they are slow but because they work by a process of seepage, filtration, and osmosis, each of which is a metaphor. Thus, the beginning may be very hard to discern, so that the process is only noticed after it has been under way for a while.

Moreover, there are more specific problems in analyzing the initial introduction of new technology.[12] Many inventions are, in fact, reinventions, which is why patent law defines what an invention is and also why litigation over patents repeatedly occurs.[13] There are numerous examples of such reinventions, including working submarines (first used in 1776 but "reinvented" in 1797 and 1879),[14] the percussion-fused hand grenade (1861 and 1905), and breech-loading rifles (for instance, 1740s, 1750s, 1780, 1839), although it can be argued that all the reinventions were "new."

However, they were not necessarily novel. The percussion-fused grenades of 1861 and 1905, although invented in different times and places, were essentially the same in how they worked (or failed to work). Innovative approaches to percussion-fused grenades, which were quite different in concept to the Ketchum of 1861 and the Russian and Japanese devices of 1905, only appeared after the start of the First World War (1914–1918). Moreover, alongside the dates given above for submarines comes the development, in the early 1910s, of reliable diesel propulsion, which ensured that the submarine could be a wide-ranging platform and could play a significant role in the First World War.[15]

How something works and, in particular, how effectively it works and is seen to work can be more significant than what it does. The standardization of performance in order to improve predictability may be more important to capability than a change in specifications.[16] Contributing to the problems of assessing success and failure in the history of technology,[17] much of new technology did (and does) not work effectively when first introduced. This is equally true of patented inventions and of present-day developments. For example, the great constructional problem with the breech-loading rifle was the escape of gas at the breech, thus reducing the propellant force, and this problem was the cause of the major delay in its adoption in the nineteenth century. Similarly, the tendency of the Gatling gun, an early machine gun, to jam delayed its large-scale introduction. The Gatling had black powder cartridges that caused a lot of fouling. In contrast, smokeless propellants caused less fouling, and therefore fewer jams. Refinements in the manufacture of cartridges also reduced jamming.[18] Jamming is an issue throughout the history of firearms.

Judging the effectiveness of such innovations is complicated by the degree to which their selling involved a deliberate attempt to conceal problems. This process was accentuated by commercial and international competition but also by the rise of publicity as an element in the more populist and news-conscious culture of the nineteenth century. As an instance of the degree to which the idea of the machine gun in part existed separately from, but linked to, the reality, Hiram Maxim, a great showman, publicly challenged other producers of machine guns to duels, using the press to advertise these events and staging them at major festivals. One of Richard Gatling's machine guns, armed with blanks, played a role in the Wild West shows staged in London for Queen Victoria's jubilee in 1887 by Buffalo Bill, William Cody.[19] American inventiveness, mechanical skill, industrial capability, and entrepreneurial promotion all combined.

At the same time, there was the established process of testing weapons, although, by the late nineteenth century, this process was often now more public, in the sense of publicized, than in the past. Thus, John Owen of the Royal Armory at Woolwich published a review of alternatives, *Compound Guns, Many-Barrelled Rifle Batteries, Machine Guns, or Mitrailleurs* (1874). There was also public debate about the merits of different forms of battleship construction.

As a result of the problems facing the development and use of weapons, it is important to discuss whether the pertinent date was the date of invention, the date it worked effectively for the first time (and how was/ is "effectively" defined, both at the time and subsequently?), the date in which it was introduced to the battlefield (a date that sheds light on factors affecting its usefulness), or the date military thinking changed in order to take advantage of what the new device allowed the operator of it to do that he could not previously do. The last factor is of particular significance for the machine gun. In this case, as in others—for example, the switch from battleships to carriers in the navies of the 1930s and 1940s—it is necessary to allow for more than stubbornness and conservatism in explaining the cautious and apparently belated response to the weapon. In part, the limited availability of machine guns when the First World War broke out in 1914, an average of only two per thousand troops, reflected the widespread assumption that a conflict would be mobile and that heavy machine guns would be an encumbrance as their value was in supporting the defense, not the offensive. During the war, lighter weapons were introduced, providing an offensive capability for machine guns.

Alongside the argument that the weapons used reflect fitness for purpose rather than a stubborn failure to adapt to change, production difficulties in making a device, as well as military or political stubbornness, nevertheless, could mean that a weapon took longer to make an impact than might be suggested by focusing on invention alone. These factors contribute to the fact that optimum technology is not always pursued and/or effective, a point indicated by German weaponry in the Second World War.[20] In this case, the focus of the Allies on mass production proved more appropriate, even though many of the resulting tanks were individually inferior to their (fewer) German opponents. Similarly, the Soviet production of primitive short-range gunpowder rockets in bulk proved more effective (at the tactical level) than the German attempt, with the V rockets, to use more sophisticated liquid-propelled technology in order to have operational or strategic impact, notably by affecting the ability or willingness of a devastated Britain to act effectively against Germany.[21] A modern instance of the problematic nature of optimum technology is provided by the American F-35 fighter and by the question of the continuing applicability of manned flight as opposed to the greater use of unmanned drones (see chapter 5).

Generally, more sophisticated weapons have a greater number of components and characteristics. As a result, the development toward effectiveness can be a complex and slow process. In order to make a significant impact, the bolt-action rifle required the invention of smokeless nitrocellulose (not gunpowder) propellants and of the box magazine in the 1890s, as well as fixed ammunition (the bullet fixed in a metal cartridge, so that the round becomes the key armament) in the 1850s and 1860s. This opened the way to mechanical developments, making possible both rapid-firing artillery and machine guns. The Dreyse needle rifle, invented in 1835, and the Chassepot rifle, adopted by the French in 1866, could be improved thanks to the invention of Poudre B (1884), ballistite (by Alfred Nobel, 1887), and cordite (1888). Thus, the effectiveness of magazine-fed bolt-action repeating rifles of the 1880s, such as the French Lebel (1886) and the German Mauser (1889), depended upon a number of technologies, and others besides, including the manufacture of ammunition. The power of such rifles was demonstrated by Western forces operating in China and South Africa in 1900.

There was a similar problem with the technologies of artillery. While ogival shells, the rifling of barrels, and big calibers were around, albeit in small numbers, in the American Civil War (1861–1865), it was not until the invention of the recoil/recuperator system in the late nineteenth century (combined with smokeless propellants) that artillery acquired the power that allowed it to dominate the battlefield. This power was seen with the international force (Western and Japanese) that suppressed the

Boxer movement in China in 1900. However, even the Russo-Japanese War (1904–1905) did not bring home fully just how destructive artillery had become, and this destructiveness was to provide a shock for the armies in 1914, in the opening campaign of the First World War.[22] This shock helped lead, first, to the resort to trenches and, then, to the apparently intractable nature of trench warfare as armies struggled to regain tactical and operational mobility.

Several processes of change may occur simultaneously but not necessarily synergistically. Indeed, they may pull in quite different directions. This tension is not automatically related to more complex issues of impact. With gas, which was used on a large scale by both sides in the First World War, there were problems of how to weaponize the forms of poison gas and then how best to use it, whether, for example, releasing it from canisters at the front line or firing gas shells.

Although gas had a deadly effect on soldiers from 1915, it proved only to be tactically important in that war, whereas submarines seemed both tactically and operationally significant and offered a strategic potential in the shape of destroying the trans-Atlantic supply systems on which the Allies depended. This potential forced a response on Britain, notably in the shape of organizing trade into convoys and requiring the Royal Navy to regard their protection as a priority. In this case, a technological development led to a technological reply, not least with the developing use of depth charges, and also to a cultural response in the shape of an emphasis on commerce protection alongside the established preference for combat between surface warships.

Gas warfare was a complex business that required a mix of technical skill, scientific knowledge, and tactical ability, as well as favorable weather conditions for operations to be successful. Aside from the problem of a change in wind direction possibly blowing gas back into the faces of attackers, as indeed happened, any attempt to exploit quickly the use of gas meant advancing into it. This problem would also have arisen had the Americans, as considered, employed tactical atomic bombs in support of the invasion of Japan scheduled for 1946.

There was also, in the First World War, the increasing resort to gas masks by defenders and their greater effectiveness, a classic instance of the development of anti-weaponry. Gas forced the pace of new equipment and tactics as effective ways of employing gas and also anti-gas defenses were adopted. Mustard gas, which harmed by contact as well as by the ingestion that had proved fatal with the earlier chlorine and phosgene gas attacks, was first used in 1917 by the Germans. Mustard gas was primarily an incapacitant, burning and blistering its victims and so compounding the serious problems facing medical and support services.[23] The possibilities of gas were grasped by the British Special Brigade Royal Engineers. British artillery made effective use of gas shells in order to silence German guns.[24] Yet, as a powerful reminder of the degree to which technology is shaped by politics and related assumptions about acceptability, the postwar revulsion against gas as a weapon led to international pressure against its use, including the 1925 Geneva Protocol, pressure that ensured that most of the combatants in the Second World War did not employ it.

To turn to another weapon of the First World War, flamethrowers were employed by the Byzantines to use Greek fire more effectively, probably from the ninth and tenth centuries. At sea, Greek fire was pumped into tubes on the bows of warships, tubes that served as flamethrowers. The use of a pressurized system was reinvented in the 1910s. However, the specifications improved thereafter. The one- and two-man flamethrowers of the First World War, as well as the wheeled and static models, were not mobile in the fashion of backpack models of the 1930s and 1940s, and they were also severely hampered by being capable of only short-range bursts.

Flamethrowers were more effective in the Second World War thanks to the invention of thickening agents that allowed the fuel to be projected a reasonable distance without being consumed in the process. Thickened fuels, especially napalm (petrol thickened with *n*aphthalic and *palm*itic acids), also stuck to the target. Napalm is one of the most lethal of weapons because, aside from killing by burning, asphyxiation due to the oxygen being consumed can be a cause of death, especially when the fuel is squirted through the slit of a bunker. The British, Americans, and Canadians also developed flamethrowers mounted on vehicles. Therefore, there was a long gestation of flamethrowers before the Second World War and the Vietnam War witnessed their full potential.

Returning to the complexities of usage, and thus the difficulties of assessing technological development, the example of the tank (see chapter 4) indicates that appropriate developments in military thinking exist not in the abstract but in terms of an often bitter debate about practicalities and purposes. The same was true of some earlier weapons and techniques, for example, gunpowder weaponry in late fifteenth- and sixteenth-century Europe and southwest Asia.

THE PROBLEMS OF PRODUCTION

There is also the issue of production. To create an effective weapon, and to lead to a relevant change in tactics, and even doctrine, is only part of the story. It is also necessary to be able to manufacture large numbers of a new weapon, and at a consistent standard, in order to replace losses, both in victory and in defeat, and to provide the resources for new operational opportunities. To do so, it was important to standardize weapons in practical designs that could be readily reproduced. This process was particularly seen with modern weaponry as a result of industrial manufacturing techniques. The extent to which this process occurred with weapons of the ancient world, for example, the catapult, is less clear. Alongside pronounced variations, so that there was no catapult per se but rather belly bows, torsion ballistae, and onagers, there were enough construction descriptions to indicate that such reproduction was possible.[25]

The benefits and problems of modern mass production accentuated production issues. A British War Office paper of 1936 for the cabinet on army reorganization noted various issues that caused delay:

> The programme of re-organisation of both infantry and artillery is retarded by the necessity of maintaining two divisions ready for immediate dispatch overseas, since units which are in process of re-organisation cannot be mobilised at short notice. . . . A considerable time must elapse between the start of the conversion of a cavalry regiment from a horsed to a mechanised basis, and the time when it is fully trained in the use of its new equipment . . . The rate of re-equipment of artillery with a new weapon does not depend merely on the production of the weapon itself, but also on the provision of adequate reserves of ammunition . . . When the design of a new tank has been settled,

it takes roughly a year (under peace conditions) before that tank is "in production," and probably another year before units are fully equipped with it and trained in its use.[26]

Serious problems have to be overcome when introducing new weapons. Johann von Dreyse's "needle" rifle, a breech-loading, bolt-action rifle, invented in 1835 and used by the Prussians, had an unprecedentedly high rate of fire, but early versions suffered from a number of design faults, including a brittle firing pin, a bolt action that was liable to jam, and a weak seal around the screw-breech. As a result, Austria, Britain, and France continued to rely on muzzle-loaders.

Such problems did not only arise with sophisticated modern weapons. For example, the development of true firearms in thirteenth-century China did not lead to the rapid displacement of prefirearm gunpowder weapons, because of problems with effectiveness, reliability, cost, and availability. In sixteenth-century Japan, however, effective guns, once introduced from abroad (from China and from the West via Portugal) by means of trade, were widely and rapidly copied, as Japan's metallurgical industry could produce muskets in large numbers.[27]

With firearms, it was necessary to deploy a number of production technologies: weapon, ammunition, ignition, and propellant all had to be considered.[28] Rifling a gun barrel to improve range and accuracy was an idea of the Middle Ages that became readily practical only with subsequent metallurgical progress. Thus, again, the dates of inventions can be misleading. Conception, production, and application occurred as very different episodes in the case of rifling. Although, in Britain, Alexander Forsyth patented the use of fulminates of mercury in place of gunpowder as a primer for firearms in 1807, the initial impact of the percussion cap, coated with fulminates of mercury, was limited, and the mass-produced metal percussion cap dates from 1822. There was a dramatic reduction of misfires as a result, which led to a great increase in firepower.

Firearms were not the only weapons to present problems. Bold Allied ideas for the use of tanks had the First World War continued into 1919, notably those of the British officer J. F. C. "Boney" Fuller, failed to take sufficient note of the problems of manufacturing and maintaining sufficient tanks. In addition, the tanks then available were far too unreliable and underarmored for any bold ideas to work (see chapter 4). The subsequent tactical and operational success of the tank, notably with German attacks in 1939–1940, led Fuller to appear more prescient than was in fact the case.

Moreover, introducing weapons into service rapidly can cause serious problems. The rush on the part of the Germans to force the V-2 rocket into service in 1944, when the war was increasingly going very badly for them, helped to lead to a high margin of error, while the lack of a reliable guidance system was also significant among its limitations. In addition, the relative ineffectiveness of the V-2 owed much to the rocket having to reenter the Earth's atmosphere so that the nose cone heated up due to friction, which meant that only a relatively small payload could be carried. Had the Germans managed to develop an ablative shield, as used by later nuclear IBCMs (intercontinental ballistic missiles), then a far bigger payload could have been fitted. This case exemplified the issue of an absent technology. Missiles also lacked the multipurpose capacity of aircraft.[29]

The use of missiles reflected the inability of the Germans to resist Anglo-American air attacks, as well as Hitler's determination to hit back, and repeated his fascination with new technology and the idea that it could bring a paradigm leap forward in military capability. In practice, albeit in very different circumstances, the Allied air assault on Germany in 1943–1945 benefited more from developing an existing technology by equipping long-range fighters with drop fuel tanks, extending their ability to protect bombers and engage with the *Luftwaffe* (German Air Force) (see chapter 5). Nevertheless, the use of planes, rather than missiles, meant that the Allies took heavy casualties in manpower.

Production factors are not the sole significant ones. In addition, as an aspect of managing both novelty and continuity in weaponry, it is important to be able to supply and repair weapons. Both are key examples of their functionality and fitness for purpose. The records of the Teutonic Order, a German crusading order of knights on the southern shores of the Baltic from the late fourteenth and early fifteenth centuries, provide ample and systematic evidence on logistics, including statements about the costs of supply and repair. New weaponry posed particular problems of supply and repair. It was difficult, for example, to maintain the Girandoni breechloader, magazine-fed rifle, which was an innovative weapon; in general, the loading mechanisms of eighteenth-century breechloaders were susceptible to clogging by powder.

In contrast, much of the importance of the introduction of single-shot breechloaders in the mid-nineteenth century, followed by that of repeating firearms, stemmed from the ability to mass-produce rifling, sliding bolts, magazine springs, and chain-feeds to a high standard, and also to provide the large quantities of ammunition required. If the requirement for ammunition accentuated logistical problems, these in turn encouraged the application for military purposes of technological advances in transport. The ideas and technology for the mass production of the interchangeable parts of muskets were developed in France and then taken into production in America at the arsenals at Springfield, Massachusetts, and Harper's Ferry, Virginia. Nevertheless, technological progress and industrial output were less effective at the latter due to the strength of craft traditions among the workers in this more isolated settlement.[30]

Effective mass production provided a substantial advantage over craft-manufactured firearms, however good the latter were on an individual basis. This advantage required a major change in the production process, a change that put a significant emphasis on skill. When American gun makers modernized Russian small arms after the Crimean War (1854–1856), they provided not only machinery but also skilled workers and advanced production techniques.[31]

In turn, improvements in technology seek to respond to the problems confronting production. Ease of manufacture in quantity can entail the avoidance of tight engineering tolerances, which require skilled workers, a requirement that poses problems as well as offering potential. Skill and quality are not fixed factors but vary according to circumstances, including the need for new skills, the character of social systems, and the willingness and ability to reassign labor if required. The evaluation of skill and quality depends in part on the capacity of manufacturing systems and on how these interact with quality control: a vital function of twentieth-century manufacture was inspection, which required skilled inspectors using precision-made testing tools.

Whatever the general peacetime improvement in the situation, war brought change. Notably, under the pressure of war, innovations in manufacturing processes were introduced while labor provision greatly changed. Alongside the need for more labor for manufacturing, and for labor with particular skills, came the overcoming of wartime limitations on provision, notably, in the two world wars, by the greatly expanded employment of women, especially in Britain, the United States, and the Soviet Union.

JUDGING QUALITY

There is also the question of how technological innovations were perceived at the time and how far they were encouraged as such. Within Western states, the institutionalization of military systems, particularly for navies from the early modern period and for artillery from the eighteenth century, ensured that the utility of new weapons and systems was carefully probed. Thus, in the 1770s and 1780s, the merits of copper bottoming ships in order to limit infestation of the timber, and therefore drag, and to improve and increase the service life of the ship were carefully considered by the British and French navies, respectively the world's leading and second navies throughout the century. The key drive was the attempt to use human ingenuity to counteract natural processes, in the shape of the damage done by marine worms to timber, an organic substance. The competitive context between these two states encouraged a search for particular advantage, and notably so as the warships of these powers were very similar.[32]

Again, in 1848–1849, British officers commanding regiments with rifle companies reported to the secretary of the Military Board on the best form of rifle ammunition.[33] Testing was a central element in proving the effectiveness of new designs, and, in the nineteenth century, this testing was reported by foreign observers and domestic commentators, including the press.[34]

Investigation did not necessarily ensure appropriate usage, not least because of a tendency to rely on existing paradigms. Thus, conservatism on the part of French military engineers thwarted proposals for new fortification architecture in the late eighteenth century.[35] Moreover, automatic rifles, around since the end of the nineteenth century, were, when tested by the British during the First World War, viewed as nothing more than weapons in which the burden of opening and closing the bolt had been automated. That is not how automatic rifles are viewed today. However, due to mechanical reasons, no automatic rifle, with the exception of the American BAR (which was more of a light machine gun) was reliable at the time of the war, although both the French and Germans used them toward the end of the war to a very limited extent. Moreover, automatic rifles were heavy: not only were they not as light as service rifles but also their need for a bigger magazine made them even heavier. In contrast, the British reorganized their infantry tactics during the war around the Lewis gun, an effective light machine gun, and these tactics and technology contributed greatly to the effectiveness of their infantry advances in 1918.

In judging technological change, there is also the issue of differentiation between similar devices, which can be as important, if not more so, than the general focus by commentators on introducing new technologies. If, for example, all bolt-action manually operated rifles are viewed as being essentially the same, it means that the Dreyse rifle of 1840 was the same as the British SMLE No. 4 of a century later, when clearly they were very different. There is, therefore, the question of the degree of change within a given technology. Similarly, modern high-velocity rifle bullets cause different sorts of wounds to musket balls because of their higher impact energies. They leave a track through the body and set up hydrostatic effects on body fluids in the area of the track. Moreover, unlike spherical bullets, conical bullets can yaw and tumble, which causes worse wounds than bullets that strike point first and aligned on their trajectory.

Change within a given technology is not a recent process. For example, weapons such as bills, halberds, swords, and spears evolved over time according to a range of factors, including changes in armor and alterations in use. Some developments were abandoned, while emulation created differences as well as similarities. More generally, differences in the technicalities of the technology concerned, so that the original or the copy might be technically better, could alter the way a weapon was used. Indeed, there is always the danger that what looks the same is regarded as being the same, which was/is very much not the case. Contemporaries had a far more acute sense of this than later commentators, but it is not always easy to discern. This sense might be artisanal or craft in character, rather than being written down.

Furthermore, the extent and consequences of hindsight are among the difficulties in assessing similar inventions; theorizing about the impact of any new development needs to take this into account. For example, there were different models and varieties over the centuries of the composite bow, which was first attested in the West in Mesopotamia in about 2200 BCE,[36] and these varieties did not operate in an identical fashion. Storing compressive and tensile energy by virtue of its construction and shape, allowing it to be smaller than the long bow, the composite bow was a sophisticated piece of engineering that seems to have been invented in various places by different peoples, although there was probably some interchange of ideas. Thus, the Turkish bow was different from the Chinese bow. The bow's effectiveness owed much to the lamination of its wood, but it was labor intensive to manufacture. Indeed, it is not safe to be too technologically deterministic and to claim that the composite bow drove out other types of bow, as it did not. The lamination of its wood was perfect for central Asia and the Middle East but entailed some limitations due to the humidity of certain important regions, notably Southeast Asia and India.

The effectiveness of the bow was greatly enhanced due to its use by horsemen, most famously the Mongols in the thirteenth century, but their success was largely due to other features of their war making, notably organization, strategy, and operational practice.[37] Similarly, with their opponents. For example, Song China (960–1279) benefited from improvements in weaponry, but these were not decisive in major battles or in the overall outcome of wars. Improvement in the firepower of the crossbow gave the Song army some advantage in wars against the Khitan, Jurchen, and Mongols, successive attackers from the north. The development of paddle-wheel warships strengthened the defensive capability of the Song navy against the attempts of the invading Jurchen in the twelfth century to cross the Yangzi River. Toward the end of the Song period, rockets propelled by gunpowder were quite conspicuous during the eventual Mongol invasion of Song China. Yet, the Song succumbed to the Mongols.

There is also the question of how change occurs. It would be mistaken to suggest that we must choose simply and solely between whether technological change is incremental and based on current knowledge, as with cannon in Europe in the eighteenth century,[38] or revolutionary. Instead, technological change is both incremental and revolutionary, at different times and in various settings. Nevertheless, the issue of emphasis has to be addressed. The problematic character of the concept of revolutionary change can be seen by considering examples from the premodern period.

Violence and warfare directed against other humans (as opposed to the killing of animals) date from deep in human antiquity and nature.[39] The development of weapons, notably worked stones, axes, spears, and bows, was important to this process, with the lengthy Stone Age, the period from prehistory down to the use of metals from ca. 7000 BCE, seeing greater effectiveness against both animals and humans.[40] Alongside the human capacity for organizing group violence, the use of weapons was highly significant in helping overcome physically stronger animals, such as bears, as well as in killing others. The development of stone blade technology was followed by the use of microlithic flints, which, mounted in wood or bone hafts, proved effective, for example, as knives and arrowheads.

Moreover, in 7,000–5,000 BCE, in both West Asia and southeast Europe, it was discovered that heating could be used to isolate metals from ore-bearing rocks. Soft metals, which melt at low temperatures—copper, gold, and lead—were the first to be used, and this use explains why copper was the basis of metal technology before iron. With the exception of the Americas, the Stone Age began to be replaced by the successive ages of metal. Indeed, the issue of technology is certainly as old as the warfare of the ages of metal because no metal weapon could have been fashioned without the technology to smelt and work metal. In the third millennium BCE, bronze, which was made by alloying copper with tin, was widely adopted, as it was stronger and more durable than pure copper. Bronze replaced not only copper but also hard stone and flint.

Metal ore is more malleable than stone, while metal weapons provided stronger penetration and weight, the key requirements for success in hand-to-hand combat, with the additional factor of the reduced bulk necessary for ease of use and mobility. Flint weapons were much sharper than their metal counterparts, but, unlike metal, did not hold their edge with use. Metal swords probably developed in Europe in the second millennium BCE. The history of metallurgy is closely linked to the development of sword blades.

The invention of steel (an alloy of iron, carbon, and traces of other elements) was a major technological development that probably occurred by accident when working iron, a common metal. The skill in pattern welding and tempering blades so that you had a soft core for flexibility and a hard skin for toughness and that would take and hold an edge emerged in different places, east and west, to produce remarkable weapons. A number of technologies were involved, illustrating the point that it is mistaken to take a weapon and equate it with a single technology and thus a particular moment and place. Smelting, forging, tempering, sharpening, and polishing were distinct and different but all necessary to the fabrication of a sword blade. Moreover, separate technologies were involved in making the hilt, which was an equally important part of the weapon. The hilt was necessary for holding the weapon and could be developed to provide protection for the hand holding it. Swords eventually became both cutting and thrusting weapons. Swords could also be used to parry, thus providing defense.

Swords, however, were of no use to anyone who had not trained in their use. The development of fighting skills was as important as the quality of the weapon. A fifteenth-century European long sword was a truly destructive instrument in the hands of a trained swordsman, and it is clear from sword manuals of that century how they were supposed to be used. As with Japanese weapons and swordsmanship, European swords required more than brute force alone. More generally, the evolution and use of bladed weapons was very much tied up with that of armor and handling techniques.[41]

The extent of revolutionary change is problematic. For example, returning to antiquity, there was a considerable overlap of flint with copper, copper with bronze, and bronze with iron, rather than a sudden and complete supplanting of one technology by another, a point that is still relevant today. In addition, the metallurgical aspects of making and processing the metals and alloys were not static, while different metallurgical processes developed in particular parts of the world. Thus, steels are not the same, geographically or historically.

Overlap was also seen with weapons. For example, the sling, a very ancient weapon, went on being used into the age of gunpowder. Although relatively short range, notably compared to the bow, the sling was dangerous, especially in the hands of experts who knew how to pick stones that would fly true to the target. The role of expertise ensured that particular areas, such as Thrace and the Balearic Islands in antiquity, became noted for their slingers. Sling-staffs, moreover, offered an improvement in projection in what was one of the longest-lasting and most neglected of weapons. As another instance of overlap, the carved capitals of the Monreale Cathedral cloister near Palermo in Sicily, dated from 1174 to 1189, depicted several types of shields, including kidney-shaped and round.[42]

More generally, aside from overlap, revolutionary change may be illusory: the timescale may be far greater than it appears to be, and the process of change may have been far from straightforward. It is also necessary to put weapons in context, not only with reference to those of opponents but also with regard to questions of combined arms effectiveness and tactics.[43] Thus, the Roman invasions of England in 55 BCE, 54 BCE, and (successfully) from 43 CE, benefited from the discipline of the Roman infantry with its short swords, javelins, and body armor. Lacking effective missile power and with little body armor, their Celtic opponents could not compete, while their chariots were vulnerable to Roman archers and their hill forts, such as Maiden Castle in Dorset, to Roman siegecraft.

THE CASE OF THE SHIELD

The development of shields indicated both the possibilities and constraints posed by the need to respond to the human body and the action-reaction cycle of military developments, in this case the response to attackers. As men have two arms, it was possible to wield both an attacking and a defending weapon simultaneously. This option would not have been possible had humans been reliant solely on weapons that required two arms, such as bows and arrows, slings, large axes, and pikes.

Shields could be readily combined by individual soldiers with their use of many handheld weapons, notably handheld spears, swords, and javelins. Shields also provided a measure of protection against missile weapons such as arrows, javelins, and the stones thrown by slings. The tactical formation of the Roman tortoise, with closely packed soldiers enjoying cover from shields held above them or to the side, amply demonstrated this: it provided protection as well as being highly maneuverable. Moreover, the metal boss turned the shield itself into an offensive weapon at close quarters.

The evolution of the early shield is unclear but reflected an adaptation of natural materials, such as wood and hide. Wooden shields were depicted in prehistoric cave paintings, as were bows. Subsequently, as the range of worked material increased, so shields could be made from more substances, which indicated an important flexibility in weaponry. To a degree, this flexibility has been lost with technological development due to the increase in specialization in specifications and functions.

The use of shields by many different premodern societies is striking. The size of shields varied greatly, as did their grip, and both were important for their capability as well as their tactical use. As with weapons and other forms of technology used in warfare across history, there was a trade-off in specifications. Central issues included the shield's weight, which was a problem on the march and, even more, during battles. If the weight was too great, then the resulting strain on the arm might create a difficulty not only in holding the shield but also in the use of weapons by the other arm. The Roman army trained with overweight weapons and shields, so that when it came to battle and marching, their muscles were well used to handling such items. Weight was related to material and also to size. The larger the size, the greater the ability to deflect blows or missiles, but there was also a loss in terms of mobility, maneuverability, and the capacity to use offensive weapons simultaneously. For cavalry, the load-bearing capacity of horses posed a different issue, and there were also practicalities of being on horseback including the horse's head, neck, and reins being in the way if a large shield had to be moved from side to side.

There were also variations in the shield's handgrip. Among the variations were the round shields in which the shield was closely attached to the left forearm, which was put inside the armband. The Greek aspis was a type of this shield but also had a grip near the rim. The main contrast to this type would be a center grip.

The development of shields also showed how premodern societies were far from static in their weapons, which then underlines our limited knowledge of how and why change occurred, as well as commenting on the assumption among scholars on the modern period that change then was automatically more frequent, rapid, and important, three criteria that are linked but also different. This development of shields can be seen in ancient Greece and Rome and in medieval Europe. The shields described in Homer's ninth-century BCE works *The Iliad* and *The Odyssey*, which clearly reflect the type seen in artifacts from Mycenean Greece, the Bronze Age culture of ca. 1580–1120 BCE, were very large. They had a central single grip and were suspended from the neck by a thong. The shield could be swung around to cover the back when in retreat.

In contrast, the *hoplon* or large, heavy shield of the later hoplites (heavy infantry) of classical Greece in the seventh to fourth centuries BCE had a central armband and a handgrip on the inside near the right edge. These shields, which offered protection from chin to knee, were, however, too heavy to slide along the arm and required the full arm and two grips to lift them. The shield-bearing armies of classical Greece were a key instance of the extent to which economic development led to state forms that could support more sophisticated and better-armed militaries.[44]

At the same time, the change in shields when hoplite phalanx fighting was adopted in Greece was not really a result of developments in the economy or the technology of product but instead a result of a change in battle techniques. In the phalanx, the right-hand side of the formation was dangerously exposed, as the soldier had to concentrate on using his spear, which was held on his right-hand side.[45] He could not easily defend himself from close attack on the right. Hence, there was a natural tendency for phalanxes to move as a block to the right as each man instinctively moved to his right to gain shelter from his right-hand neighbor. A larger shield held on the left helped provide protection. The shield was also important for the technique of the *othismos,* or pushing advance. The relationship between weapon and tactical use therefore emerges clearly.[46]

There was also development in the case of Roman shields. Under the Republic in the last centuries BCE, the legionary shield was a long oval with a single grip. In turn, the switch to a rectangular shield occurred about the time of the Emperor Augustus in the early first century CE and lasted until about 200 CE. These shields were wooden, with the rim reinforced with bronze. The grip was horizontal and was protected by a bronze or iron boss. The Romans used plywood for their shields, finding this type of construction more resilient, and were able to curve it for the rectangular shields.

Subsequently, however, there was a general switch back to an oval shield, although a few rectangular shields still show up in excavations. The change in shield types can be linked to a number of others also related to a reevaluation of Roman fighting methods to cope with the "barbarian" armies that became a greater problem for the Romans from the second century CE. These methods included a longer sword (the *spatha*) for the infantry, the use of heavy cavalry, and different infantry formations and tactics.[47] However, it is necessary to employ care in explaining changes when there is scant, if any, evidence for why decisions were taken. The auxiliary infantry employed the oval shield throughout, and this was not a reflection of technology but of the differing fighting practices of the two types of unit, legionary and auxiliary. The fighting practices are worth noting, as the nature of the enemy and its fighting methods that both types of Roman unit encountered would have been the same.

In medieval Europe, there was a shift from round-shaped shields to kite-shaped shields, probably in the tenth century, as these shields were well in use by the eleventh. Then, in the thirteenth, there was a change to smaller, more maneuverable, flatiron-shaped shields. This change can be explained in terms of fitness for purpose. The kite shield could help cover the legs of a horseman who did not have mail-armored legs, because it is thought that many horsemen fought on the ground. In contrast, on horseback such a shield could only cover one leg. Such shields were unnecessary in the thirteenth century because legs became protected by mail-armor. Large kite-shaped heavy shields would probably have been less easy to manage than round or oval shields. Large shields were also found in non-Western societies, as in North Africa where there was a use of leather *lamt* shields. These ensured that armor was largely unnecessary.[48]

Shields could be employed in both defensive and offensive tactics. Interlocking tactics provided a defensive wall, as with the Greeks and Romans, which could also serve to cover an advance. The Anglo-Saxons also used a shieldwall at Hastings in 1066, an impressive formation, especially if benefiting from terrain features, notably—as at Hastings—a slope, only eventually to fall victim in that battle to the Norman tactics of feigned retreats and the use of archers. An example of the offensive use of the shield was in broadsword and buckler tactics of the fifteenth and sixteenth centuries, for example, in Germany and Scotland.[49] However, by then the use of the shield was declining, although siege engineers employed them into the nineteenth century.

The abandonment of armor and shields had a number of causes (and contexts), but the development of bladed weapons and techniques for their use played a role. The shield could be an encumbrance, especially if weighed down by opposing arrows and spears that stayed in the shield; and the shield's usefulness declined after defensive employment of the sword developed. Moreover, staff weapons proved effective, not least Scottish spears and Flemish halberds at the beginning of the fourteenth century and Swiss pikes and halberds in the fifteenth. They offered a wall of points providing a defense that did not depend on shields.[50]

ASSESSING THE EVIDENCE

In the case of antiquity, there is the difficulty of recovering the nature of war. With the exception of those societies, such as Greece and Rome, for which we have literary evidence, only the archaeological record is present and that skews the situation. Material aspects are heavily emphasized in such a situation, and the material remains tend to determine assumptions about social and political structures and about the purposes and character of conflict. This, indeed, is the case with most of human history, and notably where the written record is weak.

To focus on more recent centuries, in contrast, is to consider only a portion of this history, but it does offer marked advantages in exposition and analysis. In particular, the variety and quantity of sources are greater for the last half millennium than for earlier periods, although this is not equally the case for all parts of the world. Indeed, the latter situation contributes to a more general Western-centricity in both discussion and analysis.

Across a far shorter timescale than the shield, and in a fashion that is easier to demonstrate, the machine gun provides an instance of incremental change, with inefficient earlier models being improved and used more effectively. In assessing change, the term "a lateral [sideways] leap" is possibly more helpful than "revolutionary," as the question of whether something is revolutionary is subjective and is very difficult to address because of the difficulty with keeping hindsight from biasing the answer. And technical change is not always "forward" in the conventional sense. Furthermore, sometimes technological advance entails simplification, although there is a tendency for it to lead to greater complication. Simplification can seem an advance but can also appear not to be innovative.

Whatever the level of complexity, supposed technical superiority may be incidental, or indeed unnecessary, if the new weapon increases the amount of damage that can be inflicted to such a level that the enemy cannot tolerate it. The latter factor, however, is far from clear: perception, and by either or both sides, plays a major role in the consideration of the effects of weapons on targets, and this perception affects use of the weapons, tactically and operationally.

Another aspect of incremental development that can entail simplification is relating new weaponry to training. The military has to be trained so that the benefits of technological change can be grasped. Royal Navy recruiters in Britain in the early 2000s produced postcards depicting modern weapons with captions such as "Awesomely Powerful. Deadly Accurate. But Without Highly Trained Weapons Specialists about as Lethal as a Pork Sausage." Training soldiers to clean and maintain weapons is also important to effectiveness, and notably so with complex weapon systems. Equally, technology may have to be simplified so that training and maintenance are readily possible.

THE WEST AND THE REST

Alongside the problems of comparing Western with non-Western developments, there are the particular issues involved in considering the latter and understandably so as the non-West is far larger and more diverse than the West. Although there are important exceptions, much of the talk about technology ignores anything outside the West or simplifies the non-West. Yet, it is acknowledged that gunpowder and, later, military rockets—the "explosives technology" that has been seen as so important in Western military history—are Asian in origin. At the same time, it has been argued that in China in the twelfth and thirteenth centuries, it was political and institutional developments, not technology in itself, that turned guns into effective military instruments, because Chinese institutions were the first to harness gunpowder to military use and to mass-produce it to make weapons.[51] Furthermore, there are examples of earlier Asian technologies, such as the composite bow and the stirrup, that were arguably superior (although the definition of "superior" is problematic) to contemporary Western technologies but that are not presented in most general histories of war as winners in the way that later Western technologies are generally so treated.

This issue of comparing West and non-West is thus related to the need for a methodological debate on how best to assess "paradigm-shifting" weaponry. The West itself is difficult to define, as it included Byzantium (the Eastern Roman Empire) and Armenia as well as the societies of Catholic Europe.[52] There is also a need, in reacting against Western-centricity, to beware of assuming that the non-West has always been underrated. Some medievalists have been all too ready to believe that everything superior in a technological sense came from the East and rather reluctant to accept Western ingenuity. The fourteenth-century treatises of Guido da Vigevano and Konrad Kyeser included designs for radically new weapons such as multi-barreled cannons and screw-powered boats.

Moreover, although there were Islamic advantages,[53] naval technology was better applied, as far as the Mediterranean was concerned, by Western powers in the eleventh to the thirteenth century and, even more, in the fourteenth century. This situation had major consequences in terms of supporting the power projection of the Crusades and, subsequently, in limiting the results of their failure in the Near East and Egypt in the thirteenth century. Although the Ottoman Turks had ships under military command earlier, notably at Constantinople in 1453 and on the Danube River at Belgrade in 1456, it was not until they developed a large and permanent navy in the late fifteenth century that the balance was redressed, and by the time of their war with Venice in 1499–1503, the Ottoman fleet was the more powerful. Moreover, as discussed in the next chapter, technology itself was, and is, not an issue that can be readily separated from the need for organizational support if naval strength was to be sustained.[54] Accepting these qualifications, the flow of weaponry is an important indication of the sense of relative advantage.[55]

The differing criteria applied to weaponry in the East and the West, and, indeed, the differing usage of the weapons, both by individuals and by larger formations, makes comparisons difficult. There is also the issue of non-equivalence: with whom can the Mongol horsemen be compared in the West, and with whom the Swiss pikemen in the East? This issue is compounded by the extent to which weapons technology should be considered in the context of operational effectiveness: does it do what it is supposed to do, and predictably so? Comparisons are weakened, or at least made more difficult, by the need to address this context.

Repeatedly, evidence is an issue. As far as old technologies, such as arms and armor, are concerned, where there is little or no documentary evidence of how they were made or used, the technologies tend to be neglected or underplayed. The material remains (which can be limited[56]) determine assumptions, but the latter can be somewhat simplistic. However, there have been advances in understanding made from the study of surviving examples in collections, including of armor, and there are also artistic depictions, which is where a lot of evidence of premodern military technology comes from.[57] Thus, early sixteenth-century muskets have been used for tests.[58] The value placed on past weapons is also instructive. There are records showing the presence of Viking swords for sale in Baghdad in the tenth century. This evidence seems to confirm the attraction of Carolingian and Viking swords in the Arabic world, which was itself remarkable for its sword-making techniques.

EFFECTIVENESS FROM ANTIQUITY TO THE PRESENT

These and other points underline the importance of seeing technology as a long-term variable, rather than focusing largely on the last six centuries, the modern age, with technology understood as, essentially, an enabler or at least an adjunct of modernity. Turning to the long term helps clarify the analytical context. For example, an emphasis on organizational factors as crucial to the understanding of the opportunities offered by weaponry, as well as to the application of technological innovation, does not relate only to recent Western history. Indeed, it is central to much of the discussion of classical and medieval warfare, although limitations with the sources create difficulties in probing the issue.

It is also necessary to avoid making capability and the course of conflict overly clear-cut. Philip II of Macedon (r. 359–336 BCE) is generally presented as beating the squabbling Greek city Thebes and its allies because he controlled a better all-arms army, while his control ensured unity of purpose for his powerful monarchy. But Philip's key victory over the city-states of Thebes and Athens at Chaeronea (338 BCE) was not easy nor a given. Similarly, the historian Polybius claimed that the Romans defeated the Macedonians because of the superiority of the legion over the less flexible phalanx, but, even so, the most serious battles in the Second and Third Macedon Wars, Cynoscephalae (197 BCE) and Pydna (168 BCE), were both close-run for the Romans, as was Magnesia (190 BCE), a key victory over Antiochus, the ruler of the Hellenistic Seleucid dynasty. At Heraclea (280 BCE) and Asculum (279 BCE), Pyrrhus, king of Epirus (r. 319–272 BCE), a relative of the Macedonian royal house, had won victories over the Roman legion utilizing the phalanx, although at Heraclea his losses were so heavy that it became the source of the term "Pyrrhic victory," one that could not be afforded.

Modern habits of thought have proved important in considering earlier situations but also, therefore, in not always understanding them. For example, when military technology works, there is a tendency to think that it is a war-winner. The American use of "smart munitions" in the 2003 Gulf War is a good example of this, but just because the munitions do what they were designed to do (and it had taken more than 60 years to achieve the level of reliability and precision seen in Iraq—and that was not 100 %) does not mean that these things will solve the basic military problem of defeating the enemy. Similarly, the major expansion in aerial and automatic surveillance in the late twentieth century, and the resulting enhancement in the quantity of intelligence information, did not necessarily lead to improved analysis, as was shown in the misleading claims made prior to the war about the existence of Iraqi weapons of mass destruction, although political factors were also at play in this case as justification was sought for an attack. More generally, there is a widespread belief that superior technology is always the answer without understanding what the question is. Bigger, faster, and higher are seen as the ultimate criteria, but such data exists in its own world of unreality.

This point was seen during the American intervention in Vietnam in the 1960s, where the Americans heralded technology as the ultimate means to defeat the enemy. Vietnam became the most bombed country in history. As discussed in chapter 5, huge technical advances were made by the Americans, with smart munitions to destroy bridges that free-fall iron bombs had failed to hit after many air raids, as well as electronic countermeasures to defeat Soviet-supplied radar and SAM anti-aircraft missiles, and airborne cavalry carried into contested landing zones by the ubiquitous Huey, which led to the development of effective helicopter gunships and reduced the need for artillery and ground transport links. To provide intelligence on the moves of opponents, the Americans developed the idea of sensors delivered by air that were monitored by continuously orbiting aircraft that would receive and retransmit sensor signals. This system looked toward the "network-centric" warfare idea of the 1990s.[59]

In all these instances, technology was harnessed to provide solutions to known problems, but the tactical and operational use of that technology did not ensure success on the ground, let alone lead to desired strategic outcomes. American air power eventually became something of a blunt instrument, if not a panacea, with President Johnson attempting, in operations such as Rolling Thunder, to bomb North Vietnam into peace talks without a broader understanding of how such an operation would stiffen North Vietnamese resolve. America's opponents, the North Vietnamese and Viet Cong, adapted to the threat by employing supposed American strengths against the Americans, frequently the resort of the weaker combatant and, therefore, in the context of decolonization struggles, an un-Western approach to battle. At the same time, the North Vietnamese use of Soviet-provided technology, notably SAM missiles and advanced radar stations, ensured that even America's much-vaunted air superiority came with a cost. The Americans, in turn, responded by using ever more sophisticated technology, but faith in technology contributed to their failure in Vietnam, although other factors were certainly involved and significant. Moreover, the emphasis should be on how the North Vietnamese fought and, finally, won the war, which they did in 1975, at least as much as on how their opponents lost it.

The extent of the impact of technology in asymmetrical contexts has become more important since 1945 because the development of atomic weaponry—especially in large quantities from the 1950s—has introduced a factor discouraging (though by no means preventing) conflict between states armed with such weapons and therefore has lessened symmetrical warfare. No major state has fought another since the end of hostilities between China and the United States with the close of the Korean War in 1953; and even then China was not yet armed with nuclear weaponry, unlike its ally, the Soviet Union, which neither engaged formally in the conflict nor used its nuclear weaponry.

At the same time, the dependence of the use of weaponry on wider cultural and political constraints has been demonstrated in the case of atomic weaponry, because since 1945 atomic bombs have not been used against opponents who lacked them and therefore were unable to respond in kind. Uneasiness over civilian casualties has become more prominent in the West in recent decades and was also seen in 2011–2012 in the response by much of the Arab world to attempts to suppress reform movements.

Mostly, technology is overrated by the military, the press, and the general public, although the evidence for this is pretty anecdotal. We do not have good means of rating technology, and therefore it is difficult to tell when someone is overrating it. However, it is clear that the military does not necessarily use a new weapon or even a better version of an existing one in a revolutionary way or even necessarily a particularly effective one.[60] Aside from the implications for war making, this situation indicates the need for caution in seeing new military technology as a cause of the transformation of war. As another point, war can be transformed without becoming more effective, as in the case of technology and, to a lesser extent, organization from 1898 to 1916.

Nevertheless, providing troops with better arms than their opponents not only enhances their effectiveness but also their confidence and morale, an important point that is frequently ignored. Thus, during the Second World War, the availability of radar for Britain helped create a sense that the Germans could be beaten in the battles of Britain (1940) and the Atlantic (1939–1945, most acutely 1941–1943). Moreover, a recent analysis of the success of the British Eighth Army in defeating the German-Italian force in Egypt under Erwin Rommel in late 1942 has emphasized morale and argued that it was linked to weaponry. When troops felt their weapons were inferior, as with the British earlier in 1942, they were less willing to risk their lives, and large numbers of uninjured British troops surrendered to attacking Germans as Rommel advanced across eastern Libya and into Egypt. This contributed to growing criticism of the Churchill government in Britain. Conversely, British superiority in firepower at El Alamein helped demoralize the Axis forces.[61] The interplay of weaponry, morale, tactics, and leadership in this case provides an instance of the more general need not to focus on supposed national characteristics.[62] In March 2012, the leadership of an army coup in Mali in West Africa cited the government's failure to provide adequate arms to confront well-armed insurgents as a key motive.

Enhanced confidence and morale can increase fighting quality but can also compromise it by encouraging a misguided confidence in the weapons themselves, or by leading to tactics in which there is a reluctance to close with the enemy for fear of affecting aspects of the weapons' performance. Instead of more resources necessarily increasing fighting quality, better quality made a more effective use of resources. This point implies that forces with superior fighting quality will benefit disproportionately from enhanced (in both quality and quantity) resources, as the Americans did against the Japanese in the Pacific in 1943–1945 in the latter stages of the Second World War. Militaries need men trained to use new weapons, and the Americans provided both in the Pacific and Europe in 1943–1945. The availability of superior firepower helped reduce casualties by lessening the need for frontal assaults and close-quarter engagement or, as happened in successive assaults on Japanese-held islands, by altering the terms of such conflict. In the absence of such resources, forces with superior fighting quality, however, can employ this quality to lessen, indeed sometimes close, the capability gap.

Technology, force structure, fighting quality, doctrine, and tasking are in a dynamic relationship. The greater capability provided by advances in platforms and weaponry makes it possible to envisage and carry out missions that hitherto had been impractical. In 2001, the Americans were able to use helicopters to lift troops into combat from ships in the Arabian Sea to Kandahar in Afghanistan, a distance of 450 miles.

NON-MILITARY TECHNOLOGY

Technological advances have had a major impact, not only in terms of weaponry but also in the varied fields on which war and military technology draw—for example, advances in food preservation, medical treatment, and communications. Materials technology, including metallurgy, ceramics, plastics, and composites, has always been hugely important. Moreover, the significance of broader technological developments can be seen in the case of the dependence of weapons technology on the ability to ensure precision. Electro-optics is a key modern instance of this process. It is a branch of technology involving components, devices, and systems that operate by a modification of the optical properties of a material by an electric field. Thus, electro-optics concerns the interaction between the electromagnetic (optical) and the electrical (electronic) states of materials. The use of lasers and infrared in modern surveillance and targeting systems provides a good example. Modern weapon systems are dependent upon electro-optics for targeting, and targeting is a key component of the systems.

Without accurate and precise targeting, the effectiveness of a weapon is greatly reduced, as the British navy discovered at Jutland in 1916 when the big guns of its warships underperformed. This was part of a general problem of underperformance that affected the world's largest navy at what was mistakenly hoped to be a decisive engagement with the Germans, translating the achievement at Trafalgar in 1805 over the French and Spaniards into the modern age.[63]

The significance of non-military technology can be traced back to prehistory, where the development of agriculture underlines the extent to which key weapons related not only to what is used in fighting but also to the tools that increase society's capabilities. In the case of agriculture, calorific production (though not necessarily nutrition) was improved, ensuring a surplus that eventually permitted specialization in human activity in the shape of full-time warriors. Humans moved from harvesting wild cereals to cultivating crops, which became large scale in western Asia and north China by about 7000 BCE, in Egypt by 6000 BCE, and in northern India and central Europe by 5000 BCE. The spread of agriculture accentuated the development of permanent settlements and led to significant innovations in irrigation and in the processing and storage of food. Metalworking and trade both became important, as food surpluses made it possible for some workers to concentrate on other tasks. In the long term, this situation was to lead to specialization in military service, as opposed to a situation in which all or most of the fit males fought.

Indeed, to reverse the usual emphasis in the discussion of war and technology, it can be argued that, far from weaponry being the key sphere for the successful application of technology in order to enhance military capability, it was these other fields in which application was most important, not least in terms of force projection, command and control, and in sustaining the level of military commitment. Much of this application entailed not the specialized usage of military developments but, rather, the employment of advances in other fields, such as barbed wire,[64] most commonly used to control animals. Earlier, experience in smelting and manufacturing bronze for bronze church bells was significant for the development of cannon founding techniques and later for copper bottoming warships.[65] A recent military review of Australian operations in Afghanistan pressed for the purchase of "commercial-off-the-shelf-equipment" for use against improvised explosive devices.[66] Advances in other fields did not require heavy investment from military-industrial complexes nor, often, government as a whole. Moreover, major companies might have more research capital and capability available, a point readily apparent in the case of modern communications equipment.

This counterintuitive point about non-weaponry technologies serves as a reminder that the inherent strength and adaptability of economies, societies, and states may be more important than the particular characteristics of their military systems. The value of this strength has been underlined as the result of a more positive focus in recent scholarship on the role of private entrepreneurs, rather than governments, in mobilizing resources for war on land and at sea.[67] This point has an application in the shape of the strength of the West on the global scale after the demise of European colonial empires, for this strength is in part a matter of economic, fiscal, and cultural power, rather than simply of military strength. "Soft power" therefore takes on value both in itself and for its military applications.

Looked at differently, the relevance of non-weaponry technologies and capability helps ensure that war can be an important forcing house for the application of developments, so that, for example, medical advances have been pushed hard in wartime, as blood typing was in the First World War. In 1927, Sir Frederick Barton Maurice, a former British major general, gave his inaugural lecture as the Professor of Military Studies, a newly created chair at King's College, London. Maurice declared:

> History shows that great changes in the character of war are normally brought about by other forces than the power of weapons (I am here speaking of war as a whole, not of the tactics of the battlefield), for the tendency is that sooner or later an antidote is found for each new form of attack. . . . [T]he deadlock of trench warfare of 1915–1918 was a revolution, which changed the character of war. But the prime cause of that change was only partly weapons, it was still more numbers; and the reason why armies of millions could be maintained in the field was, I think, first the development of railways, roads, and mechanized transport of all kinds, which enabled supplies to be brought to the front in almost unlimited quantities, and secondly the progress of medical science, which has almost eliminated the danger of epidemic disease. . . . With certain reservations as regards the sea, I would say that the changes which affect the daily lives of peoples, such as developments of transport and of communication, tend to affect war much more than do changes of weapons. [68]

TECHNOLOGY, ADAPTATION, AND TASKING

Non-weaponry technologies are important. The relationship between West and "non-West" involved, and involves, far more than force, and force involves more than technology, but the role of the latter should not be neglected. It is instructive to note how far, especially after 1850, non-Western powers sought access to Western military technology. Turkey was the leading customer of Krupp in the 1900s, as part of a process by which Balkan powers were a key market for advanced weaponry.[69] Moreover, the licensing of weaponry for manufacture became a well-developed process. Thus, the Armstrong Company, a major British arms manufacturer, obtained a licence to manufacture and sell Gatling machine guns within Britain in 1869,[70] while, after the 1965 India-Pakistan war, the Indian Air Force moved from subsonic to supersonic fighters in part by obtaining a license to manufacture the Soviet MiG-21L fighter. By the time war between India and Pakistan was renewed in 1971, seven squadrons of MiG-21 were in service. Another six squadrons were equipped with the Soviet Sukhoi Su-7 strike fighter, although the Indians also designed and built HF-24 Marut fighters. Syria's role as a key market for Russian arms was important in the Russian response to the crisis there that began in 2011.

However, the role of this diffusion has led to an underplaying of the extent to which weaponry, new and old, and both in and outside the West, became operative in particular contexts, and it needs to be considered in this perspective. In both West and non-West, these contexts owed much to preexisting tactical conventions, institutional practices, and military cultures. Thus, in 1940, French strategic and operational inadequacies, rather than deficiencies in weaponry, ensured that interwar German efforts at innovation, which had aimed at incremental improvement, produced instead a "striking and temporarily asymmetrical operational revolution,"[71] or at least—and the analytical contrast is significant—a context within which a particular operational gambit worked. Such circumstances had been lacking in 1914 when Germany had attacked less successfully, in part because the French, eventually, responded more successfully to the German breakthrough than they were to do in 1940. In Saudi Arabia, the acquisition of modern technology from the 1920s, notably Ibn Saud's use of wireless, machine guns, and trucks, both provided the government with a valuable advantage over its opponents who, outside the Hejaz, generally relied on tribal cavalry, and was employed by Ibn Saud alongside more traditional means and goals of fighting, notably the cavalry raid and the politics of winning over opponents.[72]

The extent to which the failure to ensure the adaptations necessary to make the best use of weapons has compromised the ability to exploit change, and therefore limited capability, has become a standard theme in much of the literature. The issue, however, could be reexamined in order to ask whether the need for such adaptation did not vitiate, in whole or in part, the adoption of such weaponry, a point that remains valid. Indeed, there has frequently been a clash between newly fashionable ideas about the acquisition and use of apparently appropriate state-of-the-art weaponry and less modish, but more pertinent, questions of adaptability. These questions range from specifics, such as cost and the necessary level of logistical support—for example, the availability of ammunition—to the general issues of existing military and social practices and the continuities and significant interests they represent.

When this tension is considered alongside the role that tasking, or the setting of goals, plays in military history, including the usage of new technology, then it becomes clear that the impact of technology in the military history of societies is so varied, as well as profound, that it undermines much of the commonplace analysis of enhanced capability in terms of new weaponry. For example, the double-tracking of railways in Europe prior to the First World War was important in speeding mobilization and deployment[73] but is apt to be forgotten in the focus on the machine gun. Yet this enhanced capability in communications affected doctrine and tasking, and not always helpfully. The German ability to mobilize more rapidly than the Russians encouraged the German military leadership to regard the launching of war in 1914 as a reasonable option, not least as there was the understandable belief that French-financed Russian rail improvements in Poland were eroding this advantage by making the Russian mobilization quicker, and thus exposing Germany to simultaneous operations on two fronts. This German view about the launching of war, however, proved very misguided at the strategic level, as skill at the operational level in the opening campaign could not be translated into lasting strategic success.[74]

Earlier, Helmuth von Moltke the Elder, chief of the Prussian General Staff from 1857 to 1888, had grasped the interaction of technological advance and planning, as he became proficient at appreciating how the use of railways enhanced the possible precision of planning and thus changed the nature of the decision-loop. As a reminder of the complexity of explanation, however, so also did the organizational development by the Prussians of an effective General Staff and the use, at lower headquarters, of chiefs of staff who were answerable to the General Staff in order to create an integrated army. Alongside the sense of new potential, this organizational development contributed to a focus on planning that deteriorated into dogma and failure to note wider strategic and political parameters.[75]

The fascination with military change, particularly in weaponry, and the conviction of its value, seen in much of the literature, is somewhat subverted by detailed research on how institutions really adapted to the actual problems of conflict. For example, Jenny West's conclusion about the British Ordnance Office in the mid-eighteenth century—that its traditional and unchanging methods, rather than new departures, helped the office to respond effectively to the very great demands it faced in the Seven Years' War with France (1756–1763)—is more generally applicable. This war saw Britain become the state most effective at global power projection, notably making gains from France in North America, the West Indies, West Africa, and India, and at sea and in 1762 defeating Spain in Cuba and the Philippines; but the issue of objectives is immediately apparent in this case, in that lengthy and widespread conflicts were not anticipated when Britain began hostilities in 1739, 1754, and 1775. More generally, greatly fluctuating demands for gunpowder created problems for both the Ordnance Office and gunpowder makers, while, whether in power or in opposition, politicians were unwilling to extend the power of government in the crucial sphere of gunpowder production and distribution, even though they were aware of their inadequacy.[76]

In short—and similar points could be made about the availability of sufficient cruise missiles today—the optimal effectiveness of the system was affected both by the goals that were pursued and by the parameters of the politically possible. The latter are sometimes discussed in terms of the concept of strategic culture.[77] Changes in the eighteenth century in the production of saltpeter for gunpowder in Sweden demonstrated "how interests, which are not scientific, industrial, or militaristic, still play an important role in the militarization and demilitarization of munition production."[78]

At the same time, the possible is often a matter of cost and the many factors involved in that simple word. For example, trade-offs in specifications can involve the technologically sophisticated against the possibility of more or less, as with American aircraft carriers. The American large-deck *Nimitz*-class carriers are an impressive display of strength, but their expensive two-reactor nuclear power plant has led to discussion of the value of smaller and less complex, and also cheaper, carriers. There are similar trade-offs today in air power, as between manned planes and drones and between types of the latter. In March 1942, during the Second World War, the British launched an attack that wrecked the dry dock at St. Nazaire, the only dry dock on the Atlantic coast big enough to accommodate the 42,000-ton German battleship *Tirpitz*. Thus, the requirements of the warship lessened its usefulness, although Hitler's insistence that she only go to sea when free from real risk was also a key restriction.

The point about the problematic nature of the concept of optimal effectiveness is of value for analysis of the earlier introduction and spread of gunpowder firearms, a topic considered in chapter 2. Moreover, while this spread of firearms has frequently been discussed in terms of a military revolution and the onset of modernity,[79] it is necessary to emphasize its long-term nature, not least the difficulty of establishing both an effective system of gunpowder production and a practical means of battlefield application by infantry. Once due attention is devoted to the complexity of gunpowder, it ceases to be a simple agent of historical change and becomes, instead, the product of a complex process. Like the discovery of the means to measure longitude in the eighteenth century or the development of atomic bombs in the 1940s, this process was an interaction of intellectual achievement and practical knowledge, in the context of political and social circumstances and with respect to particular strategic cultures. The German philosopher Hegel's argument that weapons arise from ideas, and that the factors that frame the latter require consideration, is instructive.[80]

A cross-cultural, historical perspective suggests that the diffusion of military practice across the world has been as important as, if not more so, than that of weaponry; although precision on this point is limited, not only thanks to a paucity of comparative research but also because the development of military institutions in response to foreign examples is variously due to both weaponry and practice, and the latter are of course related. Whatever the country and period, the understanding of technological proficiency and best practice entailed cultural issues, as the acceptance of particular weapons and their usage interacted with the varied appreciation of what was necessary and desirable. Thus, in the United States, although evidence for most soldiers is lacking, there was at least a tendency for expectations in the Civil War (1861–1865) to evolve from a series of heroic contests in which soldiers could ideally display manliness to, instead, a more incessant, machine-like battle in 1864–1865.[81] A similar process was seen in Europe with the First World War. More generally, an important cultural variable was presented by the degree to which a society was keen, or at least ready, to engage with modernity in the form of new elements of a material culture and the attitudes to go with them.

THE PROCESS OF CHANGE

What was supposedly wrought by revolutionary change requires careful consideration alongside analysis of the very process of alleged revolution. The combination of these rethinkings is to replace a "big bang" or triumphalist account. Instead, there needs to be an understanding of the degree to which incremental change not only was most common but also posed (and poses) its own problems, for both contemporaries and scholars, of assessing best practice, as well as the difficulties of determining whether it was appropriate to introduce new methods. Models of the quasi-organic search for best practice and its subsequent diffusion, as well as the language of adaptation, whether or not expressed in Darwinian terms, both make change appear far less problematic than was repeatedly the case and also distract attention from the significance of the understanding of novelty. This point is true for both new weapons and for related organizational changes; while, in addition, their political rationale has to be borne in mind,[82] as do their cost.

The use of Darwinian notions in relation to technological change is problematic, as the adoption of new weapons is in large part a matter of the development of a conflict between attack and defense and the relevant adaptation of fighting methods. Whereas animals do not have to intellectualize over how best to employ biological arms and armor, human beings do intellectualize and often get it wrong. Linked to this, the extent to which success goes to the "best" in human warfare is questionable, as it is unclear what the "best" means.

With firearms, the net effect of the application of knowledge[83] was incremental, rather than revolutionary, change; and the same was true of the earlier introduction of the stirrup, an issue that, like gunpowder, benefits from an understanding of the variety of device and practice thus summarized.[84] The genesis of the stirrup was a long one. It is possible that the Scythians of central Asia used leather loops in the fourth century BCE, although these may simply have been to help in mounting horses. These loops were not, therefore, able to provide a better fighting platform. The latter was offered, instead, by the use of rigid metal stirrups, which provided stability in motion, helping in both shock action and with firing or throwing projectiles from horseback. These actions did not depend on stirrups, and the horse had been used effectively in warfare long before they were developed, but stirrups helped make horses more effective. However, the advantage was a modest one, and the use of stirrups diffused slowly.

The incremental nature of added military value emerges clearly from this example. The effectiveness of steppe forces owed more to the techniques of cavalry use, which were by-products of nomadic lifestyle, than to the technology of the stirrup. This point remained the case with the Mongols of the twelfth and thirteenth centuries, whose use of the short stirrup helped provide a steady firing platform.

Bold statements about revolutionary transformation are frequent for many other parts of the world. Such statements reflect the academic and popular preference for finding such transformation. However, the tendency for change to be incremental involved not only technical improvement but also matching the pace of introduction, adaptation, and deployment with tactical and operational adjustments. Moreover, the consequences of new technology were often less radical than is frequently suggested. For example, there has been a major advance in the understanding of Chinese military technology,[85] and it is clear that gunpowder did not cause a radical restructuring of government or society there.

TECHNOLOGY, ORGANIZATION, AND THE PURSUIT OF VICTORY

It is useful for scholars to adopt a chronological perspective that permits a reconsideration of novelty and technological change, as with the discussion of the early modern period in Europe (ca. 1450–1790) against a medieval background.[86] Indeed, the apparent role of technological transformation in causing change and compromising (or even facilitating) continuity is linked to issues of periodization in history. These issues can lead to an excessive concern with apparent transformation as helping explain the causes and/or consequences of new periods, and albeit to a lesser extent, to interest in such technological transformation in facilitating (or not) opposition to such developments. Furthermore, both in the case of the onset of the early modern period and more generally, there is the question of how weaponry impacted on military and governmental organization, an issue that brings together technological capability and the factors that affect institutional culture, not least social context and political goals.

As a good example, the capability of the Napoleonic military in the 1800s was not so much due to new weapons, though the standardization of the French artillery in the late eighteenth century was important. Instead, organizational and command issues were crucial, not least the development of all-purpose infantry, the massing of firepower at the tactical level, and the use of mixed-armed units: their superiority over unitary structures was clearly demonstrated in the Napoleonic wars, and the mass warfare of that period had important repercussions for contemporary and subsequent debate over the organization of armed forces.[87]

With both weaponry and organization, the processes by which change and debate took place are open to discussion. Intellectual and cultural factors are important for technological and organizational enhancement, not least in terms of how problems are perceived and solutions constructed.[88] Traditionally, there is teleology at play, notably with reference to the use of science, including the very employment of the concept of military science. While being wary of such teleology, it is worthy of note that a self-conscious method of rational analysis was applied in European discussion of warfare and weaponry, especially, but not only, from the sixteenth century. Mathematics was utilized with great effect in ballistics and navigation, while, from the sixteenth century, a "knowledge nexus" had developed that was of particular value in the projection of Western power, as cartography and navigation were employed to gain conceptual understanding of the space of the world. This self-conscious rationalization also affected some military history, with a move from narratives of glory and prowess, in which the emphasis was on the manliness of individuals and groups (manliness understood in terms of honor and bravery), to, instead, attempts to discern and dissect underlying characteristics of success including technological application.

The emphasis on knowledge provides more than one way to discuss the place of technology, for knowledge includes the issue of how conflicts were analyzed differently in order to provide contrasting views on best practice[89] and also focuses on how goals were formulated and assessed. This focus is linked to the reversal of the standard approach for explaining change, by arguing that, instead of weapons dictating tactics, strategy, doctrine, and tasking, it is the assigned tasks that determine doctrine and force structure.

The latter process is even more the case now than earlier, as the range (and cost) of procurement options in weaponry are greater than hitherto. Furthermore, the institutional nature of military systems, and the particular interests and political weight of military-industrial complexes, ensure that there are bureaucratic interests and lobby groups able to press for each option. This situation returns attention to the role of choice in policy formation, and thus of strategic and organizational cultures.[90]

Technology also links to the role of culture, not only in considering a willingness to appreciate, understand and adapt new advances but also as an aspect of a more general sense of flux and new capability.[91] Thus, in an article on the "Future of War" in the American popular news journal *Newsweek* on December 25, 1944, J. F. C. "Boney" Fuller, a British major general turned commentator, wrote: "Before the present century has run its course, there is nothing fantastic in suggesting that complete armies will be whisked through pure speed a thousand miles above the earth's surface, to speed at 10,000 miles an hour toward their enemy."

Like many predictions of future warfare, this assessment proved wrong, and completely so. Earlier, visiting India in 1926 on behalf of the British War Office, Fuller had emphasized the need for the Indian Army to mechanize and had presented this as at once an aspect of modernity and a necessary response to a public that, in the aftermath of the First World War, did not want to face heavy casualties. Fuller argued that the navy and air force "were mechanized forces, materially highly progressive," but he thought the Indian Army reflected "its surroundings" in being Oriental,[92] a process and term that, in the British context, amounted to condemnation.

More generally, the sense of flux and new capability offered by the prospect of new technology can challenge established norms about conflict, as with the idea in the 1990s and early 2000s of a paradigm-shifting revolution in military affairs (see chapter 6), although these challenges themselves have usually been contested by the nature of military practice and institutional culture. The latter, however, became more sympathetic to new technology in the twentieth century. The bloody intractability of the First World War encouraged this process, not least with the conclusion that previous practices were obsolete and with the institutionalization of research. A British memorandum of 1920 for the cabinet noted, "In the early days of the War it was apparent that the existing arrangements for research and experiment in the Fighting Services were quite inadequate. This led to hurried expansion, improvisation and the creation of new establishments."[93] The British proved very successful in this process during the First World War. The tank and gas munitions were the result of official research, although nearly all the British trench warfare munitions, notably the Stokes mortar and the Mills grenade, were invented by civilian engineers.[94] Separate to such research, the history of technology as a distinct academic field largely developed in the United States only from the 1960s.[95]

ASYMMETRICAL WARFARE

Speedy movement by sea and access to air mobility have led modern advanced militaries to an enhanced capability for rapid force projection. This capability has resulted in an increase in points of contact with opponents, and most prominently since 1945 for the United States. Moreover, the pursuit of objectives, especially at a distance, frequently brings technologically very different militaries into conflict in what is known as asymmetrical warfare.[96] Such warfare poses a variety of challenges to both sides, not least depending on the degree to which the less-powerful combatant resorts to guerrilla warfare or terrorism. Each of these seeks to thwart conventional warfare by negating the concentration of effort in order to produce an overwhelming application of force. Such an application is generally valuable in conventional warfare with its focus on capability for battle.

Instead, with guerrilla operations and terrorism, war becomes a much more protracted process, one where it is necessary for counterinsurgency forces to bring political and military strategies into line in order to lessen support for opponents. To this end, technology is very useful, not least aerial surveillance and the mobility provided by airborne forces, as with the Americans in Afghanistan from 2001, but state-of-the-art weaponry alone can achieve only so much, both against guerrillas[97] and against terrorists. Furthermore, a small increase in the numbers of either of the latter can make a major difference to their effectiveness.

The idea that state-of-the-art weaponry can act as a substitute for troop numbers makes more sense for symmetrical warfare than against guerrillas or terrorists, but even for that it has limitations. In 1939, Sir John Dill, commander of the British I Corps in France, complained about the "incalculable" harm done by the British military commentator Basil Liddell Hart, an influential advocate of mobile warfare, and thus tanks, over the previous two decades. Dill wrote:

> Thanks largely to Liddell-Hart's advice, battalions were cut down. The argument was that it is fire power, not man power that is wanted on the battlefield. That may be true up to a point but at night, in fog and when the enemy uses smoke one must have men on the ground. [98]

In practice, the British army in France was seriously outfought by the Germans the following spring, but troops were certainly required for combined arms operations.

The limitations of an advanced military in conflict with motivated irregular forces are scarcely novel. In the case of Western forces, these limitations can be found before the cultural shift in Western attitudes toward war and military service seen from the 1960s, a shift that has been blamed by some commentators for the problems faced by such forces. This shift included a marked and vocal reluctance to cause civilian casualties, which makes it difficult to counter opponents who are not readily differentiated from the general population, a reluctance that affects the current use of drones. However, the failure of Italian forces against Bedouin opposition in Libya in 1911–1912 and of the American expedition of 1916–1917 to find the Mexican guerrilla Pancho Villa are instructive indications both of the more general problems confronting conventional forces and of the impact of these problems prior to the 1960s.

Furthermore, today, in the case of opposition from a domestic guerrilla or terrorist force, while military action itself is necessary to overcome opposition, it is not very helpful as a general policy of civil control to resort to politics and policing by high explosives. Domestic guerrilla opposition or terrorism indeed poses in a particularly acute form the problem that faces all militaries: war involves obliging others to heed one's will, but victory in engagements and occupying territory are only so useful in this process. Like superior weaponry, victory in engagements and occupation are far better than the alternative; but such victory and occupation do not ensure that the defeated accepts the verdict.

Moreover, in operational terms, it is difficult for victorious forces to impose their timetables on opponents who resist occupation.

Instead, as in Iraq in 2003, the victor can find itself in an unresolved situation, unable to obtain closure but denied a clear target whose defeat will ensure it. Moreover, this has repeatedly been the fate of the Israeli military since the Intifada, the rebellion in occupied territories that began in 1987. The Israeli Defense Forces, successfully developed to win quick victories over Arab states as in 1956, 1967, and 1973, and with a strong operational and tactical focus on mobility and a marked proficiency in tank warfare, have found an adjustment of doctrine and force structure difficult, in part, but certainly not only, because of the need to implement policies in the face of the serious constraints posed by domestic and, even more, international opinion.[99]

The role, however, of such constraints in limiting success should not be exaggerated, because there are instances where they have been weak but where success has still been elusive: this was true of Napoleonic forces occupying Spain in 1808–1813, of Germans occupying Yugoslavia in 1941–1944, and of the serious problems affecting the Japanese in China in 1937–1945. Although Chinese conventional forces were defeated, notably in 1937 when Beijing, Shanghai, and Nanjing were captured, followed by Guangzhou and Wuhan in 1938, the Japanese were surprised, and frustrated, by their failure to impose victory, and, within occupied areas, Japanese control outside the cities was limited.[100] There are instances of success in combating irregular opposition, for example, in the Greek Civil War, the Malayan Emergency, and the Soviet suppression of nationalist opposition in Eastern Europe in the late 1940s, but the stress should be on the inherent difficulty of the task of counterinsurgency.[101] It is far from clear why such campaigns should be slighted in the classic canon of military history with its focus on battles and related tactics, leadership, and weaponry. Discussion of Napoleonic-era warfare focuses on Napoleon's 1805–1806 campaigns and his victories of Ulm, Austerlitz, and Jena, rather than on counterinsurgency campaigns in Calabria, Spain, and Tyrol.[102]

The limitations of an advanced military do not mean that it was/is without resources in combating insurrections. Air power, for example, provided major advantages in firepower, mobility, and tempo over the previous punitive use of columns of troops.[103] The latter were slower and susceptible to ambush. Indeed, modern insurrectionary and counter-insurgency warfare can both be discussed, certainly tactically and operationally, in terms of the use of technological advances, and a key dynamic can therefore be seen in terms of responding most successfully to the innovations of the opponent.

As a prime example, the deployment and effective use of simple-to-operate, ground-to-air, heat-seeking missiles was important in the 1970s not only in conventional warfare, notably the Arab-Israeli Yom Kippur War of 1973, but also as a key acquisition for insurrectionary forces, especially those contesting Portuguese power in its African colonies.

Anti-personnel and anti-vehicle mines restricted the safe mobility of counterinsurgency forces on land, and Soviet-supplied SAM-7 missiles hit low-flying aircraft and helicopters. In addition, the guerrillas benefited from Soviet rocket-propelled grenade launchers and from the durable Kalashnikov AK-47 assault rifle, capable of automatic fire, which became the guerrilla weapon of preference. In contrast, to fire a self-loading (or semi-automatic) rifle, such as the American M1 Garand and the British L1A1, the trigger has to be pulled for each shot. The self-loading part means that a new round is chambered after each shot is fired without the rifleman having to do anything, but the weapon cannot fire fully automatic.

In Guinea-Bissau, where guerrilla activity began in 1963, the guerrillas had SAM-7 missiles from 1973. These not only challenged Portuguese air superiority but also powerfully contributed to the sense that the Portuguese had lost the initiative.[104] As a counterfactual (what if?), the possibility of the large-scale use of such weapons against American helicopters in the Vietnam War at a time when electronic jamming was limited raises interesting questions.

Similarly, these missiles, the American Stinger and British Blowpipe, proved important in the Afghan resistance to Soviet forces in the 1980s, although it would be misleading to suggest that this was the cause of Soviet failure. There were already major military and political reasons why the Red Army was failing in Afghanistan. Nevertheless, the use of missiles contributed to a sense of vulnerability and intractability. Soviet helicopters and aircraft were forced to fly higher, reducing the potential for ground support.[105] The Soviets were also forced to alter their takeoff and landing procedures, making them most hazardous. The same sense of vulnerability arose from the Afghan guerrillas' use of anti-tank grenade launchers, notably the Soviet RPG-7 model.

However, shooting off multiple flares, a relatively simple technology, proved a very effective countermeasure to heat-seeking missiles. Aircraft and particularly helicopters were provided with both flares and chaff dispensers. Chaff, which is also used on warships, distracts radar-guided missiles. Anti-aircraft missiles were countered by jamming systems but remained important as a threat to Western forces in Iraq and Afghanistan in the 2000s and early 2010s.

The ground movements of these forces were challenged, more effectively, by the use of explosive devices, both stationary and rocket-propelled. Explosive devices to counter movements by ground forces are not a modern phenomenon. The fourgasse dates from at least the sixteenth century. At Sevastopol during the Crimean War (1854–1856), the Russians added a refinement by employing a chemical ignition system that produced a flame to ignite the fuse when a soldier trod on the mine. Two glass containers (one inside the other) held chemicals that when mixed produced an exothermic reaction of sufficient intensity that the fuse was ignited. When a soldier trod on the containers they broke and the chemicals mixed.

Modern explosive devices ensured that Western dominance in firepower and mobility in Iraq and Afghanistan came with serious costs and uncertainty. They also led to an arms race between explosive devices and both protection and counterdevices, as well as to the development of relevant tactics and operational practices. Thus, in Afghanistan, alongside jamming devices, thermal imaging cameras, and airborne surveillance drones that could trigger bombs remotely came attacks on bomb-making networks and attempts to limit guerrilla safe havens and to interdict their supply routes.

Aside from countering missiles and explosive devices, there were improvements across the range of equipment both used by the American and allied forces in Iraq and Afghanistan and also developed to help in future such commitments. Drones (see chapter 5) attracted most attention but were far from alone. There were also significant improvements in the capabilities of more ordinary weapons. In the early 2010s, a collaboration between American and German companies led to the production of the XM25, a gun able to fire a bullet that explodes near the target due to computer programming, with computers inside the bullet and in the rifle and the relevant data provided by a laser range finder. The technology is designed to prevent opponents benefiting from firing from cover.

The specific capabilities of weapons might appear far removed from questions of political support for the respective combatants, but this support, as in Iraq and Afghanistan, owed at least something, if not much more, to the appearance of success. The effective use of weapons by both sides contributed greatly to the latter.

THE REPORTING OF WAR

Bearing in mind that it is the effect of technology that matters in warfare, not the technology itself,[106] the impact of technology on war is far from a constant but, instead, is affected by and mediated through the multiple contexts of military activity. In particular, the impact of technology is culture-specific, bearing in mind that cultures are not rigid entities but instead capable of development.[107] There has to be a desire for change, and technological change is therefore affected by cultural responses to innovation. Indeed, the Western expectation of technological change was important to developments in military capability and war making over the last century; developments in terms not simply of the global consequences of Western advances but also of changes within the West both in the past and today.

These changes range widely. For example, democratization in the reporting and commemoration of war has been taken a stage further with technology, although this technology is fundamentally an enabler, in the shape, in particular, of the more speedy and insistent reporting of news, while the democratization itself is the product of social shifts. Thus, the twentieth century brought newsreel, radio, television, and then e-mail and mobile phones to war reporting, and advances in filming and transmission made real-time reporting easy. In the attempted authori-

tarian Communist coup in Moscow in 1991, Boris Yeltsin's speech from
the back of a tank was reported live on CNN, thus preventing the Russian junta, which was moving tanks in its effort to seize power, from sup-
pressing the news.

Newsreel and radio first took further the nineteenth-century innovation of the war correspondent, with all the attendant problems of news
management that this posed for government. Indeed, as a positive public perception of operations was important to a sense of victory, in fact
increasingly a definition of victory, so the immediacy that first radio and
then television brought for the public created important problems. The
public, however, was still at a distance, as institutions were heavily involved in the management of news. Thus, John Turner, a British newsreel cameraman in the Second World War, took striking film of the tor-
pedoing by a German submarine of the battleship HMS *Barham* in 1941
in the Mediterranean, in which 869 lives were lost, only to find that the
film was censored.[108] In the Vietnam War, in contrast, it proved more
difficult for the American government to manage what was described
as the "First Television War."

The internet, video cameras, and mobile phones have altered the parameters of possible news management as both public and soldiers moved
into the world of iPhones and YouTube. The easy dissemination of photographs and other material can undermine the war effort as was shown
with the Abu Ghraib scandal and in 2011 with photographs of American Marines urinating in Afghanistan on dead Taliban fighters. Now,
soldiers in the field are able to communicate with family, friends, and
others at home, and this ability creates major difficulties in news management. These were made abundantly clear in 2003, when the serious
problems that American occupation forces faced in Iraq were rapidly
communicated, gravely undercutting the sense of victory that the government had sought to inculcate.

This situation also suggested that, in the future, the views of the military will play a greater role than hitherto in the perception of victory
and, indeed, as a result, that the process of conflict will be much more
closely involved in this perception. Greater ease of personal communications on the part of individual soldiers may also lead to a degree of
interaction between soldiers in the field that poses problems for mo-

rale and discipline, and in a few cases to direct communication with the enemy. Thus, rather than victory as a response to the result of war, there will come a new version of victory as a response to the process of war, with all the problems that the latter entails for cultures, or at least constituencies, that have little idea what to expect.

In short, audiences as well as soldiers will have to be "blooded" to ensure success, an issue that underlines the shifting interaction of war and culture and the manner in which technological impact is dependent on this process. Modern Western culture is uneasy about causing as well as suffering casualties. Indeed, I was told by an Israeli general in the late 1990s that he was now expected to plan operations in which there were not only very few Israeli casualties but also relatively few Arab ones. In earlier periods, direct observation or participation in conflict, or indirect participation via the military service of older male relatives, prepared much of the public for the experience of war, but in a very different fashion to the present situation.[109] As a parallel point, because of the sanitization and distancing of death, most Westerners are now unfamiliar with the sight of a dead human or with the killing of animals.

Technology, in this case the internet and mobile phones, does not operate in a vacuum. Information is a social product, and assumptions about the validity of particular views play an important role. The personalization of events is a problem with war reporting, so that the personal view of the soldier on the ground or, more usually, that of the journalist, is considered more important and more pertinent than a more considered view from someone at headquarters who has access to more facts: experience is valued more than intellect. The latter tends to be mistrusted by the public, which is liable to view information and remarks from senior staff officers as deliberate propaganda, while the front-line view is thought to be pure and untainted, a flawed belief that itself is susceptible to the insidious manipulation of information. New technology provides the public with a snapshot of incidents from a perspective that is never fully made clear, ensuring that the public's perception of war is based on a flawed presentation. A lack of understanding of the nature of war is linked to the tendency to apply civilian peacetime values to an environment that is the very antithesis of normal civil life.

CONCLUSIONS

The impact and role of technology can be qualified from several perspectives. In particular, there is often a tendency to assume that in some way "technology" is an absolute, independent of other factors. The human element in the use of, and response to, technology is frequently overlooked, but in practice there is a complex relationship among observation, experience, perspective, and perception—the last one aspect of the use of technology that is underexplored. For example, to employ the same weapon does not mean that its use is understood, and this inability to understand can lead to a failure to reproduce results. Whether something is adopted successfully may be decided by all sorts of reasons unconnected with technical merit: it is not the technology itself but the response to it that drives change.

As an instance, during the First World War, the British Livens projector was one of the most effective ways of delivering a dense cloud of gas on a specific target. The technology of the weapon itself was simple and, once the means to fire several thousand of them simultaneously had been resolved, it proved to be a devastating weapon that achieved surprise nearly every time it was used. The Germans captured some unfired projectors along with the drums they fired and copied both, but they failed to realize what made the weapon so effective and their use of it was both limited and had little success. Thus, having essentially the same weapon was not enough; tactical and operational knowledge were essential for effective use.

Furthermore, technological change is often used and perceived selectively by historians and commentators in explaining military change, in that only the successes are considered. In contrast, unsuccessful, less successful, or only partially successful ideas, inventions, and developments, such as the plug bayonet, early iron cannon, caseless ammunition, and the anti-missile laser, are overlooked or neglected. In practice, failure plays an important role in the pursuit and process of change. More generally, the assumption that there is continuity in technological improvement is simplistic. Indeed, there may be no pattern other than the one subsequently imposed after the event in order to explain what has happened, in terms of both improvement and impact.

Technological change comes about mostly in response to problems that need to be solved. This is an aspect of the extent to which broader cultural, social, and organizational issues are at stake. Indeed, alongside a perception of the essential socio-cultural foundations of technological success has come a view of technology as a direct "social construct," with social-cultural forces shaping the technology.[110] Once the technology is adopted, societies and cultural norms are themselves shaped by it, not least through the consequences of economic growth and change, but the underlying initial influences remain strong. From this perspective, warfare—the form and structure that it takes, and the technology it uses—emerges as a social construct.

Dethroning technology from the central position in the narrative and explanation of military capability and change does not, however, entail denying its importance or neglecting the degree to which warfare has autonomous characteristics. Instead, it is necessary to adopt a more nuanced approach to the different factors—material, political, cultural, social, and other—that play a role in military capability and change, considering them, not as reified concepts that compete but rather in a manner that allows for the multiple character of their interaction. That is the approach taken in this book.

1

EARLY MODERN WESTERN WARSHIPS

Technologies of Power Projection and Lethality

Killing and the ability to kill are key aspects of military history. In popular works, they also tend to crowd out other types and characteristics of technology. In particular, there is a tendency to downplay those facets that do not relate directly to conflict or to discuss them only when they are involved in battle. This contrast is less marked when considering naval history because ships serve both to project power and to provide the fighting platform. As a result, improvements in the specifications of warships serve to offer an all-round enhancement of capability, although, in detailed terms, as with other branches of military technology, an improvement in a particular specification can compromise other advantages. For example, increasing weight in order to provide greater protection can limit speed and maneuverability, a trade-off that became of major significance as armor developed in the nineteenth century in response to the increased power of naval ordnance.

Western expansion from 1450 to 1700, in what was subsequently described in the West as the early modern period,[1] provides an important instance of the linkage between military technology and key changes in world power. The extent to which global naval strength and world history altered as a result of Western warship technology is a central issue. In turn, this question relates to a number of technologies, specifically ship construction, navigation, and firepower, and these technologies have to be considered in both conceptual and instrumental terms.

A classic means of demonstrating the significance of technological change is to assess the earlier situation, notably the weapons and systems, and then to attribute developments to changes in technology. That approach, however, risks not only crowding out other reasons for developments but also treating the earlier weapons system as inherently static and, therefore, readily supplanted. As far as naval warfare is concerned, this approach, nevertheless, appears self-evident. Western cannon-carrying ocean-going warships won a series of battles in the Indian Ocean in the early sixteenth century, notably off Diu in 1509, an area where there had been no Western warships in the Middle Ages. These victories both apparently demonstrated their superiority and helped secure a new world order dominated by Western powers.[2] In turn, this order attracts attention thanks to modern interest in globalization and the development of long-distance trade links.

As with many popular concepts, there is a considerable basis for this interpretation, but it also faces limitations. First, it is necessary to give due attention to earlier changes in shipping and weaponry. The long-standing tendency to distinguish the Middle Ages from the conditions and processes of modernity and modernization has led to a repeated failure among historians who are not specialists in the period to note the dynamic character of medieval warfare. Secondly, there is a related failure to devote due attention to non-Western developments, although there are some important exceptions.[3]

SHIPS AND CANNON

Initially, the key Western developments in naval capability were made by the Portuguese, who, thanks to their location on the Atlantic edge of Europe, had an unprecedented opportunity to project power. Drawing on late fourteenth- and fifteenth-century Western changes in ship construction and navigation, specifically the fusion of Atlantic and Mediterranean techniques of hull construction and lateen and square-rigging, as well as on advances in location-finding at sea, Portuguese warships enjoyed advantages over other vessels, whether the latter carried cannon or not.

These varied advantages were a reminder of the extent to which technology was not a simple process involving changes only in one element. For example, developments in rigging permitted the Portuguese greater speed, improved maneuverability, and a better ability to sail close to the wind and thus maneuver more effectively in deep water combat, although the significance attributed to the lateen sail has been queried.[4] The ability to sail close to the wind was greater than in the case of Chinese ships.

Developments interacted. Thus, carvel building, the edge-joining of hull-planks over frames, replaced the clinker system of shipbuilding using overlapping planks. This change contributed significantly to the development of hulls that were stronger and better able to carry the heavy guns that challenged stability and seaworthiness by needing to be carried high in the hull so that they could fire above the waterline.[5]

As with other important technological changes, there was no single leap forward but instead a process of development in which there were a number of stages. The Portuguese initially relied on the caravel, a swift and seaworthy but relatively small ship, ideal for coastal exploration and navigation, as well as the *nau* or great ship, a very large carrack-type vessel that could carry a larger cargo and thus support a crew in lengthy voyages. The *nao* was the Spanish equivalent to the *nau*. However, the Portuguese subsequently developed the galleon as a vessel able to sail great distances. It was longer and narrower than earlier carracks, with a reduced hull width-to-length ratio, and was faster, more maneuverable, and capable of carrying a heavier armament. Royal support for shipbuilding also became important in Spain.[6]

Developments in ship construction were linked to changes in firepower, namely the spread of cannon. However, underlining the extent to which technological changes did not simply combine but also operated on different chronologies, it was not necessary to have a large sailing ship in order to carry cannon, because galleys were also altered in order to carry them. Indeed by the mid-fifteenth century, galleys were being built to carry cannon, and in 1513 French galleys showed their ship-killing capability at the expense of the English fleet off the French naval base at Brest. In the sixteenth century, the emphasis on firepower in galley warfare increased. These cannon were carried forward and supplemented the focus on forward axial attack already expressed by the presence of a metal spur in their bow.[7]

Yet, as a reminder of the dependence of weapons effectiveness on the platforms available, galleys could not mount the armament of sailing ships because of the requirements linked to their being rowed by large numbers of men. In contrast, in sailing ships, cannon could be fired not only from bow and stern but also from the side of the vessel. Moreover, as a sign of the process of accretional change, this ability owed much to the development around 1500 of gun-ports just above the waterline and of waterproof covers for them. These covers ensured that guns could be carried near the waterline as well as higher up, thus reducing top-heaviness and increasing firepower.[8] Such cannon, moreover, could inflict serious damage near the waterline, and, thereby, hole opposing warships. Indeed, it has been suggested that the development of more powerful "ship-killing" warships constituted a revolution in naval warfare.[9]

The cannon themselves reflected a process of accretional development, and one in which effectiveness was considered in a number of lights and was capable of a range of definitions, including that of cost. The introduction of cannon was certainly a difficult process at sea, and not only there. There was no pattern of rapid change. Wrought-iron cannon remained in use on ships until into the nineteenth century.[10] The manufacture of large cast-iron weapons was initially beyond the technological scope of the period, but, from the mid-fifteenth century, firepower was increased by the development of large cannon cast, instead, from lighter, more durable, and workable "brass," which was actually a form of bronze. Whereas brass is an alloy of copper and zinc, bronze is an alloy of copper and tin that can also include lead or zinc. Gunmetal is a form of bronze, as it includes zinc. These cannon were thick enough to withstand the high pressure from large powder charges and were able to fire iron shot with a high muzzle velocity and great penetrative force. The stone shot used in early cannon were phased out.[11]

In turn, cast-iron cannon were produced from the mid-sixteenth century. They were relatively inexpensive but were not preferred for warships as they were liable to fractures during casting and could burst when overheated through rapid firing. Cast-iron cannon did not become the leading naval cannon until after 1650, when the growth of big battle fleets was eased by the availability of cheap large-caliber cast-iron guns. Demand from purchasers interacted with the development of cast-iron technology, offering a good example of the relationship between goals and capability. Investment was encouraged by other aspects of enhanced capability, notably significant earlier improvements in gunpowder that increased the range of cannon.[12]

The impression that is created is that of a technologically driven and enabled revolution in naval power and capability, with developments in ship construction, rigging, navigation, muzzle-loaded cast-metal cannon, and heavy cannon on the broadside, all giving the West a key advantage. The latter advantage is seen in particular episodes, especially Portuguese victories in the Indian Ocean in the early sixteenth century. The arrival of Dutch and English sailing ships in the Mediterranean from the late sixteenth century, and the copying of this technology by Mediterranean powers, first the North African Barbary states and, later, Venice and the Ottoman Turks, is treated as further evidence of this process. The rise of the large specialized warship, in place of ships used for both trade and war, is also seen as a key aspect of specialization.

There are, however, significant problems with this account of a technologically driven shift in naval strength and world power. Other factors were also highly significant, notably the international context. The Chinese abandonment of long-range naval expeditions after the 1430s took a potential opponent out of the equation. In addition, alongside the strength of Portuguese warships, the success of their operations in Indian waters owed much to political factors, not least eventual Gujarati hostility to the Ottomans. The amphibious character of many Portuguese operations accentuated this point. Moreover, there was also, notably from the 1520s, willingness on the part of the Portuguese to rely on warships based on local designs and also to focus on boarding enemy ships and using armored soldiers, rather than destroying ships by cannon fire.[13] The preponderance of short-range pieces in English inventories in the 1540s supports a similar interpretation but, by 1569, the English emphasis had changed to heavy guns capable of both long ranges and devastating short-range fire.[14]

As far as technology is concerned, it is necessary, first, to consider the process of development in the West and, secondly, its impact on the world scale. It is important to avoid the teleological assumption that development was a matter simply of sinking ships through gunfire and, therefore, that the arrival of more powerful ship-killing warships (and the appropriate guns) represented a revolution. Instead, it is necessary to note the difficulties of the process. The introduction of large numbers of cannon on individual ships was a challenge for ship design, made maritime technology more complex, and greatly increased the operational and fighting demands on crews.

Furthermore, it has been argued that, as with land warfare, earlier, fifteenth-century changes were also significant. Such a shift of emphasis entails a focus on a different chronology, specifically looking at a longer-term process of development and thereby reducing the supposedly revolutionary impact of any particular stage. Kelly DeVries has written that it is necessary to focus on a "process of technological and tactical evolution which began with the advent of gunpowder weapons on land, and then progressed through the placement of these guns on board ships, their use in naval engagements as anti-personnel weapons, their increase in size and numbers, and, finally, their changes in technology, separate from similar weapons used on land, in order to produce weaponry that was effective by contemporary criteria."[15]

The progression suggested, however, is not entirely plausible, as it implies a relatively simple, sequential process. In practice, such things rarely occur in the real world. While it is clear that some developments depend upon the existence of certain others, and hence a chronological progression can be discerned as innovations are made, that does not constitute a clear lineage. Rather it is often pattern-spotting after the event, and a pattern-spotting that tends to neglect the failures and dead-end developments that add up to a non-linear progression.

In this case, a progression from anti-personnel to anti-material weaponry was probably less obvious than might be implied, as the size of weapons was not merely a question of what was technically feasible to make but a question of perception about how such weapons might be employed. The two are interlinked, but it is unwise to project small to large as a process because often it was the other way round, as with small arms ammunition.

If the focus is on shipping, the process of change was also a long one. Developments in the fourteenth and fifteenth century, particularly the increase in the number of masts, the number of sails per mast, the variety of sail shapes, and the spread of the sternpost rudder, were each of significance. The relationship between firepower and other developments was less clear-cut than has sometimes subsequently been suggested. Thus, changes in rigging, and the arrival both of cast-metal cannon and of heavy cannon on the broadside, did not all occur at once, nor were they mutually dependent. The respective significance of particular changes is difficult to assess, and this difficulty has implications for the attempt to analyze the nature and consequences of technological development.

ORGANIZATIONAL SUPPORT

There is the additional factor of the need to consider other criteria of naval capability, criteria that were related to technological development but not dependent on it. The key variables here were those of maritime context, political support, and administrative capability. The first was significant for the availability of skilled and experienced captains, navigators, and sailors, and the skill and experience required increased, as it was a case of sailing greater distances and farther from the sight of land.

Political support was highly important because of the great cost of naval power and the need for a pooling of resources in order to create and sustain it. The requirement for cannon, indeed for many cannon, accentuated the extent to which the construction, equipment, manning, supply, and maintenance of a fleet all required considerable financial and logistical efforts and posed very different issues to those of land power.

These problems were enhanced by the nature of the available technology because a key feature of the period was the lack of change in the fundamentals of construction material and propulsion method. In short, it was the lack of technological transformation that requires emphasis. The construction of large warships using largely unmechanized processes was, by the standard of the age, an immense task requiring considerable labor inputs and formidable capital investment, not least to provide large quantities of seasoned timber of the correct size.

Ships, however, generally had a life of only 20–30 years. Moreover, maintenance was expensive, as wood and canvas rotted, while iron corroded. The construction and support of warships therefore demanded not only advanced shipyards but also permanent institutions to manage them and to arrange and finance supplies. Indeed, fleets represented the major industrial activity of the period and required a comparable administrative effort.[16]

This need provides a different way to look at Western proficiency than that based on technology. Non-Western states had warships carrying cannon. The question is whether the contrast with the West rested, in the short term, not on technological capability but on the degree of political support and administrative sophistication. The latter two can be seen as helping to finance and implement technological progress in the longer term but, at any given stage of progress, it was the willingness and ability to finance and organize naval activity that was the key factor. Thus, technology emerges as an element within a wider matrix, as is always the case.

In the early modern period, the major change was the development in Western Europe of a state commitment to permanent naval power, a development that was based on political and economic factors. The presence of a number of states competing in the seas around Europe was significant, and notably because such warfare became more protracted during the sixteenth century. This commitment was matched in the case of the Ottoman (Turkish) empire in the sixteenth century.[17]

Secondly, new long-distance trade routes focusing on Western Europe led to a commitment to naval strength as a way to benefit from their trade.[18] Fleets furthering the interests of earlier territorial states had been important, notably with ancient Greece and classical Rome,[19] but, in Europe, they became more permanent and more clearly under government control in the sixteenth and, even more, seventeenth centuries.[20]

Political support could be a complicating factor as well, for example, the fashion in the early sixteenth century for very large warships, such as Henry VIII of England's four-masted *Henri Grace à Dieu* (Great Harry), which reflected the desire to make a statement about royal power as much as functional considerations. The *Great Michael*, an enormous warship built for James IV of Scotland in 1511, cost £30,000 (Scots) to construct and had running costs of £668 monthly at a time when annual royal income was less than £4,000 per year. In contrast, under Elizabeth I in the 1570s, the English built smaller and more maneuverable warships. The English warships opposing the Spanish Armada in 1588 carried 883 cannon.[21] At the same time, both the Armada and the subsequent English attack on Iberia in 1589 illustrated the limitations of naval power in this period, not least vulnerability to storms, the difficulties of combined operations, and the major supply problems posed by large fleets.

The issue of organizational sophistication is not separate to that of technology but germane to it. Both were interacting aspects of economic development, with finance and institutional processes forming common elements. Moreover, as was to be the case throughout any discussion of technology, and as remains pertinent today, the resources mobilized and produced by economic development played a crucial role in the ability to develop and apply new technological concepts. This was particularly so with metallurgy, the basis for more effective cannon, and with shipbuilding. The latter in particular saw interplay between advances in empirical practice and greater scientific knowledge, notably of hydrostatics and ship stability.[22] Quantification played an important role.[23]

Knowledge was not only acquired and disseminated through craft practices, it was also spread in publications, which became more important from the sixteenth century as printing enhanced possibilities for the systematization and dissemination of knowledge and technique. For example, Pedro Medina's navigational treatise, first published in Spanish in 1545 in Seville, a center of knowledge about exploration, was translated into English, French, German, and Italian. Medina also made astrolabes and other navigational tools. Publications ranged from theoretical and cutting-edge, such as *De Havenvinding* (1599) by the Dutch mathematician Simon Stevin, a study of determining the longitude of a ship, to works of a more artisan character, such as Henry Bond's *The Art of Apparelling and Fitting of Any Ship* (1655), which assessed the optimum lengths and thicknesses of masts, yardarms, and cordage. A similar work was Thomas Miller's *The Compleat Modellist: or, Art of Rigging* (1660), and the demand for such works was shown by it going through several editions.

The dissemination of new knowledge was a key theme, both in cartography and in navigational works, for example, Thomas Addison's *Arithmetical Navigation* (1625), which provided detailed knowledge of the effective use of naval charts and of the celestial bodies. Aside from material from mathematicians, there was also information from explorers, as with John Davis's *The Seamans Secrets* (1595), which provided advice on how to read charts and use instruments.

Moreover, the revisions of both navigational works and maps, as in the different editions of Edward Wright's *Certain Errors in Navigation* (1599), reflected an attitude to received knowledge and authority that encouraged a process of improvement. Debate was central to the process of improvement. For example, Peter Blackborrow, a sea captain, produced *The Longitude Not Found* (1678), a critique of *The Longitude Found* (1676) by Henry Bond, a teacher of applied mathematics, as well as *Navigation Rectified: or, the Common Chart proved to be the only true chart . . . with an addenda . . . proving Mercator's practical rules in navigation to be notoriously false* (1687). Although important, England was scarcely alone as a source of important publications in the seventeenth century. For example, *Hydrographie, contenant la théorie et la practique de toutes les parties de la navigation* (1643) was by the French Jesuit mathematics professor Georges Fournier.

If, therefore, technology is understood in the broadest sense, as permitting both the application of scientific and practical advances and economic development, then the technological and economic development that helped in the development and spread of printing with moveable type in Europe[24] can be regarded as making technology possible in the narrower sense of relevant aspects of military activity.

The emphasis on political and organizational support is readily pertinent in the case of naval warfare. In the early modern period, on the
global scale, there was a process of consolidation in naval power that
was not primarily due to technological factors. This consolidation involved, in particular, the ending of large-scale east Asian naval activity.
In considering this factor, it is pertinent to note the issue of timing.
Long-range east Asian naval activity was significant, with China, in the
early fifteenth century,[25] while large-scale, but short-range, activity was
very much the case in the 1590s, as Japan, Korea, and China struggled for
control of Korea.[26] Thereafter, there was neither long-range activity nor
anything on this scale. That did not mean, however, a lack of ability to
mount amphibious operations, an ability seen, in particular, in the capture of the Dutch positions in Taiwan in the early 1660s.[27]

Yet, both in regional waters and farther afield, the relative lack of
Chinese naval action is notable. This was the case, for example, during
the Manchu conquest of Ming China in the 1640s and 1650s, with neither side making much use of naval power. Thereafter, the Manchu continued this pattern. Whereas the Mongols, in the thirteenth century,
having conquered China, had used its naval resources in order to attack Japan and Java, there was no comparable activity in the case of the
Manchu. For example, war with Burma in the 1760s did not have a naval
component other than in building river-boats in 1769.[28] There was no revival in the navy to match the upsurge in piracy in Chinese waters at the
close of the eighteenth century. In a different context, that of the abandonment of expansionism, the Japanese also did not resume the major
amphibious operations seen in the 1590s.

This shift away from long-range east Asian naval activity was of major importance, both in world history and, more specifically, in naval
history. It cannot be traced to technology, or to economics, or to organization. East Asian shipping had shown an impressive long-range
capability and remained important for mercantile activity. Moreover,
although the Philippines were farther away from China than Taiwan,
the effort brought to bear against the latter could have been replicated

for the Philippines. The ability of the Chinese to campaign at a distance was to be displayed in particular in the eighteenth century, with operations mounted and sustained against Tibet, Xinkiang, Nepal, and, less successfully, Burma. The organizational capacity of the Chinese has attracted attention, and it was related to a formidable resource effort.[29] Both could have been the case for naval activity. For example, without expecting any technological enhancement, China could readily have mounted an invasion of Japan.

The key element therefore does not appear to be technology, however defined. As earlier with Mamluk Egypt, which also focused on land warfare,[30] there were resource issues, notably the availability of timber, and organizational problems, especially the disruption of Chinese naval administration and shipbuilding during the long wars with the Manchu that preceded their conquest of China. However, although naval systems could not simply be wished into existence, Manchu China had a much better basis for acting as a naval power than Peter the Great (r. 1689–1725) was to have in Russia in the early eighteenth century, not least with an established maritime tradition, a far longer coastline, waters that were open for navigation year-round, and a lack of powerful rivals able to try to close off naval options.

Yet, this basis was not to be developed, nor was there to be development in the very different political context of India,[31] although, in part, this was because the British in the late eighteenth century cut short Maratha and Mysore efforts to establish navies. These efforts are difficult to evaluate, but, alongside bold plans, notably by Tipu Sultan of Mysore in the 1780s and 1790s, there was not only powerful British opposition but also institutional weaknesses facing the development of a large fleet.[32]

The Ottoman (Turkish) empire was the leading non-Western naval power, but, despite its need to protect maritime links in the eastern Mediterranean and the pilgrimage routes to Mecca and Medina, its ambitions at sea were very much subordinated to serving as a land power and notably so by the close of the seventeenth century. Persian naval power was far more limited, although, in the 1730s and 1740s, it was possible to mount expeditions to Oman, which itself was a regional naval power.

There was no equivalent to the successive naval potency of Portugal, Spain, the United Provinces, France, and Britain. Looked at differently, the great strength the Ottomans displayed in the Mediterranean in the sixteenth century,[33] and their strength in the Black and Red Seas and the Persian Gulf, was not matched elsewhere, as the Ottoman impact in the Indian Ocean was more limited and, in the end, short term.[34] Again, perspective is significant, as the Mediterranean was important economically and politically, only for its importance to be underplayed due to a subsequent tendency to focus, from the sixteenth century, on the strategic and economic role of Atlantic naval power. The Ottomans remained a significant naval power in the Mediterranean into the eighteenth century, albeit being heavily defeated by the Russians at Cesmé off the island of Chios in 1770. This battle, one of the most decisive of the century, involved the use of fireships, a technique not at any technological cutting-edge.

NAVAL SUPERIORITY

If Atlantic naval power is under consideration, then the center of attention is not technology, as competing Western navies had essentially similar warships and armaments. In explaining, for example, Britain's naval superiority by the eighteenth century, it is not pertinent to look at better ships. Indeed, Sir Thomas Slade, surveyor of the Royal Navy from 1755 to 1771, designed a series of two-decker seventy-four-gun warships that were both maneuverable and capable of holding their own in the punishing close-range artillery duels of line-of-battle engagements, and he did so by working from French and Spanish warships in the 1740s.

Instead, the material and institutional advantages of the Royal Navy were crucial. These advantages stemmed from steadiness of financial support, commitment to maintaining a large reserve of seamen through peacetime enforcement of the protectionist Navigation Acts, and a public and political assumption that there would be extensive and sustained active service at sea. In turn, the navy safeguarded the dynamic competitiveness of the multi-lateral British Atlantic commercial system, helping give Britain a key advantage over its rivals.[35]

The lack of a crucial difference between warships and between armaments meant that there was no real technological gap between the major states; but that did not entail the absence of a contrast in capabilities between states with such fleets. Superior British gunnery was a key instance. Britain had an advantage in technology and industrial capability in its developing metallurgical industry, as well as having good seamanship and well-drilled gun crews. The last owed much to experience, demonstrating a major point in evaluating capability, namely familiarity with the use of weapons in battle conditions.

Resources and organizational sophistication also help explain the strength of the major navies as compared with other naval forces. For example, the sailing and fighting qualities of pirate ships were not different from those of warships, and the former could be very significant.[36] Instead, it was the organizational underpinning of the major navies that contrasted greatly with that of pirate forces.

DECLINING NAVAL FORMS

In the West, other forms of warship were eventually crowded out. Viking longboats had provided mobility and flexibility, and notably, with their shallow draught and prow at either end, they were suitable for inshore waters and rivers, as well as being able to travel in the open seas. The Viking tradition of longship building had continued for centuries. It remained important in the islands off west Scotland until the late sixteenth century, providing mobility and a continued capacity for raiding. In 1533, an English attempt to impose their power by using new naval technology failed when the *Mary Willoughby* was captured by longships off the Shetlands. The use of Viking-style longships in the Western Isles, especially by the MacDonalds, permitted the transport of troops to Ulster, employing Lough Foyle as the landing area, throughout the sixteenth century. Attempts to intercept the fleets by English sailing ships were unsuccessful, as were efforts to penetrate into the lochs of the Mull of Kintyre to attack the vessels at source. Only the occupation of Lough Foyle by the English finally solved the problem.

By then, the Scandinavian kingdoms—Denmark (which also ruled Norway and Iceland) and Sweden (which also ruled Finland)—had navies of a conventional European type. The shallowness of parts of the Baltic as well as its limited tides were to encourage the additional use of shallow-draught ships, especially the Swedes in the Gulf of Finland in the eighteenth century. However, these ships were different from long-boats and were also deployed as part of a navy organized around supporting ships of the line. In the Mediterranean, galleys were of minor importance by the late eighteenth century.

CONCLUSIONS

The question of why the West came to dominate the oceans is an important one, as this dominance was crucial to later world history. Alongside ships that could readily fulfill the task in the absence of similar capability on the part of non-Western powers, an emphasis on (Western) resources, organizational sophistication, and political support, as in this chapter, is more generally pertinent for the discussion of technology, although that does not mean that other issues should not be considered, as we note in the following chapters. This emphasis provides a way to consider, amplify, and contradict differences in the use of technology in various parts of the world and, therefore, contrasts in the importance of technology.

For example, it has been argued that capital-intensive military innovations were a characteristic of Western society. Geoffrey Parker has advanced this thesis as a way to link the Greeks of the fifth century BCE, the (non-Ottoman) Europeans of the Renaissance (fifteenth and sixteenth centuries CE), and more recent Western warfare, including the development of the atom bomb. Parker relates this emphasis on research and technology to a willingness to spend and an ability to pursue the intellectual understanding of natural processes and possibilities. In contrast, he argues there was a shortage of the necessary flexibility in cultures that lacked diversity and openness.[37] As with any overarching interpretation, this thesis, while helpful, has to be addressed with caution, notably because it risks primitivizing non-Western societies and then explaining their fate accordingly, an approach that has been all too common. In practice, the answer to the global contrast is multi-dimensional.

From the technological perspective, this issue also opens up the question of whether the equations of technological proficiency and application, economic strength, organizational sophistication, and political support are different for armies and navies. This potential difference is a factor when the preference of certain societies, such as Mamluk Egypt and Moghul India, for land warfare, notably cavalry, is discussed. As a result, we return again to the extent of cultural factors in explaining contrasts between Western and non-Western societies and to trying to assess these factors alongside environmental issues.[38] However, that issue does not exhaust the matter. In a sense, as throughout with the question of the impact of technology, we are left in an indeterminate situation, one that captures the interaction between material circumstances, cultural and political assumptions, and the complexities of conflict.

The exceptional nature of Western naval strength, however, was clear, and notably by the eighteenth century. John Corneille noted that when Muhammad Ali Khan, Nawab of the Carnatic, visited HMS *Kent* in 1755, he was "greatly surprised at its size and number of guns."[39] A foreign source, more particularly a self-interested British one, for the views of an Indian ruler is perforce unreliable, but there is no direct information on the latter. Moreover, no eighteenth-century Indian state had a warship comparable to the *Kent*, nor was indeed to have one.

2

GUNPOWDER TECHNOLOGY, 1490–1800

Edward Gibbon was to claim that gunpowder "effected a new revolution in the art of war and the history of mankind,"[1] a view that was common in the eighteenth century and indeed both earlier and later.[2] More recently, the widely repeated thesis of the early modern Military Revolution[3] has focused renewed attention on the issue of gunpowder technology. Improved firepower and changing fortification design, it is argued, greatly influenced developments across much of the world and, more specifically, the West's relationship with the rest of the world. In other work, I have questioned the thesis,[4] but here, first, I want to draw attention to the changes that stemmed from the use of gunpowder.

THE DEVELOPMENT OF GUNPOWDER

Gunpowder weaponry developed first in China. We cannot be sure when it was invented, but a formula for the manufacture of gunpowder was possibly discovered in the ninth century, and effective metal-barreled weapons were produced in the twelfth century. Guns were differentiated into cannon and handguns by the fourteenth.

Each of these processes in fact involved many stages, with technical issues overcome as well as the need to accept a new idea in weaponry, the explosion. As far as the earliest use of gunpowder as a propellant or explosive, as opposed to a pyrotechnic composition for, say, fireworks, is concerned, someone discovered, probably by chance, that compacting the powder in a small chamber altered the way the material behaved when ignited; or, rather, the way the combustion gases behaved. This discovery, in itself, probably led nowhere until someone else (probably) had an idea about how to harness the energy of the explosion. Several inventive leaps were necessary before any sort of recognizable weapon appeared. It is likely that there may have been a considerable time interval between the discovery of the combustible properties of what was to become known as gunpowder and the discovery that it could be used to explode things and to propel objects. This schema would be in accordance with the normal condition of technological development prior to modern industrialization. Such development was largely incremental based on experience, rather than being revolutionary and based on abstract conceptualization.[5]

From then on, ways were sought to improve both the explosive properties of the powder and the ability of "guns" to withstand the detonations. With the gunpowder mixture of sulfur, charcoal, and saltpeter (potassium nitrate), it was important to find a rapidly burning formula providing a high propellant force.[6] An increased portion of saltpeter, which provided oxygen for the gunpowder reaction, transformed what had initially been essentially an incendiary into a stronger explosive device. With cannon, it was necessary to increase the caliber and to move from pieces made of rolled sheet iron reinforced with iron bands to proper castings. The vulnerability of infantry, including those armed with gunpowder weaponry, to cavalry attack at this stage ensured that these weapons were largely used on ships and in fortifications.[7]

Knowledge of gunpowder was brought from China to India[8] and Europe in the thirteenth century, although the path of diffusion is unclear. The extent of Mongol rule, from China to Eastern Europe, may well have helped in this diffusion. Once gunpowder emerged in the West, however, a different mind-set approached the questions of improvement, which was eventually pursued with considerable energy. In the fourteenth century, gunpowder was used in cannon. The first "handgonnes" date to an English reference of the 1380s, and they were known elsewhere in the 1370s. Assessing early gunpowder weaponry is difficult due to the lack of a developed language and vocabulary for such weapons. However, much can be learned, not least from surviving weapons.[9]

Gunpowder presented the ability to harness chemical energy. Cannon indeed have been referred to as the first workable internal combustion engines, although they do not qualify if only because no cyclic process in which expansion and compression alternate (the Carnot process) occurs.

Many states benefited from switching to gunpowder weaponry, and the latter increased markedly in potency in the fourteenth and fifteenth centuries. The replacement of stone by iron cannonballs, the use of better gunpowder, and improvements in cannon transport all raised artillery capability.[10]

EARLIER FIREPOWER

In the case of both cannon and handguns, there was also the need to consider their respective value against earlier weapons. Cannon competed with siege weapons, which had a long history going back to antiquity. Siege engines included devices that came into direct contact with the walls, notably battering rams and siege towers, and those that fired projectiles, especially catapults. Mining was also used to undermine walls. Considerable technological sophistication could be involved with siege engines, and there was also a process of improvement and specialization that is relevant as a comparison with the subsequent (and shorter) history of gunpowder firearms. Works such as *On Machines* by the first century BCE Athenaeus Mechanicus reflect an interest in the possibilities of mechanization.

Catapults came in different sizes and threw projectiles that had varied purposes. Large catapults could throw heavy stones designed to inflict damage to the structure, for example, to the battlements. Medium-sized catapults launched bolts, and lighter handheld ones fired arrows and small stones designed to clear away defenders from their positions. Such anti-personnel weaponry provided an opportunity for gaining tactical dominance and for the use of siege engines against the walls. When Alexander the Great of Macedon successfully besieged the well-fortified port of Tyre in 332 BCE, during his conquest of the Persian Empire, the catapults were able to provide covering fire for battering rams employed to breach the walls, and also for boarding bridges from which troops moved into the breaches from ships. Cannon were later to provide the breaching force of the battering rams without needing their close contact, although, in the age of cannon, breaching castle walls was also still achieved by mining.

Alongside specialization in the pregunpowder age came the improvement of weapons in order to enhance their effectiveness. Bolt-shooting catapults were equipped with stands and winches, which served to build up a major tensile strength so that they could outfire handbows. Roman catapults relied on torsioned ropes. The animal sinews within the ropes of the torsion machines were there for strength. In contrast, in the composite bows, the sinews were there for flexibility, as the horn and wood gave the composite bow its strength.[11]

By the late fourth century BCE, in response to important developments in the scale of fortifications, the Hellenistic powers that succeeded Alexander's Macedonian empire were able to produce more formidable siege weapons. Siege towers became larger and heavier, able to project more power, and were also better defended, for example, with iron plates and goatskins to resist the fire missiles and catapults launched from the positions they were attacking. Flexibility in usage was crucial, an aspect that can be lost if the emphasis is on other specifications. For example, the siege towers could be assembled and disassembled, so that they could be taken on operations, but others would be made on site if timber was available. The latter capability was a key aspect of weapon use. The effectiveness of battering rams was enhanced by sheathing them with iron and mounting them on rollers, thus increasing their momentum and accuracy. At the siege of Rhodes in 305–304 BCE, there were also iron-tipped borers (made effective by a windlass, pulleys, and rollers) that were designed to make holes in the walls.

These were not the real competitors with cannon. Instead, it was the trebuchet, the most powerful siege engine in terms of the projectile that could be fired. Invented in China in the fifth to third century BCE, the trebuchet was a traction piece that contained a rotating beam placed on a fulcrum. A sling was hung from the beam, and the projectile was placed in it. On the shorter side of the beam, ropes were hung and, when they were pulled, the projectile was thrown forward. Experiments have shown that if the slings of traction trebuchets were hung onto, as is depicted in the illustrations, the arc is flattened and the ballistic force is increased, which is the way it would usually have been used in a siege. This usage is not at all like a howitzer or mortar, which is why it is not helpful to suggest that the gunpowder equivalents of the trebuchet were the howitzer and the siege mortar.

Overcoming fortifications was important in order to transform raiding into conquest. This overcoming did not necessarily require siege engines and the related logistical capability and combined arms approach, as the surrender of fortifications could follow defeat in the field or the suborning of support. The latter was particularly seen in early modern Indian warfare.[12] Nevertheless, an ability to take fortifications was important as a measure of military effectiveness.

As with other successful weapons not dependent on a secret or highly complex manufacturing process, the use of the trebuchet spread, and it was employed by both sides during the Crusades. Moreover, again as part of a common process, the weapon became more effective. In the twelfth century, the Arabs replaced the ropes, which had been pulled down by men, with a counterweight, although not everywhere or always, for the Arabs continued using the traction trebuchet at least for a century after the counterweight trebuchet appeared. By the thirteenth century, the latter had also replaced the earlier model in Europe, where trebuchets superseded torsion catapults. The latter were more accurate but could not throw such a powerful projectile. Trebuchets hurled stone balls, some of which weighed up to a massive 140 kilograms (300 pounds) and could cause great damage. Trebuchets were also more accurate than might be imagined. The last major Crusader fort, Acre, fell in 1291 to a determined Mamluk assault after its defenses had been weakened by trebuchets and by mining.

THE CHANGE TO GUNPOWDER

Nevertheless, siege engines were to be replaced by cannon. The process of replacement is instructive, as it shows the range of factors that could be involved when one weapon was succeeded by another, and also the often lengthy transition,[13] both features more generally true of the nature of technological development prior to the Industrial Revolution.[14] Improvements in the production of iron, making it possible to manufacture larger cannon, were important but did not automatically lead to change. For a while, siege engines were supplemented by and then supplemented cannon, as with Henry V of England's successful siege of the French fortress of Harfleur in 1415 prior to his victory at Agincourt.[15]

The continued use of stone-throwing trebuchets owed something to observation of their continuing value,[16] as well as to disadvantages with the new gunpowder weaponry, notably the cost,[17] although the trebuchets went out of fashion relatively quickly after cannon were deployed, with only a few appearing after 1415. Aside from in sieges, cannon were also used as field artillery, and definitely so from the early fifteenth century: the Hussites commanded by Jan Zizka used field artillery at Kutná Hora in 1421.[18]

The effectiveness of cannon, however, was limited by their inherent design limitations throughout the fifteenth century. Large siege bombards were extremely heavy and cumbersome to move and position. Great skill was required by the gunsmiths to hammer lengths of wrought iron together to ensure that the seams were able to withstand the pressures generated within the barrels. However, the use of a separate breech chamber to hold the powder and shot increased the speed of loading, with gunpowder preloaded and in a cool chamber.[19] The extent to which there was a requirement to cool down after firing is probably overstated and, therefore, the extent to which the rate of fire was correspondingly limited can be queried.

In 1552, in the siege of Kazan, the capital of an Islamic khanate on the River Volga, the victorious Russians under Ivan IV, the Terrible, employed a wooden siege tower carrying cannon and moved on rollers. This was an example of the integration of old and new methods, a process that was frequently typical of transitions from one to another but that also reflected a hedging of bets in the shape of an unwillingness to embrace the new at the expense of the old. In this siege, the Russians benefited from deploying 150 cannon in their first large-scale use of artillery, compared to 70 in the city, from their use of a mine tunneled beneath the walls, and from a simultaneous assault on all the gates.

Trebuchets were replaced by cannon, which eventually offered a greater mobility and accuracy. The employment of improved metal casting techniques, which owed a great deal to the casting of church bells, and the use of copper-based alloys, bronze, and brass, as well as cast iron, made cannon lighter and more reliable, as they were able to cope with the increased explosive power generated by "corned" gunpowder. Improved metal casting also allowed the introduction of trunnions (supporting cylindrical projections on each side of cannon) that were cast as an integral part of the barrel, improving mobility. Cannon were less bulky than trebuchets, which increased their usefulness.

In turn, the emphasis on cannon helped change tactics and also adapted to new tactics, as with the Spanish conquest of the Moorish kingdom of Granada in the late 1480s and early 1490s, a conquest that involved a number of sieges.[20] Located on the ground, cannon were far less vulnerable than siege towers to the counterbattery fire from cannon in the besieged fortress. Siege operations in 1550 were different to those of a century earlier, although there were greater differences between 1350 and 1450. The sieges of Calais in 1346–1347 and 1436 provided a clear example.[21]

There were limitations with cannon. On the battlefield, their relative immobility restricted their usefulness, as did their need for clear firing lines. Accuracy was an issue, as was the speed of fire. Running short of gunpowder and cannonballs was a frequent problem for any protracted siege. Elizabeth I of England ordered her forces (successfully) besieging Edinburgh in 1560 to take care to collect and bring back the cannonballs they had not used. In the French Wars of Religion, this problem of supply hit the royal army in 1573 in the unsuccessful siege of the major Huguenot (Protestant)-held fortified town of La Rochelle.

Moreover, in another instance of the process by which improvements are countered, that in artillery was followed by a development in fortification architecture, a process seen in India as well as in the West, and one that continued the response to the spread of trebuchets.[22] Cannon and fortifications were in a counterpointed tension, with effectiveness in part dependent on developments in the latter. The move from high stone walls to lower-profile earthen structures, able to absorb much of the impact of artillery shot while still providing shelter for defending troops (and cannon), required teamwork and logistical efforts of great scale,[23] while also posing new problems for attacking forces.

The Ottoman Turks continued to use siege towers (as well as cannon) in the sixteenth century, but they proved unsuccessful in their invasion of Malta in 1565. A large wooden siege tower was employed against the fortress of Birgu, only to be destroyed by cannon firing chain shot. This, however, was not the reason for the failure of the expedition, which instead owed much to command divisions, logistical issues, the resilience of the defense, and the ability to relieve Valetta with Spanish troops from nearby Sicily.[24] By the seventeenth century, the Turks also focused on cannon, and the age of siege engines was over.

The shift from bows to firearms offers a parallel process. Handguns had greater penetrative power than bows but also had limitations. Gunpowder itself posed serious problems if its full potential as a source of energy was to be used successfully. The issue of how the energy is released when gunpowder is detonated also relates to the size, shape, and consistency of the particles. For an even burn, the particles must be of uniform size and shape. In addition, the components of the composition have to be evenly distributed in the mixture. Gunpowder is not a single compound but a mechanical mixture of three ingredients, and that at a time when mechanical processes lacked the specifications of today, notably consistency and quality control.

When the ingredients are poorly mixed together, gunpowder does not burn at a consistent rate or with the same energy release, and these circumstances could cause sudden peaks in energy that the gun is not built to withstand. This situation was something that had to be discovered and the solution found. Such knowledge would have been considered privileged information and kept secret, a factor that affected diffusion, while also encouraging an emphasis on hiring experts who possessed the knowledge. The role of renegades was particularly important in the early modern world, as they spread knowledge across cultural boundaries, notably between Christendom and Islam.

For a long period, cannon were not strong enough to make proper use of gunpowder. This did not change until the development, around 1420, of a more effective type of gunpowder, which provided the necessary energy but without dangerously high peak pressures that could burst the barrel. The rate of ignition propagation from one grain to its neighbors was a key issue. The way to control this was by using coarser grains. Fine-grained powder did not have oxygen between the grains, and thus probably burnt with less heat than what is termed "corned powder."[25]

The composition of gunpowder evolved from what in Europe was called Serpentine to corned powder, which was in general use by about 1500. Serpentine was less stable and was liable to separate when stored or transported so that it had to be remixed on the battlefield (or a little way behind). This was dangerous, as explosive dust was produced during the remixing process. The problem was overcome by mixing the powder with water or urine, forming the wet mixture into cakes that were then dried and cut. This was the process of corning. Corning powder was more powerful, partly because of increased propulsive energy per unit of mass and partly because it burned more rapidly, so that new sorts of guns were needed to cope with increased pressures. Corned powder was more reliable and less prone to absorb moisture than Serpentine. Corning itself was a Western innovation.[26]

The chemical nature of the gunpowder reaction also caused problems, for example, when the chemical reagents lacked consistent purity. The chemistry of gunpowder and its ignition properties were not really known about until the mid-nineteenth century, shortly before it was superseded by smokeless propellants and explosives. Moreover, gunpowder ages and becomes unstable after a period of time, especially if it is not properly stored.

Problems came too from the supply of the ingredients. Charcoal and sulfur were relatively abundant, but, although powder formulation varied considerably,[27] about three-quarters of the weight of gunpowder was provided by saltpeter and this was difficult to provide. As a result, the availability of supplies could make a major difference to particular powers and conflicts, not least to the rise of English (later British) power.[28] Problems with the availability of saltpeter helped ensure that the Mon-

gols did not use gunpowder outside of China,[29] while the export of saltpeter by Elizabeth I of England to the Saadian rulers of Morocco in 1578
helped to doom Sebastian I of Portugal's crusade at the battle of Alca-
zarquivir. Sebastian was killed in this crushing defeat, most of the Portuguese bases in Morocco were then captured, and, thereafter, no effective Western military pressure was brought to bear upon Morocco until
the French did so in the 1840s. The battle is a good instance of that frequently overused term, "decisive victory."

Aside from problems with the availability of saltpeter, handgun shot
was less readily recyclable than arrows, although the lead balls could
be collected, melted, and recast, and, provided the raw materials were
available, lead shot was easier and quicker to make than arrows and
bolts. Again, the role of supplies both qualifies an account of technological capability based solely on the specifications of weapons and yet also
shows how the significance of technology brought in other factors. Difficulties in obtaining gunpowder and shot proved particularly serious in
sub-Saharan Africa, for Native Americans, and in Central Asia, but not
only in these cases.

As a reminder that specifications were important, the nature of the
projectiles used with early gunpowder weapons was a particular issue.
Spherical shot generates a large amount of aerodynamic drag (resistance),
essentially because its wake is disproportionate to its cross-sectional
area. This characteristic ensured that the projectiles of the fifteenth and
sixteenth centuries lost speed at a high rate, on average about three times
faster than modern bullets. Lower speed meant less kinetic energy on
impact, and thus less penetrative power. In addition, effects arising from
the spin of projectiles lessened their accuracy. Bullet spin creates a force
that acts perpendicular to the sideways vector of the wind, the air movement acting on the bullet as it travels. In the case of wind acting hori-
zontally on a clockwise rotating bullet, the Magnus effect induces pressure differences that cause a downward (wind from the right) or upward
(wind from the left) force to act on the bullet, which leads it to deviate
from its trajectory. A vertically acting wind causes less deviation unless
the wind speed is 9 miles per hour or more. There are several other effects that act on projectiles, the Poisson, Coriolis, and Eötvös effects.

Ballistics is a complicated field. These characteristics could not be counteracted by skill in firing.

The lower velocity of musket and pistol balls was one reason why large calibers were used, to ensure that a projectile had enough energy to cause damage. These problems help explain the replacing of musket balls in the nineteenth century, as the drag coefficient of a sphere is approximately 0.47 compared to only about 0.05 for a modern conical boat-tailed bullet. Rifling was essential so that the new bullets spun and were thus stabilized in flight, thereby obviating tumble and yaw (among other ballistic problems).

Handguns had other limitations. They had a limited range, a low rate of fire, were affected by bad weather that could spoil the gunpowder, and were not easy to make. It was estimated that in seventeenth-century India, a mounted archer could fire six arrows in the time it took a musketeer armed with a matchlock musket to fire one shot.[30] Although musketry helped give the Moroccans victory over the larger Songhai army at Tondibi on the River Niger on March 13, 1591, Songhai archers and spearmen proved effective subsequently, not least because the swampy terrain did not favor the Moroccan musketeers.[31] Much of the effectiveness of the handgun depended on the individual soldier, but he might be a poor shot, or be unsteady in igniting the lighted fuse, or otherwise in the firing process. Being a poor shot, however, was not much of a problem because the weapons were so inaccurate and were used en masse. Handguns were also not straightforward to use from horseback, as this position made it difficult to load, aim, and fire them. Pistols did not need to be used en masse to be effective, but the trick was to get very close: the tactic for a horseman armed with a pistol was to pursue an enemy and get close enough to touch the back plate of his armor with the muzzle before firing in order to ensure, first, that the shooter did not miss and, secondly, that the ball penetrated. There was little point in shooting from a moving horse at a distance of more than a few feet. Horse pistols were effectively one-shot weapons and could only be used at close quarters.

Rather than assuming that a shift from bows to arquebuses took place because they were deadly weapons, it might be that it was their lower cost compared to the crossbow that led to their adoption. The desirable specifications of weaponry were rarely in concert, and bows were no exception. Crossbows, which required far less training and physical strength than longbows, gained more penetrative power in the fifteenth century as a result of the development of steel bows. However, as a reminder of the complex trade-off in the characteristics of weapons, these bows were expensive, as tempered spring steel was a costly material to make and one that required much skill.[32]

This was not the case with longbows. Traditionally made out of a single piece of yew wood, they were easier and cheaper to make, and an experienced archer could fire an arrow every 5 seconds. Their widespread use in fourteenth-century England was a new departure that had significant consequences. At the battle of Crécy in 1346, the Genoese crossbowmen in French service were, as a result, seriously outfired by the English longbowmen, and the resulting firepower advantage was important to the crushing English victory over the French. The Genoese crossbowmen may not even have fired shots.[33]

Other spectacular victories won largely due to English longbowmen included Poitiers (1356) and Agincourt (1415). However, longbows required strength, lengthy training, and considerable expertise for proficient use. They had an average draw-weight of 100 pounds. In addition, their specifications were never improved, as were those of crossbows.

The increased place of handguns appears to have been due not to an instant acceptance of their overwhelming capability but to their use in a particular niche and by a specific group, militia who guarded city walls, a protected role that compensated for their battlefield vulnerability. From this role, the use of handguns spread, but it is no accident that the weapon was most effective when employed in concert with field fortifications, as in the battles of Cerignola (1503), Ravenna (1512), and Bicocca (1522) during the Italian Wars. The shelter of such fortifications was valuable against attacking forces, whether cavalry, pikemen, or swordsmen. At Cerignola on April 28, 1503, the greatly outnumbered Spaniards rested in defense behind a trench and earth parapet, which held attacks by French cavalry and Swiss pikemen, exposing them to fire from arquebuses. As a reminder of the difficulty of judging relative effectiveness, this defensive success was helped by the French failure, in their haste, to bring up their cannon against the Spanish fieldworks. Aside from entrenchments, a wagon-fort could also be used, with wagons joined together providing protection, notably against cavalry. The Ottoman Turks proved adept at this tactic.

More generally, interlinked problems with range, accuracy, and killing power helped guide the tactical use of firearms, as part of a learning curve that entailed an appreciation of their limitations. At the same time, firearms offered an additional flexibility in creating and dealing with tactical opportunities.[34]

One advantage of the arquebus over the longbow was that the gunner did not have to train and practice from childhood to become proficient with the weapon. Moreover, the gun was more destructive than either a crossbow or a longbow. The greater velocity and penetrative power of handguns were particularly important as, thanks to quenching rather than air cooling, improved armor was produced in sixteenth-century Europe. These advantages were very important given the early problems faced by those who adopted handguns.[35]

Handguns were inaccurate and produced a lot of smoke, so that the bore had to be cleaned regularly to prevent fouling becoming a problem, even during battle. The arquebus needed about forty actions to load and fire, so it had a slow rate of fire. The widespread adoption of the arquebus by Western field armies led to the integration of pikemen to protect the slow-firing gunners. Handling a pike not only required stamina and strength but also a fair amount of training: about thirty actions were required, but the pikemen did not need to go through them all to be effective in battle.

THE USES OF FIREPOWER

The use of firepower played an increasing role in warfare in Eurasia, notably from the fifteenth century. The change was particularly significant in the case of the Ottoman Turks. They initially relied on mounted archers but, in the second half of the fourteenth century, developed an infantry that became a centrally paid standing army, eventually equipped with field cannon and handguns. This capability helped lead the Ottomans to a series of victories that ensured that they became the key power in the pivotal area where Europe, Asia, and Africa met. In 1453, Ottoman cannon, including about sixty new cannon cast at the effective foundry of Adrianople (Edirne), played a leading role in the capture of the Byzantine capital of Constantinople (Istanbul), breaching its walls and driving off the Byzantine navy, although numerical superiority and command flexibility were also crucial.[36] Whereas the Ottomans had relied on both cannon and trebuchets in their successful siege of the city of Thessalonica in Greece in 1430, their victorious final assaults on Constantinople in 1453 and on Venetian-held Negroponte (on the island of Euboea) in 1470 were mounted through breaches made by cannon. The latter victory helped win them the dominant position in the Aegean. The Ottomans' focus on cannon was aided by the efficiency with which they operated their field foundries.[37]

The change to firearms was also marked in a series of battles, although much of the Ottoman infantry continued to be armed with bows and spears.[38] On August 11, 1473, at Başkent, the effect of Ottoman cannon and hand gunners on Türkmen cavalry led to victory over Uzun Hasan, the head of the Aqquyunlu confederacy that ruled modern Iran and Iraq. Its forces centered on cavalry armed with bows, swords, and shields.[39]

At the battle of Chaldiran on August 23, 1514, Shah Isma'il I, the Safavid leader, who had overthrown the Aqquyunlu, was, in turn, defeated by Selim I the Grim, the Ottoman sultan. Although the Safavids had used cannon in their victory over the Uzbeks at Merv in 1510, their army at Chaldiran was of the traditional central Asian nomadic type—horsed archers. In contrast, the Ottoman army was a more mixed force and included hand gunners and cannon. Thanks to their firepower and numerical superiority, the respective importance of which is difficult to disentangle, the Ottomans won a crushing victory over the Safavid cavalry. Ironically, the Ottoman cannon were also important for another reason as, chained together, they formed a barrier to cavalry charges.

Gunpowder weaponry, moreover, helped Ottoman expansion in other directions. On August 24, 1516, Ottoman firepower played an important role in the defeat of Mamluk heavy cavalry at the battle of Marj Dabiq, although other factors also came into play, and this point underlines the difficulty of separating out and evaluating specific elements. The Ottoman army was far larger, the Mamluk veterans held back, and the governor of Aleppo, who commanded the Mamluk left flank, made a secret agreement with Selim and abandoned the battle at its height. The Mamluks were not simply dependent on cavalry and, indeed, were developing an artillery corps, but it was poorly integrated with the rest of the army. Victory led to the Ottoman conquest of Syria (modern Syria and Lebanon) and Palestine (modern Israel and Palestine).

Another similar battle at Raydaniyya on January 23, 1517 resulted in the conquest of Egypt. The Mamluk cavalry was driven off by the Ottoman field guns. In contrast, although the Mamluks had about a hundred brass cannon mounted on carts, as well as handguns, their positions were outflanked by the more mobile Ottomans, who then successfully attacked the gun emplacements from the rear.[40]

On August 29, 1526, at Mohács, firepower played a major role in the defeat of the heavy cavalry of Louis II of Hungary by the invading Ottomans under Selim's successor, Suleiman the Magnificent. The Hungarians had 85 cannon, the Ottomans about 240 to 300. The Hungarian cavalry attacked, pushing back the lighter Ottoman cavalry, but was stopped by the infantry and cannon, whose fire caused havoc. The Hungarians, their dynamism spent, were then attacked in front and rear by the far more numerous Ottoman forces and routed. Louis drowned while trying to swim across a river in armor. This victory was followed by Ottoman dominance of most of Hungary, a dominance that lasted until the 1680s. In 1529, Suleiman advanced to besiege Vienna, although, besieged late in the campaigning season and assisted by a relief force, it did not fall. Gunpowder weaponry, nevertheless, had helped transform the geopolitics of the region.

The Ottoman victories, especially Mohács, in part showed up how their enemies did not appreciate the power of gunpowder weapons and, hence, highlighted their inability to use them with comparable effectiveness and their lack of suitable countermeasures. Indeed, until opposing armies were similarly equipped, the technically inferior army tended to lose, and quite spectacularly so, in no small measure due to an inability to appreciate not only the effects of gunpowder weapons but their tactical and operational usage. While technological support and superiority helped lead to victory, at the same time, technological ignorance led to defeat—different sides of the same coin. This is an element of technological change that is not usually considered. Technological superiority does not assure victory, but there has to be a willingness to accept that a technological advantage favors the enemy in order to devise suitable countermeasures. That did not happen at Mohács.

In the case of each of these episodes, it is possible to put the stress on gunpowder weaponry, but also on other factors, a process more generally the case when considering the impact of weaponry. At Başkent, the Ottomans benefited from having a fortified wagon position, from numerical superiority, and from better discipline.[41] Aside from these specifics, there are more general limitations to an account of military progress based on gunpowder weaponry. Although gunpowder provided the basis for different forms of handheld projectile weaponry, such as arquebuses and muskets, as well as artillery, nevertheless the technique of massed projectile weaponry was not new. The English employment of longbowmen in the fourteenth and fifteenth centuries abundantly demonstrated a continuity that went back to the use of javelins, bows, and slings in the ancient world. Thus, gunpowder weaponry was, for long, an agent, not a cause, of changes in warfare, and especially so in battle tactics on land.

This instance raises more general points about the difficulty of assessing technological change. First, many weapons should be understood as parts of a tactical system that helped incorporate new developments into existing patterns of use. Secondly, it is difficult to assess how much weight to put on the potential for change represented by the specifications of a given weapon and how much to focus on the constraints posed by the situation mentioned in the previous sentence. These elements contribute to the question of why gunpowder weapons did not significantly replace bladed weapons in Western armies until the sixteenth century. Rate of fire, logistics, and cost were all crucial issues, as were versatility of use and tactical awareness and the lack of any influential social group or military interest committed to firearms. A considerable body of experience and knowledge existed for the exploitation of all manner of bladed weapons, but a similar knowledge and skill base had to be built for firearms.

The limitations of firearms also played out in terms of different national military traditions. For example, handguns were adopted only slowly in France and the British Isles. In France, they initially appeared less valuable than a combination of pikemen with heavy cavalry, the latter French, the former generally hired, especially from the Swiss cantons and German states. Thus, the French lacked the infantry firepower the Spaniards deployed at Pavia in 1525. The French willingness to use cannon, but not hand gunners, underlines the need to be cautious in referring to the impact of gunpowder and, more generally, giving an undifferentiated account of innovation in weaponry.

The process by which lessons were learned played a role in innovation, as did social assumptions and practices. Tactical and operational experience of campaigning did not automatically encourage the use of firepower by either the French or the English. Campaigning in Italy in 1494–1496 in the opening campaigns of the Italian Wars (1494–1559) did not lead to a change in the structure of the French army, as they deployed very little small arms firepower in these campaigns.

Similarly, longbows continued to be important in England. The army that crushed the Scots at Flodden in 1513 contained archers, not hand gunners, while at Pinkie in 1547 the Scottish army, again principally pikemen, was badly battered by English cannon and archery.[42] Longbowmen, indeed, remained the chief deliverers of firepower in the English militia into the mid-1580s, despite the government's determination, from the 1560s, to rearm garrisons and key trained bands (militia units) with the caliver, an early gun and, increasingly, with the musket. The extent to which the militia system limited governmental control over weaponry and force structure[43] is a point of more general relevance.

Far from being centered solely on change, much of the Western discussion of war considered developments with reference to the past, and notably an exemplary view of antiquity. In his *Art of War* (1521), which was frequently reprinted, Nicolo Machiavelli tried to update Flavius Vegetius's fourth- or fifth-century *Epitoma Rei Militaris* (*On Military Matters*) by focusing on the pike and treating the arquebus as similar to missile weaponry. In his book Machiavelli expressed continued favor for the Roman order of battle, drill, and use of swords and shields.[44]

The main problem in comparing Renaissance with classical warfare was set by the major role of French heavy cavalry in the fifteenth and sixteenth centuries, not by that of firearms as they were presented as a new version of missile weaponry. As the large-scale use of the pike in the early sixteenth century in Western Europe in many respects represented a revival of the successful Macedonian phalanx of the fourth century BCE, the key development in Western infantry warfare of the period was apparently organizational, rather than technological. At the close of the century and in the early seventeenth century, the military reformers linked to the House of Nassau in the United Provinces (Dutch Republic), as well as to the German territories of Nassau, the Palatinate, Baden, Hesse-Cassel, and Brandenburg, consciously used ancient Greek and Roman models for their efforts to improve military organizations. Their limited sense of changing conditions was matched by the contemporary theoretical work of Justus Lipsius and others on the ancient Roman military.[45]

Rather than assuming a single technological innovation bringing a fundamental change, it is more appropriate to note the development of firearms in the long term, both with the shift from bows and also thanks to improvements in handguns. The latter process reflected an important flexibility with firearms. For example, the musket, a heavier version of the arquebus, capable of firing a heavier shot farther, and therefore penetrating armor, was first used in Europe from the 1520s, and its use became widespread by mid-century. Heavier shot is less affected by deviations than lighter shot, and this made it more accurate, although, at long range, accuracy was still poor. The lead ball of about 15 grams (half an ounce) that was fired could kill at 180 meters (200 yards), but it was very difficult to hit a target at more than 55 meters (60 yards).

Tactics countered the limitations of handguns, notably the use of densely packed soldiers fighting at close range so as to build up the volume of shot likely to hit a target, thus countering the affects of low individual accuracy. Moreover, the use of firearms became more important as they were integrated into combined-arms tactics. As a result, firepower came to be more important than the manpower offered by other infantry. However, that approach can represent a misleading primitivization of other infantry weapons and forms. This would be inappropriate, not least given the significance and professionalism of pikemen in the fifteenth and sixteenth centuries.

CAVALRY CONFLICT

With technology, it is always pertinent to consider the timescale. In the long term, firearms dispatched other infantry weaponry to the museum and brought cavalry to an end, but the latter development occurred in the twentieth century, four centuries after the large-scale deployment of hand gunners in Europe. Instead, in the short term, firearms offered new opportunities to cavalry, providing an aspect of its long-standing value and flexibility.[46] Those armies that used mounted archers continued to do so, albeit with some significant changes, while other cavalries adopted handguns.

In central, south, and east Asia, mounted archers remained important, in part due to problems with the availability of muskets, powder, and shot and with reloading while moving on horseback. Babur's account of his victory over the Lodis at the First Battle of Panipat on April 21, 1526, a victory close to Delhi that was crucial to the establishment of Mughal power in northern India, acknowledged the role of his artillery in defeating Lodi elephant and cavalry attacks but also put much emphasis on his mounted archers, who mounted a successful attack of their own, defeating the Lodi army.[47] On November 5, 1556, at the Second Battle of Panipat, the Mughal rulers of much of north India defeated a far larger force thanks to their use of such archers.

In the West, in contrast, firearms transformed cavalry warfare when the invention of the wheel-lock mechanism in the 1500s spread. Unlike the arquebus or musket, which required a lighted fuse, the wheel-lock relied on a trigger-operated spring that brought together a piece of iron pyrites or flint and a turning steel wheel. The contact produced sparks that ignited the gunpowder in the pistol's pan. This priming charge then ignited the main charge through a vent in the barrel. As a result, the glowing match of the arquebus or musket, which could be all too easily extinguished by rain or wind, could be dispensed with.

As a reminder of the range and trade-off of specifications, the wheel-lock mechanism was more expensive and delicate than the matchlock and more difficult to repair, and hence not common. It was better suited to the needs of cavalry, as it required only one hand to operate, but was more for men with money than for cavalry. Cavalry pistols did not become widespread until the invention of the snaphaunce and the flint-lock. Invented in about 1550 and coming into fairly widespread use from the late 1550s, the snaphaunce was an early form of flintlock but was more complicated. It was replaced by the flintlock from about 1620. Similarly, the stabbing weapons of cavalry were lighter than those of the infantry. Cavalry could fire their pistols while moving and, as three pistols could be carried, were able to fire several shots before reloading, which was useful because reloading in action was not easy. Moreover, the muzzle velocities of pistols were sufficient to cause nasty wounds if soldiers were hit.

Tactics adapted to the new weapon, which is another way of saying that its effectiveness depended on tactical innovation. Yet again, the choice of phrase is important, and not only for what is said but also for what is implied. The key tactic was the caracole, in which ranks of cavalry advanced in order and fired their pistols, before turning away from the enemy. The tactic, like Western line-ahead naval tactics, was easier to describe on paper and illustrate than to follow in practice,[48] which makes it difficult to assess. Evaluation in part has to rest on the characteristics of the weapon, but that is not sufficient as a guide to effectiveness. The caracole used by German *reiters* and others was very similar to Mongol attacks.[49]

The caracole was criticized by commentators, because they claimed that pistoleers fired from too far away and that the maneuver discouraged cavalry from closing with opposing infantry. It was understandable that they fired from too far because pistols were outranged by infantry firearms, but accuracy was so low that the standard advice was to touch the opponent with the muzzle before firing.

As with other weapons, moreover, the effectiveness of cavalry firepower depended on the opposing response. Although infantry could offer more formidable firepower than cavalry, they could also be stationary and unsupported, which left the initiative with the cavalry, and the caracole was effective against formations that were mostly pikemen. Works on cavalry warfare, such as Johann Jacobi's *Kriegs-Kunst zu Pferd: Darinnen gelehret werden die Fundament der Cavallery in vier Theilen* (Frankfurt, 1634), made much of cavalry firepower.

Cavalry, however, primarily used the sword as a shock weapon. The caracole was employed against infantry, not other cavalry who being more mobile than infantry were less willing to have pistols fired at them from close range. And the caracole required horsemen to get in close, which put them at considerable risk. It was a tactic that required discipline and nerve as well as a lot of training. Not many were prepared to do it in the way prescribed. The effect of cavalry firepower could be more wishful thinking than a reality despite some apparent success. Even with the advent of dragoons, the men dismounted to shoot and did not attempt to fire their pistols from a moving horse. It is significant that manuals that describe the caracole do so in the context of a range of tactics, which undermines the idea that the caracole was very effective in reality.

As with other weapons, however, the combined arms approach could be effective. This approach was a matter of combining soldiers each having different arms, and also of soldiers having more than one weapon. Cavalry charging with the swords after firing their pistols were particularly effective and were a challenge to heavy cavalry that did not use pistols. The lances used by the latter were insufficiently flexible as a weapon for such a struggle. At Coutras (1587) and, even more, Ivry (1590), in the French Wars of Religion, the cavalry of Henry of Navarre (Henry IV) used a mix of pistol and shock tactics with great effect.

Combined arms approaches were not always readily apparent and involved choices; and the best combination of weapons and tactics was fought out in print. Writers often had direct experience. Giorgio Basta (1540–1607) served the Spaniards as a commander of cavalry under Alessandro, Duke of Parma, Commander of the Spanish Army of Flanders and, after Alessandro's death, entered the service of Emperor Rudolf II. In his study of light cavalry, published posthumously in Venice in 1612 and then translated into French, Basta urged the value of mobility.

As a reminder of the need to abandon any one idea of development, the shift in Eastern Europe in the sixteenth century was largely to swords, not pistols. This was particularly so of the Poles, who won a series of cavalry victories in the 1600s over the Russians, Swedes and Turks, notably Kircholm over the Swedes in 1605 and Klushino over a far larger Swedish and Russian army in 1610. The mobility and power of the Polish cavalry, which relied on shock charges, overthrew their Swedish counterparts in the 1620s. Thereafter, as often happened in such circumstances, the Swedish infantry was left exposed to all-round attack and suffered heavily.[50]

These tactics affected other armies, with Gustavus Adolphus of Sweden (r. 1611–1632) ordering his first line to fire only one pistol, so that they could rapidly move to the use of their swords, with the lines behind maintaining momentum by only employing their swords. In the 1700s, in the War of the Spanish Succession, John Churchill, 1st Duke of Marlborough, made the British cavalry act like a shock force, charging fast, and he used a massed cavalry charge launched at the French center at the breakthrough climax in his most dramatic victory, that at Blenheim in 1704.

In the eighteenth century, however, the proportion of cavalry in Western armies declined as a result of the heavier emphasis on infantry firearms, the effectiveness of which increased due to the use of flintlock muskets and bayonets. As a result, cavalry came to be principally used on the battlefield to fight other cavalry, always an important role and one that ensured particular requirements for weapons and tactics. A number of factors were involved in the declining role of cavalry, which again underlines the importance of not isolating weaponry as a factor. Cultural issues, indeed, encouraged a continued stress on cavalry because its social prestige remained significant. This prestige was not restricted to the officers. For example, eighteenth-century French cavalry attracted a higher quality of recruit and received better pay. However, cavalry was about three times more expensive than infantry, was of limited value in hilly terrain and in the enclosed countryside that was increasingly more common across much (but not all) of Europe in the eighteenth century, and was less effective in the face of infantry armed with flintlock muskets and with bayonets. The success of British infantry advanced on French cavalry at the battle of Minden in 1759 was especially dramatic.

FLINTLOCKS AND BAYONETS

The mention of both weapons ensures again the need for care in assessing effectiveness and considering development. Bayonets and flintlock muskets represented different types of killing. Their combination was the key factor, as was the ability to produce the weapon in quantity and at a reasonable price. The first form of flintlock ignition system was the snaphaunce lock from the mid-sixteenth century. The more classic flintlock was developed from this in the early seventeenth century.

Flintlock firing mechanisms increased the speed and reliability of musket fire, with major consequences for effectiveness. Whereas matchlocks had been affected by wind, rain, and general humidity, the last a particular problem in the tropics, flintlocks made musket fire less dependent on the weather. In the flintlock musket, powder was ignited by a spark produced through striking flint against steel. These muskets were lighter, more reliable, and easier to fire than matchlocks and did not require a rest. The resulting increase in the rate of fire made infantry more deadly. Moreover, without the hazard of the burning matches previously used to ignite powder, musketeers were able to stand closer together, which increased the firepower per length of unit frontage. The process of loading was complex but less vulnerable than with the matchlock. In a normal loading, either pistol or musket, the regular procedure was to tear off the end of the greased paper cartridge, prime and shut the frizzen, thus covering the primed pan, and pull the hammer to half cock (a safety position to prevent premature sparking), cast about to bring the muzzle to chest level, pour the remaining powder from the cartridge down the barrel, stuff the opened end of the cartridge into the muzzle (the ball would be encased in the opposite end of the cartridge and, depending on the manufacturing method, crimped in place by twists to the cartridge above and below the ball or by a thread), draw the rammer, and ram down the charge so as to seat the ball and cartridge firmly, usually by means of two or three solid tamps to ensure it was all the way down and properly seated. The greased paper cartridge provided the wadding that both ensured increased compression and held the ball in place until the main charge exploded. While it could happen that the ball slid back down the barrel, this would have only been the case with a quick reload in a dire emergency where speed was the imperative and the target very close.

Then to fire the soldier would pull the hammer to full cock, present the muzzle down range on command, and on the command "Give fire!" pull the trigger. The soldier would return back down to the prime and load position with the flintlock at the waist ready to load and fire it all over again. When weapons were loaded and to prevent the powder from getting wet, a wooden plug called the tampion (hence the modern feminine hygiene tampon) was inserted to plug the muzzle. The closed frizzen cover held the powder in the pan and hopefully kept the priming powder dry.

For a rifled barrel, the procedure was similar but more complex. Here, rather than a greased cartridge, the rifleman would typically keep powder in a horn to prime the pan and then the charge. The ball would have to be seated. A small greased patch of cloth, or even paper wet down with saliva if nothing else was available, would be placed in the muzzle. A loose ball would be placed on top and pushed in slightly. Then a small wooden hammer was used to gently tap the ball into the muzzle and seat it. Only then could a rammer be used gently to tap the ball down the barrel. The idea was not to damage the rifling. But with a smoothbore musket, you could shove anything down the barrel as fast as possible. The more delicate rifle procedure meant that about the fastest one could safely prime and load and fire was a minute, while with the smoothbore the well-drilled infantryman could get off two to three volleys in a minute. British infantry, due to the emphasis on firing drill and discipline, could typically fire three (and occasionally four) volleys a minute. No one else could fire that fast. That contrast made a great difference once volley fire commenced at between 40 and 100 yards.

Western armies were not to experience a change in weaponry comparable to the flintlock until the introduction of rifled firearms in the nineteenth century. However, flintlocks were more expensive than matchlocks, and those developed in the early seventeenth century were used for hunting and for pistols, which further underlined their characterization as a luxury weapon. The issue of cost was magnified by the marked increase in the size of most Western armies from the 1660s and 1670s, an increase that reflected greater organizational sophistication,[51] and notably in the case of France, the army of which increased considerably under Louis XIV (r. 1643–1715), about 340,000 men in the 1690s. As a result of the greater numbers of troops to equip, it took time to introduce the flintlock as a major military weapon.

Instead, the bayonet, one of the most important and underrated innovations in military technology, was pushed first, although there was an important degree of coincidence with the flintlock. The fearsome edge of bayonets affected warfare by transforming infantry capability but, at the same time, as with many innovations, there was the risk of compromising effectiveness. In this case, the early plug bayonets, introduced in the early 1640s, were inserted in the musket barrel and therefore prevented firing. This bayonet was based on a weapon used by hunters and was named after Bayonne in southwest France; they were daggers that, if necessary, could be inserted into muskets, making them a valuable weapon against boars.

Use rapidly spread in the French army and, by the 1670s, specialized units, such as the dragoons and fusiliers, were being issued with bayonets. At the siege of Spanish-held Valenciennes in 1672, the first French bayonet attack occurred and, by the 1680s, the weapon was more common. These bayonets were essentially double-edged dagger blades that were about 30 centimeters (12 inches) long, attached to a handle that was about the same length. This handle was designed to be the same diameter as the musket's bore and was fixed in position by working the handle into the musket. In 1672, bayonets were also issued to a unit in the English army, Prince Rupert's Dragoons, that was taking part in the Dutch War as Charles II of England was allied with Louis XIV.

As with firearms, or earlier with shields, there was a process of continual innovation rather than a "big bang" of invention. In particular, the plug bayonet was replaced by ring-and-socket bayonets, which were developed in the 1680s. These allowed firing with the blade in place, as the bayonet was attached to a ring fitted round the musket barrel. Moreover, the bayonet was turned and locked in place, providing firmness in combat. However, for early ring-and-socket bayonets, the means of lock-ing them in place were sometimes very poor or completely absent. The effectiveness of bayonets depended upon the quick and secure fitting of the bayonet to the muzzle. Shooting with the bayonet fixed was not al-ways encouraged for several reasons, including extra weight, which in-creased not only the physical burden but decreased accuracy (such as it was), partly because tiredness made the musketeer drop the muzzle even lower. There was also the danger that the musketeer might spear himself on the blade when he reloaded.

As with other innovations, the development of the bayonet meant the need for choice in deciding what to do with existing weapons, both on one's own side and in the armies of opponents. The bayonet led to the phasing out of the pike, which was now redundant, partially because of the particular value of the bayonet but also due to the bayonet's role as part of a weapons system. Bayonets were a better complement to fire-arms in fulfilling the pike's defensive role against attacking infantry and cavalry and also had an offensive capability against infantry and, on oc-casion, cavalry; again, like the pike, but with the addition of firepower. As they were lighter and more mobile than pikes, bayonets had much to offer in terms of flexibility. Although drills did not change at once and tactical changes were not as rapid as might have been expected,[52] never-theless there was a switchover from pike to bayonet in the 1690s and 1700s.[53]

Firepower was greatly enhanced as a result of the replacement of pike-men. This firepower came increasingly from flintlocks. Like the earlier adoption of the arquebus, the spread of the flintlock was not instanta-neous, however; unsurprisingly so, as the cost of one was equal to the annual wages of an agricultural laborer. Nevertheless, as an indication of competitive pressure in the West in the late seventeenth century, of the clear advantage of the flintlock, and of the existing firearms' tactics, units, and doctrine that could guide its use, the adoption of flintlocks was quicker than that of the arquebus. Although French regulations permitted the use of flintlocks by some soldiers from 1670, matchlocks were not completely phased out until 1704. The arduous Nine Years' War (1688–1697) led the French, who were, notably by the mid-1690s, under greater military pressure than at any time since the mid-1670s, to decide to change over, and this was decreed by an ordinance of 1699.

Again, combined-arms tactics were significant. The impact of the flint-lock was magnified by the replacement of the pike by the bayonet, and the bayonet-flintlock combination altered tactics, helping lessen the role of cavalry. Drill focused on patterned training was crucial to infantry.[54] More generally, there was an overlapping process of evolution with fire-arms, methods of manufacture, gunpowder, and tactics. Changes in one stimulated change in one or more of the others. There was co-dependency. Moreover, the effectiveness of Western forces on the world scale was en-hanced by flintlocks, which helped encourage the copying of Western weapons and methods elsewhere in the world.[55]

This copying was aided by the long-standing ability to serve in the military of other rulers, including rulers from other religions and cul-tures. Individual careers indicated a range of service. For example, Guil-laume Le Vasseur, Sieur de Beauplar, a French military engineer, served in 1630–1647 with the forces of Sigismund III and Wladyslaw VII, suc-cessive kings of Poland, and produced a description of Ukraine, then under Polish sovereignty.[56] Military engineers helped ensure the stan-dardization and spread of Western patterns of fortification. Mathematics was a key knowledge in the design of these fortifications, as was shown in individual careers. For example, the English mathematician Jonas Moore (1617–1679) became a surveyor and then advised on the fortifi-cation of Tangier before becoming Surveyor-General of the Ordnance. In 1673, Moore published *Modern Fortification, or Elements of Military Architecture* and in 1683 a translation of Tomaso Moretti's *Trattato dell-'artigliera.*[57]

The flintlock musket was not adopted in all areas in the eighteenth century. For example, in central, east, and Southast Asia and much of Africa, the matchlock remained in use. The cost and difficulty of acquir-ing flintlocks were factors, as was the continuity of local craft practices of making matchlocks.

The introduction of the flintlock-bayonet combination also displayed the organizational sophistication of leading states in the period, one that made it possible to adopt technological change. Between 1701 and mid-

1704, the British Ordnance Office issued 56,000 muskets, the main Russian state arsenal at Tula produced an annual average of nearly 14,000 muskets between 1737 and 1778, while, in the 1760s, the French manufactured 23,000 muskets annually at Charleville and Saint-Etienne.

Standardization, and thus measurement and calculation, were key themes. In Russia, Peter the Great (r. 1689–1725), who proved a determined borrower of advanced Western methods, reorganized the Gunner's Chancellery into an Artillery Chancellery and, in 1704, appointed James Bruce its director. The Moscow-born son of a Scots officer in Russian service, Bruce had studied in London under those who would subsequently be seen as key figures in the Scientific Revolution. As director, he standardized gun calibers and introduced the use of a linear measure to show ball diameters, as well as a caliber scale, and special curves and compasses for ballistic calculation.[58]

CONCLUSIONS

Pedro Páez (1564–1622), a Spanish Jesuit missionary priest who worked in the Portuguese missions in Ethiopia, recorded the local reputation of the Portuguese as "very strong men who fought with harquebuses and bombards and would destroy them all."[59] The changes that stemmed from gunpowder weaponry were both considerable and believed to be so, but the timescale involved was lengthy. This timescale reflected not only the time taken to develop effective weapons but also that involved in the understanding of tactics that used them with particular impact, for example, in siegecraft.[60] At the same time, the timescale was such that the term "revolution" is not a helpful pairing with gunpowder.

With time, gunpowder weapons became more versatile, while the effort put into making and supplying them became central to the infrastructure and logistics of war. Developments included the use, in the Thirty Years' War (1618–1648) and the English Civil Wars (1642–1646, 1648), of lightweight "leather guns," which, in fact, were tubes of copper bound with wire and then covered in leather. Moreover, there was a use of demountable brass cannon that looked toward later screw-guns.[61] For artillery, there was also a process of mathematization, through an engagement with ballistics.

Furthermore, training patterns became more established, and a literature on usage developed. The latter encouraged consistency and eased diffusion. So did military service abroad. Henry Hexham (1585?–1650?), an English soldier who fought in the Low Countries in the early seventeenth century, published *The Principles of the Art Militarie; practised in the wars of the United Netherlands. Represented by figure, the word of command and illustration* (three parts, London, 1637–1640).[62] The cosmopolitan nature of Western culture led to the translation of works. Thus, the *Trattato dell'artigliera* by Tomaso Moretti (d. 1675) appeared in an English translation in 1673. Louis de Gaya's *Traite des Armes* (1678) was translated into English that year. The regular and formulaic nature of drill and training encouraged not just printed works but also the appearance of manuscript manuals. The latter, for example, provided the essential knowledge required by an officer.

The impact of printing by moveable type is an aspect of the significance for war of non-military technologies. Such printing rapidly spread in the second half of the fifteenth century, with a printing press established at some point in over 250 Western locations. The subsequent reorganization of the industry was more significant, with printing in the West concentrated in a smaller number of centers of publication where large numbers of titles were profitably published.[63]

This level of activity, which was not matched outside the West, permitted the dissemination of ideas, techniques, and news in print, and this dissemination of different and often contradictory material was an instance of the multi-polarity generally discussed in terms of competing states. From the perspective of this book, print was particularly important for the spread of new technology and, even more, the new techniques that made particular weapons seem useful. Publications also encouraged the standardization of usage. Publications both helped change aspects of warfare that were traditional and, in grounding new practices, encouraged the characteristics of consistency, regularity, and uniformity linked to permanent forces and bureaucratic support.

Gunpowder weaponry was deadly. The wounds caused by musket balls were serious because of their size (the Brown Bess had a caliber of 0.75 inches) and the fact that lead is soft and tends to flatten on impact with flesh and certainly on impact with bone. Sometimes, the ball would disintegrate on impact, causing even more damage. The modern equivalent is the hollow point used in some handguns. Musket balls lacked range but not hitting power. Yet, in light of the timescale, the term "revolution" appears inappropriate for gunpowder weaponry or, more specifically, for the so-called Military Revolution of the early modern West. This point has wider implications for the discussion of technology, because the frequent usage of the term "revolution" carries with it the implication that only revolutionary changes were, are, and will be of consequence. That is not the case. Nor is it the case that weapons alone explained results. The Korean response in 1597 to Chinese success over the Japanese—"Military affairs are simple. Big cannons defeat small cannons and many cannon defeat few cannon"[64]—underplayed other factors such as organizational support.

Socio-political contexts were also important. The societies of the period had hierarchical and deferential political cultures and were opposed to disruptive change. As a result, new technology was resisted or it was channeled into "socially acceptable patterns." The situation became different in the modern world, as an aspect of its civilization was the encouragement of continual technological change in order to support dynamic social arrangements and because its modern character rested on a commitment to development through modernization.[65]

3

FIREPOWER, STEAMSHIPS, RAILWAYS, TELEGRAPHS, RADIO

*Technologies of Killing, Logistics, Command,
and Control, 1775–1945*

The progress in the state of gunnery and steam navigation renders it
necessary to reconsider from time to time the principles of attack and
defence of coasts and harbours. Whatever improvements may be made in
land batteries, their entire adequacy for the purpose of defence cannot be
certain against the rapidity of steamers and the facility of their manoeuvring
power . . . but they may be powerful in combination with . . . the floating
batteries with their sides coated with thick iron plates.

—*Sir John Burgoyne (1782–1871), influential
British Inspector-General of Fortifications*

THE INCREASE IN FIREPOWER

Works on military technology commonly discuss the nineteenth century in terms of increased firepower, and especially so if the period is extended to include the First World War (1914–1918). This firepower was indeed important, whether provided by the minié bullet or steel artillery, the machine gun or recoil and recuperator artillery.[1] The machine gun, an automatic repeating weapon, was a metaphor of the application of industry to war. The employment of the very workings of the machine for further effect was seen with the recoil energy of the Maxim gun, the use of barrel combustion gases by the Browning and Hotchkiss machine

guns, and the way in which the Skoda's breech was blown back by propellant gases.

These weapons helped give Western powers a significant tactical advantage over non-Western forces,[2] leading to the knighting, in 1901,
of Hiram Maxim, a key figure in the development of machine guns.
The Gatling gun, an early machine gun, was used by the British army
in action in the Anglo-Zulu War of 1879, contributing to the devastating firepower at its victory in the battle of Ulundi. The improved firepower of artillery increased the effectiveness of relatively light pieces,
and their lightness ensured that they could be moved rapidly in difficult terrain and climate conditions. Across the world, advancing columns of Western forces benefited from support by light artillery and
machine guns. In turn, non-Western powers sought to acquire Western weaponry. In 1896, the Italians were defeated at Adwa by Ethiopians under Emperor Menelik II, whose French-made artillery was superior, although the fate of the battle involved far more than respective
strengths in weapons.[3]

New weaponry was also to transform warfare in the West, affecting
ideas of appropriate conduct there.[4] Accuracy and range increased, and
tactics changed accordingly.[5]

The accuracy and rate of fire increased in a series of steps. For example, percussion muskets (muskets with percussion caps), introduced
in the 1820s and 1830s, were followed in the 1840s by percussion-lock
rifles. Their rifled barrel gave bullets a spin, which led to a more stable,
and thus reliable, trajectory. These rifles were also less expensive to manufacture than earlier ones. Technological change became more insistent
in the second half of the century,[6] as did the ability of the industrial
economies of the West to introduce new types of weapon. Thanks to
steel production methods, especially the Bessemer steel converter and
the Gilchrist-Thomas basic steel process, steel output rose dramatically
from the 1870s on.

The heavy casualties in the opening maneuver campaign of the First
World War on the western front in 1914 reflected the greater peril of
the modern battlefield. The potency of artillery had been increased by
better sights, new propellants and fuses, steel-coated projectiles, high-

explosive fillings, and new recoil/recuperator dual systems whereby one part allowed the barrel to recoil without moving the carriage and the other part allowed the barrel to return to its original position on the carriage. This hydropneumatic and hydromechanical system was essential to quick-firing guns. The French 75 mm rapid-firing field gun, introduced by the firm Schneider-Creusot in 1893, was stable, as a result of compressed air counteracting energy, and could, as a result of its automatic fuse setter, fire twenty shells a minute up to 6 miles.

This capability posed major organizational issues, as there was a formidable challenge for munitions supplies, especially of shells but also of gunpowder. Nevertheless, the opportunities offered by improved artillery affected the maneuvers and plans of the leading powers,[7] as well as encouraging links between centralized state procurement of large quantities of weaponry, and the foundation and development of large industrial concerns, such as Krupp's, able to produce them.[8]

The destructive impact of new weaponry was already evident in the Franco-Prussian War of 1870–1871. German breech-loading, steel-barreled Krupp's artillery proved the key battle-winning weapon, although in large part because of the way in which it was used. Departing from the Napoleonic tradition of gun lines laying down frontal fire, the Germans operated in artillery masses: mobile batteries formed by enterprising officers that converged on key points, annihilated them with cross fire, and then moved on. The effective use of artillery fire as an integral part of tactical and operational planning and execution overcame the impressive defensive role of the French infantry, armed with deadly Chassepot rifles, who inflicted heavy casualties on advancing German forces.

By enhancing the rapidity, range, impact, and accuracy of fire and greatly increasing lethality, these firearms led to the "empty battlefield," as units increasingly sought to avoid exposure to fire. Thus, cavalry became more vulnerable, while entrenching became more significant for infantry, which, however, greatly compromised mobility. Indeed, the problems of recovering mobility became a key tactical, operational, and strategic element of the trench warfare of the First World War, with the combatants seeking to overcome the consequences of the very entrenching they sought in order to protect their manpower.

WIDER TECHNOLOGICAL CURRENTS

Alongside greater firepower, it is also pertinent to consider the central significance of other aspects of technology. In doing so, military technology can be linked to wider technological change, both in Western and non-Western society. The nineteenth century saw not only the industrialization that made what has been called "total war," and may more properly be termed "industrial war," materially possible,[9] and indeed also conceptually necessary; the century also witnessed a period of unprecedented development in technological capability, with ideas realized at a great rate, and the subsequent advances rapidly disseminated across the world. Nature appeared overcome and tamed, leading to a transformation of possibilities for empires.[10]

Steamships, railways, telegraphs, and radio, the key subjects of the remainder of this chapter, are all related, focusing as they do on movement and unprecedented speed, but they also form two pairs, the first relating to transport and the second to command and control. Each pair was linked to military effectiveness, both by expanding the possibilities of what could be done and by increasing the potential of existing systems. Logistical and command systems had never been static,[11] but their possibilities were now greatly expanded, and in a fashion that suggested that further changes would also be possible. This sense of inevitable change greatly contributed to the search for, and support of, technological innovation, especially from the second half of the century.

Steamships and railways used forms of locomotive steam power, as opposed to the stationary steam power of the eighteenth century classically represented by the steam engine of James Watt. New ideas and devices intended to produce effective forms of locomotive steam power were tried out in the late eighteenth century. The widespread interest in heat and motion led to experiments with the industrial use of steam power and with steam locomotion. The ideas often went back centuries, as with steam power. Nevertheless, inventions incorporated these ideas, such as that of the steam carriage by N. J. Cugnot in the 1770s and the first workable steamboat demonstrated by the Marquis de Jouffroy d'Abbans in 1783. However, these inventions did not lead to breakthroughs.

The same was true of the use of hydrogen as a lifting agent in a balloon commissioned by the French *Académie des Sciences* in 1783 and manufactured by the physicist J. A. C. Charles, who flew in it. Earlier that year, the Montgolfier brothers had employed hot air to work on a heat pump, an ancestor of the internal combustion engine. Meusnier's designs for cigar-shaped steerable balloons indicated the sense of new capabilities.

Hot-air balloons were employed by the French for tactical reconnaissance in 1794 during the French Revolutionary Wars in the campaign in Belgium, the major campaign zone. Such balloons had a clear potential for reconnaissance and artillery spotting but were also bulky, slow to inflate, and inflexible. Balloons had to be tethered in order to ensure that they did not end up over the enemy lines. They also made tempting targets. As a result of their disadvantages, Napoleon ended their use. Balloons were to be used in the nineteenth century—for example, by the Union forces in the American Civil War (1861–1865)—but very much as an ancillary capability.

The abortive development of hot-air balloons was an instance of a more general process in which new weapons, such as submarines, failed to fulfill their apparent potential.[12] The combination of technologies needed if these weapon systems were to become effective was absent, and, in its absence, they could not fulfill the hopes of their proponents. Submarines were not to be viable until technologies of underwater propulsion, detachable torpedoes, and storing or obtaining air under water could all be combined.

Similarly, rockets, in effect giant fireworks, which were introduced from the Orient to the West, lacked the guidance system and payload necessary to make them a significant challenge. Nevertheless, their apparent potential led the British to deploy them both at sea and on land during the Napoleonic Wars. Their limited effectiveness was demonstrated in 1814 during the naval bombardment of Fort McHenry, the fort protecting Baltimore from amphibious attack, an episode that led to the anthem "The Star-Spangled Banner," and in 1815 with their presence in the British army at the Battle of Waterloo.[13] Rockets were never likely to be useful until effective solid motors were devised and the payloads became more destructive, which had to wait until the 1930s and 1940s.

Just as these weapons had scant immediate effect, so also with the utilization of iron railways along which horses could pull wagons. These railways were much used in the eighteenth century, principally to move coal in England, leaving majestic structures such as Causey's Arch in County Durham, the largest freestanding arch in England since the Roman Empire. However, it was not until the application of steam power that such railways could develop into anything other than feeders to existing river and canal links, while it took longer to create a long-distance network of railways. In 1804, Roger Hopkins built a tram road in South Wales upon which Richard Trevithick tried the first steam railway locomotive engine, essentially a mobile beam engine. Yet, it was not until the 1810s that locomotive technology achieved a breakthrough as far as the railway was concerned. George Stephenson invented the locomotive in 1814 for pulling coal trains and the first public railway, the Stockton to Darlington, was opened in 1825.

STEAMSHIPS

There were already significant changes at sea in the 1810s. Wind and wood, the dynamics and properties of which had dominated naval power for millennia, became redundant within decades in what truly was a fundamental revolution in means and capability. The first steam warship, *Demologos* (Voice of the People), later renamed *Fulton* after its talented American inventor, Robert Fulton, was laid down (when construction began) in 1814. The ship was intended for the protection of New York harbor, a key anchorage, during the war of 1812–1815 with Britain, but the conflict ended before it could be used. Such a warship provided an opportunity to supplement and/or lessen dependence on coastal artillery (and therefore fortifications) and a possible means to challenge the ability of British warships to take the initiative. The likely cost of amphibious attacks was increased.

Although the Americans were first, not least with the *Savannah*—in 1819 the first steam-propelled vessel to cross the Atlantic, albeit helped greatly by her sails[14]—the British rapidly developed a steam capability at sea. Industrial capacity, notably in metallurgy and shipbuilding, by the state that put the "Industrial" into Industrial Revolution, as well as the ready availability of finance by the world's leading trading power, ensured that, even when other countries took the lead in technological innovation, Britain would be best placed to catch up and to develop what seemed appropriate. The Royal Navy initially leased small private steamships for use as tugs, but in 1821, the tug *Monkey* was purchased, providing the navy with its first owned steamship. In 1822, the *Comet,* the first steamer built for British naval service, followed. Again, it was a small ship, brig-sized and for use as a tug, reflecting the maneuverability provided by steam power and the continuing limitations of sailing vessels in light or adverse winds.

The expedition sent against the privateering base of Algiers in 1824 included *Lightning,* a steam-powered paddleship equipped with three guns, launched at Deptford in 1822. This was the first operational deployment of a British steamship. Four British-built paddle steamers were used from 1827 for the new Greek fleet then fighting for independence from the Ottoman (Turkish) Empire. This was a cause supported by Britain, notably with the sinking of the Ottoman fleet at the battle of Cape Navarino in 1827, a victory for sailing ships but the last victory of the Age of Fighting Sail. The paddle steamers encouraged interest in steam power among serving British officers. In 1830, the first purpose-built British steam warship, *Dee,* entered service.[15]

There were, however, serious limitations. Early steamships suffered from slow speed as well as a high rate of coal consumption, which limited range, not least because the storage space on these relatively small ships was limited; they also suffered from the problems posed by side and paddle wheels. Vulnerability to catching fire was an issue, as was the large amount of space taken up by wheels and coal-bunkers, which left scant room for cannon, repeating an earlier issue with the rowers on galleys, as did side wheels.

The culture of power and the nature of institutional preference were also significant. With the memory of victory over the French at Trafalgar in 1805 an abiding reference, there was a strong reluctance to throw away the existing British lead in sail-warships by embracing the new technology, which was, and is, a frequent dilemma when dominant powers were, and are, faced by new opportunities. The challenge to American air power posed by the development of unmanned flight and rocketry at the present day is a good example. The Americans have a lead in these alternative technologies, but the ability of other states to invest in the latter makes questionable the American decision to spend heavily on arguably anachronistic conventional air capability, notably with the F-35 (see chapter 5). A similar point arises with aircraft carriers. Looked at differently, to throw away a clear lead appeared (and appears) unwise. More than unreasonable conservatism was at stake.

At this stage, the military potential of steamships appeared much greater than that of railways where locomotive technology, nevertheless, had achieved a breakthrough in the 1820s. Moreover, industrialization supplied the necessary demand, capital, and skills to forward the development of railways. As with other technologies, an incremental process was highly significant. When Goldsworthy Gurney's steam-jet (or blast) was applied to George Stephenson's *Rocket* locomotive in 1829, speeds rose from 16 to 29 miles per hour, overturning widely held doubts about the impact of rapid travel on the human body. Direct drive from the cylinders and pistons to the wheels increased efficiency, as did an engine design that boiled water more rapidly, while the development of wrought-iron rails in the 1820s and 1830s was important to the success of the new system.

Yet, at this stage, it was difficult to see what the military consequences of railways might be. The most significant appeared to be the greater strength and effectiveness of the British economy. However, as Britain was not a zone of conflict, it was not clear that its role at the front of developing and financing railway technology would be significant militarily.

Instead, the military consequences of steam power seemed far more obvious at sea, not least because Britain, as the world's leading naval power and producer of coal, was best placed to use its new advantages in the development of steamships. Naval strength was regarded not simply as a deterrent against the threat from other powers, notably France and the United States in 1815–1870, but also as a proactive means to ensure respect for British interests around the world, from China to the Falkland Islands. Steam power offered strategic, operational, and tactical advantages and greatly increased the effectiveness of the Royal Navy. It replaced dependence on the wind, making voyage times more predictable and quicker, and also increased the maneuverability of ships.

Maneuverability was significant both at sea and, even more initially, in rivers, where the relatively weak power of early steamships meant that they appeared more suited to operations than on the high seas. In the First Burmese War of 1824–1826, the 60-horsepower engine of the East India Company's steamer *Diana*, a 100-ton paddle-tug built in India in 1823, allowed her to operate on the swiftly flowing Irrawaddy River. The *Diana* towed sailing ships that destroyed Burmese war boats and was crucial to the successful British advance 400 miles upriver, an advance that led Burma to terms. The threat to the East India Company's position in Bengal was ended and Britain gained coastal regions of Burma, making the latter vulnerable to subsequent attacks, as indeed proved the case in two later wars. In 1886, at the close of the Third Anglo-Burmese War, Burmese independence ended.

Steam also brought an ability to operate inshore. It became easier to sound inshore and hazardous waters and to attack opposing fleets in anchorages. The success of the British bombardment of the Egyptian-held fortified port of Acre in 1840 owed much to steamships. The contrast between operations then and when Napoleon had unsuccessfully besieged the Turkish-held fortress by land in 1799 indicated the advantages offered by naval bombardment.

On the high seas, steamships showed that they were able to cope with bad weather. The *Nemesis*, a 700-ton British iron-hulled paddle steamer, built at Birkenhead by John Laird for the East India Company, sailed through the winter gales off the Cape of Good Hope to China in 1840 and was the first such warship to reach Macao, although two lesser warships had crossed the Pacific from Chile the same year. Britain then was in conflict with China in the First Opium War, and *Nemesis* went on to destroy eleven Chinese war junks in January 1841 near Guangzhou (Canton). The totemic significance of this success seemed obvious to British commentators.

Whereas, despite worthwhile enhancements in construction, armament, seaworthiness, and navigational knowledge, there had been relatively few major changes in the nature of sailing warships over the previous century, steamships developed rapidly. Unlike sailing ships, they were not a mature system or one dependent on a natural power source, the wind, and therefore vulnerable to it. In the 1840s, the screw propeller, placed at the stern of the ship, offered a better alternative to the paddle wheel, by making it possible to carry a full broadside armament, which made the tactical advantages of steam clear-cut. Screw steamers were also more mobile. The British sloop *Rattler*, launched in 1843, was followed in 1846 by the frigate *Amphion*. Alongside screw propellers, metal hulls and fuel-efficient engines were British technological improvements that were crucial to the development of steam propulsion at sea.

Competition drove forward technology in a process that was often to be repeated with naval technology. When the French ordered the *Napoléon*, the first screw-propeller ship of the line, the British converted *Ajax* to screw propulsion. While by the start of 1854, France had the *Napoléon* and eight conversions, the British, who had outspent them heavily, had three new screw ships of the line and seven conversions. They were determined to ensure that the Royal Navy stayed to the fore.[16] The British warships sent to the Baltic in 1854 against Russia in the Crimean War (1854–1856) included no fewer than nine steam battleships, two designed as steam battleships and the other seven converted. Another four screw battleships followed later in the year.

Conversions were important to the application of technological developments, as they cut the cost of doing so. In the 1920s, aircraft carriers could be more rapidly produced by converting existing warships, a process encouraged by the limitations on ship numbers under the Washington Naval Treaty of 1922. The conversion of battlecruisers (which were less armored and faster than battleships) helped ensure that carriers were faster than the standard battle fleet, centered as it was on the battleship with its heavy armor. This basis was to be important to a key characteristic of carrier warfare, the speed of the carriers, which reduced their vulnerability to surface fire. Only one British carrier, the *Glorious* in 1940, was sunk by a battleship.

The effectiveness of steamships was enhanced by other developments in naval capability, again underlining the need not to take one factor in isolation, an element that was increasingly significant as weapon systems became more complex. Moreover, these other developments underlined the value of steam power because it did not hinder their use, as, for example, galleys had constrained that of shipboard artillery. Furthermore, these other changes emphasized the value of investing in steam power. The key developments were the linked, and counterpoised, changes in armament and protection. Naval ordnance altered radically, thanks primarily to the work of the French gunner Colonel Henri-Joseph Paixhans, who used exploding shells, not solid shot. Such shells were not new: the French had first taken shell-firing mortars to sea in the 1690s, and many people had experimented with shell guns in the eighteenth century, but the fusing problem was then insuperable.

As with submarines, it was necessary to bring together a number of specifications. In the early 1820s, Paixhans constructed a cannon and a gun carriage steady enough to cope with the report produced by the explosive charges required to fire large projectiles and to give the projectiles a high enough initial speed to pierce the side of a big ship and to explode inside. His innovations with fuse mechanisms were crucial. Paixhans invented a fuse mechanism whereby the spherical shell could be fired safely in a flat trajectory, and therefore at a higher muzzle velocity than from a high-trajectory gun or mortar. Now, exploding shells could be fired into or through the hull of a warship from the main guns, and not from mortars, and thus had greater range.

Paixhans's innovations were demonstrated successfully in 1824, and their impact was increased by his publications. As in Britain, not least with the debate over the value of steam, the calculations of naval power were advanced in public, again a feature that was to become more prominent in technological developments and debate, in part due to the cost of new systems and in part due to the new nature of public politics. The dominant position of British naval power was such that innovations elsewhere challenged Britain whatever their formal rationale. Paixhans pressed for the combination of his new ordnance with the new steamship technology, and he intended that shell-firing paddle steamers should make sailing ships of the line obsolete, destroying, in a new naval race, Britain's structural advantage over France.

This was a more practicable version of the arguments of the American Robert Fulton (1765–1815) in the 1800s and 1810s that his work with mines, torpedoes, submarines, and steamships could overthrow this advantage. In 1806, he argued that "It does not require much depth of thought to trace that science by discovering gunpowder changed the whole art of war by land and sea; and by future combination may sweep military marines from the ocean."[17] These arguments were advanced by Fulton for a number of purposes, notably obtaining British, French, or American backing. The rationale offered for his technology varied depending upon the sponsorship being sought, but there was a common theme that revolutionary change was possible and could be made imminent. Fulton offered a magic bullet for naval warfare.

In 1837, the French established the Paixhans shell gun as part of every warship's armament, but they found it difficult to manufacture reliable shell-firing guns, a classic instance of the difficulties of moving from invention to application. The French metallurgical industry was less effective than its British counterpart, a problem that was subsequently to be important in shipbuilding and that indicated the significance of industrial capability to technological development. As a consequence, the hopes of Paixhans's supporters that this new technology would enable France to threaten British naval hegemony proved abortive, even while it underlined the extent to which France seemed Britain's principal challenger. Moreover, the habitual process by which the comparative advantage of one power was lessened by the diffusion of the new technology it could deploy was shown in this instance, as the British adopted shell guns as part of their standard armament in 1838.

IRONCLADS

The new ordnance posed a terrible threat to wooden ships, but shells helped lead to their antidote, armored warships. The Korean "turtle ships" of the 1590s covered in hexagonal iron plates were used with great effect in alliance with the Chinese against the invading Japanese, although command skills were also important to the Korean naval victories. However, like the galleys of antiquity, these ships are difficult to judge as none survive.[18]

Excluding the Korean ships, the first ironclad warship, *La Gloire,* was French. It was inspired by the success of three newly built French 1,575-

ton iron-plated, wooden floating gun platforms off Kinburn in the Black Sea in 1855 during the Crimean War with Russia (1854–1856), a limited war that tested out the military effectiveness of the combatants. These platforms had been towed from France by steamships, again a reminder of the interaction and mutual dependence of developments. Kinburn was captured, as was the nearby Russian coastal fortress of Ochakov, but it proved impossible to exploit the success in order to make much of an impact on the war on land. Indeed, the key campaign of the war, the lengthy operations against the Russian Black Sea naval base of Sevastopol in 1854–1856, depended on land attack, for naval bombardments proved ineffective.

Laid down in March 1858 and launched in November 1859, the 5,630-ton *La Gloire*, however, was merely a wooden frigate fitted with 4.5-inch-thick metal plates, since the French were handicapped by a lack of iron-working facilities. Nevertheless, Emperor Napoleon III, a bellicose ruler who was determined to challenge the British, ordered five more ironclads in 1858, and they were commissioned in 1862.

Worried that their naval lead was being destroyed and concerned about Napoleon III's attempts to coerce Britain into accepting French hegemony and expansionism on the Continent,[19] the British matched *La Gloire* with an armored frigate, HMS *Warrior*, laid down in May 1859, completed in October 1861, and still afloat in Portsmouth Harbor where it forms an interesting contrast with the *Victory*, Nelson's flagship at Trafalgar in 1805, a wooden warship of note. With its iron hull and displacement of 9,140 tons, *Warrior* was more significant than the *La Gloire* and, built at the Thames Ironworks, also testified to British manufacturing capability.

The *Warrior*, which cost £377,000 (a formidable sum) to build, was a revolutionary ship design. It was actually a true iron ship, as opposed to an ironclad ship. Furthermore, with its watertight compartments below, the *Warrior* was the first large seagoing, iron-hulled warship[20] and set the pattern for the first British armored frigates. In addition to their iron hulls, the first generation of British armored frigates was on average 60 percent larger than its French counterparts.

As a reminder of the fundamentals of naval power, whether imperial or not, and of the linkage of the "home front" to military capability, the British had the experience of the world's leading merchant marine, of skilled shipbuilding, and of ambitious and innovative ship-designers such as Isambard Kingdom Brunel on which to draw. Brunel's SS *Great Britain* had been launched as early as 1843. There was a major difference in industrial capability. The French had the infrastructure to build a few big iron ships but not a new fleet, while the British, the world's leading shipbuilder, had been building large iron ships for commercial purposes for some time.

The French challenge encouraged heavy British investment in the navy, and the two powers took part in an ironclad naval race in 1859–1865 that was won by Britain with its greater resources and commitment. As with the German naval race against Britain in 1906–1912, France foolishly focused on what turned out to be a discretionary opponent, rather than building up an ability to engage successfully with rivals on land: in France's case in 1859–1865 this meant Prussia and in Germany's case in 1906–1912 France. On the other hand, alongside the totemic power of ships came the drive to challenge Britain's imperial position, which was largely based on maritime predominance.

These cases are examples of the more general significance of tasking. Due to the availability of sources, the choice entailed in the latter is more apparent for the last two centuries and for the West then, but the choice involved in tasking was certainly more generally important, both chronologically and geographically. It is a significant issue when considering the creation and use of technological possibilities. Tasking reflected the outcome of political contention. In the 1860s, radical Liberals in Britain opposed expensive ironclads and pressed for cheaper gunboats, but their argument lacked political traction.

Iron ships were structurally stronger than wooden ones and made redundant the wooden screw steamers built in large numbers in the 1850s and the very beginning of the 1860s. The shift to iron reflected not simply the vulnerability of wooden ships to shellfire but also success in overcoming the problems that had delayed the use of iron, including its effect on magnetic compasses, the fact that iron hulls fouled very much worse than wooden ones that were copper-bottomed, and the difficulties of securing sufficient consistency and quality in the iron. The last was a classic problem with materials: it was not enough to discern a superior material; it was also important to ensure consistent quality. The ability to overcome these problems reflected the strength of the British economy in the acquisition and application of relevant knowledge. Metallurgical developments were a product of the strength and sophistication of the industrial base and the latter were seen in the capacity to utilize innovations.

The changes in naval technology were at a rate that would have been inconceivable in the eighteenth century. States rapidly copied each other. Russia, which had destroyed a wooden Turkish fleet off Sinope in 1853 using shell guns during a surprise attack, invested during the Crimean War (1854–1856) in screw-propelled gunboats and, from 1861, in ironclads.[21] More generally, the real and perceived tensions between armor and armament, and between weight and maneuverability, created an inherent instability and a drive for improvement. These tensions also made it unclear how best to assess naval strength, which created a serious problem for planning.

This difficulty of assessment was an aspect of the impact of technology, and one that helps differentiate modern warfare from earlier periods in which the pace of change was generally lower and the resulting imponderables fewer. Moreover, on the whole, success in earlier periods rested more on the use of weapons as part of ably led, well-deployed, and enthusiastic forces and less on the inherent superiority of particular arms, although this contrast has to be used with care and, as so often, it is necessary not to primitivize earlier periods. In addition, fighting leadership, skill, tactical innovation, and enthusiasm all remained important to military success.

IRONCLADS AND THE AMERICAN CIVIL WAR

The potential of ironclads was shown on March 8, 1862, in the American Civil War (1861–1865) when the Confederate *Virginia* (earlier the *Merrimack*) attacked the Union warships blockading the port of Norfolk, Virginia, as part of the strategy of interdiction designed to cripple the export trade of the Confederacy and thus make it harder to raise funds and acquire arms. *Virginia* employed ramming to sink one warship and used gunfire to destroy another.

Next day, there was the first clash between ironclads in history, one that, in comparison to the engagement on the 8th, however, indicated the reduced advantage stemming from a matched technological advance. In nearby Hampton Roads, cannon shot could make little impact on the armored sides of the *Virginia* and the Union's *Monitor,* even though they fired on each other from within 100 yards. There was only one casualty in the engagement.[22] The resilience of ironclads to cannon fire was indicated by the disparity in the Civil War between the seven armored Union ships lost to Confederate mines, compared to only one lost to fire from the cannon of shore batteries.

During the war, moreover, the capability of ironclads increased, although the Union blockade was for the most part enforced by wooden warships. Whereas the *Monitor* had had two guns in one steam-powered revolving turret, the Union laid down its first monitor (a class of ship now taking the name of the original vessel invented by John Ericsson) with two turrets in March 1863, ultimately completing nine of the latter. One ship was converted to a three-turret monitor, the *Roanoke,* which was designed for the high seas, but it rolled too badly to be effective.

As a reminder that capability has to be assessed in terms of conflicts that did not occur, as well as those that did, the likely consequences of British entry into the Civil War were unclear. Such intervention appeared possible during the *Trent* crisis of December 1861, when Confederate envoys were seized from a British ship, and, subsequently, in the second half of 1862 as a result of pressure for Anglo-French action from Napoleon III and of the run of Confederate success that, in the event, ended with the Battle of Antietam on September 17. The extent to which steam power and iron ships might have changed the nature of naval warfare by this juncture was far from apparent. In part, the Union developed ironclads not only to fight the Confederacy but also in order to be able to resist the danger of British intervention, and, by doing so, the Union both built up its confidence in the event of war and reduced Britain's political leverage.[23] As a result, public relations played a major role in the discussion of technology and weapons' effectiveness, with the engagements off Norfolk on March 8–9, 1862, being much covered. Deterrence was the key issue in American capability, as, aside from the serious problems of American ships overseas obtaining coal when America it-

self lacked colonial bases,[24] its ironclads were designed for coastal service and were not really suitable for long range service on the high seas
or, indeed, service in heavy seas.[25] Thus, in contrast to the French navy,
fleet action against the British Isles was not a prospect.

The overall strategic rationale for the American (Union) navy facing the threat of a foreign war was coastal ironclads for defense and
commerce raiders for offence, possibly coupled with military operations
against apparently vulnerable (British-ruled) Canada and, perhaps, even
against British imperial bases in the Atlantic and Caribbean, such as Ber-
muda. The American navy assumed that a few marked repulses to any
British attacks along the eastern seaboard, as well as mounting losses to
the British merchant marine worldwide from American commerce raiders, would eventually dampen any British enthusiasm for war against
the Northern states. In short, the Anglo-American War of 1812–1815 was
read in a way that provided a logic underpinning a possible strategy for
what in fact were different circumstances.

Much of this strategic assumption and related operational possibilities was due to developments on a tactical level. American monitors were
designed to fight at close quarters, 1,000 yards or less. As these vessels
were largely submerged below the waterline, offering only a concentrated armor protection scheme along the exposed hull and especially
the gun turrets, it was quite reasonable to assume that enemy fire would
not be effective against this target profile until the 15-inch guns of the
monitors began to tell in response. Naval combat before, during, and
after the Civil War confirmed that reliable naval gunnery was still at earlier and more limited "Age of Sail" ranges, despite the advent of rifled
heavy cannon. Battle was still confused—noisy, clouded with smoke
(smokeless powder was not yet in use), and with accuracy always at the
mercy of the slightest pitch and roll of the vessel. As a result, the "raft"-
like feature of the monitors, as gun-platforms, made them much more
stable and tactically challenging than the high-freeboard, broadside-
firing ironclads of the European variety, which were designed for power
projection and heavier seas and which presented larger targets.

As for the hitting power of the American (Union) 15-inch Rodman
(army) or Dahlgren (navy) guns themselves, Civil War ironclad engagements proved time and again that, at effective combat ranges, no

armor afloat could possibly resist a 450-pound shot propelled by 50- to 60-pound service charges. In 1863, the CSS *Atlanta* was reduced to surrender after three hits from the 15-inch gun of the monitor USS *Weehawken,* one of which blasted a 3-foot-wide hole in her casemate armor. True, this armor was "laminated"—two layers of 2-inch iron plates. But these were rolled, wrought-iron plates, backed by 24 inches of wood. Such composite armor is more effective than solid plate of the same combined thickness. The wood was intended to prevent the spalling of the iron plates when struck, by which small pieces of iron fly off the face opposite the one struck. Furthermore, the shot in question struck at an angle, meaning that even more armor and backing was offered to resist the shot, a cored shot of 330 pounds. When armor of thickness T is sloped at 60 degrees, the horizontal thickness of the armor is twice T. Thus, if a projectile strikes at a horizontal trajectory, it has to penetrate twice the thickness of armor compared to if it struck the armor at 90 degrees to its 60-degree slope.

The same experiment was demonstrated against the 5- and 6-inch-thick armor of the CSS *Tennessee* (which was battered into surrender by the more numerous Union fleet under Farragut at Mobile Bay in 1864) and the 6-inch armor of the CSS *Virginia II* (at Trent's Reach, 1865) with similar results, demonstrating the effectiveness of the American (Union) ordnance. This capacity was important in underlining the fleet's ability not only to blockade the Confederacy but also to mount significant pressure through supporting amphibious attacks including engaging coastal positions.

The primary concern for Union ironclad designers, especially the talented Ericsson, however, was the 4- and then 6-inch armor plating of ocean-going British ironclads, from *Warrior* to *Bellerophon,* the Reed-designed "central-battery" broadside-and-sail ironclad. While the *Warrior's* armor, for example, consisted of solid rolled plates of 4.5-inch thickness, backed by 18 inches of teak and a thin iron inner "skin," the sides of the vessel were vertical; deflection would not assist resisting bombardment, as it did in the case of Confederate casemates. *Warrior's* plating was also defective at the joints.

To confirm by firsthand experience themselves, the American navy, in 1862–1863, procured rolled iron plates from the same British and French companies producing armor for their own nations' ironclad fleets. These were then backed by up to 3 feet of wood, and the targets packed against a solid hillside bank of clay. Nevertheless, 15-inch smoothbores tore ragged holes through these structures, not only penetrating the iron and wood but leaving the plates themselves "shattered" and "brittle" around the point of impact. This testing indicated an important and developing aspect of a military world in which technological innovation was seen as a central feature: both intelligence operations and testing became more significant. Uncertainty over how military forms that had not hitherto competed would perform was more prominent than when the pace of innovation had been more subdued.

The targets in the American tests of 1862–1863 argued little for actual British ironclads afloat during the American Civil War, namely *Warrior* and her sister-ship *Black Prince,* the *Defence, Resistance, Achilles,* and a few wooden ironclad conversions, all protected with 4.5-inch iron armor plates. By 1864, the U.S. Army and then Navy had already produced 20-inch guns that packed approximately double the hitting power of the 15-inch varieties. American rate-of-fire was reduced, but this mattered little when lighter-caliber weapons could effect no appreciable damage in the meantime against the turret armor of the American monitors— by 1864 up to 15 inches in thickness. Armor plates arrayed in a turret structure were also found to be innately stronger overall to resist the force of impact and, therefore, penetration, than thick slabs bolted onto the broadside. Monitor turret armor proved impervious at even point blank ranges to Confederate 10-inch Columbiads firing shot weighing 168 pounds, as opposed to the 68-pounder smoothbores of *Warrior* and her sisters. Moreover, the monitor form of the ironclad at least enabled upgrades without requiring an entirely new design of ship to float the armor of equal weight.

Thus, any European ironclad would have done well to stay clear of Union monitors, and the blockade of the American seaboard, such as that attempted by Britain in 1812–1815, eventually with considerable success, would now have been too hazardous for Britain sensibly to risk capital ships. In order to be of any real threat to the Union, the Royal Navy would have needed to invest in building and sustaining a "Brown Water" ironclad force to operate effectively in North American coastal waters.[26] In addition to the problems posed by the American monitors, the fast wooden screw steamers authorized by Congress in 1864 would, it was feared by the British, act as "a chain across the great lines of commerce."[27] This concern led to the British building fast unarmored iron-hulled warships in response so that these steamers could be engaged. Similarly, there was to be anxiety in the 1900s that fast German ships, including converted ocean liners, would outrun British warships and threaten British trade. This concern encouraged the development, in response, of battlecruisers,[28] the emphasis of which was on speed, not armor.

As another instance of the unpredictability of any British entry into the Civil War, improvements in naval ordnance also made coastal defenses, both American and British, obsolete. In a classic form of the interplay of weaponry and anti-weaponry, improvements in artillery in the nineteenth century made existing systems largely redundant, as rifled artillery, both moved on land and carried by steamships, could inflict serious damage on masonry forts, although Charleston's defenses did better than expected in 1863.[29] This change meant that the defense of harbor cities, such as Boston and New York against British attack, would have been heavily reliant on monitors. In Britain, the defenses of the naval bases were improved.[30]

GREATER NAVAL CAPABILITY

At sea, the mutually interacting need for more effective guns and stronger armor continued to cause pressure for improvement after the American Civil War. Off Punta Angamos in 1879 in the War of the Pacific (1879–1883), armor-piercing Palliser shells, fired from the 9-inch (British-produced) Armstrong guns of Chilean warships, forced the badly damaged Peruvian *Huáscar* to surrender, as the 8 inches of wrought iron on its turret had proved no defense. This battle was important because, alongside strength on land, Chilean effectiveness in part depended on the ability to mount amphibious operations against Peru, and this ability was clearly linked to the effectiveness of Chilean guns. The battle was followed by successful amphibious assaults on Peru that helped lead to Chile's success in the war. It ended the war with important territorial gains to the north.

For the leading naval powers, there was a process of rapid change in capability. Wooden-hulled ironclads were quickly superseded in the 1860s. The wrought-iron navy was followed, after experimentation with iron and wood armor, by the introduction of compound armor plate in 1877, the iron and steel navy. There were also moves toward the first all-steel warships in the 1870s with two all-steel cruisers completed for the British navy in 1879. From the 1890s, warships were increasingly built with nickel-steel plate, providing added protection without greater weight. This ability encouraged the construction of larger ships able to carry bigger guns and thus to counter the stronger armor. Greater motive power was provided by major progress in steam technology, notably the combination of high-pressure boilers with the compound engine in the 1860s, and then the introduction of the triple-expansion marine engine in 1874, although it was not used in warships until the 1880s. This engine was followed by the water tube boiler.

In place of warships designed to fire broadsides came guns mounted in centerline turrets, which were able to fire end-on, as well as to turn. Moreover, firing armor-piercing explosive shells, guns became more effective. These were ships clearly designed for battle and from the 1880s it became common for them to be called battleships, ships that were defined by their function. Guns also became more rapid firing, as breechloaders replaced muzzle-loading guns, which took a long time to load with large shells. Rifled artillery, percussion detonators, and high explosives, especially cordite and melmite in the 1880s and 1890s, also increased the effectiveness of naval power. There was also a professionalization of naval construction, with an emphasis on scientific methods of design and construction that rested on careful mathematical calculations and detailed problems, rather than on intuition and half-hull models.[31]

Yet, at the same time, there was an attempt to create what can be called anti-weapons (although all weapons are in a sense anti-weapons) by exploiting against battleships the potential offered by other vessels and weapons, namely the speed of cruisers and the development of powered torpedoes. In 1864, the modern self-propelled torpedo originated with the invention of a submerged self-propelled torpedo driven by compressed air and armed with an explosive charge at its head.[32] After Germany's dramatic victory over France in 1870–1871 in the Franco-

Prussian War, the French navy was faced with the consequences of a political focus on the continuing and now stronger threat posed by the German army, as opposed to the option of naval investment aimed against Britain, which had engaged Napoleon III during the naval race in 1859–1865.

As a result, Admiral Théophile Aube, who became navy minister in 1886–1887, and a group of thinkers known as the *Jeune École* sought to counter British naval strength by out-thinking the British. The less expensive option of unarmored light cruisers would use less coal and be faster and more maneuverable than battleships. These cruisers were also regarded as more flexible and thus better able to fulfill a range of tasks removed from the ship-killing battle-focus of battleships. Cruisers would be able to protect sea lanes; to advance imperial expansion, a major issue for France, the world's second largest trans-oceanic empire; and to attack the commerce of opponents. The far-flung British imperial economy was particularly vulnerable on the last head.

As a reminder of the need to put weapons into the context of their use, the conceptual and methodological challenge posed by the French was not only a matter of a different force structure focused on cruisers but also a mixed-arms doctrine that looked toward twentieth-century doctrine and practice, especially the attempt to combine battleship and submarine operations in both world wars and the integration of air power in the Second. However, with cruisers, the necessary speed and range were obtainable only in big cruisers, which were expensive.

Aube also favored the torpedo boat and claimed that the self-propelled torpedo made close blockades too risky. Thus, the battleship was nullified and the use of British blockade to close down French options, as in conflicts from 1689 to 1815, could be overcome. This argument prefigured German hopes from submarine and air power at the expense of Britain in the two world wars, as well as the ambitions of more minor states seeking to thwart later American naval hegemony. With blockade broken, the *Jeune École* believed that naval mobility would be ensured and that their cruisers would be able to launch a crippling war on British trade.[33]

With France apparently the most likely opponent, as well as the closest naval power, the Royal Navy had to respond to this change and challenge, but it did so unwillingly. As the practice of close blockade represented a clear operational capability and strategic asset for Britain, there was a reluctance to abandon it. Indeed, it was felt necessary in the British exercises of 1885 to plan for the establishment of a defensible advance base, so as to reduce vulnerability to torpedo attack. However, from the 1890s, the threat to the Royal Navy from torpedo attacks curtailed British interest in littoral warfare. In 1888, France completed a submarine powered by an electric battery.

As a pointed reminder of the rate at which relative capability appeared to change with new technological developments and their impact in doctrine, the 1900s and early 1910s were to witness a revived commitment to battleships. This revival was notably as a result of the prominence of the *Dreadnought,* launched by the British in 1906, a display of British technological proficiency and a proof of naval prowess. The reform of the tax system by the Liberal government led to an increase in revenue that permitted greater expenditure on both warships and old age pensions. In the design of the ship, technology was reimagined as a scientific means to ensure efficiency and economy, notably in speed and firepower. Aside from the increase in fighting power represented by this, the first large armored ship with an all-big-gun armament and turbine propulsion,[34] the *Dreadnought* seemed able to see off recent challenges. This capability reflected innovations designed to limit the risk from torpedo boats including nets, thicker waterline armor, secondary guns, searchlights, and the use of destroyers (originally armored torpedo-carrying warships) to provide protection against torpedo boats. Moreover, the move to smokeless powder ensured that torpedo boats would lack the cover provided by smoke. At the same time, Mahanian notions of command of the sea ensured that there was a strong doctrinal commitment to battleships, although, in the case of Germany, this commitment was based on a serious failure to understand the respective strength of the naval powers and the potential of the German navy.

In the event it was not torpedo boats or, later, submarines that were to doom the battleship. Instead, the development, in the 1930s and 1940s, of air power was to challenge the technology of surface firepower. The success of high-level bombers was mixed, but torpedo planes could be deadly, as with the Japanese sinking on December 10, 1941, of the British battleship *Prince of Wales* and the battlecruiser *Repulse*. When sunk, the former had the best radar suite of any operational warship in the world including close-in radar for her anti-aircraft guns as well as radar for her main guns. The *Prince of Wales,* a modern ship, also had good compartmentalization.[35]

The continued value of battleships was seen in coastal bombardments, notably in 1943–1945—for example, D-Day in Normandy (1944) as well as at Iwo Jima and Okinawa in 1945—and again during the Korean War. However, institutional politics were important in the move from battleships, notably the rise of carrier admirals to prominence in the American navy. Moreover, the enhancement of air power at sea in the 1950s, not least with developments with arrester gear and night flying, was significant.

For surface ships that were not carriers, missiles rather than guns appeared to be the future, and missiles did not require large ships. After 1960, when the last British battleship was scrapped, only the United States kept battleships in its fleet, and in the 1980s the *Wisconsin* was converted to be able to launch cruise missiles. The retirement of this ship, the last serving battleship, from the large American reserve fleet was announced in 2011. Battleships became museum pieces. Coastal bombardment by warships remained significant, as with operations by the British navy against the Argentineans in the Falklands War in 1982, but the emphasis is now on missiles, not big guns.

RAILWAYS

Despite significant improvements in capacity and running, railways lacked a comparable process of enhancement to that of warships. Nevertheless, railways proved highly significant in war. By the Crimean War (1854–1856), they were playing a role in warfare, in this case largely because the lack of Russian rail links to the Crimea hit the deployment and logistics of Russian forces. Thus, due to the weakness of its rail system, Russia was unable to realize much of the potential of its central position when attacked by seaborne Anglo-French forces able to take advantage of the capability offered by steam power. More generally, the Allies' lead in weaponry rested on a superior technical and manufacturing base.[36]

The scope of the Russian rail system again became an issue during the Russo-Japanese War of 1904–1905, in this case with the need to reinforce and sustain, across the vast distance of Siberia, the peripheral but strategically significant position in Manchuria against Japanese attack. Although, in 1904, the railway was incomplete at Lake Baikal, the Russians transported 370,000 troops to the east. Their ability to use the railways as an integrated element of strategy making, however, has been queried.[37]

In contrast to the Crimean War, in the Austro-French war in Italy in 1859, both sides employed railways in the mobilization and deployment of their forces. In the opening stage of the conflict, despite problems with single track and insufficient locomotives in Piedmont, the French moved 130,000 troops to Italy by rail in a matter of weeks, thereby helping to gain the initiative. This number includes those transported to Marseille and Toulon for subsequent movement by sea to Genoa. At the same time, the railway had as great, if not greater, of an impact on logistics as on the strategic movement of armies over great distances.[38]

The extent to which the railway had altered the relationship between amphibious attack and land defense was to be discussed by geopoliticians in the early twentieth century, notably Halford Mackinder in 1904,[39] but was already playing a role in military planning by the mid-nineteenth century. In 1854, Sir James Graham, the First Lord of the British Admiralty, wrote to Fitzroy, Lord Raglan, the Master-General of the Ordnance, about the need to defend the estuary of the Humber on Britain's east coast: "I quite concur in the opinion that the permanent presence of a large military force at Hull [the major port] is not requisite: that inland concentration, with rapid means of distribution by railroad is the right system."[40]

In the American Civil War (1861–1865), the railway, which had expanded greatly in America in the 1840s and 1850s, especially in the North, made a huge difference, tactically, operationally, strategically, and economically. At the tactical level, manmade landscape features created for railways, such as embankments, played a part in battles. Operationally, the railway created links along which troops could move. In 1862, the Confederate commander Braxton Bragg was able to move his troops 776 miles by rail from Mississippi to Chattanooga and thus create an opportunity for an invasion of Kentucky.

Such a potential was totally different to the situation during the previous wars in North America, and, if the term "revolutionary" is helpful, then the capacity to plan for rapid movement was a significant development.[41] As a result, rail junctions or river ports where steamship
services and railways were linked, such as Atlanta, Chattanooga, Co-
rinth, Manassas, and Nashville, became operationally highly significant
and the object of campaigning. Union advances targeted such junctions,
which the Confederates struggled to protect or regain.

At the same time, there was still a heavy dependence for logistics on
such traditional means as wagons and foraging. Indeed, the improvement of Union field transport was crucial to William Tecumseh Sherman's successful advance through Georgia and the Carolinas in 1864–
1865,[42] an advance that destroyed the Confederacy's strategic depth.

More generally, military plans increasingly depended on using or
threatening rail links. In 1861, Captain William Noble of the British
Royal Engineers produced a report on the defense of Canada (part of
the British Empire) arguing that the American presence on the St. Lawrence waterway was a threat to British communications, as the only railway from Montréal to Kingston, Ontario, and points farther west went
along the north bank of the river. As a result, Noble pressed for Britain
taking the initiative if war broke out with America.[43]

In 1862, in the campaign that led to the Battle of Second Manassas or
Bull Run, the Confederate general "Stonewall" Jackson hit the Union
supply route along the Orange and Alexandria Railroad, destroying
the supply depot at Manassas Junction. Later that year, the Union commander Ambrose Burnside planned to move south toward the Confederate capital, Richmond, along the Richmond, Fredericksburg and
Potomac Railroad after he had captured the river crossing point of Fredericksburg, which, in the event, he failed to do. West of the Appala-
chians, the Union forces planned both to gain control of the Mississippi
River and to advance into the Confederacy along the railways running
southeast through Tennessee and Georgia. In 1864, the Union success
in cutting rail links led the Confederates to abandon Atlanta. This victory helped ensure Abraham Lincoln's reelection, which had looked less
probable earlier in the year. The comparable campaign in the War of
American Independence had been the British surrounding of Charles-

ton in 1780, but that had been obtained, thanks to amphibious capability, by moving units across rivers, notably the Ashley and the Cooper by boat. The Patriots had held on in Charleston, only to surrender rapidly once it was bombarded.

Technology, use, and potential combined in the American Civil War to ensure organizational attention. The Union created U.S. Military Railroads as a branch of the War Department. This was part of the process of wartime mobilization, the scope of which expanded as a result of the organizational demands stemming from new capacity and needs. The function of U.S. Military Railroads included the building and repair of track and bridges. This capability provided a quick-response system to such requirements for transport links as the exigencies of the war required. As with the purchasing networks and naval dockyards created in the early modern period to sustain warships (see chapter 1), this system was necessary in order to give effect to the new technology, as well as to earlier methods, such as wagon-based logistics.

At the same time, aside from noting the weaknesses of the Confederacy's railway system,[44] it is important to put the use of the railway in the Civil War in context. The network did not necessarily influence where the campaigns were fought. Rivers probably had a greater effect on where operations were mounted, although Sherman's and Grant's remorseless offensives in 1864–1865 moved away from the shackles of a confined geography that rivers and, indeed, railways imposed. This was a manifestation of the change in the nature of conflict during the Civil War. Indeed, there were no railways in the Wilderness, and it was here perhaps more than anywhere that trench warfare made an impact. The problem with drawing an overall conclusion for the war is that, on the one hand, railways seemed to influence where campaigns and battles were fought, while others were dictated by the presence of navigable rivers; but some campaigns paid little or no direct heed to the presence of either.

Moreover, the technological aspects of railway warfare were limited. There were no major developments in the specifications of locomotives. Rail design and fabrication methods, as well as railway construction systems, were crucial to the speed of laying of new track in addition to the safety of trains on it and the speed they could travel. Changes in these were not driven forward by the Civil War, and economic developments, rather than the war, were responsible for the growth of a large-volume rail system.

On a different scale, an effective quick-response system was also created by Prussia in the 1860s. In its wars with Austria in 1866 and France in 1870–1871, Prussia won in part thanks to an effective exploitation of the railway network to achieve rapidly the desired initial deployment, thereby gaining the operational and strategic initiative. The Crimean (1854–1856) and Franco-Austrian (1859) wars had led to an understanding in Europe of the need for good rail links for military purposes. Through use of planned rail movements, the Prussians made mobilization a predictable sequence and greatly eased the concentration of forces. Uniform speed by all trains was employed by the Prussians in order to maximize their use. Military trains were also of standard length. Rail use was planned and controlled by a railroad commission and by line commands, creating an integrated system linked and made responsive by the telegraph. The number of locomotives was kept high in order to cope with a wartime rise in demand.[45]

The availability and use of railways helped both to create capability gaps within the West and also, more obviously, between the West and non-Western powers. In the latter case, railways were very important in imperial expansion. Given the fact that they were built behind the front of imperial advance, railways were not involved in conflict in a tactical sense or, usually, operationally, and this remained the case into the twentieth century; for example, with the Italian conquest of Ethiopia in 1935–1936. Nevertheless, railways could be of operational significance for advancing forces if the pace of advance was reasonably slow, and they played a key role in logistics. The latter became of greater importance as Western forces operated inland. In the absence of river routes, such operations compromised the power projection advantage of ocean steamers. Moreover, the need to use human porters for many inland operations created problems in the shape of obtaining sufficient porters and then providing them with enough food. The high death rate of porters was a significant operational element, notably in the African campaigns of the First World War in which the German colonies were conquered.

In 1896, the Anglo-Egyptian army invading Sudan built a railway straight across the desert from Wadi Halfa to Abu Hamed, the 383-mile-long Sudan Military Railway constructed across the bend of the Nile. The railway was pushed onto Atbara in 1898 and played a major role in the supply of the British forces, and thus in operational effectiveness. The British crushed the Sudanese forces at Omdurman in 1898. In the Boer War (1899–1902), the railways that ran inland from the South African ports such as Durban and Cape Town facilitated the deployment of British military resources, first against Boer advances and subsequently in the conquest of the Orange Free State and the Transvaal, although wagon trains also proved necessary.

Railways were also regarded as of strategic importance, in particular anchoring territorial interests, and their extension was a matter of governmental concern and press comment.[46] By 1906, a rail system in Russian central Asia had been created, serving strategic and economic interests and troubling British observers worried about a threat to Afghanistan and Persia (Iran), and hence to the British position in southern Asia. To the east in 1896, Russia obliged China to grant a concession for a railway across Manchuria to Vladivostok, and this Chinese Eastern Railway (CER) was constructed in 1897–1904. When the Russians advanced against the Chinese in Manchuria in 1900, the railway served as an axis of movement. The CER proved a key issue of Russian power until purchased by Japan in 1934.[47]

Communication links were sought by imperial powers and were seen as a way to strengthen their empires, politically, economically, and militarily.[48] The role of the railway therefore was strategic in the broadest sense, in that it helped in the development of the economic links that sustained and strengthened the major powers. For example, the railway was crucial in creating and improving economic links between coastal and hinterland America, as well as in integrating the frontiers of settlement with the world economy. This integration was important in the spread of ranching, with the cattle being driven to railheads, and in the exploitation of mining opportunities.

Railways were also important to the protection of empire. Faced by the rebellion of the *Métis* (mixed-blood population) in Manitoba and

Saskatchewan in 1885, the Canadian government sent over four thousand militia west over the Canadian Pacific Railway, achieving an overwhelming superiority that helped bring rapid victory. This display of capability was followed by a new increase in government subsidy for the railway that enabled its completion that year.[49] Similarly, the railways the British built in India helped ensure that troops could be moved to areas of difficulty, as in 1897 when they were sent to the North-West Frontier (of modern Pakistan) to assist in overcoming resistance among the Waziris.[50] Railheads such as Peshawar and Quetta played a key part in British planning both on that frontier and with regard to power projection into Afghanistan and, in turn, had to be protected.

In Mexico, the building of a railway across the rebel area in 1900 helped to end long-standing Mayan resistance to the Mexican government, although the effects of cholera, smallpox, and whooping cough were also significant. In 1926, the French responded to a rebellion in their new colony of Syria by building a railway into the Jebel Druze region, the center of the opposition, in order to facilitate the movement of their forces.

Railways, therefore, could play a major role, although they were of less direct use in battlefield moves. Indeed, at the tactical level, the limited mobility of troops was still very striking. Moreover, in the Third World, railways did not play a role in many areas. For example, no railways were built in Afghanistan, a country that was never brought under Western control. Indeed, across most of the world, alongside the emphasis on railways, it is important to note the continued role of horses, mules, and oxen, which, together, provided essential mobility for long-range movements away from rail links. Horses conspicuously did so for the Germans as late as the Second World War, counteracting the impression created for the *Wehrmacht* by the emphasis on tanks, notably in German propaganda. Mules were also important for the British in that war, both in Burma and in Italy.

In addition, it is necessary to appreciate the extent to which a simpler technology than that of railways, namely roads, remained significant. Usage in the nineteenth century did not yet focus on vehicles equipped with internal combustion engines, but the construction and maintenance of roads required certain techniques, such as cambering, while the technological element rested with the equipment used for construction and maintenance. The high explosives that helped break up and move large quantities of rock, as in tunnel construction, were important.

The relevance of roads in the late nineteenth century was not a case of a residual significance in the gaps between new railways, for many new roads were built. For example, road construction was crucial in New Zealand in the 1860s, when British troops were used to extend the Great South Road from Auckland over the hills south of Drury in the face of Maori opposition. By 1874, a road had been finished between Tauranga and Napier, separating two areas of Maori dissidence.

Railways remained vital during the twentieth century, for peacetime military structures, mobilization, and during wartime. They were designed for strategic and operational effect[51] and proved the major way in which troops and supplies were moved to conflict zones in the First World War. Narrow-gauge (different from standard railway tracking) light railways played an important role, as they were relatively easy to lay and maintain. These lines carried supplies and troops up to the trench lines and batteries.[52] The large-scale trench warfare of that conflict, especially on the western front, depended on the combatants' ability to provide substantial quantities of bulky and weighty supplies on a regular basis in order to support the densely packed forces necessary to maintain and defend a continuous front line as well as the large, and growing, number of heavy-artillery guns required to support attacks. The number of shells that had to be moved up for these guns was formidable.

In turn, such supply networks relied on the largely static nature of the fighting, which created major problems when advances took place, as with the Allies on the western front in late 1918. As a result, numerous labor battalions were required then to repair the railways seriously damaged by the retreating Germans.

The contrast in military activity was readily apparent where railways were sparse, as in Africa during that war and in China in the 1920s. In these cases, where the communication system was heavily dependent on human porters, the density of operations and, especially, of firepower was lower. Nevertheless, railways were also very important in these areas, although in a different fashion. Axes of advance were frequently along them, as in the fighting of the Russian Civil War of 1918–

1922 and of the Chinese warlord era of the 1920s. In China, the national rail system was a kind of modern battlefield. Most of the fighting was along, or around, or for, it. The rail system connected mostly relatively new, industrial cities. The rail plus the cities were in effect a separable realm from the countryside and its farmers. The ability to move troops by rail helped shape the conflict. Thus, in 1924, the warlord Wu Peifu depended on the rail system in order to concentrate his forces against his rival Zhang Zuolin, the Manchurian warlord.

Most troops were infantry, which underlined the significance of railways for transport and logistics. Moreover, operations often focused on a struggle to control railway centers and junctions, such as Wuhan. Communist control of Moscow and Petrograd (St. Petersburg), the hubs of the rail system, was important to operational effectiveness in the Russian Civil War, and the campaigns in the Urals and Siberia revolved to a great extent around the Trans-Siberian Railway. Furthermore, armored trains played a major role in the Russian Civil War and were also significant in China.

Despite the spread of petrol-powered vehicles, railways remained important in the Second World War, which helps explain the emphasis placed upon bombing them. This emphasis was particularly apparent in the sustained Allied air assaults on Germany and Japan, which correctly identified rail links as fundamental to the economies of the combatants and notably to the integration of their manufacturing processes and the movements of raw materials and *matériel*. The serious German and Japanese shortages of oil made coal-based rail links even more important to them, which increased their vulnerability to attack and sabotage, notably by bombing and partisan activity.

Furthermore, rail links were operationally crucial. Rail supply was very important to German operations in the Soviet Union but proved inadequate to the burden and vulnerable to sabotage. Prior to Operation Overlord, the Allied invasion of Normandy in 1944, there was a major effort to use air power to isolate the zone of hostilities, especially by cutting rail bridges across the Seine and the Loire in order to weaken the German ability to move troops into the region. The importance of rail links helps explain the significance of air attacks on bridges. Many

French towns were very heavily bombed in this effort at isolation. For example, Lisieux in Normandy was almost completely destroyed.

At the tactical level, guns could also be fired from trains. At Sevastopol in the Crimea, successfully besieged by the Germans in 1942, although only after formidable efforts, the Red Army had guns sheltering on flat trucks in tunnels that were pulled out to fire and then moved back into the tunnels.

COMMUNICATIONS

Alongside transport and logistics, communications was a key area of military operations in which there were important technological advances. Prior to modern systems of information transmission, communications was a particular complication for maneuvers at a distance beyond the range of visual signaling or sending messages by horseback. For example, in the War of American Independence (1775–1783), the nature of communications prevented the exercise of close control and made it difficult to respond to developments.

Indeed, some British operations in North America and in Atlantic waters proved object lessons in the troubles created by poor communications. In North America in 1777, instead of a coherent plan, there were two totally uncoordinated campaigns. Operating in conjunction with each other, Generals Burgoyne and Howe might have been able to wreck the two American field armies, to gain total control of the Hudson Valley, to separate New England from the Middle and Southern states, and to initiate a state-by-state pacification of hostile New England. Operating, however, as two uncoordinated roving columns, they would have achieved far less even had they been undefeated. In the event, moving into the Hudson Valley, Burgoyne was blocked by the Americans at Bemis Heights and forced to surrender at Saratoga. The British forces based in New York City farther south were not informed sufficiently rapidly to be able to provide support by advancing in strength earlier up the Hudson Valley.

Nevertheless, there was progress in communications in the late eighteenth century. Signaling at sea, which was crucial to tactical effectiveness, communications, and coordinated action, improved from the 1780s. This improvement was due to organization and practice rather than technology. A quick and flexible numerical system of signals was developed by the British. It was generally possible for a lookout to see only about 15 miles from the top of the main mast in fine weather. However, fleets positioned a series of frigates, each stationed just over the horizon, and they signaled using their sails, which were much bigger than flags and, because the masts were so tall, could be seen at some distance over the horizon.[53] This relay system was particularly important for British fleets blockading hostile ports, notably the leading French naval bases, Brest and Toulon, and their Spanish counterparts, especially Cadiz. Blockade was a key task given the difficulty of finding fleets once they had moved away from shore, as with the Spanish fleet that sailed to invade England in 1719,[54] and, indeed, because of the dependence of both sides on the same winds, the difficulty of forcing them to action.

To support blockade, there would be an inshore squadron of highly maneuverable ships that signaled, using a relay of frigates, to the main fleet, which was located a few miles off in greater safety; close inshore operations exposed ships to the danger of running aground, which was why, as in 1759, the British had different cruising stations off Brest depending on whether the winds were westerly or easterly. Improvements were made in surveillance and blockade but within a context of limited information and operational capability as well as the general problem of station keeping. Difficulties in surveillance were dramatically seen with the unexpected French arrival off Scotland in 1708, New York in 1778, and Ireland in 1795 and 1798; their successful breakout from Toulon to Egypt in 1798; and the serious problems Britain faced in 1805 in responding to the French attempt to amalgamate their naval forces prior to launching an invasion attempt against Britain. In the event, the French plan failed in 1805, which helped to demonstrate the many difficulties faced in trying to implement bold naval schemes, notably with the control and coordination of different units across an operational dimension spanning the North Atlantic.

At the same time, there were technological developments in communications. The semaphore was an important example of the increased application of scientific method to aspects of military affairs during the

French Revolutionary and Napoleonic wars.[55] Claude Chappe, who developed the semaphore telegraph, was given official approval by the French Revolutionary government in 1793. The network of semaphore stations, with an average distance of 7 miles between each, created from 1794, was extended by Napoleon to reach the cities of Venice, Amsterdam, and Mainz, all of which the French controlled.

The technology was flexible but required considerable organization. A set of arms pivoting on a post provided opportunities for multiple positions, and these constituted the message. The system had a capacity of 196 different combinations of signs and an average speed of three signs a minute. Furthermore, code could be employed. In favorable weather, one sign could be sent the 150 miles from Paris to Lille in 5 minutes, although fog, poor weather, and darkness gravely limited the system by affecting visibility, while the skill of operators was also an issue. Telescopes on the towers were used to read messages, and these towers were constructed about 5–10 miles apart. No better system of communications was devised until the electric telegraph.[56] The Paris to Lille route was important because Lille was a key base for French operations on the northeastern frontier. This frontier was under attack from Allied forces in 1792–1794, and, in turn, the French made decisive advances there in 1794.

The semaphore system was copied abroad, an aspect of the way in which what appeared to be best practice was rapidly diffused within the Western world. Chappe's work was translated into English by Lieutenant-Colonel John Macdonald, a military engineer who did much work himself on improving telegraphy, publishing *A New System of Telegraphy* in 1817. In the 1790s, the Admiralty in London was linked to the major base of Portsmouth by semaphore, while Sweden also constructed some stations. Furthermore, nine were established along the Lines of Torres Vedras, fortified positions built in 1810 by Arthur, Viscount (later Duke) of Wellington, the British commander, in a successful attempt to protect Lisbon against French attack. In good weather, a message could be sent the 22 miles from the Atlantic to the River Tagus in 7 minutes.

Nevertheless, only very short messages could be sent rapidly, while semaphore networks were very limited. In part, this was because of issues concerning visibility but also because the stations could be attacked, rather as German telegraph cables were cut and radio stations were attacked in 1914. Indeed, during the Napoleonic War, British naval forces in the Mediterranean put ashore parties in order to attack the French stations; for example, on the coast of Catalonia, which France occupied from 1808 to 1814. Napoleon investigated the possibility of a mobile semaphore system for his 1812 invasion of Russia, but it was considered unviable.

Most orders and reports were still handwritten. They were communicated on land by mounted messengers, both on the battlefield and at the operational level. Aside from the vulnerability of the messengers, who, on horseback, were necessarily conspicuous, there were also problems linked to confusion and misunderstanding, as with the charge of the British Light Brigade at Balaclava in the Crimea in 1854. This charge was mistakenly launched into Russian guns because James, 7th Earl of Cardigan, the commander on the ground, could not see what Lord Raglan, his superior on the heights, could, and there was no rapid way to check the orders. Alongside serious personal animosity between commanders, reliance on a messenger proved fatal in this case.

The electric telegraph offered a very different capability, notably at the strategic level. It provided an effective system for the transmission of messages, both overland and across the seas. The electric telegraph was invented in 1837, with the electromagnet used to transmit and receive electric signals. Moreover, the American Samuel Morse developed the simple operator key and refined the signal code, which became Morse code. In 1838, he was able to transmit ten words a minute using his code of dots and dashes.[57] Despite claims suggesting that the resulting system of telegraph cables operated like the modern internet,[58] there were significant problems in reliability, in the speed of transmission, and in the density of the network.

Nevertheless, compared to the earlier situation, the telegraph offered both rapidity and range. The latter was of great value in the co-ordination of far-flung resources, while, more generally, the telegraph facilitated the practice of strategy. As with some other technological developments, this capability also had consequences that were unwelcome, not least, in this case, because they facilitated the politicization of strategy. For example, during the Crimean War (1854–1856), the European telegraph network was extended to the Crimea, allowing Napoleon III of France to intervene in Allied operations, to the understandable irritation of his generals. It also proved possible for the British government to question and send instructions to generals to a hitherto unprecedented extent. Thanks to the telegraph, moreover, William Russell of the *Times* was able to send home critical reports about British military administration, reports that caused the government serious difficulties.[59]

At the more conventional level of directing resources, the British used the telegraph effectively in countering the Indian Mutiny (1857–1859), while it was employed extensively in 1859 in the Second War of Italian Unification. Moreover, from 1859, the Prussians sent orders for mobilization by telegraph, and the telegraph was linked to the development and use of the Prussian rail system. This linkage was very important to the effectiveness of Prussian mobilization in successive conflicts. Furthermore, during the Austro-Prussian War of 1866 and the Franco-Prussian War of 1870–1871, the telegraph was utilized to help coordinate Prussia's successful advances. Earlier, in the American Civil War (1861–1865), both sides employed the telegraph, which ensured that cavalry raiders sought to cut telegraph lines, an important indication of the vulnerability of ground-based communication systems. The use of the telegraph was enhanced by developing "trains" with insulated wires and poles on wagons designed to extend the fixed telegraph lines to the advancing armies.

The telegraph was also utilized to issue instructions for far-flung troop movements. This was very much the case for the British Empire with, for example, the dispatch of troops from India to Ethiopia in 1868 when the latter was successfully invaded. This movement helped in a concentration of forces that was easier to arrange than what had accompanied the successful British invasion of Egypt in 1801. In 1868 and, even more, when Egypt was successfully invaded again in 1882, the British benefited from the combination of steamships and telegraphs. Moreover, the opening of the Suez Canal in 1869 greatly increased operational flexibility and strategic tempo, as well as reflecting the ability to fulfill bold engineering projects and thus the significance of non-military technology. In response to the Russian advance into the Balkans, Britain moved army units from India to the Mediterranean in 1878 in a successful exercise of brinkmanship. Similarly, in 1879, the movement of troops from Ceylon (Sri Lanka) to Natal in South Africa during the nearby Zulu War was important to a surge of reinforcements in what had become very much a crisis as a consequence of overoptimistic British generalship and unexpectedly successful Zulu resistance.

Naval movements were affected by the telegraph. In 1898, Commodore George Dewey's squadron of American warships was ordered from Hong Kong to Manila by telegraph. Its arrival there and rapid total victory over the heavily outgunned Spanish squadron at Cavite were to be crucial to the defeat of Spain in the Philippines. That year, moreover, the British won their confrontation with France over competing interests in the southern Sudan, the Fashoda Crisis, without conflict, in part by manipulating information about it thanks to their control of the telegraph links. However, the major display of British naval strength in European waters was also crucial in leading the French to back down.

As a result of the value of telegraph systems, notably for far-flung empires, their planning became a key aspect of strategic policy.[60] By 1900, more than 170,000 miles of ocean cables were in use. Moreover, reliance on the new technology led to the need to take precautions. For example, in developing communication routes between Britain and India through the Middle East, the British took great care to run their telegraph route under the Persian Gulf, where it would be difficult to intercept, rather than overland along the shores, where it would be far easier for hostile locals to cut the telegraph. Nevertheless, there were still major problems with running telegraphs under the sea, and it took time to devise the appropriate technology, as the successive costly attempts to lay cables under the Atlantic demonstrated.

Telegraph lines were also seen as of operational importance in colonial warfare. As a result, telegraph systems were established to help strengthen the imperial presence; for example, when the Italians occupied Eritrea in 1885. Due to this, telegraph lines were frequently attacked by insurgents. On the North-West Frontier of India (in modern Pakistan), tribesmen cut telegraph lines in the Waziristan rebellion that began in 1937. The question, however, is whether the telegraph had a significant impact on operations or whether it merely permitted interference by those who were hitherto remote from the action. And it could play no part once battle was joined if only because those at the sharp end were out of reach.

Meanwhile, field telephones had become important from the late 1890s, being used by the Americans in the Spanish-American War (1898) and by the British in the Boer War (1899–1902). Radio, however, was to challenge the value of earlier systems.

A discussion of radio serves to introduce the theme of the impact on war of rapid developments in communications. These developments were to be of great importance at every level of war, tactical, operational, and strategic. Communication systems proved vital weapons, as well as important indicators of the modernization of war and of major changes in how it was waged. Radio was a particularly significant advance on existing methods. In 1895, Guglielmo Marconi demonstrated the transmission of messages by the use of electro magnetic waves, in 1899 he transmitted across the English Channel, and in 1901 he sent radio signals over 3,000 miles across the Atlantic. This was an important stage of development in communications, one that was not dependent on fixed links, such as telegraph cables. The British navy, which needed to control and coordinate widely separated units, was to be Marconi's best client. As a result of the new capability, radio networks were created. In 1912–1914, the Germans built a network of radio stations in their colonies: at Duala, Windhoek, Dar-es-Salaam, Tsingtao, Yap, Apia, Rabaul, and Nauru.

In war, radio was used during the Russo-Japanese War of 1904–1905, and it was also employed during the First World War. As a result, the control of radio stations was important in operations outside Europe, and the Allies made major efforts to capture the German ones in 1914. The attack on German East Africa (now Tanzania) began with the shelling of the wireless tower at Dar-es-Salaam. During the war, the use of radio made it easier for commanders to retain detailed operational control. British control of the international underwater telegraph system encouraged the Americans, especially the navy, to develop what was, by 1918, the biggest radio network in the world.[61]

Cost, conservatism, and working problems, not least the size of early radios, affected their employment, but advances were made during the 1930s, both at the strategic level[62] and at that of tactics, notably in using radios to control tank advances. Radio was increasingly seen as important to combined operations, especially land-air coordination, although coordination proved difficult to arrange in practice and also risked compromising the independent effectiveness of aircraft and tanks. The Germans, Americans, and British made major advances in the use of radios, but these were not matched by the French, Italians, Japanese, and Soviets. Instead, there was a reliance on human communications—by couriers—and on telephones, but the former were slow and the latter easily interrupted.

Radio, however, still faced problems, not least that of the effects of climate, especially in the tropics, and the serious problems of security. Encryption took time and was not foolproof, as the extensive Allied interception of German and other supposedly secure Axis systems amply demonstrated during the Second World War, while transmitting in clear was very risky.[63] Transmission by ships and submarines permitted the fixing of their location, and this proved very important in the Allied success over German submarines in the Battle of the Atlantic. Encryption and interception provided classic instances of the counterpointing of weaponry and "anti-weaponry" that was so important to technological development and impact.

During the Second World War, radio played a major role at the tactical and operational levels. For example, radio was used for carrier operations and anti-submarine patrols, as well as for directing airplanes and artillery fire. Radio was increasingly employed for short-range communications. Fitted in army vehicles and also capable of being carried by soldiers, radio increased tactical flexibility and control, making the use of artillery and air support more effective. Linked to new fire direction techniques, radio ensured that the use of indirect fire, which had been developed in the First World War, became more effective.[64]

Moreover, the inability to communicate with the men at the front in action seen with the telegraph changed as reliable radios became widespread, which was particularly the case from the 1950s. Radio contributed greatly to the speeding up of tactical moves and to the coordination required for combined operations. However, there are still problems today, notably with the means to communicate directly with air support, ensuring prompt support and avoiding casualties from friendly fire, casualties that attract greater public attention than in the twentieth century.

CONCLUSIONS

The changes in communications technologies were important in transforming the nature of war at the tactical, operational, and strategic levels. The 1859 War of Italian Unification saw France, Austria, and Piedmont all take advantage of the new technologies at a scale they had hitherto not been able to employ.[65] Again, there was a close linkage to more general developments in economy and society. Thus, the wide-ranging nature of technology emerges clearly in this example. These points could also be made about most military technologies or about civilian technologies applied to military purposes. The Western ability to operate in the tropics, an ability that was to be important to imperialist expansion, owed much to new knowledge about disease and its control. Moreover, this ability also affected areas outside the tropics, such as the American South during the Civil War. The use of quinine and mosquito nets proved important in the Union campaigns in the Mississippi Valley and more generally.[66]

There was correspondence in the *Times* about the industrialization of warfare as early as 1870. In his *War of the Future in Its Technical, Economic and Political Aspects* (1897), part of which was published in English as *Is War Now Impossible?* (1899), the Polish financier Ivan Bloch suggested that the combination of modern military technology and industrial strength had made great power warfare too destructive to be viable. If such warfare occurred, Bloch argued that it would resemble a great siege and would be won when one of the combatants succumbed to famine and revolution. He suggested that the stalemate on the battlefield that came from defensive firepower would lead to collapse on the home front as societies succumbed to the cumulative pressure.

Bloch was often to be cited by later commentators, but one of the problems with his apparently prescient view of trench warfare in the First World War is that such warfare had already occurred in the last stage of the American Civil War (although only in part of the zone of conflict and for a small portion of the war), but without it leading to prolonged stalemate. More significantly, the idea that technologically driven destructiveness alone was the cause of the stalemate on the western front is misleading, since it was firepower, tactics, operational considerations, and resources in combination that contributed to stalemate and also, crucially, to its resolution. This resolution was partly due to better technology and to better use of technology than was available when Bloch was writing.

4

THE INTERNAL COMBUSTION ENGINE

The Technology of Decentralized Power, 1910–2013

Really a fearsome sight . . . The road was on a slope of the hill, and the tanks just crawled up the slope, up the right bank nose in air, down with a bump into the road and across it—almost perpendicularly up the left bank, and down with a bump behind it and so onward up the hill without a moment's pause or hesitation.

—*B.W. Harvey and C. Fitzgerald, eds.,* Edward Heron-Allen's Journal: The Great War: From Sussex Shore to Flanders Fields, *2002*

Edward Heron-Allen's account of British tanks crossing a road on October 16, 1918, as the Allies successfully advanced against the Germans on the western front in Belgium and France at the close of the First World War (1914–1918) ably described the subordination of terrain by the new weapon. Railways and roads might seem similar in that both provided routes along which troops, supplies, and firepower could be transported. However, there was also an important contrast. Trains could not leave railways and move cross-country. In contrast, road vehicles were able to leave roads provided the terrain was suitable. This capability brought a tremendous increase in mobility. That mobility was combined with firepower in the tank, a weapon that was to grip the imagination as a key example of the transforming character of new technology. The internal combustion engine also affected naval and air warfare.

The First World War was more generally significant because of a major change in the relationship between technology and the conduct of war. Prior to 1914, technological change on land had tended to be relatively slow and, in some respects, wars had been fought despite such change. The First World War was a watershed not only tactically but also with regard to innovation and inventions. In this conflict, warfare influenced new technology that then changed the nature of war. Technological change was made in response to specific aspects of the war.

The rate of change accelerated from 1915. Entirely new munitions, such as the light mortar and the tank, emerged as a direct consequence of the war, and timely enough for them to have an impact on the war. Moreover, slightly older but still new technologies were developed very quickly so that they too had an effect on the war. Radio, aircraft, and materials technology all benefited from rapid wartime development, developments that might not otherwise have occurred for another 30 years and that fed into the changes that took place in the 1920s and 1930s.

TANKS AND THE FIRST WORLD WAR, 1914–1918

Prior to the First World War, there had been interest in armored vehicles. In 1909, Colonel Frederick Trench, the perceptive British military attaché in Berlin, reported that the Germans were proposing to subsidize power traction vehicles "of a type suitable for military use."[1] Such interest was greatly taken forward during the war as both sides sought comparative advantage, and also in response to the apparently intractable problems posed by trench warfare. As with armored warships, the process of "invention" was complicated, as the ideas that were advanced were not always viable but, nevertheless, contributed to the development of a practical weapon. In December 1914, Maurice Hankey, the influential secretary to the British Committee of Imperial Defence, suggested,

> Numbers of large, heavy rollers, themselves bullet proof, propelled from behind by motor engines, geared very low, the driving wheels fitted with "caterpillar" driving gear to grip the ground, the driver's seat armored, and with a Maxim [machine] gun fitted. The object of this device would be to

roll down the barbed wire by sheer weight, to give some cover to men creeping up behind, and to support the advance with machine gun fire.[2]

Tanks were invented independently by the British and French in 1915 and were first used in combat by the British in the battle of the Somme, on September 15, 1916,[3] and by the French the following April. Few tanks were available for use on the Somme and there was a lack of tactical understanding about how best to employ them. Nevertheless, the British employment of tanks was an aspect of their search for greater effectiveness during the lengthy Somme offensive. This search is underrated due to the habitual emphasis on the tactics of the first day, July 1, when British troops advanced in lines into devastating machine gun fire, leading to heavy casualties.

The scale of tank use swiftly increased, which was an aspect of the way in which it was possible to deploy new weapons rapidly. The British use of tanks en masse at Cambrai on November 20, 1917, was certainly a shock to the Germans. On August 8, 1918, no fewer than 430 British tanks broke through the German lines near Amiens. That November, the French planned to deploy 600 tanks to support an advance into Lorraine, and, by 1918, they had 3,000 tanks. These included the Schneider-Creusot, which carried a 75 mm gun, a powerful weapon, and the faster and lighter-gunned Renault.

The Germans deployed tanks in 1918 but did so in far smaller numbers and to less effect than the British; these tanks, some captured from the British, did not influence the outcome of the unsuccessful German spring 1918 offensives. Fewer than 60 of the large A7V tanks were in service. German industry was unable to manufacture tanks in sufficient quantities, although the failure of the offensives was largely due to a repeated lack of focus in attacking on any particular axis, rather than a shortage of a particular weapon system; in short to operational-strategic rather than tactical-operational issues. Nevertheless, the shortage of tanks was an aspect of a more general weakness of motorization and mechanization on the part of the Germans. This weakness proved operationally significant, as the German ability to sustain breakthroughs and break-out in the spring offensives was thereby limited.[4] Moreover, the strength and determination of the continued Allied resistance was important. The first tank versus tank action occurred on April 24, 1918, near Villers Bretonneux, between German A7Vs and British Whippets and MkIVs, during a German infantry attack. At least one A7V and one Whippet were knocked out by tank gunnery, and the Whippets retreated because they were outgunned, although it was not realized at the time that they had been engaged by enemy tanks.

At the tactical level, tanks seemed to overcome one of the major problems with the offensives against trenches that had hitherto proved so unsuccessful and costly in manpower during the First World War: the separation of firepower from advancing troops, and the consequent lack of flexibility. Instead, by carrying guns (cannon) or machine guns, tanks made it possible for advancing units to confront both positions hitherto not suppressed by artillery fire and counterattacks. The latter had repeatedly served to blunt the impact of break-ins into opposing trench lines and break-outs through them. Tanks, indeed, offered precise tactical fire to exploit the consequences of the massed operational artillery bombardments that preceded attacks. Moreover, they could smash through barbed wire and cross trenches. Tanks could also be hit by rifle bullets and machine guns without suffering incapacitating damage, although bullet strikes caused the armor to spall (each bullet strike caused a spall of metal to fly off inside of the panel adjacent to the strike), which was why tank crews wore mail visors to protect their eyes.

Tanks offered mobility, not only in breaking open a static battlefield but also in subsequent operations. A memorandum of June 1918 from the British Tanks Corps Headquarters claimed,

> Trench warfare has given way to field and semi-open fighting . . . the more the mobility of tanks is increased, the greater must be the elasticity of the co-operation between them and the other arms. The chief power of the tank, both material and moral, lies in its mobility, that is, its pace, circuit, handiness, and obstacle-crossing power.

Now, the tank commander had to make sure he was not too far in advance of the infantry:

> whilst formerly he merely led the infantry on to their objective protecting them, as best he could, now he must manoeuvre his tank in advance of them

zig-zagging from one position to another, over-running machine guns, stampeding away and destroying the enemy's riflemen and all the time never losing touch with the infantry he is protecting. This increased power of manoeuvre of the Mark V Tank demands an increased power of manoeuvre on the part of the infantry.[5]

While the value of tanks and their likely future consequences attracted much attention from commentators, commanders had to decide how best to employ tanks and how to combine them with infantry and artillery. This was an issue made dynamic by the variety of tank types, and by actual and possible developments in them.

Yet, as a reminder of the need to understand limitations as well as potential, it is necessary to note how far the value of tanks was lessened by their problems, which included durability but also firepower and speed. During the First World War, the British light infantry mortar in practice was more effective, more reliable, and more capable of providing flexible infantry support than the tank, which was underpowered, undergunned, underarmored, and unreliable. Moreover, it was difficult for the tank crew to communicate with each other, let alone with anyone outside the tank, and this problem made it harder to get a tank to engage a target of opportunity and lessened tanks' flexibility in contrast to the infantry. The British all-weapons platoon of 1917 and 1918, in which infantry had the means to engage many different kinds of target without calling in artillery support, was a very effective tool. In these platoons, Lewis guns, hand and rifle grenades, riflemen, and Stokes light infantry mortars were used together. Tanks, in contrast, had the potential for flexibility but often were unable to fulfill that potential.

One of the biggest problems with tanks was that the crews were subjected to heat and noise to almost unbearable levels. Clean air was a problem. Every time the tank went over rough ground, the crew was thrown around. These factors helped ensure that operating a tank for long periods was stressful and difficult. Although circumstances have eased, they are still difficult.

The value of tanks in the First World War was also affected by the difficulty of providing sufficient numbers of them, which reflected their late arrival in wartime resource allocation and production systems. Tank numbers rose rapidly but were still small compared to the numbers of infantry and artillery. The British, moreover, suffered from a failure to produce sufficient spare parts.

The ability to devise anti-tank tactics was also significant, as German anti-tank measures were quite effective. Wherever tanks met real resistance, they did not do nearly as well as anticipated, a situation that was to recur in the Second World War. The use of artillery against tanks was particularly important in this respect and reflected both the plentiful availability of artillery pieces on the western front and the extent to which the incremental nature of improvements in artillery was a matter of tactics as well as of technology and numbers. Field guns firing high-explosive shells proved effective at knocking out the poorly armored tanks of the time. In addition, anti-tank mines were introduced: shells buried with the fuses just below the surface pointing up. At Cambrai on November 20, 1917, sixty-five British tanks were destroyed thanks to direct hits by German artillery fire, although the majority of losses were due to mechanical fire and to being stopped by ditches. To operate most effectively, tanks needed to support, and to be supported by, advancing artillery and infantry. When the attack resumed at Cambrai on November 21, more British tanks were lost due to inadequate infantry support. British manuals set out infantry/tank co-operation, for example, SS 164 in May 1917 and SS 214 in August 1918, but it proved difficult to ensure.

The need for support[6] as an aspect of combined-arms or mixed operations was a lesson that had to be learned repeatedly during the following century, and in the face of contrary pressure from enthusiasts for tanks alone, pressure that increased as their speed and mobility rose. For example, during the Second World War the British Eighth Army encountered serious problems in conflict with the German *Afrika Corps* in North Africa in 1941–1942 because British armored advances lacked sufficient support; this tactic had to be replaced by the British before success could be achieved at the second battle of El Alamein in 1942. Appointed commander of the Eighth Army, General Bernard Montgomery felt it necessary to dismiss the colonels of tank regiments who were unwilling to accept the need for combined arms operations. At El Alamein, he made plentiful use of artillery in order to help open a way through the German defenses.

During the First World War, British successes at Cambrai (1917) and, more significantly, Amiens (1918) provide misleading examples of the usefulness of tanks. Aside from the importance of artillery in each battle, most of the tanks engaged at Cambrai and Amiens subsequently broke down or were otherwise immobilized within a few days. Many tanks broke down even before reaching the assault point, and in battle tanks rapidly became unfit for service, understandably so given their technical problems. For these reasons, there was a reaction in British circles against the use of armor after August 1918, and, instead, an even stronger focus on artillery-infantry coordination, as well as an interest in cavalry exploitation. Moreover, the French tanks contributed little to the unsuccessful Nivelle offensive of 1917.

There was also the problem that guns fixed in the hull of the tank, the French pattern, proved poor at engaging with targets, whereas the British location of guns in sponsons on the side of the tank was linked to the guns' ability to move laterally and vertically. The disadvantage of a fixed gun was not really solved until the Swedish S tank of the 1970s, as its sophisticated suspension system aided engaging with the target. However, Sweden's pacific foreign policy leaves the effectiveness of this tank unclear.

Had Allied tank production been at a greater level, then tanks might have made a larger contribution in 1918, but the frequently repeated claim that massed tanks would have made a significant difference to Allied capability had the war continued into 1919 is contentious. As the war did not continue, the claim could play a major role in postwar discussions about tank capability. However, even assuming that the tank could have been mass-produced in order to manufacture the huge numbers required, which had not been the case hitherto, the same basic problems of unreliability, slow speed, vulnerability to anti-tank measures and field guns, undergunning, poor intercommunication capabilities, and limited obstacle-crossing capability, nevertheless, would have remained.

There is little to suggest that tanks would have performed well. If the British tanks of the 1920s are considered as an extension of the line of development from the First World War, it is difficult to see how they would have been decisive in 1919. Furthermore, this approach ignores the anti-tank technologies that would have been developed by the Germans. Indeed, the chances are that anti-tank guns would have been superior to the tanks.

The rapid development of tanks and, even more, aircraft was an impressive aspect of the application of technology during the First World War, but, in terms of that conflict, the provision of the large numbers of heavy artillery pieces required when bombarding trench lines and of shells was more significant. This provision entailed important qualitative improvements in the production of munitions. For example, in Britain, cooperative group manufacture was introduced whereby each manufacturer within the group made some of the components. This process permitted inspection to be carried out at one location, the premises where the components were put together, instead of at the premises of each manufacturer, thereby speeding up production.

INTERWAR YEARS

The concept of a "tank" was unclear, which was why so many different types abounded in the British army of the 1920s and 1930s. At this stage, speed and maneuverability attracted more attention than firepower and armor. Linked to this, tank technology did not match the capabilities of opposing artillery. As a result, the tank was too underdeveloped to realize the expectations of commentators such as J. F. C. "Boney" Fuller and Basil Liddell Hart. It was easier to suggest a role than to ensure the technology, tactics, and doctrine to make tanks effective on the battlefield.

The significant developments in the interwar years included the Christie suspension, used on the Soviet T-34 series, and sloped armor, as well as bigger-caliber guns, although none was bigger than about 75 mm. A great deal of research and development went into armor (the nature of the steel, its construction and thickness), engines, transmissions, and suspension. The latter had a huge impact on cross-country ability.

Tank design was very dependent upon tactical doctrines. The British, for example, were fixated on the "infantry-tank," which, although quick, was undergunned and underarmored. In practice many of the

German tanks of the era were little better. Many of the British designs of the Second World War came out of this sort of thinking. Anti-tank gun technology far exceeded tank technology in the 1920s and 1930s, partly because a gun had only to fire a high-velocity projectile on a flat trajectory, whereas a tank had to do a great more besides.

Lieutenant-General Sir Philip Chetwode, deputy chief of the (British) Imperial General Staff, argued in 1921 that tank specifications and tactics ought to focus on colonial commitments rather than the possibility of conflict with other regular forces. Indeed, Germany then only had a limited and lightly armed army as the result of the disarmament terms of the Versailles Peace Treaty of 1919, while the Soviet advance into Europe had been stopped by the Poles outside Warsaw in 1920 and the Soviets had been driven back. Chetwode pressed accordingly for tanks to be armed with a machine gun, not a heavier gun, and for training in the use of tanks against opponents equipped with artillery and machine guns but not tanks.[7] His comments also illustrate how poorly the potential of armored forces was understood by many in the 1920s and, indeed, the 1930s; although, as Douglas Haig pointed out in 1927, it was unclear that mechanized forces were suitable on many terrains.[8]

The use of tanks in imperial warfare faced difficulties. Confronting serious opposition in Morocco in 1922, Spain used light French tanks, the first deployment of tanks in Africa. However, unable to keep up, the infantry could not prevent the tanks from being disabled by Moroccan stone-throwers, while many of the tanks' machine guns jammed due to faulty ammunition.[9] On the whole, the focus in imperial warfare was on armored cars, not tanks.

Meanwhile, however, growing interest in tanks was affecting the perception of other arms. In 1926, Colonel Lindsay, the Inspector of the (British) Royal Tank Corps, was in no doubt that cavalry was too vulnerable, and linked this to wider questions of the role of technology:

All civil evolution is towards the elimination of manpower and animal power, and the substitution of mechanical power. History shows that the military mind has usually lagged behind in its appreciation of civil evolution and its possibilities . . . in the army we must substitute machine and weapon power for man and animal power in every possible way, and that to do this we must carefully watch, and where necessary foster, those trends of civil evolution that will help us to this end.

Lindsay was certain that this capacity was linked to industrial capability: "We are the nation above all others who can develop the mobile, mechanical and weapon-power army, for we have long service soldiers and a vast industrial organization." Other military commentators, however, were less happy about the wisdom of dispensing with cavalry and, instead, urged its combination with mechanized forces.[10]

It was also unclear which vehicles and what capabilities would be most appropriate. Thus, in 1927, Field-Marshal Sir George Milne, the chief of the (British) Imperial General Staff, told the officers of the experimental Mechanised Force that it was necessary to have vehicles that would be immune to poison gas. As an indication of the sense of transience, Milne also claimed that "in a very few years the petrol engine itself will have to give way to something else."[11]

THE SECOND WORLD WAR, 1939–1945

The tanks of the Second World War were scarcely the same weapon as their predecessors of 1916–1918. This was just as well as they were expected to engage in a very different war, one characterized by greater mobility, both tactically and operationally, while tanks were also used across the range of land operations, from the deserts of North Africa to the islands of the Pacific, as well as in amphibious assaults. In particular, there was a very large-scale use of tanks in the conflict between Germany and the Soviet Union on the eastern front from 1941, whereas in the First World War tank use had focused on the western front. Planning and policy helped frame key responses to the new challenges requiring and facing tanks, but there also was a considerable degree of improvisation, as with the German need on the eastern front to adapt to poor roads and the dust that hit tank engines.[12]

During the Second World War there were difficult trade-offs in tank warfare between speed, armor, armament, durability, and ease of production, and these trade-offs occurred in a context made more dynamic and difficult by the need to shape change effectively and, in particular, to respond to the action-reaction cycles posed by developments in opponents' weaponry, both tanks and other anti-tank weapons. Tanks drew together a number of technologies, capabilities, and doctrines, and the tank became more a part of an integrated system in the Second than the First World War. Armor and firepower were crucial to success in battle, both to dealing with opposing tanks and with artillery/infantry defenses. In contrast, questions of reliability, range, refueling, and mechanical support were important to breakthrough operations. Engineering was also significant. The ability to negotiate difficult terrain depended on the suspension system as well as on the type of tracks.

Given the numbers of tanks required, ease of production was a key factor. Unlike the Germans, the Americans and Soviets concentrated on weapons that made best use of their capacity for mass production because they were simple to build, operate, and repair, such as the American Sherman M-4 tank. The ubiquitous Sherman, which evolved into numerous versions all intended to increase firepower against German armor as well as to enhance protection from German guns, was a feat of production but not of advanced technology. Neither was the Soviet T-34. The first T-34 models were very crude inside, and there was no upgrading until 1944. The bigger Soviet KV series, which led to the JS series, were also crude inside.

In contrast, German tanks were complex pieces of equipment and often broke down. Much German armor, moreover, was no better than Soviet armor, or indeed worse. In 1941, the Soviet KV-1 and T-34 tanks proved superior to their German opponents.[13] However, for long, the British and Americans had tanks that did not match their German rivals. The British Infantry Mark I, Matilda, Valentine, Crusader, Churchill, and Cromwell tanks suffered from inadequate armor, and the first four were undergunned. In the Tobruk campaign in North Africa in June 1942, the Crusader proved mechanically poor, while the British lacked an effective anti-tank gun and could not match German tank-artillery coordination. The Sherman was underarmored and undergunned for much of the war. When Anglo-American forces invaded France in 1944, the best German tanks were technically better in firepower and armor—the Tiger and Panther, for example, being superior in both to the Sherman—but the unreliability and high maintenance requirements of the costly Tiger tank weakened it, and there were also serious problems with the Panther.

The quality gap that favored the Germans against the Anglo-Americans was closed by late 1944 and 1945, as new Allied tanks appeared. Bigger guns came because of the need to penetrate thicker armor at long ranges. The Sherman was up-gunned and up-armored to counter tanks such as the Tiger I and the Panther but was of little use against the Tiger II. Generally, the German 88 mm gun of the Tiger tanks and the German anti-tank guns outranged the Allied tank guns. The British introduced a modified Sherman known as the Firefly, which was fitted with a 17-pounder (76.2 mm) gun, firing APC: armor-piercing capped rounds, which could penetrate German armor at long range. For much of 1944, this was the only Allied tank that could take on the Tiger I. Up-gunning, the Americans introduced a higher-velocity 76 mm gun to their Shermans in mid-1944, but the 76 mm needed new high-velocity armor-piercing ammunition (HVAP) to penetrate the front plates (100 mm thick) of Panthers and Tiger Is. This ammunition was introduced when it was found that existing ammunition would not do the job.

More generally, the thickening of armor and its increased sloping, especially in German and Soviet designs (the MkV Panther was a response to the T-34, both of which made use of glacis plates sloped at 60 degrees), led to the response of increased velocity and hitting power, so that discarding sabots with subcaliber rounds and armored caps, among other innovations, were introduced, including the use of tungsten carbide cores (the subcaliber projectile). This stress on performance in tank combat helped compensate for the earlier American emphasis on tanks that were fast and maneuverable, an emphasis that reflected the cavalry ethos and the focus on maneuverability.

As an aspect of attritional warfare, the closing stages of the war saw the introduction of more heavily gunned tanks. Delayed as a result of a lack of support in senior military circles, the American M-26 Pershing, fitted with a 90 mm gun, first saw action in February 1945, but full production did not begin until March 1945. Only twenty saw action in Europe, but this tank was to serve well in the Korean War (1950–1953). The difficulty in destroying the heavy tanks led in the Second World War to the tank-destroyer fitted with a 90 mm gun. These were, in effect, self-propelled anti-tank guns. The British finally produced well-gunned and armored tanks with the Comet, which had a 77 mm gun, though no sloped armor, but did not enter service until March 1945, and the Centurion (sloped armor as well as good gun), which was developed toward the end of the war but too late to see service.

OPPOSING THE TANK

Tanks dominated the imagination for ground warfare in the twentieth century. They had their limitations, however. A limitation that is more generally significant was the development of what can be termed anti-weaponry, a development that is an aspect of the "interadoption" more generally seen with military change,[14] although to an extent all weapons are anti-weapons. Anti-weaponry moves in concert with weaponry, so that the Crusaders improved their fortresses, notably by building concentric castles, in response to the Islamic development of siege weaponry.[15] There was to be a similar process in the West in the sixteenth and seventeenth centuries in order to provide defense against siege artillery. The tank was no exception. This anti-weaponry tends to receive insufficient attention, which is a mistake, as the anti-weaponry helps define the possibilities presented by existing new weapons and leads to pressure for development to confront particular challenges.

The responses to the tank provide a good example. In the First World War, a range of weapons was used against tanks: mines, artillery pieces, and machine guns. Armor-piercing bullets fired by the last, and low-velocity shells from artillery shells, were of particular significance. In the interwar period, there was a development of high-velocity guns that used solid shot to penetrate tank armor by kinetic energy. These guns were mounted in tanks and in carriages that were towed in the field. In 1930, George Patton, then a major in the American army, argued that the effectiveness of tanks had been reduced because "now every arm has its quota of antitank weapons which are quite effective."[16] In 1934, the British Committee of Imperial Defence pressed for anti-tank guns for the infantry.

The availability or not of opposing anti-tank guns was important to the relative success of German offensives in the early stages of the Sec-

ond World War. In 1939, the Germans were helped in their attack on Poland by the weakness of the Polish army in anti-tank guns and training.
However, as an important indication of the limitations of armor, a German tank advance into Warsaw on September 9 was stopped in street
fighting by Polish anti-tank guns and artillery. Moreover, many German
tanks broke down during the campaign. Partly as a result, having conquered Poland, the German army was not in a state to attack France
shortly afterward. German success in Poland owed much to the use of
rapid armored advances but more to strategic and operational factors,
notably that Poland, once the Soviet Union had joined in on the German
side, was attacked from all sides and, from the outset, had weakened its
defense by trying to hold all of its frontiers. Furthermore, France and
Britain, Poland's allies, were not in a shape to mount an attack on Germany's western frontier.

In their offensive on the western front in 1940, the Germans benefited from the British lack of an effective anti-tank gun, although, again,
far more was at stake in their victory, and the use of weaponry was more
significant than the weapons themselves. In 1940, the key element in
this use was strategic, in particular the misguided deployment of what
could have been important French reserves and the related failure to respond to the German axis of advance.

In contrast, Soviet anti-tank gun defenses inflicted serious casualties
on attacking German tanks in 1941–1943. Again, however, other factors,
notably strategic and operational, were responsible for German success
and failure in 1941–1943, as for success in 1940. As far as tanks were concerned, the German advance into the Soviet Union in 1941 suffered not
only from the strength of the defense but also from problems in sustaining the offensive, notably a shortage of gasoline and spare parts, and
the difficulties posed by poor transport routes in the Soviet Union.

As an instance of the more general process of competitive development, improvements in tank specifications during the Second World
War created problems for anti-tank weaponry, with thicker armor leading to pressure for more powerful weapons. This was particularly the
case with stronger Soviet and German tanks. The thick armor of the
heavier Soviet tanks deployed in 1941 proved resistant to German anti-
tank shells.[17]

The relationship between gun, ammunition, armor, and targeting system is at the heart of the dynamic between tanks and anti-tank weaponry, although, to repeat the mantra, this dynamic is both set and molded by doctrine, tactics, and fighting quality. From the Second World War, although not always before, tanks were mobile anti-tank gun platforms. Indeed, the German 88 mm (formally an anti-aircraft gun) and the British 17-pounder were both anti-tank guns that were fitted to tanks. But, as the Americans discovered with their 76 mm gun, ammunition fired by the guns made all the difference to effectiveness, indeed lethality. The anti-tank rounds developed in the Second World War were fired by both anti-tank guns and by tanks. Armor during this conflict was essentially ever-thicker steel, although spaced armor was also used by the Germans to counter shaped-charge anti-tank rounds typically fired by infantry, such as the American bazooka and the British PIAT.

The advantage of the anti-tank gun was its relative cheapness to make in comparison to a whole tank. The problem with the infantry anti-tank weapons, such as the Bazooka, was how close the operator had to get to the target before firing, which was not the case with anti-tank guns. One huge advantage over the tank was the small size of anti-tank guns, which meant they could be concealed easily so that tanks could be ambushed, as by the Germans in Normandy in 1944. Anti-tank guns were far less vulnerable than tanks to observation and to air, tank, and artillery attack. Moreover, anti-tank guns did not break down or need gasoline. Thus, when combined with anti-tank ditches, as by the Red Army against German attack at Kursk in 1943, the anti-tank gun could prove very effective.

In response to stronger tanks, anti-tank guns developed, leading to guns with larger calibers, for example, 105 mm (not 88 mm) German guns, as well as longer barrels and better projectiles. The last entailed alternatives to solid armor-piercing shot, which had proved limited against hardened armor. Hollow-charge chemical energy projectiles, which threw a jet of molten gas against armor, were one response.

Frequent improvement was necessary for anti-tank guns and for infantry anti-tank weapons. The Americans first used the Bazooka anti-tank rocket in 1942 but failed to upgrade it as tanks got heavier. The Germans, however, developed the design into the more powerful *Panzerschreck* rocket grenade. They also developed the handheld *Panzerfaust* anti-tank rocket launcher. These weapons were part of the upgrading of German infantry weaponry seen also with the MG42 light machine gun, which was deployed from 1943, offering a very high rate of fire.

Other weapons against tanks included those mounted on aircraft, both guns and rockets, which, used by the Allies, were significant in the difficult battle for Normandy that followed the Allied invasion on June 6, 1944. Air superiority and support helped compensate for the Allied inferiority in tank design. Specialized aircraft for tank-busting had an offensive range that weapons on the ground lacked. The Soviet Ilyushin Il-2 Stormovik and the British Typhoon were particularly effective. The British favored using the 60-pound semi-armor-piercing rocket, while the Soviets employed a HEAT bomblet. But large caliber guns were also used, such as on the Hurricane and the German Ju-87 Stuka, while the Americans dropped napalm in Normandy, Brittany, and the Pacific, on tanks as well as bunkers.

Motorized (self-propelled) tank-destroyers also had a major impact; effective German versions were matched by American tank-destroyers armed with 76 mm and 90 mm guns. Anti-tank and anti-aircraft guns were fitted to these tank-destroyers, which were in effect lightly armored or simpler tanks fitted with powerful guns. The Americans used M10, M18, and M36 tank-destroyers. The first two carried guns that were unable to penetrate German tank armor, but the M36, armed with a 90 mm anti-aircraft gun, proved effective. The first M36 arrived in service in France in September 1944.

The Germans used a similar concept but with turretless tanks, such as the Hetzer and the Jagdpanther, as did the Soviets with the ISU122. Thus, there was an overlap of technological developments in tanks and anti-tank systems. In a sense, the British Firefly was a tank-destroyer. There were as many variants of tank-destroyers as tanks. The reason for fitting the guns to vehicles, including half-tracks and other vehicles, was mobility.

The effectiveness of anti-tank weaponry ensured that mixed or combined-arms formations were more effective than those that focused solely on tanks. In February 1945, Montgomery, then commander of the British 21st Army Group, argued that close co-operation with infantry was needed in order to overcome anti-tank guns: "I cannot emphasize too strongly that victory in battle depends not on armored action alone, but on the intimate co-operation of all arms; the tank by itself can achieve little."[18] Indeed, commanders of armored units urged their officers to wait for support rather than charging in.

This tactic was a sensible response to the German skill in defensive warfare, especially the careful siting of anti-tank guns to destroy advancing tanks. In July 1944, Sir Richard O'Connor, the commander of the British 8th Corps in Normandy, instructed the commander of an armored division to "go cautiously with your armor, making sure that any areas from which you could be shot up by Panthers [tanks] and 88s [anti-tank guns] are engaged. Remember what you are doing is not a rush to Paris—it is the capture of a wood by combined armor and infantry."[19] Such advice was necessary given the heavy tank casualties suffered by the British in the Battle of Normandy at the hands of German anti-tank guns. Neither the vegetation, notably the readily defended hedgerows of the *bocage,* nor the density of forces made armored advances easy in this campaign. The situation proved very different with the successful Soviet advances of 1944–1945 in easier terrain in Eastern Europe and (1945) Manchuria.

Aside from the defensive firepower, the question of engineering and logistical support for tanks was a serious hindrance to mobility for the Allies and the Germans in France in 1944. The dominance of air power by the Allies was also a major problem for the Germans. Yet, by 1944–1945 the effectiveness of tanks in large numbers was shown in the Soviet use of mobile tank armies for deep envelopment in maneuver-style warfare.[20] This effectiveness was shown at the expense of the Germans in Eastern Europe and also, in August 1945, in the rapid Soviet defeat of the large Japanese army in Manchuria.

POST-1945

Tanks were not suited to or available for many of the conflicts that followed 1945. Revolutionary forces tended not to have any, while the terrain and vegetation of the areas in which they operated were often not well suited to tanks. This was the case, for example, with the Viet Minh's campaigns against the French in Indo-China in 1946–1954, campaigns that largely focused on the heavily wooded interior of North Vietnam, notably in the Dien Bien Phu operation of 1953 in which French troops parachuted into a valley were successfully outgunned by Viet Minh artillery and overrun by infantry attacks. In 1959, Allen Dulles, the director of the CIA, explained to the American Senate Foreign Relations Committee that in Cuba "what you need against guerrillas are guerrillas. . . . It is rough country, and there is no use sending tanks and heavy artillery up there."[21] The Batista government had fallen there at the start of the year to Fidel Castro's left-wing guerrilla-style insurrection, without the Americans intervening. There was also the problem—which affected, for example, the combatants in the Arab-Israeli war of 1948–1949—that the major powers that manufactured tanks were not necessarily willing to supply them to other states.

However, the situation in the Middle East was very different by the time of the next Arab-Israeli war, in 1956 between Egypt and Israel, in large part because the diffusion of advanced weaponry became a way to obtain, secure, and support protégés. In 1955, the Soviets, through Czechoslovakia, agreed to provide hundreds of tanks, 200 MiG-15 fighters, and 50 Ilyushin-28 bombers to Egypt. In contrast, France, then, because of its endangered colonial position in Algeria, opposed to the pan-Arab nationalism of Colonel Nasser of Egypt, armed Israel.[22] In 1965, concerned about rising Soviet influence in Egypt, President Lyndon B. Johnson agreed to sell tanks to Israel. The rivalries of the Cold War thus ensured the spread of technology even as patrons and protégés changed. American support for Israel replaced that of France. Arms supplies were not only the case with the Arab-Israeli struggle. In 1978, Soviet-supplied tanks helped Ethiopia defeat Somalia. The variety of sources of supply was indicated by the Pakistani air force in 1971, which contained American and French planes as well as Chinese-built MiG-19s and planes that had originally belonged to the German *Luftwaffe*.

At the same time, the confrontation between the Soviet-led Communist bloc and the American-led West for long focused on Europe, where their land forces were massed and faced each other across the border between West and East Germany. As a result, the North European Plain appeared the clear cockpit of any future war, with planning accordingly,[23] and this encouraged an emphasis on tanks by both sides and the related development of armor-based doctrine.

Tank attacks were regarded as the key means by which the Red (Soviet) Army would advance: the Soviet Union had a major advantage in tank numbers as well as considerable experience from the Second World War. In response, NATO countries sought to deploy heavy defensive tanks with guns able to penetrate the armor of the heaviest Soviet tank, such as the Conqueror, with its 120 mm gun, that the British deployed in 1955. Other specifications also improved. To cope with supplies, multi-fuel engines were a focus of development after 1945, so that tanks could run on any fuel, but these engines introduced a further element of complexity and cost. Moreover, the ability to aim and shoot accurately while moving, a key ability if mobility was to be retained and vulnerability lessened, only followed the development, in the 1950s–1960s, of complex stabilized gun systems, fast traversing turrets, and good targeting systems. This combination enabled tanks to have high first-shot kill capabilities.[24]

These tanks were primarily designed for conflict in Europe. A wish to counter the possibility of Soviet attacks and, also, to have an alternative to the response of a massive retaliation by atomic weaponry encouraged American planners, notably in the army, to seek a strong conventional posture as a deterrent and as an aspect of the policy of flexible response. The Americans prepared for limited war[25] as well as large-scale atomic conflict. Flexible response, advocated by President John F. Kennedy (1961–1963), led to a stress on alternatives to nuclear warfare, in other words conventional forces, which meant a heavy reliance on tank and anti-tank warfare.

The commitment in Vietnam, which dominated American military attention from 1963, distracted attention from this operational and tactical means by driving home the extent to which limited warfare did not necessarily mean a reprise of the European stage of the Second World War, which had required such weapons. However, after the Vietnam War ended for the United States in 1973, its military returned to an emphasis on mobile conventional warfare based on tanks and planes, the two linked in the concept of an air-land battle.[26] This stress on what was presented as the operational dimension of war looked toward the methods that were to be used by the Americans in defeating Iraq and its Soviet-supplied weaponry in 1991.

At the same time, there were significant developments in anti-tank weapons. After the Second World War, anti-tank guns were progressively supplemented by missiles, which proved a winner in combating both tanks and aircraft. In the Arab-Israeli Yom Kippur War of October 1973, Israel's American-built tanks proved vulnerable to the Soviet Sagger ground-to-ground missiles used by the Egyptians, although the Israelis, whose focus on aircraft and tanks had led to a neglect of artillery, argued that the best anti-tank weapon was another tank. In a striking illustration of the continuing difficulties of assessing relative capability, claims varied (and still vary) over the effectiveness of tanks and missiles in that conflict. The Israelis claimed that their tank losses were overwhelmingly to other tanks, whereas the Egyptians stressed the role of their missiles.[27]

As with battleships, there were trade-offs with tanks, arms, armor, and speed again proving crucial factors. Thus, the Soviet T-54/55 and T-62 tanks used by the Syrians in the Yom Kippur War benefited from being simple to use, thus requiring less training, and easy to maintain, and they were also armed with powerful guns, while they could move a longer distance on a single tank of fuel than the tanks of their Israeli opponents. The last was both tactically and operationally significant. Moreover, unlike the Israelis, the Soviets had fully integrated night-vision sights. However, the compact frames of the Soviet tanks left little space or ventilation for their crew, which tired them out, while, combined with thin side armor, this feature accentuated the problem of crew vulnerability to penetrating rounds. The limited depression angle of the main gun also ensured vulnerability, as the Syrian tanks could not adopt a "hull down" position in order to engage. In contrast, the Israeli Centurion, an older, British-supplied model, albeit updated, was heavily armed, had a good long-range gun, and could readily depress this gun, thus exposing little of the tank. In conflict with Pakistan in 1971, the Indians, defending the east bank of the Tawi River, countered this problem with their T-54 tanks by the use of well-prepared defensive positions.

Conflict in 1973, as on other occasions, owed much to the impact of the trade-off of different specifications, as, crucially, mediated by a training that in 1973 was better in the Israeli case. In the event, the Syrian tank crews fought less well, not least because of a lack of flexibility. Moreover, the Syrians lacked adequate combined arms capability, with poor artillery and infantry support proving key elements. A misuse of Soviet operational art was another important element.[28] Egypt and Syria lost about 2,250 tanks in the war, and the Israelis 840.

The trade-off in specifications and the role of training remained significant in other tank clashes. Demonstrating the problems of translating technology and technique successfully, the misuse of Soviet operational art displayed by the Syrians in 1973 was also seen with the North Vietnamese failure to make the best use of tanks in their 1972 Spring Offensive in South Vietnam. At the same time, their tanks proved vulnerable in this campaign to technological advance in the shape of American helicopter-fired wire-guided missiles and anti-tank weapons.[29]

In the 1991 Gulf War, the Iraqi tanks were both technically inferior and poorly used. The Iraqis dug them in, believing that this would protect them from air and tank engagements, but they failed to understand the capabilities of both precision munitions and up-to-date tank gun technologies that ensured a high first-shot kill capability even when only part of the turret was visible. In the 2003 Gulf War, the Soviet-supplied Iraqi T-55s and T-72s that were not destroyed by air attack could not prevail against the American M1A1 Abrams tank.

Since the Vietnam era, tanks have proved to be very vulnerable to helicopter gunships firing anti-tank missiles. In the Iran-Iraq War of 1980–1988, the Iranians benefited from the use of missiles against Iraqi tanks, with helicopters firing missiles. More generally, tanks repeatedly proved vulnerable to weapons other than other tanks, and the range of such weapons increased. They included the Thunderbolt II, an aircraft that was supposed to be an inexpensive anti-tank platform for missiles, and the Vulcan cannon, a very effective anti-tank weapon. In Lebanon in 2006, Hezbollah's mines and its Soviet anti-tank missiles challenged the Israeli armor advancing in the shape of the heavy Merkana tank, which had hitherto provided a key capability advantage over Israel's opponents on land.

Moreover, the sophistication of anti-tank missiles has improved. As with other technological developments, this improvement was a matter of enhancements in existing types as well as the introduction of new types. Thus, there were improvements in wire-guided missiles, from the Soviet Sagger model introduced in 1963, to the more accurate Soviet Metis-M (1978). There was also the addition of laser-guided anti-tank missiles such as the Russian Kornet-E (1994). The Yom Kippur War was a reminder of the effectiveness of cheap, handheld anti-tank and anti-aircraft weapons.

Thanks to missiles, the tank increasingly seemed vulnerable in close combat, especially in urban areas. It also appeared obsolescent because of the cost in resources and manpower entailed in losing and even maintaining tanks. However, there have been attempts to lessen vulnerability to anti-tank weapons, notably with improvements to armor so that it responds better to being hit by missiles, and also by jamming devices. There has been significant progress in both directions; for example, by the use of composite armor and of explosions to detonate incoming rounds on impact rather than letting them penetrate. Modern composite armors combined with reactive explosions to give tanks unprecedented protection from other tanks and from anti-tank weapons fired on the ground but, the Gulf Wars of 1991 and 2003 revealed, are less effective when targeted by aircraft dropping smart bombs or using a Vulcan cannon. In 1991, the Allied air force destroyed 1,300 of Iraq's 4,200 tanks, as well as 850 of its 2,800 armored personnel carriers.

However, the true effectiveness of current armor is, for those outside the military, a matter of speculation since the performance (and indeed the composition) of the armor is secret. This progress in protection has greatly affected other specifications, such as weight and cost, and there are still serious vulnerabilities. Moreover, even if destruction can be avoided, damage remains a central problem not least as, due to cost, the number of tanks available has fallen. The cost of replacing damaged tank tracks is formidable, let alone that of dealing with engine problems. Anti-tank, like anti-aircraft, weaponry continues to indicate the effectiveness and importance of anti-weapons.

Nevertheless, although the demise of the tank has been predicted since it was invented, technical responses, if not solutions, to the continuing problems of firepower, mobility and armor show that the tank is here to stay, at least until there is a major change in the parameters of land conflict. In 2010, the United States had 6,302 main battle tanks, while China had 2,800. The evolution of the tank and the anti-tank response is a process that is self-sustaining. The idea of deflecting explosive damage was also seen in new ways of creating combat boots designed to transfer the blast energy away from the heel toward the shinbone, which can be more easily reconstructed.[30] Similarly, troops have been provided with changes to their uniform to offer pelvic protection, notably Kevlar underpants designed to limit groin injuries.

ARMORED CARS AND VEHICLES

The vulnerability of tanks to anti-tank weaponry is important, but too much of the discussion of gasoline-fuelled vehicles relates to tanks. There has been insufficient attention to other vehicles, both combat vehicles and support vehicles. The former are a wide-ranging group, including some types of mobile anti-tank and anti-aircraft guns, but the most important are armored cars and armored personnel carriers. Each tends to be underrated, but they are important, both in their own right and for what they show about the general problem of discussing advances in weaponry.

Armored cars were more vulnerable than tanks in conventional warfare, both to tank fire and to artillery. Although valuable for the British against the defending Turks in conquering Palestine and advancing into Syria in 1918, they did not play a major role in the First World War and, as a result, their potential significance in the 1910s has been underrated. There is no inherent reason to focus solely on symmetrical warfare: conflict between similarly armed forces. Armored cars had advantages for other types of conflict, as well as being lighter, and more mobile, than tanks. A British General Staff minute of September 1919, circulated to the War Cabinet by Winston Churchill, as secretary of state for war, focused on the achievements of British armored cars on the western front in France in 1918, adding:

> It is to be noted that these results were obtained in so-called trench warfare, that is when there is no open flank to manoeuvre round. Imagine the possibilities of half-a-dozen such units boldly handled in conjunction with light tanks and a cavalry force where there is an open flank! . . . In all Eastern theatres the value of these cars is constantly being brought to notice, while for internal troubles and industrial "unrest" they are an admirable specific.[31]

The minute's understanding of the range of possible tasking was instructive for the issue of assessing effectiveness.

Armored cars proved useful in the interwar period, for example, for the British in controlling northern Sudan, the drier and unforested part of the country.[32] Moreover, the Poles made good use of armored cars and motorized infantry against the Red Army in 1920, providing firepower to supplement the cavalry. In 1925–1927, the French used armored cars against the Druze rising in Syria. In subduing Libya in 1928–1932, the Italians employed columns of armored cars and motorized infantry. Reza Shah of Iran deployed armored cars and lorries, operating on new roads, against tribal rebellions in 1929 and 1932, and these rebellions were suppressed.

However, armored cars were greatly eclipsed by tanks in the Second World War and Cold War. As a result, they are ignored in standard guides that cover weapons, for example, *The Oxford Companion to World War II* (1995). Nevertheless, armored cars and armored personnel carriers played a role in both wars, the latter providing infantry with a mobility that was designed to match the tempo offered by modern armor. Armored cars played significant reconnaissance and pursuit roles, notably staying in touch with the retreating enemy, in the Second World War. The first armored personnel carrier was used in the First World War: an Mk IX tank. In the Second World War, armored personnel carriers were employed to a limited extent by the Allies and the Germans. The former (Kangaroo) used converted Canadian Ram tank hulls, while the Germans deployed half-tracks, as did the Americans, who also used the amphibious Buffalo.

Armored personnel carriers were deployed in large numbers in the Cold War as efforts were made to mechanize the infantry. Armored fighting vehicles and personnel carriers were also used in conflicts in the Third World. The Nigerian army used them with considerable effect in the bitter fighting to suppress Biafra, the would-be Ibo separatist state in eastern Nigeria in 1967–1970. In its 1971 war with Pakistan, India deployed Polish wheeled and tracked and Soviet wheeled armored personnel carriers. In the Yom Kippur War in 1973, the Syrians deployed about 1,000 Soviet-provided BMP-1 infantry fighting vehicles and BTR armored personnel carriers. In practice, however, they found it difficult to use their weapons systems effectively.[33] Such vehicles, moreover, were more vulnerable than tanks and could be less flexible. In 1979, in the conflict that ended with the invading Tanzanians overthrowing President Idi Amin of Uganda, light anti-tank weapons were used to destroy armored personnel carriers, which were largely road-bound.

There were also armored fighting vehicles that included characteristics of the tank. For example, the Warrior, which was brought into service by Britain in the 1980s, moved on tracks and had the commander and gunner stand in a turret. The Warrior has a 30 mm cannon, a 7.62 mm chain machine gun, and an external camera fitted with night vision. Designed for conventional warfare, the Warrior was still in service in the 2010s in Afghanistan.

Since the Cold War ended in 1989 1991, there has been a revival of interest in both armored cars and armored personnel carriers, and the two, indeed, have overlapped in function. This revival can be seen with the development of the American Stryker armored vehicle. The Americans in the late 1990s developed the Army After Next Project, focusing on a new generation of weapon systems able to respond rapidly to all circumstances. This capability entailed airlift, which encouraged the development of smaller, lighter fighting vehicles that could be used to equip light infantry units. The plan was to be able to field a combat-ready brigade anywhere in the world in 96 hours and a division in 120 hours, a key enhancement in capability contrasting with the situation in 1990 when Iraq invaded Kuwait and the distant and relatively slow Western forces had been heavily dependent on sea transport.[34]

The Stryker, an American eight-wheeled medium-weight armored vehicle, became the platform of choice, providing a mobile, armor-protected combat system, and with each vehicle able to connect with all the information systems serving the unit. A sense of greater effectiveness was to be derived from the comparison between the difficulties experienced by the Americans in Mogadishu, Somalia, in 1993,[35] when trying to rescue two downed helicopters, and the far less costly experience of a Stryker unit facing a similar task in Iraq in September 2004.[36] In 2010, the United States had 6,452 armored fighting vehicles.

The improved armament of Land Rovers, Warriors, and other British vehicles operating in Afghanistan and Iraq was also instructive. Such an armament is necessary in order to deal with the challenges of rocket-propelled grenades, improvised explosive devices (IEDs) or roadside bombs, and suicide bombers. Indeed, the need to provide protection in mobility has led to a reevaluation, with the emphasis in vehicles now more than in the past on the protection than the firepower side of the equation. There is an overlap with the use of such vehicles for security purposes. Policing missions in politically difficult environments were frequently supported by armored personnel carriers, as with Chinese response to Tibetan ethnic discontent in western Sichuan in 2011. New combat vehicles are built with V-shaped hulls specifically designed to project outward the kinetic energy of an exploding bomb. However, in a form of arms race, the creators of IEDs have made them more powerful.

TRUCKS

An emphasis on protection was also enhanced because of the increase in logistics requirements on the part of major forces. This increase reflected greater operating sophistication and requirements, ranging from ammunition to types of fuel. The specialization and need for operational tempo that diminished the possibilities of using civilian resources were also important. Morale is also linked to the fulfillment of the troops' assumptions about living standards, and the latter have risen sharply over the last century. At the time of the 2003 Gulf War, General Mike Jackson, the head of the British army, made caustic remarks about the British troops' requirements for lavatory paper.

The resulting requirements for supply capability were increasingly met by mechanized transport in the Second World War. In part, this provision reflected the extent to which the British and American armies were already mechanized and had access to oil. The limitations of rail networks, as well as serious wartime damage to them, further encouraged the use of mechanized transport. The United States was particularly important in the spread of such transport, not least because of the provision of American trucks (lorries) and jeeps to allies, especially to the Soviet Union. The mobility showed by the Soviet forces in their major advances of 1944 in Eastern Europe, notably Operation Bagration, owed something to the provision of these trucks. The availability of mechanized transport in the form of lorries and trucks was a measure of American mass production. The greater the availability of mechanized transport, the more it was used. In addition, some military trucks and transporters were specialized vehicles, such as tank transporters, amphibious vehicles, and gun tractors, wheeled and tracked. In each case, mechanization was important to the greater potential and effectiveness of the weapon.

In turn, the reliance on mechanized transport, as well as on tanks, increased the need for oil and thus the strategic and operational importance of seeking to control oil-producing areas. Most were under Allied control, including oilfields in the United States (more important than today), Venezuela, the Middle East, and the Caucasus, as was most refining capacity and oil tankers. At the same time, deficiencies in mechanization, issues with oil supplies, and the availability of horses all ensured that the Germans and Soviets continued to make a major use of horses, including to the close of the war. Italy and Japan also made great use of horses.[37] The significance of oil supplies helps explain the importance of Allied air and submarine attacks on Axis oil systems, including oilfields, such as in Japanese-occupied Sumatra, and refineries, notably Ploesti in Romania. Concern about air attacks on Ploesti was one reason Hitler gave for his (unsuccessful) determination to hold onto the Crimea in 1944. Thanks to Allied submarine attacks on oil tankers, the Japanese did not derive the anticipated benefit from the oilfields overrun in Borneo and Sumatra in 1941–1942. The importance of tires also led to the stockpiling of rubber in the 1930s[38] and to measures to manufacture synthetic rubber.

Lorries became even more important after the Second World War, because of the end of large-scale use of the horse, the spread of oil supply facilities, and not least because so much campaigning occurred in regions, such as Southeast Asia, the Middle East, and across Africa, where rail networks were sparse. Moreover, the very emphasis on insurrectionary warfare meant that operations were generally conducted in difficult terrain and economically marginal areas. Again, these operations put an emphasis on road, not rail, transport. However, this emphasis was lessened because insurrectionary movements frequently used human porters, notably along the Ho Chi Minh Trail in Southeast Asia during the Vietnam War, while counterinsurrectionary forces enhanced mobility and lessened vulnerability to ambushes by employing air-drops and helicopters, again particularly during the Vietnam War.

In conventional conflict, such as the Arab-Israeli wars of 1948–1973, the three Indo-Pakistan wars of 1947–1971, and the Somali-Ethiopian conflict over the Ogaden region in 1977–1978, lorries were appropriate for fast-moving operations in often flat and arid or semi-arid terrain. Lorries proved the best way to move supporting troops and supplies.

The flexibility of unarmored vehicles was also seen in conflict. Thus, in 1983, the Libyan invasion of neighboring Chad, reliant on Soviet doctrine and training, deployed armored vehicles. In contrast, the Chad forces benefited from light vehicles and a raider's desire for mobility and employed mortars and anti-tank rockets in order to inflict heavy casualties on the Libyans.

These tactics were employed again in the "Toyota War" of March 1987, with the Libyans losing over three thousand troops, and much of their armor, as they were driven from most of the north of Chad. At the same time, as a reminder of the need to be cautious in drawing conclusions, in this case on the value of "low-tech" solutions, the Libyans also suffered because of French intervention, notably the use of aircraft against Libyan ground forces, while intelligence supplied by American aerial surveillance was also significant.

More recently, the conflict in Libya in 2011 indicated similar conclusions. The anti-Gaddafi insurgents made plentiful use of unarmored vehicles, both to transport themselves and to mount weapons, especially anti-aircraft guns; and these vehicles provided a mobility that helped explain rapid changes of fortune in the campaigning. At the same time, the heavier conventional units of the Libyan army, both mobile (tanks) and static (artillery), were more deadly; but they were countered, and then seriously damaged, by Allied air power despite the serious problems the latter faced due to a lack of reliable reconnaissance information. The provision of Allied advisers and arms, notably firearms, night-warfare optics, and communication equipment, also helped the generally poorly organized rebels who captured the capital, Tripoli, that August, over-throwing the Gaddafi regime.

There is always a danger in reading too much from isolated episodes, and still more from a particular vision of modernity. To argue the obsolescence of the tank from the growing success of anti-tank weaponry, or the primacy of un- or less-armored vehicles, is possibly to draw too much from the present situation. Tanks faced serious problems when used by the Israelis against well-prepared opponents but proved militarily effective when employed by the Americans in Fallujah, Karbala, and Kufa in Iraq in 2004,[39] and again when deployed by the Syrian government against domestic opposition in 2011.

In particular, about 270 tanks were used in August 2011 in order to overcome resistance in the city of Hama, a major center of opposition. Having been deployed to blockade the city, contributing to the dislocation of opposition, the tanks broke through barricades, a capability that lighter-weight armored vehicles would have found more difficult. The tanks' machine guns subsequently proved more effective than the Molotov cocktails and stones thrown at them. However, the use of force was unable to stop the Syrian opposition. This serves as a reminder of the difference between output, in the form of military activity, and outcome. At the close of 2011, tanks had been pulled back in Syria but were still located on the edge of cities ready to be moved in, while armored cars were in the city of Homs. In addition, in February 2012, twenty tanks were among fifty vehicles used when the Ethiopians captured the city of Baidoa, a major center of the al-Shabaab militia movement in Somalia. However, in 2012 the Syrian government increasingly lost control of the domestic situation.

The need to have a broad definition of the capability of military vehicles is clear. So also is the degree to which an effective industrial base is significant for their manufacture and availability, as is the availability of oil to deploy this type of weaponry. Technological reliability and competence in its use are crucial to the effective utilization of any military technology. As far as the use of mechanized transport is concerned, this capability is much more due to the effect of changes in civilian society than those in the military.

The argument that wars are fought to gain control of oil is overly simplistic, but the availability of oil is certainly very important for warfare, and notably for the use of the internal combustion engine. The dependence of modern military systems on a range of materials, including not only oil but also rare metals, such as tungsten, underlines the vulnerability of these systems to any disruption of the global trading systems described in terms of globalization.

In turn, modern navies have found themselves called upon to be able to protect these trading systems, as notably with action against Somali pirates in the late 2000s and early 2010s. The pirate attacks themselves reflected the range of technologies involved in asymmetric conflict and the extent to which each side advances in a different fashion, by improving their own distinctive practices as well as by adapting to those of their opponent.[40] This process will continue as technologies are used and shaped in accordance with particular tasks.

5

A NEW SPHERE

Air Power, 1903–2013

Development in aircraft design and construction is rapid in these days.

—*British Ministerial Committee on Disarmament*
  dealing with Air Defence, 1934

BEFORE THE FIRST WORLD WAR

Air power is a key area of discussion when considering military technology. It provides examples of dramatic changes in capability and also links past and present with consideration of the future of warfare. Moreover, the nature, impact, and limitations of air power and warfare have been the subject of extensive analysis.[1] Manned heavier-than-air flight, first officially achieved by the American Wright brothers in 1903, was a key instance of the enhancement of fighting capability through totally new technology. Flight, or at least the use of the air, had had an earlier role in warfare with balloons, which were used by the French for reconnaissance in the 1790s, but its capability was now transformed. Imaginative literature, such as that of the novelist H. G. Wells, had prepared commentators for the impact of powered, controlled flight. Science fiction possibly gave some inspiration as to how airships could be used, as in *John Carter of Mars* (1912). In 1908, Count Zeppelin's LZ-4 airship had flown over 240 miles in 12 hours, leading to a marked revival of interest in airships, and in Britain in 1909 there was a scare about a possible attack by German airships.

However, from 1909, when Blériot made the first aeroplane flight across the English Channel, the focus switched to aircraft. A British report on changes in foreign forces during 1910 noted:

> Great activity has been displayed in the development of aircraft during the year, particularly in France and Germany. The main feature in the movement has been the increased importance of the aeroplane, which in 1909 was considered to be of minor military value. This importance was due partly to the surprising success of the aeroplane reconnaissances at the French manoeuvres, and partly to the successive disasters of the Zeppelin dirigibles [gas-filled airships].... Aviation schools have been started in almost every country.[2]

Aviation rapidly became a matter for international competition and therefore anxiety. As Lord Northcliffe, the influential British press baron, remarked, "England is no longer an island." In contrast to the naval race with Germany, but drawing on similar worries, there was concern in Britain about the bombing of its defenseless strategic targets and cities in any war with Germany; although, in 1909, when the chief of the British Imperial General Staff sought views on the likely effectiveness of airships and planes, he met with a skeptical response from General Ian Hamilton, who was unimpressed about the possibilities of bombing. Hamilton wrote, "the difficulty of carrying sufficient explosive, and of making a good shot, will probably result in a greater moral than material effect."[3] Similarly, General Ferdinand Foch, director of the French *École Supérieure de la Guerre,* argued in 1910 that air power would only be a peripheral adjunct to the conduct of war. Nevertheless, the French Directorate of Military Aeronautics was created in 1914.

New developments were frequent and rapid in the early 1910s. In the United States, the first aircraft takeoff from a ship occurred in November 1910 and the first landing on a ship in January 1911.[4] In 1911, Britain, which rapidly integrated air power into army maneuvers, established an air battalion and, in 1912, the Royal Flying Corps.[5] Aircraft were first employed in conflict during the Italian-Turkish War in 1911 and the Balkan Wars of 1912–1913. Grenades were dropped from the air on a Turkish army camp on October 23, 1911, and Turkish-held Edirne (Adrianople), besieged by the Bulgarians in 1913, was the first town on which bombs were dropped from an airplane. However, the use of aircraft had scant impact on operations in any of these conflicts, although the Italians benefited from the development of aerial photography, using it to correct their maps.[6]

By 1914, the European powers had a total of over 1,000 airplanes in their armed forces: Russia had 244, Germany 230, France 120, Britain 113, and Austria about 55. Most of these machines were little more than flying boxes, as they were slow, underpowered, and unarmed. The issue of armament did not really arise until after the outbreak of the First World War in 1914.

THE FIRST WORLD WAR

Aircraft were first used at any scale in the First World War (1914–1918), in which they played an important role, not only in fighting other aircraft but also in influencing combat on the ground (and at sea). The value of aircraft reconnaissance was quickly appreciated, not least because in 1914 aircraft provided intelligence on the moves of armies in the opening campaign on the western front, particularly the crucial change of direction of the German advance near Paris. By creating both an exposed flank for one German army and a gap between two of them, this change opened the way for a successful French counterattack in the Battle of the Marne.[7] The significance of reconnaissance was indicated by the fighter evolving as an armed reconnaissance plane protector, followed by as an armed aircraft for shooting down opposing spotters.

At the tactical level, reconnaissance aircraft proved especially valuable in helping direct artillery fire. In 1915, General Sir Charles Callwell, critical of the initial Allied plan for the attack on Gallipoli as a purely naval operation, remarked, "As a land gunner I have no belief in that long range firing except when there are aeroplanes to mark the effect."[8] Thus, in a classic instance of combined operations, artillery accuracy was believed to rest on reports from air spotters. Moreover, aircraft had an operational effect, as when the Turkish columns advancing across the Sinai Peninsula toward the Suez Canal in 1915 were spotted by British planes.

"Seeing over the hill" altered the parameters of conflict, but, despite capabilities including strafing troops and tanks, aircraft were not yet a tactically decisive nor operationally predictable tool. Their role had been grasped, but execution was limited.

The ability of airplanes to act in aerial combat, nevertheless, was enhanced during the war as specifications changed rapidly with increases in aircraft speed, maneuverability, and ceiling making it easier to attack other planes. Engine power rose and size fell, while the rate of climb of aircraft increased. The need to shoot down reconnaissance aircraft resulted in the development of the fighter, which led to the interrupter gear. This synchronizing gear was developed by a Dutchman, Anthony Fokker, but Fokker was sued for patent infringement by Franz Schneider, a Swiss engineer, and the case continued until 1933 despite the courts finding in favor of Schneider every time. Schneider, who worked for *Luftverkehrs Gesellschaft,* had patented a synchronizing gear in 1913. In addition, Raymond Saulnier, a French aircraft designer, patented a practical synchronizing gear in April 1914. But neither his nor Schneider's was reliable enough for use in combat, partly because of inconsistencies with the propellants used in the machine-gun ammunition, which led to misfires.

Fokker's synchronizing gear was utilized by the Germans from April 1915 and copied by the British, showing once again how war accelerated technological development but, with equal speed, resulted in another stalemate of sorts. This gear enabled airplanes to fire forward without damaging their propellers, and thus to fire in the direction of flight. The Fokker Eindekker aircraft, which the Germans deployed from mid-1915, gave them a distinct advantage and enabled them to seek the aerial advantage over Verdun in the key battle on the western front in early 1916. Vulnerability to German fighters was swiftly demonstrated. Harold Wyllie, a squadron commander in the British Royal Flying Corps, wrote in 1916, "sending out F.E.'s [F.E. 26s] in formation with Martinsydes for protection is murder and nothing else."[9]

The eventually successful French attempt to contest the German advantage reflected their deployment of large groups of aircraft and the fact that they now also had planes with synchronized forward-firing machine guns, both of which allowed them to drive off German reconnaissance airplanes. In turn, in the winter of 1916–1917, the Germans gained the advantage, thanks in part to their Albatross D-1, only to lose it from mid-1917 as more and better Allied planes arrived.

The superior synchronizing gear (the CC Gear) invented by the Romanian engineer George Constantinescu employed no mechanical linkages but a column of fluid in which sonic pulses were transmitted. This was not a hydraulic system because of the use of the pulses. It was more reliable than mechanical systems and allowed for a faster rate of fire. The CC Gear was fitted to British machines from March 1917, notably the Gloster Gladiator. Moreover, because Constantinescu's theory of sonics was kept secret, the Germans failed to copy the gear from shot-down aircraft because they wrongly assumed the device to be purely hydraulic and could not make it work.

Despite significant Allied advantages, notably in 1918, the Germans did not lose in the air as they were to do in the Second World War, and this contrast, in large part, indicated the relatively more limited capability of First World War aircraft, including in range, speed, altitude, acceleration, maneuverability, armament, and payload.

There were also developments in tactics during the First World War. Aircraft came to fly in groups and formation tactics developed. Aircraft also became the dominant aerial weapon: their ability to destroy balloons and airships with incendiary bullets spelled doom for the latter. The German Zeppelin airship had impressed contemporaries as a bomber, but its vulnerability to aircraft swiftly became apparent.

The British Royal Naval Air Service conducted the first effective bombing raids of the war in 1914 when planes carrying 20-pound bombs flew from Antwerp, then still in Allied hands, to strike Zeppelin shells at Düsseldorf and destroyed an airship. As with any munition, the key element was not the bomb but the fuse, and fuses had to be developed specifically for aerial bombs. Bombing became more frequent, and ambitions about its effect increased. The Germans launched bomber attacks on London in 1917 because they believed, possibly due to reports by Dutch intelligence, that the British were on the edge of rebellion. As a result, the attacks were intended not so much to serve attritional goals but rather to be a decisive war-winning tool.

The use of bombers, notably the German *Gotha*, reflected the rapid improvement of capability during the war, as science and technology were applied in the light of experience. The *Gotha* Mark Four could fly for 6 hours at an altitude of 21,000 feet (4 miles or 6,400 meters), which made interception difficult, had an effective range of 520 miles, and could carry 1,100 pounds (or 500 kilograms) of bombs. Furthermore, the crews were supplied with oxygen and with electric power to heat the flying suits.

The first (and deadliest) raid on London, a daylight one on June 13, 1917, in which fourteen planes killed 162 people and injured 432, not least as a result of a direct hit on a school that killed 16 children, led to a public outcry. This slaughter was met—in the rapid action-reaction cycle that characterized advances during the war—by the speedy development of a British defensive system involving high-altitude fighters based on airfields linked by telephones to observers, an instance of the combination of new technologies. The effectiveness of this system led to heavy casualties among the *Gothas* and to the abandonment of daylight raids. More seriously, the rationale of the German campaign was misplaced because, far from hitting British morale, the bombing led to a markedly hostile popular response, and at a time when relative war-weariness was becoming increasingly significant. This response remained the case even in the winter of 1917–1918, when the Germans unleashed four-engine *Zeppelin-Staaken* R-series bombers, able to fly for 10 hours and to drop 4,400 pounds (or 2,000 kilograms) of bombs.[10] The German bombing did not have strategic effect. It did not break British morale and was not capable of inflicting significant economic damage. As a consequence, bombing lacked the potential of submarine warfare.

By the close of the war, the extent and role of air power had dramatically expanded. By the armistice in November 1918, the British had a western front force of 2,600 airplanes as well as many in service elsewhere, and, that September, a combined Franco-American-British force of 1,481 was launched against the Germans in the Saint-Mihiel Salient, the largest deployment thus far. In 1917, German airplanes destroyed moving French tanks in Champagne. Supply links came under regular attack from the air, inhibiting German and Austrian advances in 1918 and affecting the Turks in the Middle East that year.

Airplane production had risen swiftly. In 1914, the British Royal Aircraft Factory at Farnborough could produce only two air-frames per month, but their artisanal methods were swiftly swept aside by mass production. Air power also exemplified the growing role of scientific research in military capability: wind tunnels were constructed for the purpose of research. Strutless wings and airplanes made entirely from metal were developed. Huge improvements in design, construction, engines, and armaments turned the unsophisticated machine of 1914 into a potent weapon during the course of the war.[11]

THE INTERWAR YEARS

The alarm raised in sections of British society by German air attacks encouraged postwar theorists to emphasize the potential of air power, not least as a progressive and necessary alternative to the slaughter and delay of trench warfare.[12] During the war itself, the consequences of strategic bombing—either to disrupt industrial life or to cause civilian casualties—were, in fact, limited. Indeed, despite the First World War, the impact on war of aircraft was largely untried, so that commentators of the 1920s and 1930s had little practical knowledge on which to base their theories. At the same time, they were able to sustain prewar assumptions about the potential of air power, assumptions that drew on a strong sense of elitism.[13]

Air-power theorists emphasized the bomber. For 1919, the British had planned long-range bombing raids on German cities, including Berlin, with large Handley Page VI 500 bombers, although the war ended before their likely impact could be assessed. Nevertheless, in one of the episodes that repeatedly grabbed attention for air power enthusiasts, one of the planes successfully flew the Atlantic in 1919. Moreover, in 1925, Brigadier-General William (Billy) Mitchell, a key and vocal figure in the early propagation of American air power, told the presidential inquiry on air power that the United States could use Alaska to launch effective air attacks on Japan, which was already seen as a major and growing threat to American interests in the Pacific and the Far East.[14] This aerial capability appeared to offer an alternative to naval power, although the effectiveness of the latter was enhanced with the development of aircraft carriers and carrier doctrine and tactics. In the 1930s, naval aviation came to play a significant role in American naval exercises.[15]

Drawing on prewar ideas about air power, including the apparent potential of the airship,[16] aircraft were used extensively after the First World War for military tasks within and beyond the boundaries of empire. The British Royal Air Force (RAF) bombed Jalalabad and Kabul during the Third Afghan War in 1919, tribesmen in Central Iraq in 1920,[17] Wahabi tribesmen from Arabia who threatened Iraq and Kuwait in the 1920s, and many other targets.[18] In Somaliland, the twelve DH-9s of the RAF's Unit Z brought the necessary combination of force and mobility, and the Dervish stronghold at Taleh was bombed in 1920, greatly affecting Somali morale. In the Far East, the French used aircraft to help overcome opponents and maintain order in Morocco, Syria, and Vietnam. Air power had become a vital ingredient for imperial control. Bombing suggested that artillery could be replaced, increasing the mobility of ground troops.

There were also advances in technique and technology, as in the mid-1920s, when Arthur Harris, later a key figure in the British bombing of Germany but then commander of a squadron in Iraq, rigged up improvised bomb racks and bomb-aimer sights in slow-flying transport planes, as their slowness was conducive to accuracy.[19] Gasoline, incendiary, and delayed-action bombs were all employed in the 1920s. Planes were developed or adapted for imperial policing duties, for example, the Westland Wapiti, a British day-bomber in service from 1928 to 1939 that was used for army coordination, especially on the North-West Frontier of India. In 1922, the Vickers Vernon, the first of the RAF's troop carriers, entered service. It was based in Iraq.

However, in 1922, the General Staff of the British Forces in Iraq observed, in a military report on part of Mesopotamia, "Aeroplanes by themselves are unable to compel the surrender or defeat of hostile tribes,"[20] a lesson that repeatedly needs to be relearned. Moreover, opponents on the ground soon learned not to be overawed but, rather, to take cover, return fire, and adopt tactics that lessened the impact of air attack. This process affected the British[21] and French, and also the Americans in their operations against the nationalist Sandinista guerrilla movement in Nicaragua. This point was not only true for Western powers. Amanullah, king of Afghanistan, used planes he had obtained from the Soviet Union against tribal opponents, but the latter prevailed in 1929 and he was overthrown.[22]

In the 1920s and 1930s, major advances in aircraft technology, including improved engines and fuels and variable pitch propellers, provided opportunities to enhance military aircraft. This was particularly so for fighters in the mid- and late 1930s, as wooden-based biplanes were replaced by all-metal cantilever-wing monoplanes with high-performance engines capable of far greater speeds, for example, the American P-36 Hawk, German Bf 109,[23] and (less good) Soviet I-16 Rata. The British developed two effective and nimble monoplane fighters, the Hawker Hurricane and Supermarine Spitfire. Alongside early warning radar, they were to help Britain resist the German air onslaught in 1940. In the 1930s, the range and armament of fighters, and the range, payload, and armament of bombers, all increased, notably with the introduction of the American B-17 bomber. Major advances in technology included all-metal monocoque construction and retractable undercarriages.

It was necessary to keep up with the advances made by other powers, and a failure to do so could have dire consequences. Although only a few years of development separated them, the Polish air force was outdated and no match for the German *Luftwaffe* (air force) when the latter attacked in 1939, and the French *Armée de l'Air* suffered from a lack of good aircraft, a shortage of pilots, and poor liaison with the army when the Germans attacked in 1940. The Soviet air force, which had been advanced in some respects in the early 1930s, not least in the development of long-range bombers able to attack Japan, was outclassed by the *Luftwaffe* when Germany invaded in 1941. As a key instance of the diffusion of Western techniques, Japan also developed a modern air force. In 1933, the British Chiefs of Staff Sub-Committee referred to the Japanese air force as having "air equipment and a standard of training fast approaching that of the major European Powers" and presented it as "the predominant factor in the air situation of the Far East."[24]

The likely effectiveness of the new aircraft caused much discussion, a key instance of the way in which technology affected the political and public mood. A report from a British diplomat in Spain during the Civil War circulated to the cabinet in 1937 claimed "the Nationalist air forces that smashed the iron ring of defenses round Bilbao were almost entirely made up of German machines piloted by Germans. The final attack was launched by eighty of these bombers in the air at one time, and they created havoc."[25] The adherents of the new theory of the effects of hostile air power on societies played on the fear of stalemate, or at best attrition, on the front line in any future war, and the belief that only devastating air attacks on civilians would end this impasse.

In Britain, there was strong concern about the likely impact of the German bombing of civilian targets. The Chiefs of Staff Sub-Committee reported in September 1938 on the dangers of war with Germany, focusing on the bombing threat: "there is some reason to believe that the German air-striking force *if concentrated against this country alone*, might be able to maintain a scale of attack amounting possibly to as much as 500–600 tons per day for the first two months of war."[26]

The major impact on public morale of German raids on London in the First World War seemed a menacing augury. It was believed, in the words of the ex- and future prime minister Stanley Baldwin in 1932, that "the bomber will always get through." Air Commodore L. E. O. Charlton developed these themes in *War from the Air: Past-Present-Future* (1935), *War over England* (1936), and *The Menace of the Clouds* (1937).[27] Publications and films emphasized the threat from bombing. In the event, the German air assault in 1940–1941, the Battle of Britain and the Blitz, proved less deadly than had been anticipated.

The speed of aircraft posed great problems for anti-aircraft fire, not least by challenging the processes used in ballistics. It was necessary to track rapid paths in three dimensions and to aim accordingly. Research in the United States was directed accordingly at making effective what in effect was an analogue computer. This research looked toward the development in the 1940s of cybernetics and the idea of systems that were human-machine hybrids.[28]

Even more dramatic ideas were also advanced. In his presidential address to the American Rocket Society in 1931, David Lasser discussed the potential of rocket shells, which could carry their own fuel, and of rocket planes flying at over 3,000 miles per hour and threatening "an avalanche of death."[29] These ideas looked toward German ideas during the Second World War, including for long-range bombers, multi-stage rockets, space bombers, or submarine-launched missiles, which, it was planned, were to be used for attacks on New York City and Washington.[30] Such technology appeared to offer an alternative to a German naval power projection that Allied naval strength precluded, and it also seemed to be a way to hit the American home front and American industrial capability.

THE SECOND WORLD WAR

In the event, conventional air attack was important to the German offensives of the early stages of the Second World War. Air support was important to their success. Despite the vulnerability of the German Ju-87 or Stuka to modern fighters, ground-support dive-bombing proved valuable, especially in Poland (1939), Norway (1940), France (1940), and Greece (1941). Furthermore, the terror bombing of cities—for example, Warsaw in 1939, Rotterdam in 1940, and Belgrade in 1941—was seen as a way to break the will of opponents and certainly helped lead to a sense of total vulnerability, encouraging surrender, although the bombing of London in 1940–1941 did not bring Britain to terms. Pursuing air dominance and air-land integration,[31] the *Luftwaffe* was designed to further operational warfare with a limited scope and range, which made it deadly in 1939 and 1940 against Poland and France. However, the *Luftwaffe* was unsuccessful in strategic warfare, such as the Battle of Britain in 1940, or war with the Soviet Union, or the ability to project itself into the Atlantic.

The inadequately prepared and poorly planned Germans were outfought in the sky when they attacked Britain in 1940 in the Battle of Britain. The RAF had this potential because it possessed aircraft that were the equal to those in the *Luftwaffe*,[32] while the Germans never deployed their full strength at any one time.[33] Moreover, the British outproduced the Germans so that losses in fighters were quickly made good because of more efficient manufacture. The British outproduced the Germans with replacement fighters during the Battle of Britain because German manufacture was not maximized for war, while Britain quickly developed an efficient system that drew on superior British engineering and management. In addition, Britain benefited from an integrated air-defense system. Alongside the good fighters, there were effective sensors, notably radar, and the appropriate command and control mechanisms for controlling the firepower. The *Luftwaffe* was also primarily intended to act in concert with German ground forces, something that was not possible in this self-contained aerial battle.

The *Luftwaffe* was unable to defeat the RAF and thus failed to gain the air superiority over the English Channel and southern England necessary for *Operation Sealion,* the invasion that was projected although with inadequate planning, preparation, and resources. The viability of *Sealion* was dubious even had the Germans achieved air superiority over southern England. There were other fighters farther north and west, as well as the potent threat posed by the Royal Navy. Moreover, the Germans had no experience or understanding of amphibious operations. They lacked proper landing craft. The towed Rhine barges they proposed to rely on could only manage a speed of 3 knots and would have failed to land a significant number of troops had any of them managed to reach the south coast.[34]

Similarly, German air power had serious deficiencies in affecting the war at sea, not least because coordination with the navy was very poor. Despite having acquired bases in Brittany in 1940 from which long-range planes could threaten shipping routes in British home waters, a potential lacking in the First World War, the *Luftwaffe* failed to devote sufficient resources to the Battle of the Atlantic against Allied shipping.

Instead, air power greatly helped the Allies in the struggle against German submarines. The Allies had long-range aircraft capable of sinking submarines, such as the British Sunderland and the American Liberator. Coming to the surface in order to attack or refuel, submarines were vulnerable to air attack. The provision of long-range patrol planes and escort aircraft carriers and the acquisition of air bases in the neutral (Portuguese) Azores proved crucial to Allied victory, notably in closing the "Air Gap" over the mid-Atlantic. Submarines were also visible when they were below the surface if they were at insufficient depth. The snorkel enabled submarines to run their diesels and remain submerged, but not at sufficient depth to avoid detection from the air. A submarine just below the surface was perfectly visible from the air so that submarines operating in waters within range of the anti-submarine patrols had to be either on the surface to enable aircraft watches to be continuously maintained or far enough below the surface to prevent detection from the air. The development of a series of devices, including improved radar and more effective searchlights, was important in the struggle against submarines. From 1943, ASVIII radar (a version of H2s) combined with the Leigh light were highly effective at detecting and targeting submarines. Doctrinal and tactical changes were also significant, for example, different patterns of firing depth charges. Communications intelligence in the shape of the timely decryption of U-boat radio messages proved very important in thwarting attacks and in hunting for submarines.[35]

Against the Soviet Union on the eastern front from 1941, German air power was of tactical value, but it lacked the capability to achieve operational and strategic goals. In part, this lack reflected the specifications of the German planes, notably the absence of long-range bombers, but there were more serious problems arising from the space-force ratio, with the Germans not having the number of planes necessary in order to have an impact across the very extensive range of the battle zone. There were also the problems posed by the rapid Soviet revival of their air force, which had been devastated in the initial German attack. The extent to which, despite serious losses in this attack, much Soviet industry remained beyond the range of German power proved important to this revival. In order to provide protection for their forces on the ground, the Germans had to devote large numbers of planes to destroying Soviet aircraft.

Moreover, notably from 1943, the Allied air assault on Germany led to the diversion of German planes from the eastern front to western Europe, principally in order to provide fighter-interceptors but also to make retaliatory bombing raids on Britain, the so-called Baby Blitz. The Germans devoted much of their war industry to the manufacture of fighters and anti-aircraft guns designed to protect Germany, which was an important strategic consequence of the Allied Combined Air Offensive.

Far more German industrial capacity was used for these goals than for the manufacture of tanks. As with many counterfactuals (what ifs), this point raises questions about the likely consequences had priorities been different. It is important not to assume that the transfer of resources, including manufacturing plant and skilled labor, to other priorities was (is) easy, but it is a significant issue, not least because priorities were debated at the time.

During the Second World War, alongside failures in execution, there were also major advances in air capability. In part, these advances were a matter of better aircraft, although there was also an improvement in such spheres as the doctrine and practice of ground support and anti-submarine warfare, at least for the British and Americans. Moreover, the training of large numbers of aircrew was a formidable undertaking, although it paid off, particularly for the Allies. For example, in the Pacific, there was a growing disparity in quality between American and Japanese pilots, a matter of numbers, training, and flying experience. The loss of trained pilots at the Battle of Midway in 1942 proved particularly damaging for the Japanese. By 1944, they had a new carrier fleet replacing the carriers sunk by American dive-bombers at Midway, but it had a crucial lack of experienced pilots.[36]

At the same time, it would be foolish in stressing training to neglect the extent to which the Americans by 1943 and, even more, 1944 benefited in the Pacific and over Europe from better aircraft, as part of a more general improvement in Allied capability, as the potential of the industrial base was deployed in a way that the United States had not been able to do in the early stages of the war. Whereas the Japanese had not introduced new classes of planes, the Americans had done so, enabling them to challenge the Zero fighter that had made such an impact in the initial Japanese advances. Entering service in 1940, the Zero was superior in performance to available American planes, notably the Wildcat; at this stage of the war, the Zero was more maneuverable than most planes. However, aside from American improvements thanks to training in new dog-fighting tactics, the introduction of the new Corsair (entered service 1942) and Hellcat (1943) ensured that the Americans had planes that outperformed the Zero, while, as their specifications included better protection, they were able to take more punishment than Japanese planes. The Japanese had designed the Zero with insufficient range, and also with the safety of their pilots as a low priority. It lacked armor and self-sealing fuel tanks.

The role of air power in the Pacific War underlined its more general effectiveness at sea where the number of units, and therefore targets, was limited, unlike on land. Aircraft carriers proved particularly prominent targets, as with the major American victories over the Japanese at Midway in 1942 and Leyte Gulf in 1944. Neither Germany nor Italy had aircraft carriers.

The provision of improved aircraft was also important to the British and later Anglo-American air offensive against Germany. In August 1941, a British strategic review noted, "Bombing on a vast scale is the weapon upon which we principally depend for the destruction of German life and morale."[37] On May 19, 1943, Winston Churchill commented, in an address to a joint session of the U.S. Congress, that opinion was "divided as to whether the use of air power could, by itself, bring about a collapse of Germany or Italy. The experiment is well worth trying, so long as other measures are not excluded."[38]

Precision daylight bombing, however, was never as successful as prewar advocates claimed it would be, although problems were not appreciated until experience made them clear. The major problems with bombers were the bombsight and navigation systems. Accurate bombing was a technical issue. Not only was bombing highly inaccurate much of the time, but it was also very costly in aircrew and aircraft. When ground-mapping radar was fitted to British heavy bombers, accuracy increased, but there were still problems with identifying the target, even in daylight and without anti-aircraft guns or enemy fighters; and accuracy remained heavily dependent upon the skill of the pathfinder aircraft that preceded the bombers in order to identify targets. The technology to make precision daylight bombing possible did not really exist. Indeed, until the advent of the smart bomb, which was used from the Vietnam War, precision bombing is a largely misapplied term. There were some notable exceptions, such as the bombing of Amiens prison in 1944 by Mosquitoes of the RAF, but that was down to precision flying and experience rather than technology, although it is hard to see many other aircraft of that time achieving the same outcome.

Despite the limited precision of bombing by high-flying planes dropping free-fall bombs, strategic bombing was, in the event, crucial to the disruption of German logistics and communications, largely because the less precise area bombing that was used as an alternative to precision bombing was eventually on such a massive scale. An article in the *Times* of May 1, 1945, significantly entitled "Air Power Road to Victory . . . 1939 Policy Vindicated," claimed that reductions in oil output due to air attack had affected German war potential in all spheres, and that "neither his air force nor his army was mobile." Indeed, the German oil system had been deliberately and successfully targeted in the bomber offensive.

More generally, area (rather than precision) bombing disrupted the German war economy, although it also caused heavy civilian casualties, notably, but not only, at Hamburg in 1943 and Dresden in 1945. Moreover, by 1943, Anglo-American bombing had wrecked 60 percent of Italy's industrial capacity and badly undermined Italian morale, encouraging the sense that Mussolini had failed. This belief contributed greatly to his overthrow that year, although the Allied invasion of Italy was more significant.

The air attack on Germany also led to the Germans diverting much of their air force and anti-aircraft capacity to home defense, rather than supporting front-line units, and also to an emphasis on the production of anti-aircraft guns rather than other pieces of artillery. For example, the success of the British Dambusters raid in breaching German dams near the Ruhr in 1943, and thus in hitting the production of the hydroelectric power that helped industrial production, led to a major commitment of anti-aircraft guns, labor, concrete, and other resources to enhancing the defenses of these and other dams. This commitment resulted in a reduction in the availability of concrete and workers for work on the defenses of the Atlantic Wall against Allied invasion.

The casualties inflicted by bombing have since become a matter of great controversy, notably in Germany but also in Britain, but too little attention has been devoted to the expectations, from both domestic opinion and the Soviet Union, that major blows would be struck against Germany prior to the opening of the "Second Front" by means of an Anglo-American invasion of France. The delay of this invasion, from first 1942 and then, far more, 1943, led to great pressure for alternative action. As such, it matched the pressure on the Western Allies in the First World War to mount attacks in 1915 and 1916, in order to reduce the strain on Russia, pressure that led both to the Gallipoli operation of 1915 and to offensives on the western front. In 1942–1943, the comparable pressure was encouraged by Allied concern about a possible separate peace between Germany and the Soviet Union. There were, indeed, tentative soundings. As far as the domestic mood in Britain was concerned, the Germans had not only begun the bombing of civilian targets during the Second World War but, with the coming of the V-1s and V-2s in 1944, also launched missiles against British cities, again causing heavy civilian casualties.

However, especially prior to the introduction of long-range fighters, bombers were very vulnerable. The American B-17 was heavily armed in the belief that the aircraft could defend itself, but reality proved otherwise. German day-fighters learned to attack head-on because the B-17's top turret could not fire forward. As a result, in a classic instance of the action-reaction cycle, a forward-firing chin turret with two remotely operated .50-caliber Brownings was added with the B-17G. There were also tactical issues. B-17s were supposed to fly in box formations of four, designed to provide mutual fire support, but once the box was broken, the aircraft became easy targets. Diving steeply onto the formations, or attacking from above and behind, gave the German fighters the edge.[39]

Cripplingly heavy casualty rates occurred in some raids, for example, those of the American Eighth Air Force against the German ball-bearing factory at Schweinfurt in August and October 1943. Nineteen percent of the planes on the August 17 raid were lost. The majority of the bombers were lost to German fighters, with anti-aircraft fire and accidents accounting for the rest. The target of these raids reflected the belief that advanced manufacturing was important to the war economy and an important target. Conversely, the Soviets benefited because much of their industrial plant was beyond the range of the *Luftwaffe*. So also was all of that of the United States.

The absence of a need to defend American industrial capacity was a contributory factor to the ability there to focus so many resources on production for overseas operations, including the application of new advances in the mass production of improved weaponry. There was also a labor dimension. The American emphasis on a mechanized and relatively high-tech military entailed (by relative standards) a stress on machines, not manpower, in the American army. As a consequence, a larger percentage of the national labor force worked in manufacturing than in the case of Germany or Japan. Cultural factors also played an important role, as the Americans (like the Soviets and British) were far readier to use women in manufacturing than either the Germans or the Japanese. American agriculture was also more mechanized than its German and Japanese counterparts. Furthermore, the speedy expansion of the fiscal strength of the American federal government played a significant role in encouraging an unprecedented surge in war production.

The Allies aimed strategic bombing against aircraft factories, industry, transport, political targets, and civil society. However, it proved difficult to produce an effective offensive system, let alone vindicate the hopes of prewar theorists eager to see air attack as a swift means to victory. British night attacks on Berlin from November 18, 1943, until March 31, 1944, which, it had been promised, would undermine German morale, led instead to the loss of 492 bombers, a rate of losses that could not be sustained. In the British raid on Nuremberg of March 30–31, 1944, 106 out of the 782 bombers were lost, with only limited damage to the city and few German fighters shot down. This failure resulted in the end of the bomber-stream technique of approaching the target.

Strategic bombing, however, was made more feasible by four-engine bombers, such as the British Lancaster and the American B-29, as well as by heavier bombs and developments in navigational aids and training. British night bombing was improved by much electronic and radar equipment, which the Germans countered with developments of their own. The Lancaster had a very advanced communications system for its time, and British-built Lancasters were fitted with the R1155 receiver and T1154 transmitter, ensuring radio direction-finding. As an instance of action-reaction cycle, the Lancaster's H2S ground-looking navigation radar system, however, could eventually be homed in on by the German night-fighters' NAXOS receiver and had to be used with discretion. The H2S was supplemented by Fishpond, which provided additional coverage of aircraft attacking from beneath and displayed it on an auxiliary screen in the radio operator's position. Fishpond was designed to counter German night-fighters with upward firing cannon fitted in the fuselage so that they could fly parallel with the bomber but under it before shooting it down. Monica, rearward-looking radar designed to warn of night-fighter approaches, served, however, as a homing beacon for suitably equipped night-fighters and was therefore removed. Similarly, the ABC radar-jamming equipment could be tracked by the Germans, leading to heavy casualties. The development of radar was shown with the Village Inn, a radar-aimed rear turret fitted to some Lancasters in 1944. Moreover, with Oboe and Gee-H, the British developed very accurate navigation systems.

There was also an improvement in the bombs themselves. Thus, the British attempts to sink the German battleship *Tirpitz* were finally successful thanks to the development of the 12,000-pound Tallboy bomb, two of which hit the ship in November 1944.

Because heavily armed bomber formations lacking fighter escorts proved less effective in defending themselves than had been anticipated, the introduction of long-range fighter escorts for the bombers was important, especially the American P-38s (Lightnings), P-47s (Thunderbolts), and P-51s (Mustangs). Both of the latter used drop fuel tanks, which enabled fighters to reach German airspace and still engage in dogfights. The Mustangs, of which fourteen thousand were built, were able not only to provide necessary escorts for the bombers but also, in 1944, to seek out German fighters and thus win the air war above Germany. This success contrasted with the *Luftwaffe*'s failed offensive on Britain in 1940–1941, an offensive that had been less well supported. The drop fuel tanks were key to the ability of the Mustangs and Thunderbolts to hunt German fighters over Germany.

The Mustangs' superiority to German interceptors was demonstrated in late February and March 1944, when, especially in "Big Week," major American raids in clear weather on German sites producing aircraft and oil led to large-scale battles with German interceptors. Many American bombers were shot down, but the *Luftwaffe* also lost large numbers of planes and pilots. The latter were very difficult to replace, in large part because German training programs had not been increased in 1940–1942, as was necessary given the scale and length of the war, and this problem helped to ensure that, irrespective of aircraft construction figures, the Germans would be far weaker. The large number of German pilots shot down in 1943–1944 ensured a decline in German quality, not least because there was insufficient training time (and fuel) for the new generation of pilots. The key element of skill was demonstrated by Erich Hartmann, the highest-scoring German ace, whose achievement was not so much due to the superiority of his Bf109 over Soviet fighters (or even Mustangs, of which he shot down four in one sortie in June 1944) but his skill in using the machine at his disposal.

Toward the end, the Germans, suffering from their loss of control over Romanian oil production in 1944 as a result of the Soviet advance, could not spare the fuel for training, while a lack of training time was also a consequence of the shortage of pilots. In 1943, the Allies did not yet have sufficient air dominance to seek to isolate an invasion zone, but, by the time of the Normandy landings on June 6, 1944, the Germans had lost the air war.[40] This contrast with the earlier situation, like that in the Battle of the Atlantic against German submarines, was one of the reasons why the Allies were wise to delay the opening of a second front by invading France until 1944. The shortage of fuel encouraged the process by which members of the *Luftwaffe* were used for ground warfare.

The Allied invasion of Normandy in 1944 also displayed other advantages of air power in the shape of delivering troops by parachute and glider landings. These troops proved important in securing the flanks of the Allied landings, notably by dropping American parachutists behind Utah Beach and by British glider-borne troops seizing Pegasus Bridge to the east of the British landings. The botched American air-drop was not helped by the planes being flown by crews who had no night drop experience and an unexpected bank of cloud that made the pilots disperse wildly for fear of collision. What was remarkable about the dispersed troops on the ground was that the vast majority went about trying to fulfill their tasks even though they were often with men they did not know.

However, the effectiveness of the parachutists owed much to the rapid advance of troops from the landing sites, as the former lacked the necessary armaments to resist armored attack. As yet, there had not been the development of helicopters, which were to provide the basis for new capabilities in vertical envelopment, ground support, and resupply.

On D-Day, much of the supporting firepower for the invasion force was provided by British and American warships, whereas bombers proved unable to deliver the promised quantities of ordnance on target on time. The targeting of the Atlantic Wall fortifications by warships and bombers was not as good as it should have been so that many of the casemates and bunkers were not hit, while the Allies overestimated how effective shells and bombs would be against concrete. Most gun emplacements that were put out of action by warships or bombers along the Atlantic Wall had their guns badly damaged rather than their concrete casements or bunkers destroyed in the action. However, the Normandy campaign also saw the successful use of close-air support for Allied land forces, notably with the cab-rank system provided by the 2nd Tactical Air Force.[41]

At a strategic level, the transport capabilities of aircraft were seen in the Anglo-American delivery of nearly 650,000 tons of *matériel* from India over the "Hump," the eastern Himalayas, to the Nationalist forces fighting the Japanese in China in 1942–1945. This achievement represented an enormous development in air transport.[42] Another key capability was provided by aerial intelligence, which became crucial to Anglo-American operational planning.[43]

By late 1944, the American air assault on Japan itself was gathering pace. Initially, the American raids were long distance and unsupported by fighter cover, as fighter range was less than that of bombers. This situation led to attacks from a high altitude, which reduced their effectiveness. The raids that were launched were hindered by poor weather, especially strong tailwinds, and by difficulties with the B-29's reliability, as well as the general problems of precision bombing within the technology of the period.

From February 1945, there was a switch to low-altitude night-time area bombing of Japanese cities. The impact was devastating, not least because many Japanese dwellings were made of timber and paper and burned readily when bombarded with incendiaries, and also because population density in the cities was high. Fighters based on the recently conquered island of Iwo Jima (3 air hours from Tokyo) from April 7, 1945, could provide cover for the B-29s, which had been bombing Japan from bases on the more distant island of Saipan since November 1944. Carriers could not provide a base for planes of this size and air attacks of this scale. Thus, the dependence of technology on operations was abundantly shown, in the shape of the hard-fought American conquest of island bases: Saipan had been captured in the summer of 1944. Japan's overrunning in 1942 and 1944 of air bases in China that the Americans had hoped to use as an alternative was significant in shaping American strategy and the geopolitics of conflict that provided a context for the application of technology.

Weaknesses in Japanese anti-aircraft defenses, both planes and guns, eased the American task and made it possible to increase the payload of the B-29s by removing their guns. Although the Japanese had developed some impressive interceptor fighters, especially the Mitsubishi AbM5 and the Shiden, they were unable to produce many due to the impact of Allied air raids and of submarine attacks on supply routes, and they were also very short of pilots. In 1944–1945, American bombers destroyed over 30 percent of the buildings in Japan, including over half of the cities of Tokyo and Kobe. The deadliness of bombing was amply demonstrated.[44]

JET AIRCRAFT

In 1930, Frank Whittle, a British air force officer, patented the principles that led to the first gas turbine jet engine, which he first ran under control in 1937. His innovation was rapidly copied, and the Germans in 1939 and the Italians in 1940 beat the British jet into the air. The jet fighter, however, arrived in service too late to affect the course of the Second World War.

A similar point could be made about guided bombs and rockets, on both the Allied and Axis sides. Accuracy was a major problem for the guided weapons developed by both sides.[45] The Germans used Fritz-X radio-guided bombs against ships in the Mediterranean in 1943. Some were sunk, notably the Italian battleship *Roma* on the way to surrender to the Allies, while others suffered severe damage, but some bombs missed. The Germans also used the Henschel Hs293 radio-guided glider bomb quite successfully and sank up to seven ships with it. The Germans also employed these bombs against bridges in Normandy in August 1944, but less successfully.

In 1944, jets entered service: the British Meteor capable of 490 miles per hour/788 kilometers per hour, and the German Messerschmitt (Me) 262. The Allies found that the speed of the latter (540 mph/870 km) made it difficult to tackle. The tactics of the Me-262 posed serious problems for the Allies. It could seize the initiative effectively, diving at high speed through the Allied fighter screen and continuing under the bombers prior to climbing up in order to attack the bombers from behind. If, however, the Me-262 was involved in a dogfight, it was vulnerable, as it had a poor rate of turn. There were also efforts to catch it when even more vulnerable, on takeoff and particularly as it was coming in to land. The plane had slow acceleration.

Moreover, the Germans had insufficient numbers of the Me-262 to transform the course of the war, as they hoped they could do till near the war's close;[46] and the plane's late entry into the war was also significant, as was a shortage of trained pilots. The Germans had only focused production on the Me-262 after considerable delay, in part because Professor Messerschmitt was also keen to continue work on his projected Me-209, a conventional piston-engine plane. There was also separate work on other jet planes, the Arado Ar-234, which was designed as a jet bomber and reconnaissance aircraft, the Ju-287, a four-engine jet bomber, the Me-163 rocket plane, and the He-162.

Allied air raids also caused delays and problems, not least a shortage of fuel, exacerbating the serious difficulties in the German economy arising from poor organization and the mismatch of goals, systems, and resources. This mismatch was seen, for example, in the shortage of raw materials that led to problems with blade fractures in the turbine rotors and of fuel that limited the number of planes that could be put into service. Hence technology was dependent upon resources and fuel sources. This situation was a more serious problem than Hitler's views on the use of the plane, although these were significant. Only 564 Me-262s were built in 1944. Furthermore, the plane had problems, both with the engines and due to its inadequate rate of turn. Many were lost in accidents, in part due to poor reliability.

A problem with the early jets was the lack of thrust from the engines at low speeds, which made dog-fighting difficult. And if the throttle was applied too quickly at slow speed, there was a danger of flameout. This instance demonstrates the importance of engine technology (and materials technology) in the evolution of air power.

To a degree, Hitler squandered the German lead in jet-powered aircraft because of this preference that the Me-262 should not be used as an interceptor of Allied bombers, despite its effectiveness in the role, but rather as a high-speed bomber. Indeed, in June 1944, he ordered its name changed to *Blitzbomber*.[47] Interest in the use of the plane as a bomber led to delay. By the end of the war, 1,430 Me-262s had been built. The plane was subsequently manufactured in Czechoslovakia, where it served in the air force as the Avia S-92 until 1957.[48]

Jet aircraft developed rapidly after the Second World War. The first successful carrier landing of a jet aircraft took place on HMS *Ocean* in December 1945, while the Korean War (1950–1953) saw the first dogfights between jet aircraft. The Communist Chinese intervened in the war in 1950 in support of the North Koreans and against the American-led UN forces backing the South Koreans. The Communist Chinese had only created an air force in November 1949, and their Soviet-trained pilots lacked adequate experience and were equipped with out-of-date Soviet planes. However, the Communist forces were supported by the advanced MiG-15 fighters of the Manchurian-based Soviet "Group 64." Soviet aircraft operated over the Yalu River on the North Korea–China frontier from November 1, 1950.[49] The Soviets initially fought American Shooting Stars, Starfires, and others, and they were no match for the MiG-15, but the introduction of the American F-86 Sabre provided a slightly superior plane. The newer jets turned the balance one way and back again.

Organizational factors were important to American success over Korea, as the rotation system employed by the Soviet pilots greatly undermined their continuity of experience and thus effectiveness. The tactics of dog-fighting had to change because of the higher speeds of jets, which prevented the sort of dog-fighting seen in the Second World War. What had worked with piston engines could not be made to work with jets because of the higher speeds and g-forces when turning, although all the aircraft still used guns, not missiles. The Americans inflicted far heavier casualties in the air and were able to dominate the skies, with serious consequences for respective ground support, although the absence of adequate command integration limited the American exploitation of this advantage.

At the same time, the value of air support did not diminish the heavy American reliance on ground firepower in order to blunt Chinese attacks, and understandably so given the damage that could be inflicted by artillery as well as the problems bad weather created for aircraft. When James Van Fleet became commander of the American Eighth Army in Korea in 1951, he insisted on a greatly increased rate of artillery fire, including 300 rounds per day per 105 mm howitzer. In resisting the Chinese offensive from May 17 to 23, 1951, the twenty-one artillery battalions assigned to the Tenth Corps fired 309,958 rounds.[50]

The Chinese dictator Mao Zedong had been encouraged by success in the Chinese Civil War (1946–1949) to believe that the technological advantages, especially in air power, which the Americans enjoyed, could be countered, not least by determination. However, as had been the case with the Japanese in the Second World War, American resilience, resources, and fighting quality were underestimated by the Chinese. In the sole war between great powers since the Second World War, the Chinese advance, initially successful in driving the Americans from what became North Korea, was then repeatedly checked.

It was not until the introduction of reheat (the afterburner) in the early 1950s that supersonic flight became feasible. The afterburner adds fuel to the air that has already passed through the turbine and adds a huge amount of thrust very quickly. The afterburner can be switched on by the pilot when he needs extra thrust, a process known as running wet.

In the 1950s, jet fighter-bombers, such as the American F-84 Thunderjet, made their first appearance, and they came to play a major role, replacing more vulnerable Second World War period planes. The Americans also deployed long-range jet bombers (B-47s and B-52s), as well as jet tankers (KC-135s). Doctrine was molded by institutional need and politics as much as technology, notably with the emphasis on strategic nuclear bombing rather than close air support, a preference that suited the American air force.

The greater capability of jet aircraft, the extent of the area of operations, and the extent to which the United States did not wish to commit ground troops in much of it led to the enhanced use of air power in the Vietnam War, compared to that over Korea. Over half the $200 billion spent on the war, a sum far greater than that expended by other Western powers on decolonization struggles, went on air operations, and nearly eight million tons of bombs were dropped on Vietnam, Laos, and Cambodia. Indeed, South Vietnam, where the Americans were helping the South Vietnamese resist North Vietnamese and Viet Cong attacks, became the most heavily bombed country in the history of warfare. There were also major American bombing offensives against North Vietnam, which were designed to fulfill both operational and strategic goals: to limit Northern support for the war in the South, and to affect policy in the North by driving the North Vietnamese to negotiate. These goals were not fulfilled to the extent anticipated. In part, this failure may have been due to the limits placed on the bombing of the North, especially, in 1965–1968, the harbors, notably Haiphong, through which Soviet military assistance arrived; but the air war also raised more general questions about the effectiveness of bombing.

However, as in other conflicts, there was a learning curve, with increased effectiveness in the delivery of air power reflecting improved technique as well as weaponry. This was seen in 1972, both in the Linebacker bombing offensives against the North and in opposing the North Vietnamese Easter Offensive in the South. Greater effectiveness in 1972 owed something to bombing the North Vietnamese harbors but was also due to a marked improvement in American air capability that reflected both the displacement of earlier doctrine, in response to the varied needs of the Vietnam War, and the use of laser-guided bombs. The latter compensated for earlier limitations of accuracy in bombing caused by flying at high altitudes above deadly anti-aircraft fire.[51]

As with the tank, the bomber did not come into its own until the advent of smart munitions. When the Americans tried to hit bridges in Vietnam, they largely failed despite many raids. A single bomb, a Paveway I laser-guided bomb dropped by an F-4 Phantom on the mighty Thanh Hoa Bridge, a key link on the supply route from China, on April 27, 1972, achieved an effect that numerous sorties and tons of ordnance had failed to achieve earlier during Operation Rolling Thunder. The bridge was subsequently hit twice more with Paveways. Thus, irrespective of the skill of the pilots, the bomber was only as good as its ordnance. However, precision-guided munitions are much more expensive than unguided iron bombs.

As an instance of the competitive advance of technology, the Americans had used electronic jamming in order to limit attacks on their planes by missiles and radar-controlled guns, only for the North Vietnamese to aim at the jamming signals.[52] As a result, countermeasures aircraft were an essential element of any attacking force. The United States also benefited in 1972 from advances in ground-based radar technology, which helped in the direction of B-52 strikes.

The range of capabilities offered by technological advances and also of specifications required was further demonstrated by the greatly increased use of helicopters. They were important in supplying positions and in applying the doctrine of air mobility: airlifted troops, including the new 1st Cavalry Division Airmobile, brought mobility and helped take the war to the enemy. The Americans flew about 36,125,000 helicopter sorties during the war, including 7,547,000 assault sorties, in which machine guns and rockets were used, plus 3,932,000 attack sorties. Over 2,000 helicopters were lost to hostile causes (and many others to accidents), but heavier losses had been anticipated. Helicopters had become more reliable, more powerful, and faster than in the 1950s, and their use helped to overcome guerrilla challenges to land supply and communication routes.[53]

Air power became increasingly significant in the Vietnam War as unwillingness to suffer casualties and then a wish to limit and, finally, end the ground commitment led to an increase in efforts and research into means of removing the soldier from the battlefield. Alongside air power came developments such as scatter mines, submunitions, and camouflaged listening devices, as well as body armor and specialized munitions, such as flechettes. Air power did not lead to American victory, but it played a major role in preventing defeat in the 1960s and early 1970s. Moreover, air power provided the context in which a compromise peace could be negotiated. The absence of American air assistance in 1975 when a new North Vietnamese offensive conquered South Vietnam indicated the importance of air support, although the conquest also reflected the contrasts in fighting quality and determination between the combatants, as well as more specific flaws on the part of much of the South Vietnamese military leadership and officer corps.

Air power was also very important, and increasingly so, in the Arab-Israeli wars. This importance was clearly displayed in the Six Days War in 1967 when Israel mounted a preemptive attack on Egypt in order to deal with the growing aggression of its unpredictable ruler, Colonel Gamal Abdul Nasser. The Israeli assault began on June 5 with a surprise attack on the Egyptian air bases, launched by planes coming in over the Mediterranean from the west, in other words not the direction of Israel. The Egyptians, who had failed to take the most basic precautions in protecting their planes on the ground, lost 286 planes in just one morning. In addition, their runways were heavily bombed, which reduced their value to Egypt's remaining planes and also reduced the usefulness of these planes. Nasser falsely claimed that the Americans and British had been responsible for the air assault.

Gaining air superiority rapidly proved crucial to the subsequent land conflict, as Egyptian ground forces were badly affected by Israeli ground-support attacks. Jordan joined in that day on the Egyptian side, only to have its air force destroyed by the Israelis, and the West Bank was subsequently overrun by them, their ground forces benefiting greatly from air superiority. The same fate affected Syria, with the Golan Heights overrun. The Israelis benefited greatly from the sequential nature of their campaigning, notably being able to focus first on Egypt.[54]

Air power proved important anew when large-scale conflict resumed in 1973 in the Yom Kippur War. In 1968, the United States had decided to provide Israel with F-4 Phantom jets, an important step in the definition of the Arab-Israeli struggle in terms of the Cold War. Nevertheless, in 1973, Israel's air power was badly affected by the Egyptian use of effective Soviet anti-aircraft missiles. However, once the Egyptian armor had advanced beyond the range and cover of supporting fire, it was badly mauled, and the Israelis eventually prevailed both in the air and on the ground.

In 1978, Israel advanced into southern Lebanon in an attack on the Palestine Liberation Organization. In this operation, the Israeli advance benefited from close air support. In 1982, Lebanon was invaded anew, the Israelis gaining the advantage over the rival Syrians who were established there. Again, air power proved important. The Syrians initially fought well, but, once their missile batteries in Lebanon had been knocked out and their air force badly pummeled by Israeli aircraft armed

with American Sidewinder missiles and supported by electronic countermeasures, the Syrians proved vulnerable to Israeli attack, now bol-
stered by clear mastery in the air.[55] The enhanced capabilities of anti-
aircraft weapons ironically also made them more vulnerable to such
electronic countermeasures, which was an instance of the limitations
of more sophisticated weaponry.

The Sidewinder illustrated the development of weapon types. The
AIM-9L was the first "all-aspects" variant of the Sidewinder. It could
be fired head-on, which opponents were unprepared for. Previous variants had to chase the target, and therefore had to be fired from behind
it. All-aspects capability was a considerable technological advantage
in aerial combat. First used in combat by the Americans against two
Libyan-flown Soviet-made SU-22s in 1981, this version was employed in
the Falklands War of 1982, where it had an approximately 80 percent kill
rate and was responsible for shooting down seventeen Argentine planes.
Previous variants had a kill rate of only 10–15 percent.

Israeli air (and tank) power proved less effective in Lebanon in 2006
than in 1982. Air operations were unable to end rocket attacks on Israel, including on the major city of Haifa, attacks that led many Israeli
civilians to move south temporarily. About five thousand rockets were
fired by Hezbollah, dramatically confounding Israel's capacity for deterrence, a capacity that was an intended consequence of military superiority. However, a large percentage of the long-range Hezbollah rocket
systems were destroyed in 2006. In a wider strategic perspective, Iran
appears to see Hezbollah's strength in Lebanon as a deterrent to Israeli
air action against Iran's nuclear program, which is a reminder of the potentially interacting character of different military capabilities, and notably so in the case of deterrence.[56]

Jet aircraft also enhanced the auxiliary functions of air power, supply, and reinforcement. Air power could be used to move large numbers of troops overseas more rapidly than ships. In response to disorder
in the Dominican Republic in the West Indies in the spring of 1965, the
United States airlifted 23,000 troops in less than 2 weeks. Considerable
Soviet airlift capacity, in turn, was demonstrated in resupplying Egypt
and Syria during the Yom Kippur War, and in Angola in 1975, helping to
thwart a takeover by pro-Western forces. Airlift was very significant in
supporting pro-Soviet Cuban intervention in Africa: in Angola, Ethio-

pia, and elsewhere. Indeed, the Caribbean island of Grenada acquired strategic significance as a result of the development of its airport by the Cubans as an airlift base, and concern about this capability helped explain American invasion in 1983. Soviet airlift capacity increased in the 1970s, with the development of long-range heavy-lift transport aircraft and an increase in the number of transport planes to 600 by 1984.[57]

Due in part to airlift, airports became key points of operational importance, and seizing control of them became a crucial goal in coup attempts. Soviet troops were flown into Czech airports on the night of August 20–21, 1968, when the Czech government was overthrown thanks to a Soviet-led invasion, most of which was mounted by land. The Antonov transport aircraft that were used in 1968 were able to move tanks as well as troops.

The effectiveness of air power, however, was a matter of contention. The defeats of Iraq in 1991 and 2003 were seen as, in large part, triumphs for American air power and concepts of air power. Iraqi air defenses were rapidly overcome and effective support was then provided for ground operations. Stealth and precision were characteristics of air attacks that overcame the entire Iraqi air-defense system. Technology played a major role, both with enhanced weaponry and with the use of precision-guided munitions. Thermal-imaging laser-designation systems guided bombs to their targets, and pilots launched bombs into the "cone" of the laser beam in order to score a direct hit.[58]

However, in 1999, the effectiveness of the major NATO (North Atlantic Treaty Organization) air assault on Serbia that was designed to achieve a Serbian withdrawal from Kosovo was called into question. This assault suffered the loss of only two aircraft, but the subsequent Serbian withdrawal from Kosovo revealed that NATO estimates of the damage inflicted by air attack, for example, to Serb tanks, had been considerably exaggerated. Benefiting from the limitations of Allied intelligence information and its serious consequences for Allied targeting, and from the severe impact of the weather on air operations (a large number cancelled or affected), the Serbs, employing simple and inexpensive camouflage techniques that took advantage of terrain and wooded cover, preserved most of their equipment, despite ten thousand NATO strike sorties.

The NATO operations in Serbia highlighted several serious problems with sophisticated technological weapon systems. Not the least of these is the unrealistic expectation among the public, and also among part of the military, for every operation to be conducted "clinically" and with near 100 percent success. Aside from the point that nothing is 100 percent reliable, there is the issue of the decline of reliability with complexity. Human error, the weather, and the actions of the enemy, the last a major factor often ignored by the press, the public, and even the military, all affect outcomes. Moreover, there is the problem that failure is not always understood in terms of the decisive cause of it. In addition, unfulfilled expectations lead to false conclusions. As far as 1999 was concerned, the Serbs were very canny, while NATO was often deprived of that most essential ingredient for success, good intelligence. The lack of success in hitting Serb tanks showed the importance of having special forces on the ground to light up targets with lasers, although bad weather would still have been a factor.

The air assault in 1999 also revealed the contrast between output (bomb and missile damage) and outcome: the air offensive did not prevent the large-scale expulsion of Kosovar civilians from their homes by the Serbs, and this expulsion actually increased as the air attack mounted. The eventual Serb withdrawal may have been due more to a conviction, based in part on Russian information, that a NATO land attack was imminent. The crisis indeed suggested that air power would be most effective as part of a joint strategy, as with the NATO intervention in Libya in 2011, although in Libya the situation on the ground was more propitious than in Kosovo in 1999. Although the damage to the Serbian army from air attack was limited, the devastation of Serbia's infrastructure, in the shape of bridges, factories, and electrical power plants, was important, not least because it affected the financial interests of the elite as well as their morale and the functioning of the economy. Thus, there was a marked contrast between the limited tactical, and possibly more effective strategic, impact of air power.[59] Success lay in hitting the infrastructure rather than the military.

American air power also played a major role in Afghanistan in the overthrow of the Taliban regime in 2001. The air attack helped switch the local political balance within Afghanistan. Impact analysis, however, revealed that bombing was subsequently less effective in support of the ground operations near Tora Bora in December 2001 and in Operation Anaconda, east of Gardez the following March. This decline in effectiveness was attributed to the Taliban ability by the time of the Tora Bora campaign to grasp the relevant parameters of air power and to respond by taking advantage of terrain features that could be used for camouflage and cover. The differences between effort, output, and outcome were amply demonstrated in Afghanistan,[60] although the Americans had greater air effectiveness than the Soviets had done in Afghanistan after the introduction of Stinger mobile surface-to-air missiles in 1996. These missiles limited the freedom of the Soviet Mi-24 helicopter gunships.[61]

In 2003, against Iraq, the Americans made particular use of JDAMs (joint direct attack munitions), which used GPSs (global positioning systems) to convert dumb bombs into smart munitions. This bolt-on guidance package is superior to infrared and laser guidance systems, which can be disrupted by poor weather conditions. JDAMs are not affected by poor visibility or bad weather. An upgrade that included a terminal laser guidance system enabled the bomb to hit a moving target. This system was first used on operations over Iraq in 2008.

Air power is seen as having a clear role in counterinsurgency (COIN) warfare. It constrains opponents' freedom of maneuver and options, and thus plays a part in shaping the battle space.[62] In 1994, the Mexican Armed Forces used helicopter gunships and rocket-equipped aircraft to support their successful attempt to retake the towns seized in the Zapatista guerrilla uprising in the province of Chiapas.[63]

ATOMIC BOMBS

The Second World War was brought to a rapid close in 1945 when the dropping of two atomic bombs by the Americans demonstrated that Japanese forces could not protect the homeland. At the Potsdam Conference, the Allies had issued the Potsdam Declaration, on the evening of July 26, demanding unconditional surrender as well as the occupation of Japan, Japan's loss of its extensive overseas possessions, and the establishment of democracy in the country. The alternative threatened was "prompt and utter destruction," but, on July 27, the Japanese government decided to ignore the declaration. Atom bombs were dropped on Hiroshima and Nagasaki on August 6 and 9, respectively. This devastation and the revelation of total vulnerability transformed the situation, leading the Japanese, on August 14, to agree to surrender unconditionally, although that decision also owed something to Soviet entry into the war on August 8, invading Japanese-occupied Manchuria, which removed any chance that the Soviets would act as mediators for a peace on more generous terms.

The creation of the atomic bomb was the culmination of an intense period of rivalry between the powers in conception and application. That the atomic bomb was created in the United States was indicative not only of the intellectual resources available to it but also of the nature and scale of activity possible for an advanced industrial society. It was the product not only of the application of science but also of the powerful industrial and technological capability of the United States and the willingness to spend about $1.9 billion in rapidly creating a large new industry, a sum that is far larger in current values.[64] The electromagnets needed for isotope separation were particularly expensive and required 13,500 tons of silver. Major industrial concerns were able to apply their expertise, resources, and manufacturing techniques to participate in the Manhattan Project to make the bombs, the chemical company DuPont producing the necessary plutonium. The American belief in the certainty of improvement through technological progress played a significant cultural role in encouraging support.[65]

The Germans and Japanese were both interested in developing an atomic bomb, but neither made comparable progress. The *Uranverein,* the German plan to acquire nuclear capability, was not adequately pursued, in part because the Germans thought it would take too long to develop. The German conviction that the war would, or could, be finished long before the bomb would be ready was encouraged by their numerous military successes in 1939–1941, but it was an instance of overconfidence adversely affecting the development of new technologies. The Germans were also affected by hostility to what the Nazis termed "Jewish physics," as well as the consequences of overestimating the amount of U-235 required to manufacture a bomb.[66]

In some respects, the use of atomic weaponry suggested the obsolescence, and indeed limitations, of recent military practices. More people
were killed in the American conventional bombing of Japan earlier in
1945—the firebombing of Tokyo alone on March 10, the first major low-
level raid on the city, killing more than 83,000 people in one night—
but that campaign required far more planes and raids: on March 10, 334
B-29s were sent, of which 14 were lost.[67] Indeed, the use of atom bombs,
like, at a far more modest level, that of jet aircraft by the Germans in the
closing stages of the war in Europe, pointed the way toward a capability
for war in which far fewer units were able to wield far more power. This
situation is especially relevant for symmetrical warfare.

At the same time, the new use of atomic weaponry in 1945 reflected
not the limited capacity of preexisting forms of warfare but the extent
to which they had created a military environment in which, in the event
of determined conflict between major powers, success was almost too
costly, while failure definitely was. In short, a form of total warfare existed that would, it was hoped, now be short-circuited by modern warfare in the shape of the atomic bomb, the latter a logical consequence of
strategic bombing doctrine. The heavy Japanese and American losses
suffered from campaigning in Iwo Jima, Okinawa, and Luzon earlier in
1945 suggested that an Allied invasion of Japan, in the face of a suicidal
determination to fight on, would be very costly. The Japanese homeland
army was poorly trained and equipped and lacked mobility and air support, but, fighting on the defensive, it would have the capacity to cause
heavy casualties, particularly as it was unclear how to obtain the unconditional surrender that was an Allied war goal. General Douglas MacAr-
thur remarked in April 1945 that his troops had not yet met the Japanese
army properly, and that, when they did, they were going to take heavy
casualties.[68]

A rapid and complete victory seemed essential in order to force Japan
to accept terms that would neutralize its threat to its neighbors. In addition, it was necessary to secure the surrender of the large Japanese forces
in China and Southeast Asia. The dropping of the atom bombs showed
that the Japanese armed forces could not protect the nation, and it was
therefore a major public blow to Japanese militarists. A statement issued

on behalf of President Harry Truman shortly after the first atomic bomb was dropped on Hiroshima declared,

> Hardly less marvelous has been the capacity of industry to design, and of labor to operate, the machines and methods to do things never done before, so that the brain child of many minds came forth in physical shape and performed as it was supposed to do. . . . It was to spare the Japanese people from utter destruction that the ultimatum was issued at Potsdam. Their leaders promptly rejected that ultimatum. If they do not now accept our terms they may expect a rain of ruin from the air. . . . We are now prepared to obliterate more rapidly and completely every productive enterprise the Japanese have above ground in any city. We shall destroy their docks, their factories, and their communications. Let there be no mistake; we shall completely destroy Japan's power to make war.

Critics of American policy claim that the dropping of the bombs represented an early stage in the Cold War, with their use designed to obtain peace on American terms and both to show the Soviet Union the extent of American strength—in particular a vital counter to Soviet numbers on land—and to ensure that Japan could be defeated without the Soviets playing a major role. These goals may have been factors, but there seems little doubt that the prime use of the bombs was to avoid a costly invasion. Truman wrote on August 9, "My object is to save as many American lives as possible, but I also have a human feeling for the women and children of Japan."[69]

Had the war lasted until 1946, the destruction of the rail system by American bombing would have led to famine, as it would have been impossible to move food supplies. There were already systematic American bombing attacks on Japanese marshalling yards and bridges. One important technological advance of the nineteenth century, the railway, was now newly vulnerable to a weapons system that was not conceived of then. There would also have been more deliberate large-scale bombing attacks on the cities. Aside from the raid on Tokyo on March 10, 1945, there had been heavy raids on April 13 and 19 and May 23 and 25.[70] Similarly, there were heavy raids on Nagoya on March 12 and 20 and May 14 and 16. The Japanese anticipated the loss of twenty million citizens if an invasion was mounted. The dropping of the second atomic bomb suggested that such losses could be inflicted without the Americans taking any casualties themselves. The apparently inexorable process of destruction seen with the dropping of this bomb on Nagasaki had a greater impact on Japanese opinion than the use of the first atomic bomb. The limited American ability to deploy more bombs speedily was not appreciated.[71]

Beliefs in inevitable security, inherent exceptionalism, and technological utopianism all underlay the Americans' sense that they alone should have the bomb.[72] In January 1946, Major-General Leslie Groves, the head of the atomic bomb project, warned, "Either we must have a hard-boiled, realistic, enforceable, world-agreement ensuring the outlawing of atomic weapons or we and our dependable allies must have an exclusive supremacy in the field, which means that no other nation can be permitted to have atomic weapons."[73] However, America's nuclear monopoly, which appeared to offer a means to coerce the Soviet Union without being fully mobilized, lasted only until 1949.

Then, thanks in part to successful spying on Western nuclear technology, the Soviet Union revealed its development of an effective bomb that was very similar to the American one. This development had required a formidable effort, as the Soviet Union was devastated by the impact of the Second World War, and it was pursued because Joseph Stalin, the Soviet dictator, believed that only a position of nuclear equivalence would permit the Soviet Union to protect and advance its interests. Nevertheless, such a policy was seriously harmful to the Soviet economy, as it led to the distortion of research and investment choices, and militarily questionable, as resources were used that might otherwise have been employed to develop conventional capability.

Even when the United States alone had the bomb, however, the value of the weapon was limited, as it was insufficiently flexible (in terms of military and political application or acceptance of its use) to meet challenges other than that of full-scale war. Thus, the United States did not use the atom bomb (of which they then indeed had very few) to help their Nationalist Chinese allies in the Chinese Civil War (1946–1949), and their allies lost. Similarly, American possession of the bomb did not deter the Soviets from intimidating the West during the Berlin Crisis of 1948–1949.

Nevertheless, the availability of the bomb in the late 1940s encouraged American reliance on a nuclear deterrent, which made it possible to hasten demobilization after the Second World War and to focus on the U.S. Air Force (which was created in 1947), leaving the United States more vulnerable when the Korean War (1950–1953) broke out.[74] For example, there was a grave shortage of artillery units in 1950, while Strafford Barff, the director of British Information Services in Chicago, noted on July 31, 1950, "The inadequacy of American arms and reported inefficiency of some officers and men have come as a great shock."[75]

In this conflict, the American government decided in 1950 not to drop atomic bombs. Instead, the war was fought with a strengthened conventional military, although, in 1953, the use of the atom bomb was threatened by the United States in order to secure an end to the conflict, which indeed occurred.[76]

This outcome encouraged the view that nuclear strategy had a major role to play in future confrontations, as indeed did the cost of fighting the Korean War, in which the advance of Chinese forces had inflicted considerable damage on American forces in early 1951, and the extent to which the conflict had revealed deficiencies in the American military. The war caused a revival in the American army but also led to its growing concern with readiness. Meanwhile, as the NATO countries were unable to match the build-up their military planners called for, there was a greater emphasis, especially from 1952, on the possibilities of nuclear weaponry, both as a deterrent and, in the event of war, as a counterweight to Soviet conventional superiority. The extent to which British and French forces were committed to resisting decolonization struggles, notably the French in Indo-China (and, from 1954, Algeria) and the British in Malaya, contributed to NATO's weakness in western Europe.

The need to respond to Soviet conventional superiority on land and in the air also encouraged an interest both in tactical nuclear weaponry and in the atom bomb as a weapon of first resort. The tactical nuclear weapons that were developed, such as the recoilless Davy Crockett spigot gun, which had a range of 1.25 miles (120 mm M28) and 2.5 miles (155 mm M29), were treated as a form of field artillery. Ground-launched nuclear missiles were intended for a range of targets, including bringing down Soviet bombers.[77] The British followed the Americans, with the army establishing in 1957 its first surface-to-surface missile regiment. This was equipped with Corporal missiles, a tactical nuclear delivery system capable of delivering a 20-kiloton nuclear warhead over a range of 50–80 miles. Its guidance system, however, proved unreliable.

The need to deal with Soviet numerical superiority also led to the development of non-nuclear weapon systems. These included multiple targeting with air-to-air missiles, high first-shot capabilities with tanks, and the sort of munitions that there is now pressure to ban. Although these technological approaches were not initially very successful, the systems became much more effective, but at huge cost.

The use of the atomic arsenal as weapons of first-strike or resort (in other words without prior opposing use) was pushed by Dwight Eisenhower, NATO's first Supreme Allied Commander from 1950 until 1952 and U.S. president from 1953 until 1961. Aware of NATO's vulnerability, he felt that strength must underpin diplomacy for it to be credible. As president, Eisenhower's New Look emphasized strategic air power and downgraded conventional ground forces, much to the anger of the generals.[78] The number of divisions in the army fell from eighteen in June 1956 to fourteen by that December. In December 1955, the NATO Council authorized the employment of atomic weaponry against the Warsaw Pact, even if the latter did not use such weaponry. The American nuclear stockpile rose from 369 weapons in 1950 to over 27,000 by 1962.

Planning the use of such weapons, and how to respond to that by the Soviets, encouraged a modeling of military options, not least employing the new laboratory and computer systems of MIT (the Massachusetts Institute of Technology) and RAND. This modeling, employing calculations that could not be made by the brain, was an important instance of the impact of technological development on the context within which new weapons were assessed. The manufacturing and use of weapons had to be discussed in terms of such systems. Quantitative analysis came to play a major role, both in assessing effectiveness and in seeking to control the all-important issue of financial costs.[79] The revolutionary prospect of Armageddon held out by nuclear warfare[80] encouraged planning and prediction through modeling.

The Cold War following so speedily on the Second World War helped ensure that the large-scale mobilization of science for military ends, which began in the First World War and was very prominent in the Second, was sustained. The institutionalization of government direction of, and support for, scientific research encouraged this process, which, in turn, contributed to a conviction of continual technological change.[81] Research, and even more its use, was scarcely value-free. For example, there was an emphasis on the need for unlimited testing of nuclear weaponry and on the difficulties of implementing any test ban.[82]

More generally, technological advances changed the nature of the skill-base. Thanks to weaponry in which machinery played a major role—for example, complex automatic systems for sighting—skill, rather than physical strength, became even more important for soldiering. Moreover, the industrial-age mass production that had been so significant in the world wars was replaced by technological superiority as a central factor in weaponry, and therefore in the economic capability of military powers.

As a key instance of the application of new knowledge, computers, from the 1960s, transformed operational horizons and command and control options. The American Defense Advanced Research Projects Agency took major steps to enhance computing, contributing in the process to the eventual creation of the internet. It also developed a Strategic Computing Initiative that was responsible for advances in technologies such as computer vision and recognition and the parallel processing useful for code-breaking. Code-breaking required the capacity rapidly to test very large numbers of possible combinations.[83] Such technological advances were more effective because they were grounded in earlier organizational developments.[84] The British military was also important in the development of computing. Wartime code-breaking was followed in the United States and Britain by the use of computers in fire-control systems, for example, naval defense against air attack.[85] Military institutions and research were important to other branches of the economy, being central, for example, to technological developments and application in communications.

Effective in heavy industry, although the many tanks produced had pretty crude driving mechanisms by Western standards, the Soviet Union failed to match such advances in electronics. Moreover, the shift in weaponry from traditional engineering to electronics, alongside the development of control systems dependent on the latter, saw a clear correlation between technology, industrial capacity, and military capability. The Soviet Union fell behind militarily, and notably in the 1980s in response to what has been seen as an "information technology revolution."[86] This growing gap with American capability contributed to a Soviet sense of failure that led to pressure for a new politico-economic system, pressure that unwittingly contributed to the unraveling of the Soviet Union by Mikhail Gorbachev, who came to power there in 1985.

Meanwhile, as a reminder of the variety of uses of technology, nuclear power was developed not only as a form of ordnance but also as a means of propulsion. Indeed, it became the key means for powering large aircraft carriers, from the USS *Enterprise,* and submarines. Only nuclear-powered submarines can remain submerged indefinitely. Diesel submarines have to surface to recharge their batteries.

BALLISTIC MISSILES

Dropped from planes in 1945, the potential of atomic weaponry was swiftly to be transformed by the development of ballistic missiles. In 1957, the Soviet Union launched Sputnik I, the first satellite to go into orbit. The launch revealed a capability for intercontinental rockets that brought the entire world within rapid striking range, and thus made the United States vulnerable to Soviet attack, both from first-strike and from counterstrike. Missiles created a vulnerability that had been far weaker in the case of manned bombers. Satellites also offered other capabilities, being used for reconnaissance from 1961 and for communications from 1965.

The development of ablative shields, made from composites, some of them similar to those used in armor, was important to the success of intercontinental ballistic rockets. Many test firings of the German V-2 had proved unsuccessful because the rocket broke up on reentry, and, although the cause was never conclusively determined, it was probably a combination of instability, vibration, pressure, and heat. It was not until the 1950s that the ablative heat shield was devised because of the need to protect a nuclear warhead from burning up in the atmosphere when it reentered. Such a shield works in a complex way; part of the process makes use of the high temperatures on reentry so that the resin in the outer layer is turned to gas by the heat and the heated gas is carried away.

In strategic terms, rockets threatened to give effect to the doctrine of air power as a war-winning tool advanced in the 1920s and 1930s, at the same time as their greater speed and range, and lower vulnerability, rendered obsolescent the nuclear capability of the bombers of the American Strategic Air Command, particularly the B-52s deployed in 1955. Thus, the American lead had been leapfrogged,[87] rather as French shell guns and ironclads had threatened to do to the British Royal Navy in the 1830s—1850s (see chapter 3). The development of intercontinental missiles altered the parameters of vulnerability for civil society and ensured that space was more than ever seen in terms of straight lines between launching site and target. Nikita Khrushchev, the Soviet leader, declared in August 1961 that as the Soviet Union had placed Gagarin and Titov in space, they could be replaced with bombs that could be diverted to any place on Earth.

The threat to the United States from Soviet attack was highlighted by the November 1957 secret report from the American Gaither Committee. On January 18, 1960, Allen Dulles, the director of the CIA, told the Senate Foreign Relations Committee that "one of the key facts behind Soviet diplomacy lies in their view of their increasing power in the military field, particularly missiles."[88] The strategic possibilities offered by nuclear-tipped long-range ballistic missiles made investment in expensive rocket technology seem an essential course of action, since they could go so much faster than airplanes and, unlike them, could not be shot down.[89] Sputnik also appeared to prove Soviet claims that they were overtaking the Americans in technological capability, which contributed to a sense of crisis in the United States in the late 1950s.

The United States had also been developing long-range ballistic missiles, using captured German V-2 scientists, particularly Wernher von Braun and many of his team from the research and testing station at Peenemünde, and the Americans fired their first intercontinental ballistic missile (ICBM) in 1958. The attempt to give force to the notion of massive nuclear retaliation entailed replacing vulnerable manned bombers with less vulnerable submarines equipped with ballistic missiles and also with land rockets based in reinforced silos. In July 1960, off Cape Canaveral (subsequently Cape Kennedy), the American submarine USS *George Washington* was responsible for the first successful underwater firing of a Polaris missile. In February 1962, the Soviet R-21 missile followed suit. Meanwhile, in 1961, the Americans commissioned the USS *Ethan Allen*, the first true fleet missile submarine.

Submarines could be based near the coast of target states and were highly mobile and hard to detect. They represented a major shift in force structure, away from the U.S. Air Force and toward the Navy, which argued that its invulnerable submarines could launch carefully controlled strikes, permitting a more sophisticated management of deterrence and retaliation, an argument that was also to be made by the British navy.

Other states followed the United States into submarine-launched ballistic missiles. In 1962, in what became known as the Nassau Agreement, John F. Kennedy, the American president, and Harold Macmillan, the British prime minister, decided that the Americans would provide Polaris missiles for a class of four large nuclear-powered British submarines that were to be built, although American agreement was dependent on the British force being primarily allocated for NATO duties. In 1968, the first British Polaris test missile was fired from HMS *Resolution*, the British navy's first nuclear-powered ballistic missile submarine, which had been laid down in 1964. Polaris remained in service until 1995, being succeeded by Trident. Also benefiting from the transfer of American nuclear technology, the French commissioned their first ballistic missile submarine in 1969.[90]

The effect of the destructive potential of intercontinental nuclear weaponry was unclear, which increased the significance of this weaponry. It served to enhance the possibility of a nuclear war, by increasing interest both in defining a sphere for tactical nuclear weapons and in planning an effective strategic nuclear first-strike. However, there was also an inhibiting effect, lessening the chance of a great power war, or increasing the probability that such a conflict would be essentially conventional. The risk of nuclear destructiveness made it important to prevent escalation to full-scale war and thus encouraged interest in defining forms of warfare that could exist short of such escalation.

In the early 1960s, U.S. concern about the nuclear balance increased. Kennedy had fought the 1960 presidential election in part on the platform that the Republican administration under Eisenhower had failed to maintain America's defenses. Eisenhower's vice president, Richard Nixon, was the Republicans' unsuccessful candidate. Kennedy aimed for a strategic superiority over the Soviet Union and increased defense spending accordingly.

Concern about missiles rose to a peak during the Cuba crisis of 1962, when the Soviet Union deployed them in Cuba. These missiles had a range of 1,040 nautical miles, which made Washington a potential target. The Soviet intention was to guarantee Cuba from American attack and thus protect a newly significant protégé, but the deployment of missiles also shifted the balance of terror between the United States and the Soviet Union in the Soviets' favor. In October, the United States imposed an air and naval quarantine to prevent the shipping of further Soviet supplies, prepared for an attack on Cuba, and threatened a full retaliatory nuclear strike. The Cuban leaders, Fidel Castro and Che Guevara, wanted a nuclear war, which they saw as a way to forward world socialism. However, the Soviet Union climbed down, withdrawing its missiles, while the United States withdrew its Jupiter missiles (which carried nuclear warheads) from Turkey and agreed not to invade Cuba. Possibly the threat of nuclear war encouraged the United States and the Soviets to caution, although both sides had come close to hostilities.[91]

In the 1960s, both the United States and the Soviet Union built up their missile forces. However, in 1965, Robert McNamara, the U.S. secretary of defense, felt able to state that the United States could rely on the threat of "assured destruction" to deter a Soviet assault. Thanks in part to submarines, a dispersed weapons system, there would be enough missiles to provide an American counterstrike in the event of the Soviets launching a surprise first-strike and inflicting considerable damage on the American mainland. Nuclear warfare appeared to promise mutually assured destruction (MAD), as submarines could not be found easily and the missiles from each side would theoretically cross in flight.

The logic of deterrence, however, required matching any advances in the techniques of nuclear weaponry, and this was one of the most intense aspects of the Cold War. The evolution of missiles involved developments in detection and countermeasures, but there was also the evolution of rocket motors, of the materials from which the motor casing is made—wire-wound composites, and of the composition and use of the fuel. For example, in 1970, the United States deployed Minuteman III missiles equipped with multiple independently targeted reentry vehicles (MIRVs), thus ensuring that the strike capacity of an individual rocket was greatly enhanced. This meant that any American strike or counterstrike would be more effective. The United States also cut the response time of their land-based intercontinental missiles by developing the Titan II, which had storable liquid propellants enabling in-silo launches, which reduced the launch time.[92] The precision of guidance systems moreover was increased as was information for targeting.

Meanwhile, the destructive power of nuclear weapons had increased when the atomic bomb was followed by the hydrogen bomb. The latter employed a nuclear explosion to fuse atoms together, a transformation that released an enormous amount of destructive energy. Work on this bomb had been carried on unsuccessfully during the Second World War but was stepped up after the Soviet atomic test of August 1949, as the Americans sought to reconfirm their nuclear superiority. The American hydrogen device was first tested on November 1, 1952, producing an explosive yield of 10 megatons. As this device had not been weaponized, it was not really a bomb or what was soon called a superbomb, but this development followed swiftly. In less than a decade, the destructive force released in 1945 had been made to seem limited. Whereas the bomb dropped on Hiroshima had 13.5 kilotons of TNT equivalent, the United States in 1954 tested one with 15 megatons of TNT equivalent, over a thousand times more powerful.

Alongside a level of lethality that proved difficult to comprehend came a rapid closure of the capability gap, and one that was speedier than in the case of the atom bomb. The Soviet Union tested an intermediate type of hydrogen bomb in August 1953, and in November 1955 conducted a test showing it possessed the knowledge to build a hydrogen bomb. Britain followed in 1957, China in 1967, and France in 1968.[93] These weapons, however, were not followed by the cobalt bomb, mentioned in 1950 by Leo Szilard, a prominent nuclear physicist. This was to bring life on Earth to an end by covering the planet with radioactive particles.

The American nuclear position in the 1970s was challenged by the Soviet response, part of the action-reaction cycle that was so important to the missile race. The Soviets made major advances in the development of land-based intercontinental missiles, producing a situation in which war was seen as likely to lead to MAD, as both sides appeared to have a secure second-strike capability. Since the end of the Cold War, declassified Warsaw Pact documents have revealed that in the 1970s the Soviets planned a large-scale use of nuclear and chemical weapons at the outset of any attack on western Europe. In 1977, the Soviets deployed SS-20 missiles. Mobile, accurate, and armed with nuclear warheads, they were designed to be used in conjunction with conventional forces in an invasion of western Europe. Moreover, in an interview published in the *New York Times* of February 25, 1998, Kanatjan Alibekov, an official in the program, revealed that the Soviet Union had prepared anthrax, smallpox, and plague virus cultures for delivery by intercontinental ballistic missiles.[94]

Concern about attack by ballistic missiles led to American interest in a "Star Wars" program, the Strategic Defense Initiative (SDI). Outlined by President Reagan in a speech on March 23, 1983, this program was designed to enable the Americans to dominate space, using space-mounted weapons to destroy Soviet satellites and missiles, and thus overthrow the balance of terror between the United States and the Soviet Union. Subsequently, these ideas were to be applied in considering how best to challenge other states with long-range missiles, particularly North Korea. The ability to use such weaponry effectively was (and is), however, unclear. This was especially so because of the possible use by opponents of devices and techniques to confuse interceptor missiles.

The rise to power in the Soviet Union in March 1985 of Mikhail Gorbachev, a leader committed to reform at home and good relations abroad, greatly defused tension. Although he supported the army in claiming that the American SDI could somehow be countered,[95] Gorbachev was willing to challenge the confrontational worldview outlined in KGB reports. For example, he was convinced that American policy on arms control was not motivated by a hidden agenda of weakening the Soviet Union, and this conviction encouraged him to negotiate. Moreover, the cost of the Soviet military was a heavy burden on the economy, lessening the possibilities of growth and of winning popular support. The arms race reflected the advantage the West enjoyed in electronic engineering, as well as higher economic growth rates and more flexible economic and organizational processes than those in the Soviet Union. The

Western prohibition on the export of advanced technology was also significant, and in 1974 the United States banned the export of powerful computers to the Soviet Union and its allies.

For long, the Soviet belief in the apparently inevitably insoluble contradictions of Western capitalism ensured that they failed to appreciate the mounting crises their economy, society, and political system were facing. However, the situation changed under Gorbachev. In December 1987, the Soviet government signed the Intermediate Nuclear Forces Treaty, which, in ending intermediate land-based missiles, forced heavier cuts on the Soviets, while also setting up a system of verification through on-site inspection. As a reminder of the political consequences of weaponry, this agreement helped push the German question to the fore as West Germany was the base and target for short-range missiles. In July 1991, START 1 led to a major fall in the number of American and Soviet strategic nuclear warheads.[96]

At the same time, existing missiles were enhanced. The American Trident II D-5 sea-launched missile, deployed from 1990, was more accurate than earlier missiles, while the ability to use the W-88 warhead with the missile increased explosive yield.[97] Alongside developments in "conventional" nuclear warheads, there was also investigation of the prospect for different warheads. One pursued by the Americans, largely in a theoretical fashion, was the hafnium bomb, which was seen as a way to produce a flood of high-energy gamma radiation. As the release of energy from the nuclei does not involve nuclear fission or fusion, such a bomb would not be defined as a nuclear weapon. So far, however, such research has not led to practical applications.

More generally, understandably concerned about the acquisition of weapons of mass destruction by "rogue states" such as North Korea[98] and Iran, the Americans seek a technological means to ensure security, a difficult goal at the best of times. Research is encouraged by particular tasks. Thus, the construction of underground plants for manufacturing and storing weaponry and related material, notably uranium-enrichment plants in Iran, led to the development of bunker-busting bombs, although the likely effectiveness of the latter remained unclear, not least because of advanced Iranian research on stronger concrete. Sensitivity to the use of atomic weaponry resulted in a commitment to more lethal non-nuclear weaponry.

CRUISE MISSILES

Cruise missiles provided a key gain in military capability from the 1980s and were important to military planning in the last stage of the Cold War and to post—Cold War warfare. These unmanned missiles were valuable because they could deliver precise firepower without the risks, costs, and limitations associated with air power. In their planning for conflict with the Soviet Union in the 1980s, the United States intended to respond to any attack by using cruise missiles to inflict heavy damage on Soviet armor advancing across West Germany. These missiles can carry conventional warheads or use tactical nuclear weaponry. They can be fired in all weathers and can be launched from a variety of platforms. The Soviet Union also developed such weaponry.

Tactical nuclear warheads were not used, but, in the Gulf War of 1991, cruise missiles and precision-guided bombs were employed by the United States to provide precise bombardment. At that stage, cruise weaponry had a crucial advantage over air power due to the extent to which American planes still did not use precision-guided munitions: 9,300 precision-guided munitions were dropped in that war, but most of their aircraft were not equipped, nor their pilots trained, for their use and, instead, employed unguided munitions, which made up 90 percent of the aerial munitions used. Earlier, in the Linebacker I and II campaigns in Vietnam in 1972, there had been extensive and effective use of precision-guided munitions, but the focus was still on iron bombs. The flexibility of cruise missiles was such that they could be launched from land, sea, and air. Thus, the battleship USS *Wisconsin* was converted to ensure that it could launch missiles as well as fire guns when operating against Iraqi forces in 1991.

Subsequently, the United States fired seventy-nine sea-launched cruise missiles at terrorist targets in Afghanistan and Sudan in 1998, an impressive display of force but not one that stopped the terrorists. Indeed, Osama bin Laden was able to raise funds by selling missiles that did not detonate to the Chinese, who were interested in cutting-edge American military technology. Cruise missiles were also used against Serbia in 1999 as part of a combined NATO air and missile assault designed to ensure that Serb forces withdrew from Kosovo. In 1998, the submarine HMS *Splendid* achieved Britain's first firing of a cruise missile, which had been bought from the United States. The following year, *Splendid* fired these missiles at Serb targets in Kosovo as part of NATO operations there. During the successful attack on the Taliban regime in Afghanistan in 2001, cruise missiles were fired from Allied warships in the Arabian Sea. By then, air attack had also improved as the availability of dual-mode laser and GPS guidance for bombs increased the range of precision available.

In the attack on Iraq in 2003, the precision of the American cruise missiles and their attacks on Baghdad were presented as the cutting edge of a "shock and awe" campaign that ushered in a new age of warfare. This account, however, was seriously overstated and it proved necessary to defeat Iraqi forces on the ground. The following year, there was speculation that any Chinese invasion of Taiwan would be countered by a Taiwanese cruise missile attack on the Three Gorges Dam in the Yangzi Valley, exploiting a key point of economic and environmental vulnerability.

Other states also developed cruise missile capacity. In 2004, Australia announced it would spend up to $450 million on buying air-launched cruise missiles with a range of at least 250 kilometers. Chinese nuclear-powered attack submarines are designed to deploy land-attack cruise missiles as well as anti-ship ones. In 2011, Taiwan claimed that its missile capability would counter any hostile activities by the aircraft carrier China had acquired and was making operational.

The key to effective cruise missiles is guidance and targeting systems that allow precise targets to be hit at long range. Otherwise, they are no better than the German V-1 rocket of the Second World War. Information in the form of precise positioning is crucial to the effectiveness of cruise missiles. They exploit the precise prior mapping of target and traverse by satellites using a global positioning system, in order to follow predetermined courses at a set height to targets that are actualized for the weapons as grid references. The digital terrain models of the intended flight path facilitate precise long-distance firepower, while the TERCOM guidance system enables course corrections to be made while in flight.

Such methods reflect the importance of complex automatic systems in advanced modern weaponry. The force multiplier characteristics of weaponry have been greatly enhanced and have become more varied. Industrial-age mass production has been replaced by technological superiority as a key factor in weaponry, not least because of the transformation of operational and tactical horizons by computers. This capability has also encouraged a premium on skill, which leads to greater military concern about the quality of both troops and training. This concern encouraged pronounced military support for a professional volunteer force, rather than conscripts.

DRONES

A good instance of this skill was the expertise required to direct UAVs (unmanned aerial vehicles) and RPVs (remotely piloted vehicles). These platforms are designed to take the advantage of missiles further by providing mobile platforms from which they can be fired or bombs dropped. Platforms do not require on-site crew and thus can be used without risk to the life or liberty of personnel. As a consequence, they can be low flying, as the risk of losses of pilots to anti-aircraft fire has been removed. This is important given the extent to which the fate of captured pilots has—since that of Gary Powers, the pilot of an American U-2 reconnaissance plane shot down by the Soviets in 1960, and, more consistently, of American pilots in the Vietnam War—become a major propaganda issue.

In addition, at least in theory, the logistical burden of air power is reduced by the use of unmanned platforms. So also is the cost, as they are less expensive than manned counterparts, and there are big savings on pilot training. No matter how complex they become, drones will always be cheaper than manned aircraft. Unmanned platforms are also more compact and "stealthy" (i.e., less easy to detect), while the acceleration and maneuverability of such platforms are no longer limited by g-forces that would render a pilot unconscious.[99] The lack of a crew means that

drones offer an alternative to planes greater than that provided by helicopters. The potential offered by the latter has arguably not been sustained,[100] which further increases the potential for drones.

The Vietnam War saw the development of drones. From August 1964
until their last combat flight on April 30, 1975, the USAF Strategic Reconnaissance Wing flew 3,435 Ryan 147B reconnaissance drones over
North Vietnam and surrounding areas. About 354 were lost to all causes.
Experiments were also carried out to develop drones for combat operations. In 1999, unarmed American drones were used extensively for surveillance over Kosovo in order to send information on bomb damage
and refugee columns; and, in Afghanistan from 2001, Iraq from 2003,
Pakistan, and Yemen, armed American drones were employed as firing
platforms. The 26-foot American Predator with its operating radius of
500 miles, flight duration of up to 40 hours, cruising speed of 80 miles
per hour, and normal operating altitude of 15,000 feet is designed to destroy air-defense batteries and command centers. It can be used in areas
contaminated by chemical or germ warfare. The Predator has been supplemented by a range of other drones with different ranges and functions. Drone attacks increased greatly under President Obama, from
nine in Pakistan in 2004–2007 to 205 in 2008–2010.[101] Having peaked
in 2010, with 117 strikes killing over 800 insurgents, the number of attacks fell in 2011–2012, in part due to disagreement with Pakistan, but
drone attacks increased against targets in Yemen. In the 2010s, moreover, Britain and France began joint development of drones.

The increasing use of ever more sophisticated drones suggests that
they will come to play an ever bigger role on future battlefields. By the
early 2010s, researchers were trying to teach drones to follow human
gestures so that they would be able to follow the directions of deck han-
dlers and thus use aircraft carriers. It is likely that anti-drone drones will
swiftly develop, repeating the process seen with aircraft in the 1910s.

In the clash between Israel and Hezbollah in Lebanon in 2006, both
sides used drones, with the Israelis making particularly marked use of
them as an aspect of their aerial dominance and attack capacity. Iranian-
supplied drones were used not only by Hezbollah but also by Sudan,
where one was allegedly shot down in March 2012 over the rebel province of Southern Kordofan. The difficulties encountered by Israel in

Lebanon in 2006 indicated the contrast between force projection and military output, which missiles have greatly enhanced, and, on the other hand, predictable outcomes, in the shape of a successful resolution of the crisis. More generally, this is a problem with all weaponry. At the same time, even if air power cannot end insurrections, it can be important in helping counter them.[102]

ARMS RACES

A major expansion in the advanced weaponry held by a number of states from the late 1990s proved an important change. This expansion was particularly acute in South India. First India and then Pakistan tested nuclear weapons in 1998. That year, Pakistan also test-fired its new *Ghauri* intermediate-range missile, while India fired its new long-range Agni 2 missile the following year: its range is 2,000–3,000 kilometers, extending to Tehran and covering most of China and Southeast Asia. In March 2003, both states test-fired short-range surface-to-surface missiles that could have been used to carry nuclear warheads.[103] Pakistan, in turn, sold weapons technology to other states, including North Korea, Iraq, Iran, Libya, and, probably, Egypt and Syria. Saudi Arabia probably funded the Pakistani nuclear-weapons program and in the late 1980s purchased long-range Chinese missiles. From 1998, Iran tested its *Shahabz* missile. With a range of 1,300 kilometers (812 miles), this missile is able to reach both Israel and American forces located in the region.

Atomic proliferation faces serious practical difficulties.[104] Nevertheless, weapons programs were (and are) designed to provide regimes with the ability to counter the military superiority or plans of other states. Thus, North Korea saw atomic weaponry as a counter to American power, while Syria sought to develop chemical and biological weapons as well as an atomic capability, in response to Israeli conventional superiority. Japan, in turn, felt threatened by North Korea's rocketry, leading, as a result, to Japanese interest in anti-missile defenses and in satellite surveillance, while Israel built up a substantial stockpile of nuclear bombs in response to the chemical weapons of its Arab neighbors. In 2003, Libya abandoned its nuclear program, but Iran proved unwilling to follow suit even after its violations of nuclear safeguards were exposed.

From 2006, this issue caused a serious crisis in relations between Iran and the West, with Iran unwilling to back down in the face of international pressure and in 2011–2012 threatening to close the Strait of Hormuz to international trade. In these and other cases, the advantages apparently offered the Americans by cruise missiles and other advanced military technologies did not lead to the policy outcomes they had sought in the case of the Iranian response. On the other hand, it was better to have these capabilities than not to do so. Moreover, the Iranian threat to close the strait proved redundant in January 2012 when the American aircraft carrier *Abraham Lincoln,* supported by five other warships, sailed through in order to underline the right of passage under international law.

THE CASE OF THE F-35

Meanwhile, air power was developing and using new capabilities, including stealth technology. Whereas only about 10 percent of the aerial munitions employed against Iraq in 1991 were "smart" or guided, the percentage in 2003 was about 70. In 2006, moreover, the Americans conducted tests in which aircraft employed synthetic fuel as part of their jet fuel. However, the rise of cruise missiles and drones led to serious questions about the future value of manned flight.

This issue was to play a role in the response to the biggest military program in history, the American F-35 Joint Strike Fighter. This is the latest in a series of projects for a single plane for that function; for example, the TFX of the 1960s, which became the F-111 built by General Dynamics while the carrier variant, the F-111B, was cancelled. The contract for what became known as the F-35 was awarded to Lockheed Martin in 2001, and, at that time, it appeared to have a lot to offer and to be value for money. The F-35 was designed as a comparatively inexpensive tactical aircraft intended to achieve air superiority and as a ground-attack tool. The F-35 was also seen as at the cutting-edge in technology, as it was planned with the stealth capability that defeats radar recognition as well as with advanced software and sensors. Designed to replace at least four other types in service, the F-35 was intended as the central

American fighter for the next half century as well as the basis for allied air forces.

It was planned that the United States would purchase 2,443 F-35s ensuring that, alongside orders from allies, at least 3,000 could be ordered from the outset. This bulk order was intended to produce major efficiencies of scale, both in procurement and in subsequent maintenance and support. In doing so, it was planned to counter the great expense of producing and delivering a new aircraft. These costs were such that the economic viability of air power had diminished, notably as measured in the number of firms and countries able to manufacture aircraft and the number of countries capable of supporting a significant state-of-the-art air force. As a result, coalitions of interest between a number of purchasers were required, as with the F-35 or the Eurofighter Typhoon fighter.

These coalitions of interest underline the extent to which political decisions played, and play, a key role in purchasing weapons. For example, in 1963, India bought MiG-21 fighters from the Soviet Union, rather than British Lightnings, in order to demonstrate India's distance from the West. Subsequently, American support for Pakistan encouraged the Indians to stick with the Soviet Union and, then, Russia. In turn, improved relations with the United States from the mid-2000s led India to show greater interest in purchasing American fighters and helped lead Japan to settle on the F-35 in 2011. In 2012, India preferred French to British fighters. Read back, this factor of political preference, which appears so obvious in the modern world, suggests the need for caution when criticizing what appears to be the acquisition, and therefore use, of suboptimal technology in the past.

Deliveries of the F-35 to the United States military were supposed to start in 2010, but, by the summer of 2011, the date for entering service had been postponed to 2016. Moreover, the average price of each plane had nearly doubled, from $81 million to $156 million, and program costs had risen to $382 billion. The cost of operating and sustaining the aircraft has also risen significantly, ensuring that the F-35 would be more expensive than the planes it was intended to replace. The scale of America's fiscal crisis, which, in part, is due to expensive wars in the 2000s, made this unacceptable.

Moreover, changes in the strategic environment and the nature of weaponry make the value of the F-35 increasingly questionable. There is doubt about its stealth capacity and its related ability to cope with the most modern air-defense system that it may have to face. Range is also an issue. Whereas the United States had nearby bases from which to confront the Soviet Union, Iraq, and Iran—for example, in Abu Dhabi— the range of about 600 miles is less helpful in opposing China, whose deployment of new planes, including Su-30 MK2 fighters and JH-7A fighter bombers, increases its challenge at sea.[105] However, the development of anti-ship missiles by China able to challenge American aircraft carriers, notably the DF-21F intermediate-range ballistic missile fitted with a maneuvering reentry head containing an anti-ship seeker, poses a major problem. As a result, the carriers may have to operate well to the east of Taiwan, in other words beyond the range of the American navy's F-35s. The new anti-carrier technology has led to a call for doctrinal flexibility in defining the role of carriers as they cease to be the clear supreme arbiter of (American) naval power.[106] Obsolescence for the F-35 was further underlined by planned developments for rival weapon systems, both drones and hypersonic cruise missiles.

In addition, the F-35 indicated classic problems that need to be borne in mind when discussing effectiveness. The F-35's costs and performance were compromised by the plane being expected to fulfill many roles, which, in turn, led to an overly complicated design. In particular, the F-35 was intended for the American air force, replacing its F-16s and A-10s, as well as for the navy, providing a conventional takeoff and landing version (the F-35B) to replace its F-18s, and, also, for the marines, to replace their AV-8B jump jets with a short takeoff and vertical landing version (the F-35C). Aside from its much more limited range and payload, the last caused particular problems, both with structure and propulsion, and it was placed on "probation" in 2011 (although it subsequently came out of it). The F-35C caused problems with the location of its arrester hook, based on the plane's radar-avoiding stealth "design," proving inadequate for catching the wire on landing. That was not the sole issue for there are also difficulties in integrating and testing the complex software that runs the F-35's electronics and sensors. In August 2011, test flights were stopped when a defective valve in the power system was discovered. This was part of a crisis of system failures that saw the F-22 Raptor grounded after a defect was found with its oxygen system. Indeed, the F-22 has been beset by problems since it began to enter service in 2006.

CONCLUSIONS

The F-35 may prove to be an expense too far and an entirely unnecessary system. Indeed, the loss of all or part of the program was mentioned in late 2011 as a possible outcome of defense cuts.[107] At any rate, the fate of the F-35 reflects the rapid rise of obsolescence but also the abiding issues of confusion in goals, limitations in function, and changing tactical, operational, and strategic parameters. These factors will remain important. At the same time, it would be mistaken to treat air power simply as a lesson in failure. The hopes of its advocates were frequently misplaced, notably in terms of outcomes or political consequences, but air power has dramatically changed equations of firepower and mobility. Both in its own right and as part of combined arms operations, air power has made maneuver warfare a more central part of conflict and thus increased the tempo of war.

6

REVOLUTION, TRANSFORMATION, AND THE PRESENT

Modern military power is based upon technology, and technology is based upon computers. . . . We [the Soviet Union] will never be able to catch up with you [the United States] in modern arms until we have an economic revolution. And the question is whether we can have an economic revolution without a political revolution.

—*Nikolai Ogarkov, Chief of the Soviet General Staff, 1983,*
  cited in the New York Times, *August 20, 1992*

The literature on recent, current, and future warfare is dominated by the language of change and modernization. As is the general pattern in modern culture, change and modernization are descriptive, prescriptive, and normative, being equated with improvement. Relative performance or promise is defined according to these emphases, as are the conflicts seen as worthy of attention by scholars, and therefore, in a circular sense, as contributing to their analyses. Such an approach to modernization, however, begs the question of what is a modern, let alone a more modern, style of military operations? This question is one of recurring relevance for military history and for understanding present and future situations, and thus links the Revolution in Military Affairs (RMA) discerned in the 1990s and 2000s to earlier episodes of what have been presented as military revolutions.

The focus for analysis is a key issue in every case. For recent and current developments—leaving aside the argument that war, indeed violence, is becoming less common,[1] an argument that can be queried—Western commentators did and do not generally define as modern the operations of non-Western forces, whether current or recent, regulars or irregulars. These "little wars," some of which, in fact, are far from little, are slighted, although in practice conflicts such as those in Congo and Sri Lanka are as typical, if not more, of the circumstances of warfare around the world than the American-led Coalition invasion of Iraq in 2003 that, in contrast, attracts disproportionate attention as a description of modern warfare. This focus on Iraq was dimmed by the American commitment in Afghanistan, but the common emphasis was on America's role. The stress on discussing Iraq and Afghanistan will probably continue until the next major war involving the United States. If that conflict is with Iran, North Korea, or China, and the focus is therefore on symmetrical warfare, then Afghanistan will probably be regarded as a false turning. Conversely, if there is a large-scale intervention in Somalia or Cuba, and the focus is on asymmetrical conflict, then the situation will be different.

Turning to more specific issues of current policy, a sense of technological excellence plays a leading role in procurement debates, but there is a key strategic context in these debates, that of the present. As a consequence, there is the customary danger of present military and political needs crowding out future options. This process is particularly understandable given the extent to which these needs are posed in the shape of difficult crises and in light of the problems created by serious financial constraints.

The net result of such presentism, however, is likely to be a more profound weakness for powers, including the United States, when confronting in the future what turns out to be a different military crisis. Responsibility will lie not only with the alternative priorities, notably social welfare, in part reflected by these financial constraints—a target of criticism by military commentators—but also with the military's (and politicians') frequent tendency to focus on the present and to fail to give sufficient weight to alternative military challenges. Thus, in one light, this chapter, and indeed the book as a whole, involves a call for more strategic thinking, by military and non-military alike, and indeed for a reconceptualization of strategy, in terms of both content and timescale.

Overall, any need for the reconceptualization of strategy and military thought suggests a multiple approach to military modernity and, crucially, an emphasis on its diversity. Such an approach, however, does not accord with technological triumphalism, nor indeed with the tendency of governments and militaries to overestimate their own ability to achieve success, while also underestimating the complexity and problems of transition to whatever is defined as modern. Technological triumphalism, whether or not expressed in terms of the RMA, and the dominance, precision, and rapidity of its network-centric weapons systems, provides a crucial aspect of this tendency.

A different perspective for relativism in the judgment of military developments is offered by the reflection that the standard models explaining how change occurs pretend to an inappropriate objectivity. The action-reaction and task-response models suggest that military effectiveness is, in large part, a matter of responding rapidly and obviously to events and to the needs set by ably defined goals. However, this approach underplays the extent to which perception, rather than automatic optimalization, is integral to practice in both processes: action-reaction and task-response.

A similar problem, again relating to the assumption of inherent efficiency, is posed by the notion that the spread of the methods of a paradigm, or leading, power readily creates a cultural space, or region of similar activity and norms, in war making and indeed bridges such spaces as this spread takes place. In place of this notion, the emphasis should be on how the selective character of borrowing military ideas and practices, both within and between such regions, reflects the need to employ with care analytical terms such as "modern" or "Western" warfare. These terms should not be treated as if they readily described an inherent reality or process of emulation and diffusion. The same is true for warfare of other terms such as Oriental or non-Western or Muslim or Third World,[2] and this point needs to be borne in mind in the categories used in this book.

An emphasis on the need to employ categories and analytical concepts with great care is not the sole conceptual point of relevance. There is also the problem posed by the assumption that perfect rationality is possible in the selection of appropriate weaponry, tactics, strategy, and doctrine. Such a point can be taken further by asking questions about the misleading tendency to assume that confrontations, and therefore military tasks, are predictable, with corresponding consequences for doctrine, training, and procurement. The absence of predictability is understood but then tends to be ignored.

Terrorism (possibly linked to intrastate challenges) and resource struggles are two important instances of actual and possible unpredictabilities. The varied challenges they pose include, in the case of the former, the need for military reconfiguration in response to terrorism. Such a reconfiguration is from deterrence-orientated structures and doctrine, which are currently the key forms in relations between states, to a response-orientated situation. Whether or not in response to terrorism, this transformation could, and can, be seen as necessary, both to advance the interests of individual states, such as Britain and the United States, and also, were it to be possible, to help sustain a world order based on cooperation and progress.

Yet, the transformation to more responsive, and thus active, military forces and doctrines can also be seen as likely to ensure a high level of confrontation, if not conflict, not least because there is no agreement on the character and goals of such a world order. The latter point challenges liberal attempts to create an order based on legal codes centered on human rights, as well as more neo-realist interpretations that, in a contrasting fashion and with a different goal, focus on power.

The focus on power returns us to the issue of the RMA or, as it is now usually termed, Transformation. More widely cited than defined and meaning too many things to too many people, the RMA, like Transformation, in practice had a number of meanings and associations,[3] which, in combination, suggested its usefulness to its advocates but also its misleading character. The imprecision, not to say vagueness, of meaning is something the RMA shared (and shares) with a large number of other terms, including, in the military field, strategic culture, let alone culture.

In trying to understand the meaning and use of the term, it is particularly helpful to focus on its context. The RMA was a military analysis and ideology of the time, rather than, as with many categories and concepts, a description created by later commentators. Indeed, the RMA was symptomatic of a set of cultural and political assumptions that tell us more about the aspirations of the 1990s and early 2000s than they do about any objective assessment of military capabilities. In particular, the RMA reflected the desire for unquestioned potency without any matching need to accept conscription, a war economy, or many casualties, and, in part, can therefore be seen as a response to the decline of the warrior ethos and to the growing gap between society and the military.[4]

Although the intellectual history of revolutions in military affairs owed much to Soviet thinking and planning,[5] the RMA also reflected the assertion of Western, more particularly American, superiority, as well as the ideology of mechanization that had long been important to American military thought and the influence of the vision of future war developed in the wake of the Second World War.[6] This ideology and vision were crucial, for capability, if not worth, was defined in a machine age—especially, but not only, in the United States—in terms of machines, which were then used to assert and demonstrate superiority. Reflecting the values of American society, there was a preference for seeking technological solutions to military challenges.[7] For "lives saturated with technology,"[8] the machine was the measure of existence and the proof of value. This process was encouraged by suggestions that machines would acquire an ability to substitute for human decision making. At the least, a society that had moved into a new information age appeared to offer suggestive glimpses about the future nature of war.[9]

A focus on machines also seemed to provide a ready measure for assessing the strength of different states and, indeed, civilizations. Strength could not only be assessed, even measured. It was also apparently possible to shape the changing equations of strength by investing in new capability at the cutting edge of technological progress.

Thus, the RMA was an expression of the modern secular technological belief system that is prevalent in the West and that easily meshes with theories of modernization that rest on the diffusion and adoption of new technology and related concepts. Moreover, it was particularly crucial to Americans that the RMA was an American-led military revolution. That character apparently underlined American proficiency and also offered a way to look at the world in which this proficiency appeared to be without end, or at least would be redefined in terms that the Americans were confident they could determine. If change was to be understood in terms of movement along a line in a graph, then it appeared important to be at the head of the line as well as determining the axes of the graph. This approach derived from an inadequate understanding of technological change, which does not occur as a linear progression despite the common belief that it does.

The concept of the RMA was also based on the notion that order and pattern can be found in all things, when in fact chaos is the natural state. And while some degree of order is necessary for matters of whatever hue to be described and discussed in a meaningful way, that does not mean the order or pattern actually exists. The notion is too dependent on perception and movable goalposts.

More specifically, in accordance with a long-term tendency in American military (and political) thinking,[10] the RMA met the American need to believe in the possibility of high-intensity conflict and of total victory, with opponents shocked and awed into accepting defeat, rather than, in contrast, offering the ambiguous and qualified nature of modern victory. For Americans, the victory that was fit-for-discussion was provided by a discussion that ran together confident analysis with rhetoric. A survey of American officers in 2000–2001, prior to the terrorist attacks of 2001, indicated confidence in America's ability to control the terms of an engagement against a competent adversary, alongside a lack of knowledge about future threats outside their tactical specialties.[11] The latter point, however, was also true of other militaries.

In addition, the certainty of the RMA appeared to offer the Americans a defense against the troubling threats posed, first, by the spread of earlier technologies, such as long-range missiles and atomic warheads, as well as of new ones, notably bacteriological warfare, and, secondly, of whatever might follow. As such, technology in the shape of the RMA apparently offered safety and an ability to rise above the world, a long-standing drive. Providing apparent invulnerability, the RMA seemed to keep the Americans ahead and safe, as well as suggesting that the

American military capabilities were more effective, and that their operations would be more proficient, than the model of German blitzkrieg; a model that itself was very influential in the United States with the military and with civilian commentators.[12]

The relationship between technology and safety was taken on board by politicians who understood both the need to offer the public security and the possibility of doing so by making hitherto unknown technological capabilities provide protection against risk. George W. Bush, during his campaign for president, told an audience at the Citadel, a prominent American military academy, in September 1999 that the best way to keep the peace would be a redefinition of war on U.S. terms. Once elected, he declared at the Citadel in 2001 that the first priority would be to speed the transformation of the military. Indeed, the sense that already established military structures and systems, notably in the army, were part of the problem, and not a key means to the solution provided by new technology, helped explain the very poor relations between Donald Rumsfeld, Bush's unfortunate choice as secretary of defense from 2001 to 2006, and many of America's senior commanders. A number of the latter proved adept defenders of established institutional practices, but appropriate skepticism was also voiced about aspects of the prospectus for change.

This tension between Rumsfeld and many of the commanders was related to the totalizing culture and prospectus offered by the RMA and the transformation of the military that was its institutional and doctrinal expression and that helped justify unprecedented expenditure and major changes in policy. The belief in clear problem and obvious solution proved potent, especially in a political and institutional culture that did not welcome ambiguity or doubt, a point also true about many commentators on the military. Ironically, a number of those today who advocate COIN (counterinsurgency) doctrine as the ultimate solution to everything said the same earlier, and also in a misleading fashion, about the RMA and Transformation.

In practice, no matter how sophisticated a military technology and system, safety is elusive, as the technology and system have deficiencies and imperfections that will be exploited by opponents who, anyway, have their own capacity to improve. The deficiencies and imperfections of sophisticated technologies can never be eliminated, but the effort to do so increases and the cost increases accordingly, while the trade-off between effort, cost, and achievement diminishes rapidly. Nothing will ever be 100 percent effective 100 percent of the time. Indeed, the greater the complexities of a system, the more likely it is that effectiveness will fall off sharply because of the amount of maintenance time necessary to make it work as intended.

The RMA suggested novelty as the key theme of the 1990s, but, in practice, there was more continuity in American capability and war making, not least because it was Cold War weaponry, training, and doctrine that were employed and tested, particularly in the 1991 Gulf War with Iraq. The speed and completeness of Iraq's military defeat encouraged a belief in a revolutionary change in war, although other military skills played a greater role in American success.[13] The American use of Cold War assets in 1991 involved, in particular, the new grasp and use of the operational dimension of war, a grasp that had developed in the 1980s as a maneuverist doctrine was implemented to aid planning for a mobile defense of western Europe in the event of Soviet attack.

This doctrine and planning was linked to the post-Vietnam revitalization of the American army, a revitalization that involved a process of transformation or, at least, redirection so as to focus on conflict with the Red Army rather than prepare for another Vietnam-style conflict. New weapons played a role as part of this doctrinal, strategic, operational, and tactical reevaluation. In the 1991 Gulf War, the Americans used the Blackhawk helicopter, introduced in 1979; the M1A1 Abrams tank, deployed by the army from 1980; the Bradley Fighting Vehicle, designed to carry a squad of infantry and armed with a TWO (tube-launched, optically tracked, wire command data link) missile system, introduced in 1981; and the Apache attack helicopter, equipped with radar and Hellfire missiles, introduced in 1986. The Americans also used airplane stealth technology.

In the early 1990s, the stress on agility and flexibility already seen in the American army in the 1980s was linked to a new interest in light forces connected with remote sensors and weapons.[14] Information technology was employed to enhance situational awareness. The result was Force XXI, which sought to network battlefield information systems. To assess the concept, a division-size experimental force was designated in December 1994 and adapted accordingly. A brigade-scale test carried out in 1994 had revealed a lack of familiarity with new computerized equipment, as well as the absence of the tactics necessary to exploit new capabilities. There was more success in the Advanced Warfighting Experiment in 1997, when a digitized task force was tested against a conventional opponent.

As secretary of defense, Rumsfeld created the Office of Force Transformation, appointing a retired vice-admiral, Arthur Cebrowski, as its director. Cebrowski was very committed to the idea of network-centric warfare and its role in capability enhancement.[15] As a reminder that technological possibilities are assessed in terms of the politics of strategy, Rumsfeld responded to Cebrowski's ideas by using them as an opportunity to challenge established Pentagon processes and current American commitments. He felt that the Pentagon was overly bureaucratic and that it had failed to adapt to the post–Cold War world and to the military needs and opportunities this world represented. In particular, Rumsfeld argued that the military should focus on war winning and not on such peacekeeping as the Kosovo mission of 1999, and that the route to the former was a smaller and more adaptable military. This argument also proved a way to criticize what was presented as the naive liberal nation-building of the Clinton administration. Ironically, intervention in Afghanistan and Iraq was to lead George W. Bush into far more ambitious and expensive nation-building.

Reconfiguration played a major role in the adoption of new technology. Transformation entailed a move from large "platform-centric" formations and units, such as armored divisions, to groupings that were orientated on particular missions and that were designed to act in a more agile fashion. These groupings grew on, and were located in, a matrix of networks of sensors, information processors, deciders, and shooters, networks that were to have multiple and rapid links and not to require a large hierarchy of control. Thus, "network-centric" warfare was the goal, as it was believed to take military capability to a new plane of effectiveness. Doctrine and technology were to be shaped and enhanced as a synergy. Much of the technology was focused on overcoming the problems of command and control posed by the large number of units operating simultaneously, and on fulfilling the opportunities for command and control gained by successfully overcoming this challenge. As a result, sensors, processors, deciders, and shooters could be aggregated to achieve a precise mass effect from dispersed units, a method that was also seen as lessening vulnerability. This process represented a version, in a very different context, of the concentration on the battlefield of the Prussian forces that Moltke organized with his effective staff system.

Advocates of the RMA progressed to talking about "space control" and the "empty battlefield" of the future, where wars would be waged for "information dominance"—in other words, control of satellites, telecommunications, and computer networks. The American military thus contrasted their information grids and networks, which were to be safeguarded in wartime, with hostile ones that had to be destroyed. The latter idea readily served a variety of technologies, notably air power and cyberwarfare. Integrated communications technologies were designed to enhance offensive and defensive information warfare capability, analyzing and disseminating unprecedented quantities of information, while better communications permitted both more integrated fire support and the use of surveillance to enable more accurate targeting. With intelligence, reconnaissance, target acquisition, and attack combined, firepower was regarded as brought to fruition.

The suppression of enemy defenses could therefore be achieved swiftly, as indeed occurred in Iraq in 1991 and 2003, providing an opportunity for moving onto other targets. Each objective was to be achieved rapidly in accordance with political and military needs, not least, in the latter case, getting within opposing decision cycles and thus operating more swiftly and effectively. Surveillance capability also enabled commanders to have greater knowledge of the locations of their own units, as with the use of the American Blue Force Tracker system during the successful invasion of Iraq in 2003,[16] not that this prevented "friendly fire" incidents that, in part, arose from the pace of advance and the tempo of activity.

Some of the discussion of the RMA, not least the emphasis on network-centric warfare, implied or even assumed that the world is an isotropic (uniform) surface, made knowable, pliable, and controllable by new technology,[17] notably the digitization of the world's surface and the usage of this information for GPS (global positioning system) networks. In part, both assumptions and practice represented a bringing to fruition of the computer revolution that had begun in the 1940s and that had been military in purpose from the outset.[18]

In the context of the RMA, the capability of unmanned platforms was enhanced by designing them to work within systems or networks that bring together dispersed sensors and units and different types of weapons, and, moreover, from a number of environments: space, air, land, and sea. These systems operate on the basis of high and sustained rates of information and therefore require the overcoming of any threat to the sensors, notably those located in satellites. By 2000, American military surveillance satellites, with their digital sensors and their almost instantaneous transmission over encrypted radio links, had a resolution of better than 100 millimeters (4 inches).

The potential of surveillance became a major international issue in 2002–2003, as the United States claimed that satellite information made it clear that Iraq was stockpiling weapons of mass destruction and evading the ground-search program being carried out by UN inspectors. This episode apparently highlighted the extent to which it was possible to overcome one of the major characteristics of totalitarian regimes— information management. In practice, the information obtained by surveillance was pushed too far in order to serve political preconceptions. There were no such weapons. Aerial surveillance proved less reliable than human intelligence might have done, but the lack of agents on the ground in a brutally effective totalitarian state had encouraged a reliance on aerial surveillance, a situation that recurred with North Korea and Iran.

America is at the forefront of surveillance and Transformation technology, although it is not alone in its development goals and, moreover, in order to recoup some of the cost, is likely to sell advanced weapons to allies. It is difficult, however, to control the process of technology transfer. For example, in 2000, the Americans threatened action if Israel, which had benefited greatly from such transfer, sold an airborne radar system to China that could be used against America's vulnerable ally Taiwan. Other militaries, however, did not match American priorities in Transformation. There was a major difference between the modest European commitment to network-enabled capability and the deeper American turn to network-centric warfare, and this contrast continues to be the case and is part of the reason for American concern about European interoperability.[19]

The RMA can be located very much in terms of a particular moment in American strategic thought and military politics, one of boldness of conception about America's ability to act as a force for good, a boldness held in liberal as much as neo-conservative circles.[20] Indeed, those who touted the RMA and the quest to achieve it helped to get the United States into the military and fiscal predicament it faced by the mid-2000s. At the same time, as a reminder of the danger of drawing a clear causal relationship between technology and policy outcomes, the practices and ideas summarized as the RMA and Transformation could serve to support a range of Western political strategies, including those of both isolationists and interventionists. Tasking was not predetermined by technology, although it was certainly influenced by a sense of technological opportunity and affordability.

In practice, in the context of the 2000s, and specifically the views of the George W. Bush administrations (2001–2009), the RMA particularly lent itself to the cause of American unilateralism, and this cause was most clearly espoused by neo-conservatives. At the same time, unilateralism was more generally a characteristic of American attitudes, and the neo-conservative use of it drew on a long tradition. The combination of unilateralism and the RMA can then be assessed in the context of both serving as responses to the *relative* American decline in a more multi-centered world, indeed being assumptions about how best to resist this decline and means to do so. This relative decline began in the 1960s with the rise in the Japanese and German economies and the inflationary pressures in that of America. Such decline markedly gathered pace over the last decade with the rapid rise of China and India and the fiscal problems of the United States.[21]

In the discussion of military technology, Chinese naval plans take central stage in the early 2010s and as part of a more general improvement in Chinese capability including J20 fighters and BeiDou, China's own GPS system. The development of Chinese nuclear-powered submarines equipped with long-range nuclear ballistic missiles (three submarines by 2010 compared to fourteen for the United States) has led the United States to revitalize its anti-submarine capability, which had been downgraded with the end of the Cold War and the collapse of the Soviet Union. The development of a Chinese anti-satellite capability posed another challenge, threatening not only the American concept of "Star Wars" but also the satellite intelligence and links central to American strategic, operational, and tactical capability.[22] Having put the emphasis on asymmetric responses,[23] the Chinese now can also hope to mount a viable symmetrical challenge to the United States. The Chinese have been greatly influenced by the American ideas of the RMA, and this led from 1993 to a Chinese emphasis on air, naval, and missile forces, rather than on the army, and from the early 2000s to an emphasis on what the Chinese call informatization, or modern command and control systems.

Alongside misplaced optimism, American belief in the RMA, at least in part, can therefore also be considered an attempt to overcome a sense of decline, or at least challenge, and a reality of relative decline. The "systems capable of sustained operations at great distances with minimal theater-based support" that were called for in the 2001 Quadrennial Defense Review were designed to enable the United States to counter the challenge posed by new, potentially hostile, capabilities.

At the same time, it is important to be cautious about suggesting too much coherence and consistency in the idea of an RMA, a point that is underlined by consideration of military revolutions that are supposed to have occurred earlier, and that also pertains to subsequent ideas of COIN. A less harsh view than that just summarized can be advanced if the RMA and Transformation are presented, instead, as applying, at all levels, advances originally focused on the tactical level.[24] Alternatively, they can be seen as doctrines designed to meet political goals, and thus to shape or encourage technological developments and operational and tactical suppositions accordingly; rather than, as an alternative, allowing technological constraints to shape doctrine and thereby risk the danger of inhibiting policy.

That defense of the RMA and Transformation rests on a pertinent conceptual point. Nevertheless, in reality, much discussion of the idea of successive revolutions in military affairs, especially but not only in the United States, did seem to suggest a technology-driven and defined warfare. This concept of military revolutions was extended to past, present, and future, as with the focus on supposed firepower revolutions in medieval Europe, notably those linked to the English use of longbowmen and, subsequently, to the increased reliance on gunpowder.[25]

However, it is necessary to understand not simply the limitations of the new technology but also the limitations of a technology-driven account of capability and change. This understanding entails the realization of the misapplication of tactical capabilities and lessons, such as effective air support, to operational goals, and of operational lessons, for example, about maneuver warfare, to strategic goals. Such a misapplication readily stems from the tendency to take an overly optimistic view of technological capabilities and from the disinclination, in contrast, to appreciate the political dynamics and measures of strategic goals and issues.

This preference can lead to the illusion that fresh technologies can, and thus will, bring new powers, and, therefore, that problems can be readily banished. That is not the appropriate military analysis and tasking for the twenty-first century. Thus, picking apart the RMA is not some parlor game but instead is crucial to the assessment of Western capability and the discussion of future tasking and doctrine. Understanding serious problems, including what went wrong, is important to the process of planning. "Network-centric warfare" responded to the American desire, from the mid-1960s, to remove the soldier from the battlefield, but it is a unrealistic and hazardous goal because there is no system that cannot be overcome, either by newer, bigger, better systems or by older systems that are used skillfully. As digital systems become more sophisticated, the ability of commanders, indeed of systems, to recognize an enemy will be undermined by countersystems that will disguise digitally (or by simpler means) potential threats to an attacker. Once a system reaches a certain level of sophistication, it becomes increasingly vulnerable to simpler systems, and it is highly likely that military hardware that relies on computer systems will be affected by malware specifically designed to attack particular systems. Missiles may come to carry computer virus payloads designed to attack the computer systems of aircraft, communications, and fire control. Computer systems fail, and, once they have, the hardware they service is useless. Thus, computer systems, rather than being a strength, are a weakness, not least because they reduce the reliability of a weapon system. The F-35, Tornado II, and similar aircraft require complex support systems to ensure they work. The Tornado is inherently unstable and cannot fly without its computer system, although the instability, combined with the computers, makes it highly maneuverable.

Although challenged by recent experience, the concept of the RMA continues to exert a powerful sway on the American military and public imagination. In part, this sway probably is an effect of nothing more than a vague apprehension that technology is changing more quickly and influencing war more fully than at any time before. People who feel this way are ripe for arguments of technological determinism and keen to find a new magic bullet.[26] As a consequence, the effect of the RMA lingers, even as the specifics of the argument collapse under closer scrutiny. Despite this collapse, there are still proponents of the argument, notably advocates for an RMA focused on the success in Iraq in 1991 and 2003, with the problems that came after 2003 downplayed.[27] Instead, the Iraq War and Afghanistan both suggested that technology provided a force multiplier but still required "boots on the ground." In Iraq in 2009, the tide was turned against the insurgents by the "surge" in American troop numbers combined with effective local diplomacy aimed at winning support, rather than by high-technology weaponry.

The discussion of the RMA is pertinent to the present consideration of technology and warfare, because the related idea of Transformation now provides the key basis for much Western perception of the issue. Even though warfare since 2003 in both Iraq and Afghanistan led to a major qualification, if not, in some circles, loss in confidence in the RMA, the same set of assumptions remains pertinent, not least in the desire and drive to find a new set of weapons that will deal with the issue and help lead to a recovery in confidence. Indeed, the extensive use of drones arises in part from this need. Moreover, the problems of recent years in Iraq and, even more, Afghanistan have led to increased interest in the use of air power for counterinsurrectionary warfare.[28]

At the same time, there has also been far more interest in the role of politics in such warfare, not least by altering the equations of support for both sides. Yet, politics relies on force, notably in enabling governments to demonstrate their authority and their ability to protect real and potential supporters,[29] a point that lay behind Western military policy in Iraq and Afghanistan. In short, there is no clear pattern of causation between relevant factors but rather interacting linkages.

CONCLUSIONS

Belief in the need for, and possibility of, Transformation is a key aspect of the willingness to invest in new systems. This belief and willingness is an instance of a long-standing process in which claims of new potency are advanced to ensure procurement.[30] It is unclear how far the existing disjuncture between such ideas and, in contrast, the practice and reality of current war involving Western powers will narrow if there is a further embrace of technology through the use of enhanced unmanned vehicles and other weapons systems discussed as aspects of Transformation. This question is important to the perception of the possibilities offered by improved weapons and reminds us that assumptions about likely success and appropriate behavior are important, alongside more mechanical accounts of the drive for victory through enhanced effectiveness.

Returning to the point made at the outset of this chapter, it would be mistaken to consider the present largely in terms of the commitments and ideas of the United States, whether or not other major powers are also added. Instead, focusing on "average" military states, it is clear that technological factors are significant, but less so than for major powers. The relevant doctrine, weaponry, training, and other military systems are focused far more on tasks within the state or, at most, also involving its neighbors, rather than farther afield. In 2005, for example, the Philippines decommissioned its last jet combat aircraft, while its navy currently lacks anti-missile defenses. Moreover, some states have deliberately focused on a style of warfare very different to that of the United States. Under Hugo Chávez, Venezuela's military adopted a doctrine of "asymmetric warfare" as a response to any American attack, although political posturing play a role. In the cases of such states, in an instance of the idea of geographies of knowledge,[31] there is no reason to think in terms of RMA or Transformation.

This situation has two major implications, first suggesting that the overall value of referring to the present situation in these terms is limited and, secondly, underlining the need to think of a different set of concepts and categories in assessing developments outside the leading powers. On the whole, there is little that is new in these cases and, instead, the emphasis should be on the political circumstances that lead to the use of force[32] and (separately) help determine its effectiveness. The far greater firepower and mobility enjoyed by regular forces as opposed to irregulars are the central difference in technological terms for minor as well as major powers, and that contrast, certainly, is far from new. Its impact, however, very much depends on the political situation.

7

INTO THE FUTURE

The year 2000 will be "now" soon, if we ever make it. . . . But maybe the
planet will have exploded by then, or been devastated by uranium fires and
throw-outs, and a little napalm and laser beams gone wild, on the side.

—*Janwillem van de Wetering, The Japanese Corpse, 1977*

The future recedes continually, at least for humans, unless it is ended for
us by destroying the Earth or human life on it. The elusive character of
the future means that modernity, the condition of the present seen as
looking toward the future and making it possible, also changes. Thus,
any discussion of current warfare in terms of modernity and modernization risks rapid anachronism.

This indeterminacy and unpredictability at the present time is linked
to another characteristic: the manner in which views of future circumstances so often prove mistaken. That, however, is not simply a case of
assuming technological capabilities that do not in the event arise. Instead, there is the abiding need to relate these capabilities to world developments that may provide opportunities, needs, and resources for
such capabilities or, conversely, may thwart their development or application. As a result, we are returned anew to the issue of context. Any
discussion of future warfare involves consideration of the wars to come,
and the latter entails an understanding of possible variations in tasking.

This is a matter both of tasking from and for civil society and also tasking by and for the military.

Both civil society and the military are important in tasking, and they are also mutually supportive. In theory, the military across most of the world is under civilian (political) control. Moreover, with the exception of states in which the military owns significant portions of the economy, notably (but not only) Burma, Indonesia, and, to a lesser extent, China and Egypt, the military is totally dependent on the political process for its finances. In practice, however, tasking is affected by the military because, despite these limitations, it is able to influence the situation, both due to its expertise and because of a tendency to see strategy as a military process rather than as a political one in which governmental priorities are defined and plans for their implementation drawn up. This tendency, however, is mistaken, as the military focus on winning the war frequently leads to a downplaying both of important cost implications and of other ways to pursue goals, in short of strategic issues and options.

In general, and there are significant variations, notably in countries in which the military plays a major role in politics, the military prefers to focus on tasking and strategy as processes under their control, defined in accordance with their interest, and greatly affected by changes in the technology of war. The "give us the tools and we'll finish the job" approach presupposes that the job is fairly clear-cut. The latter, however, is less apparent if the politics behind tasking (as well as the politics involved in tasking) are considered.

Technological considerations play a number of roles, but they can be seen across a continuum, from providing the means to fulfill goals to helping to define the latter or, indeed, to transform the context in which they are considered and asserted; the last is an issue with the RMA and Transformation. A latent tension between providing means and defining goals affects the discussion of military development and the reasons for, and processes of, change. In practice, both means and goals are involved.

Technological change is designed in response to perceived needs: the cost of such research means that it does not take place in the abstract. Instead, force-structure and posture decisions reflect images of warfare.[1] At present, much of the assessment of future high-tech confrontation or war depends, at least in the short term, on two concepts: synergy (profitable combination) and information warfare. The former relates essentially to means, the latter to means and the redefinition of goals. Both synergy and information warfare are seen as of importance to the rivalry of major powers, which indeed was the suppressed theme of the international relations of the 2000s and is becoming more overt in the 2010s.

Indeed, at the same time that the "War on Terror" engaged the bulk of American, and in fact British, attention,[2] a deterioration of relations affecting China, India, Russia, and the United States was of considerable importance. This deterioration led to public shows of friction, such as, in 2007–2008, Russian opposition to American plans to extend the ballistic missile defense shield to cover eastern Europe, and to encourage Georgia and Ukraine to join NATO, as well as Russian withdrawal in 2007 from the Conventional Armed Forces in Europe Treaty. Hostilities between Georgia and Russia in August 2008 can very much be seen in this context, as Georgia looked to the United States for support. The cooling of relations between the United States and China was of particular significance, as the alignment between the two powers in the 1970s had brought a crucial improvement in the strategic position of the United States and, thus, the West. The linkage of this cooling to that between the United States and Russia and to the improvement in relations between Russia and China contributed to a geopolitical transformation with major consequences for strategic needs and opportunities, and thus for the possible character of future conflict.

The concept of synergy suggests that, in any future conflict, success will hinge on the ability to achieve a successful combination of land, air, sea, cyber, and space forces, an ability that requires the development of new organizational structures, as well as careful training of commanders and units and appropriate systems of command, control, communications, and information appraisal and analysis. The heavy American investment in military infrastructure in space in the 2000s and 2010s indicates the commitment to such a synergy. At the same time, the problems of coordination were suggested by the mismatch between the arrival time of the satellites and the delay of relevant ground equipment, notably the ground-based terminals of the Advanced Extremely High Frequency Program, which is designed to provide nuclear-safe communications. The American upgrading of the satellites that provide the global positioning system reveal the need for continual advances, in this case against anti-satellite radio-jamming techniques.

Advanced technology, and a sense that technology could, would, indeed must, continue to advance, and that this advance has to be planned for, greatly contributes to ideas of synergetical warfare. These ideas reflect an awareness of the requirement for a more sophisticated command and planning environment, and also a need to do more than simply respond to the possibilities created by new weapons. Instead of treating these factors in isolation, their impact is to be multiplied by careful cooperation within, and outside, of new organizational structures. Thus, for example, if high-speed aircraft are developed, capable of "skipping" on the upper atmosphere of the Earth and of transporting troops anywhere in the world within 2 hours, their successful operational usage will depend, to a considerable extent, on such cooperation.

In the shorter term, it is more likely that the upper atmosphere will be used for the delivery of ordnance. Although not without major problems, notably in terms of ensuring accuracy, such power projection is, and will be, less problematic than that of moving troops at hitherto unprecedented speed. In the early 2010s, the Americans tested the Falcon, a hypersonic (above Mach 5 speed) weapon system propelled into space by a rocket that then moved on a preset trajectory to attack a target on Earth. There is no equivalent for the movement of troops. Indeed, the characteristics of humans, in the shape of their tolerance to circumstances—for example, g-forces—would need to be reengineered to match even a portion of the possibilities for weapons and delivery systems.

POLITICAL FACTORS

The possibility of such a transformation of human characteristics lies in the future. More feasibly for the present, a true military revolution, in the sense of an abrupt change, would possibly be not so much a new type of weaponry but rather a new form of soldiery within current circumstances. That would mean not new types of humans, a major technological and ethical challenge, but, instead, a major change, such as a return to the citizenry under arms, and, indeed, a reliance on such an outcome. However, such a return, although periodically suggested by non-specialist commentators, is definitely not necessary or appropriate in terms of modern military technology. Instead, most military equipment requires high levels of skill on the part of the soldiers. Some skills can be replaced, in part by the use of the machinery, notably aiming, but there is still the need on the part of humans to assimilate and respond rapidly to a range of information inputs, and this situation creates requirements for a high level of skill.

That does not mean that conscription is not possible. The equation varies by country, notably with reference to their social politics and political culture, thus underlining the extent to which the military is an aspect of politics; this is a situation broader than the argument that war is politics by other means. An ability to raise large numbers of troops does not preclude an emphasis on advanced weaponry. Iran, a state that has the ethos and organization necessary for mass mobilization, as it showed in its 1980–1988 war with Iraq, is currently developing or purchasing and integrating weapons with specialized high-tech capability, such as missiles, submarines, and, probably, atomic weaponry, and a similar point can be made about North Korea.

Whatever the political culture of the individual state, the possibility of shifting to conscription and the character of the resulting military are affected by the nature of the available technology. The likely speed of a future major war is such that there would not be the time, during the conflict, for combatants to move from specialized to mass forces, nor would there be sufficient advanced weaponry for these troops. Even if militaries were to be divided between advanced forces, using new technology, and lower-grade units, the quantity of resources necessary to provide for mass conscript armies, as well as the problems of counteracting the individualism, hedonism, and lack of fitness characteristic of modern Western society, are such that conscription is highly unlikely.

Moreover, this is also true of many non-Western societies. Indeed, the division here between Western and non-Western societies is far less than was the case in the 1960s and 1970s when Mao's China appeared to be the non-Western archetype and sought to lead non-Western guerrilla movements accordingly, notably in Africa and Southeast Asia. Currently, the leading non-Western military powers are China, Japan, and India, and each is affected by the social characteristics already mentioned. That, however, does not mean that rising consumerism and individualism in a China that is still under authoritarian one-party control will have the same impact as in democratic India and Japan.

In the case of Japan, there are powerful cultural, political, and social restraints on the military in response to the anti-militarism following defeat in the Second World War. While Chinese ambitions and strength, combined with continued and dangerous North Korean unpredictability, make a powerful case for an enhanced Japanese military, the political situation within Japan currently makes this impracticable. In addition, the fiscal problems facing Japan also affect the prospects for greatly increased military investment, both in legacy systems and in new military possibilities, although, as the world's third largest economy, Japan is able to support a formidable military.

In the West, looking to the future, the language of total commitment in, or close to, war will probably be employed to explain, justify, and encourage economic direction, the retrenchment of consumption, and the curtailing of civil liberties, rather than the mass mobilization of potential combatants. Phrases such as War on Poverty, War on Cancer, and War on Drugs provide indications of the direction of popular sentiment and political concern, and also clearly involve non-military technologies. Nevertheless, although the number of troops raised in the United States during the 2000s was limited and was supplied by volunteers including reservists, and not by conscripts, the War on Terror was also employed in the United States both as a justification for military commitments and as an opportunity to develop new military technologies, notably unmanned aerial vehicles for surveillance and firepower. Moreover, as the problems of stabilizing Iraq after the Second Gulf War of 2003 suggested, counterinsurgency operations could be very lengthy.

The use of the military for counterinsurgency policing purposes requires a higher density on the ground, and thus more troops. British interest in the early 2010s in expanding the Territorial Army, a reservist force, relates to this issue, as did the American debate from the 2000s about the use of reservists. A parallel process might be seen in the case of states that confront long-term problems with violent domestic opposition, such as India, not only in Kashmir from an Islamic separatist movement but also from left-wing guerrilla forces across much of eastern India. The issue in such states will possibly be addressed by increasing the number of paramilitary police or the paramilitary character of the police, although in Turkey, it is the conscript-based army that leads the struggle against Kurdish separatists. Looked at differently, the use of the army helps militarize the Kurdish issue.

The new version of the American army's *Field Manual 3–0, Operations,* released in February 2008, emphasized the need to understand post-conflict stability operations as an important role by making them equal with traditional priorities. The first task in practice overlaps greatly with the functions of other agencies of government in such a crisis, as well as of non-governmental organizations, but, in a situation like Iraq after the Second Gulf War, there is an important military dimension to the task. Moreover, this dimension is likely to remain significant, notably if the emphasis is to be on counterinsurgency warfare.

As will emerge, this perspective will appear less pertinent if the focus is on regular warfare and the perspective that of confrontation with China. On January 5, 2012, President Barack Obama announced a new "strategic guidance" for the United States designed to respond to challenges and to meet fiscal imperatives. As well as abandoning the assumption that America must be able to fight successfully two different major ground wars at once, a task that the 1990s' reduction in the size of the army had made less easy, the new plan assumed that, in place of a large counterinsurgency operation, America should focus on an Air-Sea battle capability and doctrine designed to provide readiness against China.

It is therefore possible to suggest a regional contrast between Western militaries most concerned with counterinsurgency capabilities and international intervention accordingly, notably the European powers, and those focused on regular warfare, which will probably be the case for Japan, a Western military by training, weaponry, and doctrine. The

United States may well be moving from the former to the latter category, especially if a concentration on confronting China leads to a fall in army numbers. The dependence of military affairs on tasking is clearly revealed in this case.

Turning to the more distant future, and considering technologies that are in early stages at the present, it is possible that different types of combatants will be created in the form of robots, cyborgs, and clones. It is more likely that advances in knowledge of the brain and in genetic engineering may alter what can be expected from human warriors. The latter (like other humans in the future) will probably be enhanced organic entities with cybernetic implants. Increased knowledge of the brain may also provide opportunities for action against combatants. Advances in material science will lead to designer materials with inherent capabilities to sense and modify their behavior or functionality.[3] At a different level, the possibility of using electro-magnetic pulses may be developed in order to provide tactical, operational, and strategic capabilities.

Some of the discussion of the long-term may appear fantastical, but the world of robotics is already present to a degree in the form of automatic weapons that may be controlled from a distance, including not only drones but also weaponry on airplanes not themselves under the control of the pilot. Moreover, it would be very surprising if there is no military application of advances in other fields, such as genetic engineering. Such developments might not alter the political paradigms and purposes of warfare, but they could certainly alter the conduct of war.

CYBERWARFARE

A sense of new possibilities as already present was captured by the interest in cyberwarfare in recent years. Its use is shrouded in a degree of mystery, as states that are not at war with each other do not rush to claim credit for hostile acts. Nevertheless, it looks as though the (probable) Israeli use of cyberwarfare helped to delay the Iranian nuclear program, notably with the use of the Stuxnet malware virus in 2009 in order to sabotage the centrifuges employed to enrich uranium. This attack complemented what appears to have been a policy of assassinating scientists. Israel has certainly tried to develop a major cyber capability as an alternative to more conventional warfare. The military and political risks of an air assault on Iran's nuclear program encouraged the use of alternatives, while the public discussion of both risk and alternative led to a greater understanding of technological options. This was also seen with evaluation of the Iranian threat in 2011–2012 to close the Strait of Hormuz, a threat that brought Iranian missiles as an element into opposition with American naval capability, notably with the revelation in March 2012 of a recent American evaluation of the possible consequences of an Israeli attack on Iran.

There also appears to have been a series of cyberattacks on Western governmental computer systems originating from official sources in China and Russia, notably a Russian cyberassault on Estonia and Chinese attacks on American and Japanese military and economic targets. Both Russia and China have been particularly active in this field, and this activity is clearly designed to provide a means to offset the conventional advantages enjoyed by the United States. There have also been efforts to reverse-engineer the Stuxnet malware virus. The vulnerability of American financial markets to cyberattacks emerged in electronic trading at the time of market instability in 2008 in the period when Lehman Brothers collapsed.

With cyberattacks, we are already in the stage of actuality, not speculation, but, as yet, this new technology has not reached the state of any fully fledged conflict. What that will mean in practice and whether it will be possible to provide adequate defenses against sustained attacks are unclear. The noted military historian Michael Howard has suggested that cyberwarfare may make even nuclear deterrence obsolete and may enable minor powers, including non-state actors, to equalize the battlefield.[4]

Electronic warfare across a broad range suggests the possibility of destroying the organizational processes of a target society and, therefore, has an almost science-fiction quality to it. These possibilities are linked to the idea that the so-called Revolution in Military Affairs did not really occur in the 1990s and early 2000s but is actually occurring now.

Against this interpretation, it can be suggested that possibly the RMA, or rather a revolution in military affairs, is always just over the horizon, with present predictions and promises brought to fruition in future success. Moreover, as another critique of claims that are frequently made, the idea of an RMA is centrally bound up with the way in which advocates proclaim the value of their program and policies.[5]

Yet, even if these caveats contain a considerable degree of accuracy, there nevertheless appears something recognizably different about the relationship between humans and lethality suggested by weapons, such as those of cyberwarfare, in which the destructiveness of this lethality is not so much a matter of physical destruction. The response to cyberwarfare may be a different form of internet so that what needs to be separated from the rest to protect it will be developed. The current cyberattacks will not be possible with such a system, although attacking methods will doubtless develop.

QUESTIONS OF PRIORITIZATION

In addition to cyberwarfare, the future may bring smart means of transporting munitions to the target so that tanks and aircraft will be redundant. This would be a revolutionary change as opposed to bigger and better versions of what already exists. The readiness, however, of military commanders to support such change is unclear. The case of air power makes it clear that many are reluctant to move from manned to unmanned flight. For example, the British Royal Navy is heavily committed to a new generation of jets and is putting very little effort into even considering options for drones. In this case, the role of procurement decisions in favor of carriers already taken in response to recent ideas and images of force and warfare is highly significant.

At the same time, problems of prioritization come to the fore, for both present and future, because, although it is possible to draw links between new and future weapons, not least by repeating mantras of joined-up warfare and combined operations, there are still important differences between, say, electro-magnetic pulses, robotic vehicles such as drones, and altering the fighting characteristics of soldiers. To bundle all changes, or potential changes, in a given era into a revolution in military affairs—

for example, the enhanced air power of the 2000s alongside the research into space weapons systems and low-yield nuclear technology—is to risk suggesting a misleading coherence. In practice, there may be not only no such coherence but also contradictions between the supposed constituents. These contradictions are a matter of serious competing resource demands, as well as problems in the very different relationship between potential usage and existing ethics.

Questions of doctrine and tasking also play a role. The ability to conceive of, and implement, organizational and operational means for coordinating new weapon systems as well as new and existing ones should not be assumed. Tasking demands most attention, as it will help determine investment and this investment will be crucial to the move from ideas to implementation. The extent to which the key issue for the West at present is posed by either Great Power confrontation, notably between China and the United States but also Russian pressure on Europe, or, on the other hand, by insurrectionary movements, in Europe or elsewhere, underlines the question of the choice of technology and, indeed, the technology and, more particularly processes, of choice. The specifications of weaponry required in these two cases are very different, not least because the former suggests a symmetrical warfare, in which it will be necessary to counter advanced anti-weapons, whereas that will not be the case in the second case.

DIFFUSION OF WEAPONRY

However, the diffusion of weaponry at present is such that insurrectionary movements can readily receive state-of-the art weapons. Indeed, this provides a way for major powers to fight via surrogates, as, repeatedly, in the Cold War. The transportation possibilities of the age of aircraft are such that earlier hindrances affecting this diffusion can be overcome. As a result, Iranian arms, such as rockets, were flown to Syria to be moved by land to the Hezbollah movement in neighboring Lebanon in order to threaten Israel and thus play a role in Israeli calculations about the impact of any attack on Iran. This movement helps explain the strategic importance to Israel of the overthrow of a pro-Iranian government in Syria. However, an element of continuity in the diffusion of weaponry is provided by attempts to prevent the movement of arms by sea, both by interception on the high seas and by a blockade near the destination. This situation can be seen with Israeli action against arms shipments to the Gaza Strip. Naval action has also been used against North Korean arms movements.

The transfer of weapons is not the same as that of productive capacity, but the relative ease of borrowing capability, by gift, trade, purchase, and espionage, serves as a reminder of the difficulty of maintaining a lead in technology, and notably, provided the industrial infrastructure to permit production is present in both countries. Indeed, the continued spread of advanced engineering and electronics will ensure in the future that the Western dominance of cutting-edge weaponry and the relevant control systems will probably be increasingly challenged. However, American investment in research on such weapons and systems is currently unmatched, and it is unclear how far the nature of China's military-industrial base is able to support comparable development, let alone more effective weaponry.

Instead, China has been dependent on large-scale arms purchases from Russia including fighters, submarines, and surface warships, which has helped keep the Russian arms industry buoyant, although, at the same time, Russian naval capability has declined significantly, not least in terms of the seaworthiness of its warships. In February 2012, the Russian government announced it would spend about $100 billion by 2020 to modernize its military-industrial complex. However, although expenditure was eased by the profits received from being the world's second biggest arms exporter, this pledge was an election-season announcement, as well as an instance of a more general series of commitments that Russia cannot currently afford. This issue draws attention to the additional money Russia receives from rises in energy prices, a position shared by Iran and Venezuela, both also opponents of the United States. This point underlines the need for American strategists to address energy prices and links. The former would benefit from steps to increase production and to limit and change consumption, which includes raising taxes on fuel, while the question of energy links requires active steps to lessen dependency on potentially hostile energy sources by America's allies, notably Japan and Europe.

The Chinese carrier, laid down by the Soviet Union in 1985, was purchased as an unfinished hull from Ukraine in 1998 and began its sea trials in August 2011. The speed of Chinese economic growth suggests that China will become a more major arms manufacturer. China may become the world's biggest economy by 2018, and its defense budget, a fifth of America's in 2011, may match it by 2025. This capability is seen as a threat by China's neighbors. However, there are dangers in extrapolating trends, as well as in neglecting questions of the effectiveness of investment and the consequences of China's lack of military experience.

As a consequence of the diffusion of weaponry, there is far less variation in the weaponry used on land than there was in 1850. That, however, does not mean that all militaries have identical weapons, or that they use weapons in the same fashion. Instead, the very diffusion of such weapons as semi-automatic firearms, rocket-propelled grenades, and missiles has focused attention on training and usage. This focus might appear to subvert a technological analysis of warfare based on weaponry and related systems. However, looked at differently, the very emphasis on usage arises from the given stage of weapons technology shared by much of the world on land. The situation is very different at sea and in the air, let alone with regard to cyberwarfare.

A hierarchy of military sophistication exists, but the experience of terrorist movements suggests that there will be attempts to ascend or bypass the hierarchy by using deadly weapons such as sarin gas. Moreover, recent research work on H5N1 (bird flu) has increased its ability to transmit the virus between humans and led to concerns about security and exploitation by terrorists.

Terrorists use weapons that are fit for purpose, in that they do not require much training, as with suicide bombs, and that have a disproportionate destructiveness, so that the small number of terrorists can achieve a major impact, at least in terms of killing large numbers. This process will encourage terrorist movements to persist with the attempt to find the silver bullet in order to achieve maximum disruption despite their weakness in numbers and their lack of state organization. Thus, terrorist movements have a particularly strong interest in the idea of technological capability. This interest was seen in the response to developments in explosives in the nineteenth century. At the more mundane level of working-class discontent in Britain, the invention of friction matches in 1826 by the Stockton chemist John Walker, and their subsequent manufacture as "strike anywhere Lucifers," made arson easier.

The ability of al-Qaeda terrorists to grab attention and transform priorities by means of their air attacks on New York and Washington in 2001 was a warning of what could happen if more advanced technologies were to be employed by terrorists.[6] At the same time, as far as deadliness is concerned, intent can be more potent than the means by which it is made real: numbers can readily be killed with the use of relatively simple weapons.

Moving from terrorism, technology has also proved important to both sides in contemporary asymmetric wars: for irregulars with Kalashnikovs (semi-automatic guns) and Semtex (plastic explosive) as well as for regulars with drones. The likely consequences of weaponry in asymmetric conflicts play a role in confrontations, such as that between Iran and the United States in 2011–2012. The Iranian threat to close the Strait of Hormuz through which moves about 35 percent of the world's oil traded by sea was countered by the American Bahrain-based Fifth Fleet, and that led the Iranians to focus on asymmetric capability. The key weapon is the guided missile based on a number of platforms, on land, at sea, and in the air. Mobile land-based missile batteries are designed to thwart American aircraft: from the air, there is the *Karrar* armed drone and, at sea, the *Zolfaqar* speedboat, which is able to travel at 80 miles per hour and to launch *Nasr* anti-ship cruise missiles. *Ghadir* midget submarines, domestically produced and based on a North Korean type, as well as mines, contribute to the Iranian capability. Given American firepower, heavy casualties are anticipated by the Iranians in the event of an attack, but it is hoped to employ "swarming" tactics in order to inflict losses on American warships despite the electronic defenses of the latter.

FITNESS FOR PURPOSE

The concept of fitness for purpose for a variety of combatants, and across a range of activity, is crucial. This concept subverts the idea of a technological hierarchy, not least because any stress on the role of technology as it is actually used in society poses a question mark to simple ideas of modernization.[7] In practice, weapons and the other technologies of war are developed and adopted, as well as being maintained and adapted, because they fulfill purposes. Yet, these very purposes or tasks can be redefined in terms of the potential created by new technologies and the wish to give effect to this potential. Indeed, tasking has been greatly affected by new technologies, not least as space has been reconceptualized and as new resources are pursued. Both processes will continue. The effect of global warming on Arctic geopolitics is already apparent as new shipping routes have been opened up and both merchant and warships are built accordingly.

The rapid and unprecedented increase in world population will create unprecedented pressures focused on existing and new sources of key resources, notably water, food, and energy. As a result, advanced ways of providing both will be significant for militaries in order that they will be able to operate effectively, and more effectively than their opponents, in areas of resource shortage. The safe and rapid conversion of waste water into drinkable water is a significant instance, as is the development of storable solar power as a means to enhance the use of weapons, platforms, and communications. The increase in the population is focused on urban areas, which will contribute greatly to a congested battle space.[8] Such a battle space will lessen technological advantages and complicate military options. This will be particularly the case in counterinsurgency struggles directed against violence in populous areas, such as northern Nigeria in the early 2010s where the Boko Haram Islamic fundamentalist movement has been linked to numerous bomb attacks, both on Christians and on government agencies.

It is unlikely, in the very long term, that units and militaries still reliant on legacy technologies, weapons, and platforms from the twentieth century, such as tanks and aircraft carriers, and even jet aircraft and atomic weaponry, will be deployed. Instead, such technologies, which date from the first half of the twentieth century, will probably be superseded. For the American navy, which will be at the forefront of any confrontation with China, there will be a greater emphasis on surface ships and submarines firing missiles rather than on carriers, of which they had eleven in 2010, while developing technologies, such as electro-magnetic discharge defenses and electric drive, will require a new class of naval vessel.[9]

Moreover, there is no reason to believe that the process and pace of future change will be limited or inconsequential. Far from it. Yet, the imponderables include not only human capability but also the availability of the necessary resources, especially of energy and materials. The resources issue emerges very clearly in the failure to develop capability in space to the anticipated extent. Indeed, if the future of warfare may include conflict with other beings in this or other galaxies, then it is possible that the human ability to wage war may have been compromised by the failure to press ahead with potential developments in space travel and existence.

However, as with capability on Earth, there are questions of functionality and practicality. In the former case, it is even more the case in space than in the Earth's atmosphere that reliance on human beings may be a constraint on activity. Indeed, the space-time equations of the solar system may only encourage military means that do not have this constraint. Secondly, as far as practicality is concerned, the need to think in terms of conflict with other beings that have not been discovered, let alone analyzed, is scarcely to the fore. The distance even to nearby stars makes intergalactic wars unlikely. The use of space for warfare between humans is far more pertinent, but so far many of the bold ideas advanced in the 1980s, not least relating to talk of "Star Wars," have not been brought to fruition.

RESOURCE ISSUES

Cost is a central issue in prioritization, although, in the future, it may be the very existence of resources that becomes more pressing for force structure and deployment. The availability of trace minerals, such as tungsten, required for specialist manufacturing projects is a key issue. Such minerals are important in military technologies, for example, armor-piercing shells, cruise missiles, and strengthened steels. Cost, however, may come more to the fore as societies struggle with the burdens of growing populations and economic and fiscal problems. Past developments suggest that the latter will certainly be a key concern. Russia saw a decline in military expenditure in the late 1990s due to fiscal crisis, followed by a rise thanks to increased energy prices. The east Asian boom of the early 1990s saw a number of bold plans to develop new military capabilities, but the 1997 currency crisis led to cancellations, only for economic growth in the 2000s and 2010s to bring a revival of expenditure on new procurement. Submarines designed to affect the naval situation in the South China Sea were an important aspect of this procurement,[10] with Vietnam ordering six from Russia. Concern about China's rising military expenditure and increased assertiveness helped ensure that other east Asian powers pressed ahead with new programs, notably in Japan and India but also in Vietnam and South Korea. The fiscal crisis of the late 2000s and early 2010s has had a comparable impact in the West to the east Asian crisis of the late 1990s and ensured that Asian military expenditure exceeded that of Europe in 2012, although in per capita terms the European expenditure remained higher.

Economic and fiscal crises do not inherently mean a stop to new military expenditure, both because the emphasis may be on cutting spending in other areas and because in the military sphere there may be a stress on how best to use new technology in order to save money while retaining capability. Within militaries, indeed, fiscal issues exacerbate the tension between investing in existing systems or the future. This question has been thrown into prominence by the growing cost of the military as a labor force, notably with pay and social welfare. Both, but especially the latter, in the shape of health benefits, are a particular problem as far as the United States is concerned.[11]

There is no real sign that Western governments will be able to grasp the mettle of military welfarism. Attempts to limit benefits modestly have led to outcries in the United States and Britain, and politicians and military leaders have failed to explain the extent to which these costs, and more general issues of military remuneration, are hindering future effectiveness. The over-officered nature of these (and many other) militaries is also a factor, with pension-padding (increased payment at the close of careers in order to enhance pensions) being a particular problem. Looking to the future, these and related issues of militaries as producer lobbies may well hinder the development of weaponry in particular contexts.

This restraint on investment in new capabilities is one that is cultur-
ally varied, with China, notably, not having to face the same military
social-welfare commitments, although the role of the military in China's
politics, foreign policy, and economics represents a more serious distortion. More generally, the costs of the soldiery will encourage expenditure on labor-saving weaponry. To that extent, there is a strong parallel
between the military and other forms of economic activity. Moreover,
the impact of social conditions emerges in such examples.

CONCLUSIONS

As noted throughout this book, tasking is a key element. The future
may well throw conflict between states, notably over resources—for
example, water in south and southwest Asia and northeast Africa (the
Nile basin)—to the fore. Equally, the stress instead may be within states,
namely on how best to control volatile populations who have little chance
of fulfilling their hopes of life opportunities, let alone reaching or sustained desired living standards. In the case of tension, even conflict,
within states, the weaponry employed is likely to be "low tech" compared to that used in conflict between states. For example, the planes
employed in an attempt to overawe riotous crowds, as with those of the
RAF that sought to overawe crowds threatening strategic railways during the Quit India campaign in 1942–1944,[12] will fly far more slowly than
those in such international conflict. There will also be an emphasis in
conflict within states on non-lethal firearms, not least because casualties, even injuries, caused by military action are highly contentious.

Such weapons' specifications, however, do not mean that there is necessarily a lack of sophistication. There will be an overlap with the weaponry used for policing but also a need to deal with the anti-weaponry
employed by rioters. The latter may become more deadly, but the root
problem is the mismatch between the potential offered by a great number of rioters and the likely far smaller number of soldiers. So again, political contexts come to the fore.

There are also broader questions of cultural identity. Whereas in the
past the adoption of technological change was constrained in societies

and contexts in which there was opposition to change,[13] the nature of modern civilization is one in which technological change is seen as a constant, while improvement is regarded as a necessity. There is resistance to some aspect of this change, while improvement itself is contentious, but the commitment to the status quo is limited. The military is a central part of this process.

CONCLUSIONS

Today your government and its military advisors appear to have accepted the concept that the way to defeat Communism in Vietnam is by bombing when clearly the precepts garnered from World War Two should have told them that ideas cannot be dislodged by bombs.

—*J. F. C. "Boney" Fuller, British military theorist,*
  to an American correspondent, July 1965

Rather than offering a reprise of the arguments already made in the book, this chapter focuses on a number of key themes. The need to strike a balance between bold claims for technology and attempts to minimize its role is a major point. Moreover, as in all historical works, the nature of the evidence is a key element. For much of history, it is difficult to assess the impact of technological change in part because evidence of how conflict was waged was limited or speculative.[1] This issue is a particular problem with warfare prior to 1500 in the West, and with much non-Western warfare prior to 1850, but not only then. In addition, the evidence that survives both about the course of battle and concerning why events occurred is often ambiguous. As a local observer of the battle of Oudenaarde (1708) noted, "In this battle more happened than we could see or hear of because it was impossible to remember everything."[2] Moreover, theories are frequently advanced on a limited basis, as with the argument that, during the First Civil War in England (1642–

1646), there was a rapid progress in cavalry tactics from the caracole to shock charges.[3]

Nevertheless, progress in understanding is possible, not least because of advances in battlefield archaeology[4] but also due to a greater scholarly concern than hitherto with non-Western history. Furthermore, scholarship on other aspects of combat, notably on training, cohesion, and morale, has provided a better idea of the readiness and resilience of units.[5] This scholarship makes it possible to make more informed use of arguments about the effectiveness of weapons drawing on particular engagements. Conversely, for some readers, this scholarship can introduce a level of unwelcome complexity.

Throughout, technology emerges as an important factor in affecting the results of conflict, but a factor that operates as one of those considerably influencing warfare, rather than as a determining cause of success. In part, aside from the quality of use, the effectiveness of technology depends greatly on the actions of opponents, which, indeed, is true of any element of conflict. These actions can multiply or limit capabilities. For example, the firepower advantages from 1943 of Western forces fighting Japan proved particularly useful in dealing with Japanese mass attacks. These attacks were encouraged by the Japanese belief in the determining role of spirit or morale, a belief that had greatly influenced Japanese doctrine in the 1920s and 1930s. At the same time, it was necessary for Western forces to devise and implement appropriate tactics, such as all-round concentric fire zones. Moreover, fighting the Japanese also showed the limits of high-tech firepower. In the Pacific and Burma, their defenses often withstood nearly everything thrown at them. The ultimate American weapons on the islands of Iwo Jima and Okinawa in 1945 against well-entrenched Japanese forces that could not retreat and did not intend to surrender were flamethrowers and explosive charges, employed by very low-tech riflemen.

The number of combatants involved in the Second World War and the availability of plentiful source material in a number of media, including extensive oral records, ensures that that conflict provides the best way to evaluate the impact of specific technologies, such as air power, tanks, submarines, and aircraft carriers. Repeatedly, it is the case that multiplying the number of examples provides qualifications of conclusions about capability based on fewer examples. This point is more widely relevant for the nature of research and indeed the use of evidence in constructing more general accounts of military history. For example, with submarines in the Second World War, an account based on the German U-boat campaign in the Atlantic would suggest (eventual) failure, whereas one focused on the (eventually) successful American submarine assault on the Japanese would be far more favorable about the tactical, operational, and strategic capabilities of submarine warfare.

Such conclusions are significant, as these campaigns were the last major ones in which submarines were used in conflict and, therefore, affected the understanding of their capability during the Cold War and subsequently, as well as that of anti-submarine weaponry, tactics, and doctrine. While technology helped determine the perception of submarine warfare,[6] this perception was heavily influenced by the experience of conflict.

A less common instance is provided by the value of fixed fortifications. Before the Second World War, there had been much investment on them, notably with the French Maginot Line, but also, for example, with the Finnish Mannerheim Line, the Dutch Water Line, the German West Wall, and the American fortifications to protect Manila Bay. Their record and those of fortifications constructed during the war was mixed. The Atlantic Wall built by the Germans to defend the French coast against Allied invasion showed in 1944 that ferroconcrete was very resistant to high explosive, but fortifications could be blasted through by artillery, as the Soviets did with the Mannerheim Line in 1940. This success brought their Winter War to Finland to the successful conclusion that is generally neglected due to the usual focus on earlier Finnish successes. None of the fortification systems mentioned above prevented failure.

Instead, as with other weapon systems, fortifications proved most effective as part of a combined-arms force, while, in strategic terms, the combined dimension was also dependent on an appropriate plan. As far as the combined-arms capability was concerned, fortifications required a flexible, supporting counterattack defense, because bunkers were vulnerable to attack and, once engaged, the occupants were trapped inside unless a counterattack hit the attackers when they were held up by the bunkers. While ferroconcrete is very resistant to high explosive, all bunkers and casemates needed apertures for guns, access for their crews, and ventilation. With the right tactics and weapons (demolition charges, flamethrowers, grenades, and tanks), most fortifications could be taken by attacking the occupants through these apertures, although it was time-consuming and tiring. In 1944, the Germans lacked sufficient mobile forces forward enough in Normandy to act in co-operation with the fixed coastal defenses attacked by the Allies on D-Day. Despite the cost involved in their construction, the coastal defenses on the invasion beaches were damaged or rapidly outflanked on June 6. The Atlantic Wall neither prevented the landings nor seriously impeded them, the American experience on Omaha Beach notwithstanding. Even there, the troops still managed to get ashore and press inland in a matter of hours. They were not thrown back into the sea.

Moreover, the subsequent use of other such defenses to delay the Allies' capture of ports, notably Cherbourg, was countered by the Allied ability to supply their forces across the beaches, an ability that was crucial to the success and tempo of the Allied campaigning.[7] This ability entailed a key logistical flexibility that relied on technological innovations such as floating harbors as well as an undersea oil pipeline transporting oil from England.

The lack of an appropriate plan was seen with the Maginot Line in 1940. These impressive fortifications protecting France's border with Germany directed the German attack farther north, in the event through the Ardennes in southern Belgium, although the French thought the attack would come across the Belgian plain north of the River Meuse. In response to both the threat and the reality of German attack, the French, however, proved unable to devise an adequate plan for effective mobile warfare, or at least one that worked in the campaign of 1940.

Similarly, the American attack on the German West Wall, protecting Germany's frontier, in late 1944 was inappropriate, in part because the terrain and weather helped the defenders but also because the recent rapid tempo of the American advance across France and Belgium had not prepared them for such fighting. This example underlines the need to study technologies in context. The task is always significant. If fortifications are assessed, it needs to be decided whether they were primarily designed to deter attack, delay advances, or make them costly, and also which criterion is most appropriate.

In the case of fortifications, as of other systems, technology is significant in the weaponry employed, in the means of deploying and supporting power, and in wider questions about the industrial strength and capacity of particular societies. This strength and capacity are important for the ability to innovate, produce, and sustain weapons and other means of war, and also for the economic activity that creates the wealth to fund military expenditure and, even more, advances in military capability.

The causes of conflict are also a variable that can be affected by technological change. Aside from greatly speeding up the decision-making processes of both diplomacy and war, developments in communications are also transforming the nature of political societies. Whereas the bulk of the population was illiterate and removed from the political process in most countries in the eighteenth century, and in many well into the twentieth, there has since been a process of mass politicization in which changing assumptions about the rights of a new entity, the public, have been linked to altering means for expressing and seeking to influence their views, from the daily press to modern electronic communications.

This development relates not only to external warfare but also to domestic conflict. Thus, the riots in England in August 2011, notably in London, indicated the potential of new, handheld means of personal communication, such as Blackberrys, in mobilizing and directing large-scale riots. The internet, laptop computers, and mobile phones have also become part of the stock-in-trade of insurrectionary movements, for example, the Taliban in Afghanistan.[8] As such, communications overlap operational issues in the field with the processes of political mobilization and expression. Indeed, the close linkage between the two owes much to the potential of modern communications and to the rapid exploitation of this potential.

The political dimension of conflict and its outbreak, notably the attempt to maintain cohesion and morale and to weaken those of opponents, is such that this use of communications will become more important in the future. It will probably be accompanied by attempts, by both commanders and opponents, to reach individual combatants, which will transform the nature of morale. Moreover, in their use of communications, insurrectionary movements, like the terrorist groups with which they overlap, deploy the means otherwise employed by states, companies, and civil society. As such, they may challenge the basis of future order.[9]

Technology emerges from a consideration of past, present, and future as highly important. Although technology does not only mean bigger and more expensive, it has become, across time, more potent, more significant, and more central to military policy.[10] As an instance of greater sophistication and potency, it is instructive to compare the shields discussed in the introduction, or the simple metal-bashing of single-sheet body armor that prevailed for most of history, with the complex body armor currently in use. The latter is more complex because it has to do a different job compared to the armor of earlier times and works on different principles. Modern body armor is designed to dissipate the energy of bullets and, to that end, is composed of a number of materials.

Similarly, across a brief period, there has been a major enhancement in the protection of tanks, with composite armor and techniques, such as contact explosions (reactive armor), used to deal with penetrating projectiles. The process of experimentation is important to this and to other enhancements but so also is the accumulated knowledge, notably of materials and ballistics, that links military and non-military technologies, helping, indeed, to make the distinction somewhat redundant.

To be effective, the use of new systems has to be grounded in pertinent tactics and doctrine, let alone strategy. Superior force employment is more significant than superior equipment.[11] In short, technology can be a shortcut to nowhere unless its employment is ably planned. This is notably because output, in the shape of greater lethality, does not produce the desired outcome, in the form of opponents being cajoled to accept policy prescriptions. An understanding of this mismatch is significant for any discussion of military effectiveness, but the mismatch does not mean that technology is without great value. Output is highly significant even though it cannot dictate outcome. In arguing in this study that the use of and belief in technology have to be contextualized, I am not suggesting that this should lead to a denial of role. Instead, as with other key variables, such as political developments and cultural parameters, there is a potent interaction.

Ironically, each of these three—technology, politics, and culture—is also involved in the perception of the respective roles of the others. This last point tends to be underplayed, but the impact, on both the military and civilians, of images of war, actual and fictional, current and potential, is significant for the way in which technology is perceived. In particular, concepts of manliness and honor do not relate solely to hand-to-hand combat and physical strength, as they once did. Instead, man has also been linked to the glamour of the machine, notably with movement. This glamour has played a central role in the fascination with air power, a form of warfare in which the emphasis is on the individual combatant, not the reinforcing crowd, notably of ground crew and control staff, that is, in fact, crucial if aircraft are to operate at all. Thus, reliance on the machine is not separate from current Western concepts of honorable conflict. These equations affect attitudes toward the use of (unmanned) drones, although, significantly, they certainly do not prevent their use.

The impact of such concepts, which themselves are far from constant, on the reception of new technology is not a new factor. It can be seen in the response to firearms, both in the early modern period in the West and in non-Western societies such as Egypt and Japan, and also in the debate in the late nineteenth and early twentieth centuries over the continued value of cavalry. In part, the adoption of new technology can be related to the extent to which the weaponry can be used to respond to the anxieties raised in such debates. Thus, tanks and planes provided psychological opportunities apparently comparable to those offered by cavalry.

Far from acting as a constant factor across time, technology has expanded humanity's ability to operate in a number of environments, especially under the water and in the air, and has enhanced human specifications, notably of speed. As a result of this expansion, the importance of technological factors has been enhanced: for capability, for relative effectiveness, and for governmental, institutional, and popular perception. Moreover, there is no reason to believe that this process will necessarily become less significant in the future.

The rapid rate of population increase, which itself owes much to technological advances, especially in medicine, public health, and food supply, is contributing greatly to serious pressure on resources. In addition, as far as any matching rise in production is concerned, there is the possibility that technological advance might become less possible or effective in particular spheres. However, the possible availability of less technology, or less technological change, does not mean that the effectiveness of what exists or can be established will necessarily be diminished. Furthermore, the process of efficiency savings enhancing the use of resources, seen in so many fields, will also be apparent in military technology. Again, this process will increase the significance of this technology.

Cost has always been a key issue in military activity, but it became a more significant factor with a marked rise in the pace of technological change from the nineteenth century. This pace led to a rapid obsolescence that drove up costs. In turn, the rising cost of developmental work then was such that, by the 1870s, the costs had to be ameliorated by selling more arms to foreign governments, which brought new technologies to more states than hitherto. By the second half of the twentieth century, the costs of development were such that armaments firms merged and formed arrangements with other firms, while governments combined to share project costs, as with much European military procurement at present. Costs also led to bold claims for the capabilities of new weapons, claims frequently unjustified because the weapons were either ill conceived or underdeveloped. Moreover, costs resulted in pressure to pursue new technological developments, while these developments were also presented as a way to tackle costs. This element is unlikely to cease.

The emphasis on change helped drive the shifting balance between cyclical and progressive technological development. In past centuries, weapons like the pike or war elephants might be readopted on a cycle of millennia, whereas more recently obsolescence has become the norm. This change can also be seen in relevant non-military technologies, contributing to the long-standing relationship between the impact of weapons technology and of non-military counterparts such as transport, communications, and medicine.

The conclusion is readily apparent. The cultural turn in military analysis was an appropriate response to the technological triumphalism of the RMA.[12] However, cultural interpretations are pushed too far if they lead to a new form of determinism or to a denial of any significant role for technology, whether narrowly or widely defined. Instead, the impact of technological factors remains highly important, not least in a dynamic interaction with other contextual factors. Moreover, technology will play a major role in the future. Technology remains fundamental to warfare, even though technologically determined models of the latter, such as those favored by the concept of Revolutions in Military Affairs, now or in the past, are not sustainable.

POSTSCRIPT

What happened in the past and the accounts we offer of it: history is inevitably affected by the interactions of its two facets. And so also with military history. Presentism is a key issue when considering these accounts and thus our enquiry into what happened. Presentism indeed is a theme of this book, notably with the discussion both of the RMA and of how the belief in military revolutions has affected the consideration of earlier episodes of technological change.

Present-day issues come to the fore in considering the needs for technological capability and advantage. In particular, the possibility of confrontation, if not conflict, with China lead to different concerns to those if Iran is the key issue, and, even more, if the emphasis remains on Afghanistan or similar COIN operations. The American strategic reevaluation of January 2012, with its focus on the Asia-Pacific region and its stress on air and naval capabilities, is of major significance not just for the United States but also for its allies and potential opponents. The Pentagon's "strategic guidance" document issued that month declared that "U.S. forces will no longer be sized to conduct large-scale, prolonged stability operations" and "We will of necessity rebalance toward the Asia-Pacific region."[1]

The likelihood that COIN operations will be supplemented, at the very least, if not replaced by confrontations with well-armed powers, notably China, raises the probability that there will be a stronger interest in the respective merits of rival high-tech weaponry. COIN operations have led to the use of such weaponry, notably with unmanned aerial vehicles, but the situation will be very different if both sides have advanced weaponry and require an ability to destroy that of their opponents.

Such confrontations and conflicts may well lead to a rereading of past episodes, to a repositioning in the literature of the importance of superior weaponry, and to a redefinition of such superiority. This process of reading from the present is more significant in military history than is sometimes allowed, but it also helps explain why, at one time, there are many accounts of the past and not one definitive version.

Among these accounts—it is important to note, in a book on technology—are criticisms of such power. One of the most poetic was that by George, Lord Byron, in his account of the sea in the fourth canto of *Childe Harold's Pilgrimage* (1812), published while Britain was battling Napoleon and was clearly the world's leading naval power:

> The armaments which thunderstrike the walls
> Of rock-built cities, bidding nations quake,
> And monarchs tremble in their capitals,
> The oak leviathans, whose huge ribs make
> Their clay creator the vain title take
> Of lord of thee, and arbiter of war—
> These are they toys, and, as the snowy flake,
> They melt into thy yeast of waves, which mar
> Alike the Armada's pride [1588] or spoils of Trafalgar [1805].

> (Byron, *Childe Harold's Pilgrimage*, 1812, canto 4, verse 181)

Notes

PREFACE

The epigraph is from the short story *The Bruce-Partington Plans* by Arthur Conan-Doyle published in the collection *The Last Bow*. The story is set in London in 1895.

1. A. J. Echeverria, *Imagining Future War: The West's Technological Revolution and Visions of Wars to Come, 1880–1914* (Westport, Conn., 2007).

2. D. Edgerton, "From Innovation to Use: Ten Eclectic Theses on the Historiography of Technology," *History and Technology* 16 (1999): 111–136, and "Innovation, Technology, or History: What Is the Historiography of Technology About?" *Technology and Culture* 51 (2010): 680–697; G. Raudzens, "War-Winning Weapons: The Measurement of Technological Determinism in Military History," *Journal of Military History* 54 (1990): 403–434; and B. C. Hacker, "Military Institutions, Weapons, and Social Change: Toward a New History of Military Technology," *Technology and Culture* 35 (1994): 768–834.

3. F. Cochet, *Armes en Guerre, XIXe–XXIe siècles: Mythes, symboles, réalités* (Paris, 2010), 259.

4. R. I. Barendse, *The Arabian Seas: The Indian Ocean World of the Seventeenth Century* (Armonk, N.Y., 2002), 454.

5. C. Gray, *Perspectives on Strategy* (Oxford, 2013).

6. K. DeVries, "'The Walls Come Tumbling Down': The Myth of Fortification Vulnerability to Early Gunpowder Weapons," in *The Hundred Years War*, ed. L. J. A. Villalon and D. Kagay (Leiden, 2005), 429–446.

7. T. Benbow, ed., *British Naval Aviation: The First 100 Years* (Farnham, UK, 2011).

INTRODUCTION

1. L. Freedman, *The Revolution in Strategic Affairs* (Oxford, 1998).

2. T. G. Mahnken, *Technology and the American Way of War since 1945* (New York, 2008), 4–6.

3. B. E. Seely, "The Automotive Transportation System: Cars and Highways in Twentieth-Century America," in *A Companion to American Technology*, ed. C. Pursell (Oxford, 2005), 247.

4. R. J. Overy, *Why the Allies Won* (New York, 1995).

5. Similar claims were made on the back of my *Tools of War* (London, 2007), but I was not responsible for the "blurb" for a book that was very much initiated by the publisher.

6. M. R. Smith and L. Marx, eds., *Does Technology Drive History? The Dilemma of Technological Determinism* (Cambridge, Mass., 1994); and L. Marx, "In the Driving-Seat? The Nagging Ambiguity in Historians' Attitudes to the Rise of 'Technology,'" *Times Literary Supplement,* August 29, 1997, 3–4.

7. This subject is more obscure than is generally appreciated. A. Williams, *The Knight and the Blast Furnace* (Leiden, 2002).

8. C. Smith, "*Dreadnought* Science: The Cultural Construction of Efficiency and Effectiveness," in *The "Dreadnought" and the Edwardian Age,* ed. R. J. Blyth, A. Lambert, and R. Rüger (Farnham, UK, 2011), 135–164.

9. L. Sondhaus, *Navies in Modern World History* (London, 2004).

10. R. Whatmore, "Shelburne and Perpetual Peace: Small States, Commerce, and International Relations within the Bowood Circle," in *An Enlightenment Statesman in Whig Britain: Lord Shelburne in Context, 1737–1805,* ed. N. Aston and C. C. Orr (Woodbridge, UK, 2011), 262.

11. J. P. Bertaud and D. Reichel, *Atlas de la Révolution Française: L'Armée et La Guerre* (Paris, 1989), 69–70; and G. E. Rothenberg, *The Art of Warfare in the Age of Napoleon* (Bloomington, Ind., 1977), 123–124.

12. For the case of the computer, P. Atkinson, *Computer* (London, 2010), 10–13.

13. E.g., for the interrupter gear, see chapter 5.

14. There were already drawings of underwater vehicles in late fifteenth-century editions of Vegetius.

15. C. Martin, "The Complexity of Strategy: 'Jackie' Fisher and the Trouble with Submarines," *Journal of Military History* 75 (2011): 448–449, 469.

16. S. B. A. Willis, "Fleet Performance and Capability in the Eighteenth-Century Royal Navy," *War in History* 11 (2004): 383.

17. B. Marsden, "Blowing Hot and Cold: Reports and Retorts on the Status of the Air-Engine as Success or Failure, 1830–1855," *History of Science* 36 (1998): 373–420.

18. P. Wahl and D. R. Toppel, *The Gatling Gun* (New York, 1965).

19. J. Ellis, *The Social History of the Machine Gun* (Baltimore, 1975), 34; A. Smith, *Machine Gun: The Story of the Men and the Weapon That Changed the Face of War* (London, 2002), 93, 97; and J. Keller, *Mr. Gatling's Terrible Marvel: The Gun That Changed Everything and the Misunderstood Genius Who Invented It* (New York, 2008), 221, 26, 173.

20. R. Overy, "Doctrine Not Dogma: Lessons from the Past," in *Doctrine and Military Effectiveness,* ed. M. Duffy et al. (Exeter, 1997), 42.

21. A. A. Siddiqi, *The Red Rockets' Glare: Spaceflight and the Soviet Imagination, 1857–1957* (Cambridge, 2010).

22. For a less critical view, A. Echevarria, *After Clausewitz: German Military Thinkers before the Great War* (Lawrence, Kans., 2000).

23. T. Cook, *No Place to Run: The Canadian Corps and Gas Warfare in the First World War* (Vancouver, 1999).

24. A. Palazzo, *Seeking Victory on the Western Front: The British Army and Chemical Warfare in World War One* (Lincoln, Neb., 2000).

25. E. W. Marsden, *Greek and Roman Artillery: Technical Treatises* (Oxford, 1971); and T. Rihll, *The Catapult: A History* (Yardley, Pa., 2007).

26. NA. CAB. 24/265 fols. 220–221.

27. S. Morillo, "Guns and Government: A Comparative Study of Europe and Japan," *Journal of World History* 6 (1995): 75–106.

28. B. J. Buchanan, ed., *Gunpowder: The History of an International Technology* (Bath, 1996).

29. M. J. Neufeld, *The Rocket and the Reich: Peenemünde and the Coming of the Ballistic Missile Era* (Washington, D.C., 1995).

30. K. Alder, *Engineering the Revolution: Arms and Enlightenment in France, 1763–1815* (Princeton, N.J., 1997); and M. R. Smith, *Harpers Ferry Armory and the New Technology: The Challenge of Change* (Ithaca, N.Y., 1977).

31. J. Bradley, *Guns for the Tsar: American Technology and the Small Arms Industry in Nineteenth-Century Russia* (Dekalb, Ill., 1990).

32. R. Cock, "'The Finest Invention in the World': The Royal Navy's Early Trials of Copper Sheathing, 1708–1770," *Mariner's Mirror* 87 (2001): 446–459.

33. BL. Add. 49016 fols. 7–26.

34. *Trewman's Exeter Flying-Post,* December 13, 1882, for new rifle for British army, and April 11, 1883, for explosives.

35. J. Langins, *Conserving the Enlightenment: French Military Engineering from Vauban to the Revolution* (Cambridge, Mass., 2003), esp. 325–357, 361–428.

36. It may have appeared in Mongolia earlier.

37. T. May, *The Mongol Art of War: Chinggis Khan and the Mongol Military System* (Yardley, Pa., 2007).

38. M. H. Jackson and C. de Beer, *Eighteenth Century Gunfounding* (Washington, D.C., 1974).

39. J. S. Levy and W. S. Thompson, *The Arc of War* (Chicago, 2011).

40. T. Pollard and I. Banks, eds., *War and Sacrifice: Studies in the Archaeology of Conflict* (Leiden, 2007).

41. E. Oakeshott, *The Sword in the Age of Chivalry* (London, 1981). See also his *The Archaeology of Weapons: Arms and Armour from Prehistory to the Age of Chivalry* (London, 1960), and *European Weapons and Armour: From the Renaissance to the Industrial Revolution* (North Hollywood, Calif., 1980). On the fifteenth century, S. Anglo, *The Martial Arts of Renaissance Europe* (New Haven, Conn., 2000).

42. D. Nicolle, "The Monreale Capitals and the Military Equipment of Later Norman Sicily," *Instituto de Estudios Sobre Armas Antiguas* (1980): 91.

43. For opposition to technological determinism, F. E. Rey, "Weapons, Technological Determinism, and Ancient Warfare," in *New Perspectives on Ancient Warfare,* ed. G. Fagan and M. Trundle (Leiden, 2010), 21–56.

44. P. Connolly, *Greece and Rome at War* (London, 1981), 45, 51–54.

45. Connolly, *Greece and Rome,* 42.

46. A. Schwartz, *Reinstating the Hoplite: Arms, Armour and Phalanx Fighting in Archaic and Classical Greece* (Stuttgart, 2009).

47. J. Howard-Johnston, "Byzantium against Persia and Islam, 530–750," in *The Medieval World at War,* ed. M. Bennett (London, 2009), 21–22; and S. James, *Rome and the Sword: How Warriors and Weapons Shaped Roman History* (London, 2011).

48. D. Nicolle, "Arms and Armor Illustrated in the Art of the Latin East," in *The Horns of Hattin,* ed. B. Z. Kedar (Jerusalem, 1992), 332, and "The Capella Palatina Ceiling and the Muslim Military Inheritance of Norman Sicily," *Instituto de Estudios Sobre Armas Antiguas* (1983): 50.

49. H. Talhoffer, *Medieval Combat: A Fifteenth-Century Illustrated Manual of Swordfighting and Close-Quarter Combat,* ed. M. Rector (London, 2000).

50. K. DeVries, *Infantry Warfare in the Early Fourteenth Century: Discipline, Tactics, and Technology* (Woodbridge, UK, 1996); and J. Waldman, *Hafted Weapons in Medieval and Renaissance Europe: The Evolution of European Staff Weapons between 1200 and 1650* (Leiden, 2005).

51. P. A. Lorge, *The Asian Military Revolution: From Gunpowder to the Bomb* (Cambridge, 2008).

52. D. Nicolle, "Byzantine and Islamic Arms and Armour; Evidence for Mutual Influence," *Graeco-Arabica* 4 (1991): 299–300.

53. J. France, "Technology and the Success of the First Crusade," in *War and Society in the Eastern Mediterranean, 7th–15th Centuries,* ed. Y. Lev (Leiden, 1997).

54. L. Casson, *Ships and Seamanship in the Ancient World,* 2nd ed. (Princeton, N.J., 1986); G. Deng, *Maritime Sector, Institutions and Sea Power of Premodern China* (Westport, Conn., 1999); and J. B. Hattendorf and R. W. Unger, eds., *War at Sea in the Middle Ages and Renaissance* (Woodbridge, UK, 2003).

55. J. J. Cooke, "Anglo-French Diplomacy and the Contraband Arms Trade in Colonial Africa, 1894–1897," *African Studies Review* 17 (1974): 27–41.

56. D. Nicolle, "Arms of the Umayyad Era [661–750 CE]: Military Technology in a Time of Change," in *War and Society in the Eastern Mediterranean, 7th–15th Centuries,* ed. Y. Lev (Leiden, 1997), 10.

57. For valuable recent works, C. J. Rogers, ed., *The Oxford Encyclopedia of Medieval Warfare and Military Technology* (Oxford, 2010); and K. DeVries, *Medieval Military Technology,* 2nd ed. (Toronto, 2012).

58. P. Krenn, P. Kalaus, and B. S. Hall, "Material Culture and Military History: Test-Firing Early Modern Small Arms," *Material History Review* 42 (1995): 101–119; and T. Richardson, "Ballistic Testing of Historical Weapons," *Royal Armouries Yearbook* 3 (1998): 50–52.

59. S. J. Deitchman, "The 'Electronic Battlefield' in the Vietnam War," *Journal of Military History* 72 (2008): 869–887.

60. I am most grateful for advice from Anthony Saunders on this topic.

61. J. Fennell, *Combat and Morale in the North African Campaign: The Eighth Army and the Path to El Alamein* (Cambridge, 2011), esp. 283–285.

62. A. Converse, *Armies of Empire: The 9th Australian and 50th British Divisions in Battle 1939–1945* (Cambridge, 2011).

63. N. J. M. Campbell, *Jutland: An Analysis of the Fighting* (London, 1986); and A. Gordon, *The Rules of the Game: Jutland and British Naval Command* (London, 1996).

64. A. Krell, *The Devil's Rope: A Cultural History of Barbed Wire* (London, 2002).

65. R. Martello, *Midnight Ride, Industrial Dawn: Paul Revere and the Growth of American Enterprise* (Baltimore, 2010).

66. P. Connolly, *Counterinsurgency in Uruzgan 2009* (Canberra, 2011), 69.

67. C. R. Phillips, *Six Galleons for the King of Spain: Imperial Defense in the Early Seventeenth Century* (Baltimore, 1986); J. Glete, *War and the State in Early Modern Europe: Spain, the Dutch Republic and Sweden as Fiscal-Military States, 1500–1600* (London, 2002), esp. 215; and D. Parrott, *The Business of War: Military Enterprise and Military Revolution in Early Modern Europe* (Cambridge, 2012).

68. F. B. Maurice, *On the Uses of the Study of War* (London, 1927), x.

69. J. A. Grant, "The Arms Trade in Eastern Europe, 1870–1914," in *Girding for Battle: The Arms Trade in a Global Perspective,* ed. D. J. Stoker and J. A. Grant (Westport, Conn., 2003), 28–31.

70. C. Trebilcock, *The Vickers Brothers: Armaments and Enterprise 1854–1914* (London, 1977).

71. W. Murray, "May 1940: Contingency and Fragility of the German RMA," in *The Dynamics of Military Revolution 1300–2050*, ed. W. Murray and M. Knox (Cambridge, 2001), 173; and E. O. Goldman and L. C. Eliason, eds., *The Diffusion of Military Technology and Ideas* (Stanford, Calif., 2003), 349.

72. L. McLoughlin, *Ibn Saud: Founder of a Kingdom* (Basingstoke, UK, 1993), e.g., 122.

73. D. N. Collins, "The Franco-Russian Alliance and Russia's Railways, 1891–1914," *Historical Journal* 16 (1973): 777–788; and D. Stevenson, "War by Timetable: The Railway Race before 1914," *Past and Present* 162 (1991): 163–194.

74. A. Mombauer, *Helmuth von Moltke and the Origins of the First World War* (Cambridge, 2001).

75. D. Showalter, "From Deterrence to Doomsday Machine: The German Way of War, 1890–1914," *Journal of Military History* 64 (2000): 708.

76. J. West, *Gunpowder, Government and War in the Mid-Eighteenth Century* (Woodbridge, UK, 1991).

77. J. Black, *War and the Cultural Turn* (Cambridge, 2012), pp. 5–7.

78. T. Kaiserfeld, "Chemistry in the War Machine: Saltpeter Production in Eighteenth-Century Sweden," in *The Heirs of Archimedes: Science and the Art of War through the Age of Enlightenment*, ed. B. D. Steele and T. Dorland (Cambridge, Mass., 2005), 288.

79. J. R. Hale, "Gunpowder and the Renaissance: An Essay in the History of Ideas," in *Renaissance War Studies* (London, 1983), 389–390.

80. G. W. F. Hegel, *Naturrecht und Staatswissenshcaft um Grundrisse* and *Grundlinien der Philosophie des Rechts* (1821) [*Natural Law and Political Science in Outline; Elements of the Philosophy of Right*], translation from T. M. Knox (ed.), *Hegel's Philosophy of Right* (Oxford, 1967), 212.

81. D. A. Mindell, *War, Technology, and Experience Aboard the USS "Monitor"* (Baltimore, 2000), 144.

82. G. Rowlands, "Louis XIV, Aristocratic Power and the Elite Units of the French Army," *French History* 13 (1999): 330.

83. For a useful case study, E. Lund, *War for the Every Day: Generals, Knowledge and Warfare in Early Modern Europe, 1680–1740* (Westport, Conn., 1999).

84. A. E. Dien, "The Stirrup and Its Effect on Chinese Military History," *Ars Orientalis* 16 (1936): 33–56.

85. J. Needham and R. D. S. Yates, eds., *Military Technology: Missiles and Sieges, Science and Civilization in China* (Cambridge, 1995).

86. A. Ayton and J. L. Price, "The Military Revolution from a Medieval Perspective," in *The Medieval Military Revolution: State, Society and Military Change in Medieval and Early Modern Europe*, ed. A. Ayton and J. L. Price (London, 1998), 16–17.

87. D. Gates, *The Napoleonic Wars 1803–1815* (London, 1997).

88. R. Friedel, *A Culture of Improvement: Technology and the Western Millennium* (Cambridge, Mass., 2007).

89. Regarding the Spanish Civil War, M. R. Habeck, *Storm of Steel: The Development of Armor Doctrine in Germany and the Soviet Union, 1919–1939* (Ithaca, N.Y., 2003).

90. B. R. Posen, *The Sources of Military Doctrine: France, Britain and Germany between the World Wars* (Ithaca, N.Y., 1984); M. E. Brown, *Flying Blind: The Politics of the U.S. Strategic Bomber Program* (Ithaca, N.Y., 1992); E. Rhodes, "Do Bureaucratic Politics Matter? Some Disconfirming Findings from the Case of the U.S. Navy," *World Politics*

47 (1994): 1–41; K. M. Zisk, *Engaging the Enemy: Organization Theory and Soviet Military Innovation, 1955–1991* (Princeton, N.J., 1993); and P. J. Dombrowski, E. Cholz, and A. L. Ross, "Selling Military Transformation: The Defense Industry and Innovation," *Orbis* 48 (2002): 526–536.

91. A. J. Echeverria, *Imaging Future War: The West's Technological Revolution and Visions of War to Come, 1880–1914* (Westport, Conn., 2007).

92. Rutgers University Library, New Brunswick, N.J., Fuller papers, Box 4, report on India 1926, pp. 4, 48. For Fuller on weapons, J. F. C. Fuller, *Armament and History: A Study of the Influence of Armament on History from the Dawn of Classical Warfare to the Second World War* (London, 1946).

93. Committee on Co-ordination of Scientific Research, January 19, 1920, NA. CAB. 24/97, p. 460.

94. G. Hartcup, *The War of Invention* (London, 1983); and A. Saunders, *Reinventing Warfare 1914–18: Novel Munitions and Tactics of Trench Warfare* (London, 2012).

95. B. E. Seely, "SHOT, the History of Technology, and Engineering Education," *Technology and Culture* 36 (1995): 739–772; and J. A. Staudenmaier, "Rationality, Agency, Contingency: Recent Trends in the History of Technology," *Reviews in American History* 30 (2002): 168–181.

96. G. J. Bryant, "Asymmetric Warfare: The British Experience in Eighteenth-Century India," *Journal of Military History* 68 (2004): 431–469.

97. D. M. Drew, "U.S. Airpower Theory and the Insurgent Challenge: A Short Journey to Confusion," *Journal of Military History* 62 (1998): 809–832, esp. 824, 829–830; and C. Malkasian, *A History of Modern Wars of Attrition* (Westport, Conn., 2002), 205.

98. Dill to Field Marshal Montgomery-Massingberd, former chief of the Imperial General Staff, September 25, November 18, 1939, LH., MM. papers 10/14.

99. A. Bregman, *Israel's Wars, 1947–93* (London, 2000).

100. L. Lincoln, *The Japanese Army in North China, 1937–1941: Problems of Political and Economic Control* (Oxford, 1975).

101. I. F. W. Beckett, *Modern Insurgencies and Counter-Insurgencies* (London, 2001).

102. However, see recently C. J. Esdaile, *Outpost of Empire: The Napoleonic Occupation of Andalucía, 1810–1812* (Norman, Okla., 2012).

103. D. Omissi, *Air Power and Colonial Control: The Royal Air Force 1919–1939* (Manchester, 1990).

104. M. Dhada, "The Liberation War in Guinea-Bissau Reconsidered," *Journal of Military History* 62 (1998): 592.

105. S. R. McMichael, *Stumbling Bear: Soviet Military Performance in Afghanistan* (London, 1993); and L. W. Grau and M. A. Gress, eds., *The Soviet Afghan War: How a Superpower Fought and Lost* (Lawrence, Kans., 2002).

106. E. Goldsworthy, "Warfare in Context," *RUSI Journal* 148, no. 3 (June 2003): 19.

107. Black, *War and the Cultural Turn* (London, 2011).

108. J. Turner, *Filming History: The Memoirs of John Turner, Newsreel Cameraman* (London, 2002).

109. J. France, *Perilous Glory: The Rise of Western Military Power* (New Haven, Conn., 2011).

110. W. E. Bijker, T. P. Hughes, and T. I. Pinch, eds., *The Social Construction of Technological Systems: New Directions in the Sociology and History of Technology* (Cambridge, Mass., 1987); D. Mackenzie, *Inventing Accuracy: A Historical Sociology of Nuclear Mis-*

sile Guidance (Cambridge, Mass., 1990); M. R. Smith and L. Marx, eds., *Does Technology Drive History? The Dilemma of Technological Determinism* (Cambridge, Mass., 1994); and G. Spinardi, *From Polaris to Trident: The Development of U.S. Fleet Ballistic Missile Technology* (Cambridge, 1994).

1. EARLY MODERN WESTERN WARSHIPS

1. This period is usually considered to last until the late eighteenth century.

2. C. Cipolla, *Guns, Sails and Empires: Technological Innovation and the Early Phases of European Expansion 1400–1700* (London, 1965).

3. Major recent ones include K. Chase, *Firearms: A Global History to 1700* (Cambridge, 2003); S. McGrail, *Boats of the World: From the Stone Age to Medieval Times* (Oxford, 2001), P. A. Lorge, *The Asian Military Revolution: From Gunpowder to the Bomb* (Cambridge, 2008); and G. Casale, *The Ottoman Age of Exploration* (Oxford, 2010).

4. I. C. Campbell, "The Lateen Sail in World History," *Journal of World History* 6 (1995): 1–23.

5. R. Gardiner and R. W. Unger, eds., *Cogs, Caravals and Galleons: The Sailing Ship, 1000–1650* (London, 1994); and I. Fried, *The Good Ship: Ships, Shipbuilding and Technology in England, 1200–1520* (Baltimore, 1995).

6. I. V. Maroto, "The Art of Shipbuilding in Spain's Golden Century," *History of Technology* 30 (2010): 79.

7. J. F. Guilmartin, *Gunpowder and Galleys: Changing Technology and Mediterranean Warfare at Sea in the Sixteenth Century* (Cambridge, 1974).

8. N. A. M. Rodger, "The Development of Broadside Gunnery, 1450–1650," *Mariner's Mirror* 82 (1996): 301–324.

9. G. Parker, "The *Dreadnought* Revolution of Tudor England," *Mariner's Mirror* 82 (1996): 269–300.

10. R. D. Smith, "Wrought-Iron Swivel Guns," in *The Archaeology of Ships of War*, ed. M. Bound (Oxford, 1995), 104–113.

11. K. DeVries and R. D. Smith, *The Artillery of the Dukes of Burgundy, 1363–1477* (Woodbridge, UK, 2005).

12. A. B. Caruana, *The History of English Sea Ordnance, 1523–1875, vol. 1, The Age of Evolution, 1523–1715* (Rotherfield, UK, 1994), but see review by R. R. Brown, *Mariner's Mirror* 84 (1998): 100–102; B. Lavery, *The Arming and Fitting of English Ships of War, 1600–1815* (Annapolis, Md., 1987); J. F. Guilmartin, "The Earliest Shipboard Gunpowder Ordnance: An Analysis of Its Technicalities, Parameters and Tactical Capabilities," *Journal of Military History* 71 (2007): 649–669; and R. D. Smith, *Rewriting the History of Gunpowder* (Nykobing, Denmark, 2010).

13. A. da Silva Saturnino Monteiro, *Portuguese Sea Battles, vol. 1, The First World Sea Power, 1139–1521; vol. 2, Christianity, Commerce and Corso, 1522–1538* (Lisbon, 2010).

14. R. D. Smith, "Port Pieces: The Use of Wrought-Iron Guns in the Sixteenth Century," *Journal of the Ordnance Society* 5 (1993): 6–8.

15. K. DeVries, "The Effectiveness of Fifteenth-Century Shipboard Artillery," *Mariner's Mirror* 84 (1998): 396.

16. R. Romano, "Economic Aspects of the Construction of Warships in Venice in the Sixteenth Century," in *Crisis and Change in the Venetian Economy in the Sixteenth and Seventeenth Centuries*, ed. B. Pullan (London, 1968), 59–87.

17. C. Imber, "The Reconstruction of the Ottoman Fleet after the Battle of Lepanto," in *Studies in Ottoman History and Law* (Istanbul, 1996), 85–101.

18. J. D. Tracy, ed., *The Rise of Merchant Empires: Long-Distance Trade in the Early Modern World, 1350–1750* (Cambridge, 1990), and ed., *The Political Economy of Merchant Empires* (Cambridge, 1991).

19. L. Carson, *Ships and Seafaring in Ancient Times* (Austin, Tex., 1994); and J. R. Hale, *Lords of the Sea: The Epic Story of the Athenian Navy and the Birth of Democracy* (New York, 2009).

20. J. Glete, *Swedish Naval Administration, 1521–1721: Resource Flows and Organisational Capacities* (Leiden, 2010). See, more generally, J. Glete, *Navies and Nations: Warships, Navies and State Building in Europe and America, 1500–1860* (Stockholm, 1993), and *Warfare at Sea, 1500–1650: Maritime Conflicts and the Transformation of Europe* (London, 2000).

21. T. Glasgow, "The Shape of the Ships That Defeated the Spanish Armada," *Mariner's Mirror* 50 (1964): 177–188; and P. Hammer, *Elizabeth's Wars* (Basingstoke, UK, 2003), 149.

22. L. D. Ferreiro, *Ships and Science: The Birth of Naval Architecture in the Scientific Revolution, 1600–1800* (Cambridge, Mass., 2007).

23. J. Bennett and S. Johnston, *The Geometry of War, 1500–1750* (Oxford, 1996); and A. W. Crosby, *The Measure of Reality: Quantification and Western Society, 1250–1600* (Cambridge, 1997).

24. A. Pettegree, "Centre and Periphery in the European Book World," *Transactions of the Royal Historical Society*, 6th ser., 18 (2008): 101–128.

25. L. Levathes, *When China Ruled the Seas: The Treasure Fleet of the Dragon Throne, 1405–1433* (Oxford, 1994).

26. Y. Park, *Admiral Yi Sun-shin and His Turtleboat Armada: A Comprehensive Account of the Resistance of Korea to the 11th Century Japanese Invasion* (Seoul, 1973); and S. Turnbull, *Samurai Invasion: Japan's Korean War, 1592–1598* (London, 2002).

27. T. Andrade, *Lost Colony: The Untold Story of China's First Great Victory over the West* (Princeton, N.J., 2011).

28. Y. Dai, "A Disguised Defeat: The Myanmar Campaign of the Qing Dynasty," *Modern Asian Studies* 38 (2004): 166.

29. P. C. Perdue, *China Marches West: The Qing Conquest of Central Eurasia* (Cambridge, Mass., 2005); and Y Dai, *The Sichuan Frontier and Tibet: Imperial Strategy in the Early Qing* (Seattle, 2009).

30. A. Fuess, "Rotting Ships and Razed Harbors: The Naval Policy of the Mamluks," *Mamlūk Studies Review* 5 (2001): 67–70.

31. A. C. Roy, *Mughal Navy and Naval Warfare* (Calcutta, 1972).

32. P. Macdougall, "British Seapower and the Mysore Wars of the Eighteenth Century," *Mariner's Mirror* 97 (2011): 299–314.

33. A. C. Hess, "The Evolution of the Ottoman Seaborne Empire in the Age of the Oceanic Discoveries, 1453–1525," *American Historical Review* 74 (1970): 1892–1919; and P. Brummett, *Ottoman Seapower and Levantine Diplomacy in the Age of Discovery* (Albany, N.Y., 1994).

34. G. Casale, *The Ottoman Age of Exploration* (Oxford, 2010).

35. D. Baugh, "What Gave the British Navy Superiority?" in *Exceptionalism and Industrialisation: Britain and Its European Rivals, 1688–1815*, ed. L. P. de Esosura (Cambridge, 2004), 235–257.

36. A. Tenenti, *Piracy and the Decline of Venice, 1580–1615* (Berkeley, Calif., 1967); and W. Bracewell, *The Uskoks of Senj: Piracy, Banditry and Holy War in the Sixteenth Century Adriatic* (Ithaca, N.Y., 1992).

37. G. Parker, "The Limits to Revolutions in Military Affairs: Maurice of Nassau, the Battle of Nieuwpoort (1600), and the Legacy," *Journal of Military History* 71 (2007): 366–369.

38. J. Black, *War in the World, 1450–1600* (Basingstoke, UK, 2011).

39. M. Edwardes, ed., *Major John Corneille: Journal of My Service in India* (London, 1966), 55.

2. GUNPOWDER TECHNOLOGY, 1490–1800

1. E. Gibbon, *The History of the Decline and Fall of the Roman Empire*, ed. J. B. Bury, vol. 6 (London, 1897–1901), 12. See also vol. 4, 167.

2. C. J. Rogers, "The Idea of Military Revolutions in Eighteenth and Nineteenth Century Texts," *Revista de História das Ideias* 30 (2009): 397–399.

3. See most prominently M. Roberts, *The Military Revolution 1560–1660* (Belfast, 1956); G. Parker, *The Military Revolution: Military Innovation and the Rise of the West, 1500–1800*, 2nd ed. (Cambridge, 1996); and C. J. Rogers, ed., *The Military Revolution Debate: Readings on the Military Transformation of Early Modern Europe* (Boulder, Colo., 1995). For a regional example, W. Cook, *The Hundred Years War for Morocco: Gunpowder and the Military Revolution in the Early Modern Muslim World* (Boulder, Colo., 1994).

4. J. Black, *War in the World, 1450–1600* (Basingstoke, UK, 2011), *Beyond the Military Revolution: War in the Seventeenth-Century World* (Basingstoke, UK, 2011), and *War in the Eighteenth-Century World* (Basingstoke, UK, 2012).

5. J. Landers, *The Field and the Forge: Population, Production, and Power in the Pre-Industrial West* (Oxford, 2004).

6. E. Gray, H. Marsh, and M. McLaren, "A Short History of Gunpowder and the Role of Charcoal in Its Manufacture," *Journal of Materials Science* 17 (1982): 3385–3400; and J. Wisniak, "The History of Saltpeter Production with a Bit of Pyrotechnics and Lavoisier," *Chemical Educator* 5 (2000): 205–209.

7. P. A. Lorge, *The Asian Military Revolution: From Gunpowder to the Bomb* (Cambridge, 2008), 32–44. See also L. C. Goodrich and F. Chia-Sheng, "The Early Development of Firearms in China," *Isis* 36 (1946): 114–123; and J. Needham, *Military Technology: The Gunpowder Epic* (Cambridge, 1987), and *Gunpowder as the Fourth Power, East and West* (Hong Kong, 1985).

8. I. A. Khan, "Origin and Development of Gunpowder Technology in India, 1250–1500," *Indian Historical Review* 42 (1977): 20–29, and "Early Use of Cannon and Musket in India, 1442–1526," *Journal of the Economic and Social History of the Orient* 24 (1981): 146–164.

9. R. D. Smith and K. DeVries, *Rhodes Besieged: A New History* (Stroud, UK, 2011), 49–50.

10. K. Chase, *Firearms: A Global History to 1700* (Cambridge, 2003); and A. W. Crosby, *Throwing Fire: Projectile Technology through History* (Cambridge, 2002).

11. E. W. Marsden, *Greek and Roman Artillery: Historical Development* (Oxford, 1969).

12. J. Gommans, *Mughal Warfare* (London, 2002).

13. K. DeVries, *Medieval Military Technology*, 2nd ed. (Toronto, 2012).

14. Landers, *The Field and the Forge*.

15. K. DeVries, "The Impact of Gunpowder Weaponry on Siege Warfare in the Hundred Years War," in *The Medieval City under Siege,* ed. I. A. Corfis and M. Wolfe (Woodbridge, UK, 1995), 227–244.

16. B. S. Hall, *Weapons and Warfare in Renaissance Europe: Gunpowder, Technology and Tactics* (Baltimore, 1997), 20–23.

17. P. Purton, *A History of the Late Medieval Siege, 1200–1500* (Woodbridge, UK, 2010).

18. H. Nicholson, *Medieval Warfare* (Basingstoke, UK, 2004), 89.

19. K. DeVries and R. D. Smith, "Removable Powder Chambers in Early Gunpowder Weapons," in *Gunpowder, Explosives and the State: A Technological History,* ed. B. Buchanan (Aldershot, UK, 2006), 251–265.

20. W. F. Cook, "The Cannon Conquest of Nasrid Spain and the End of the Reconquista," *Journal of Military History* 57 (1993): 43–70. See also J. Vogt, "Saint-Barbara's Legions: Portuguese Artillery in the Struggle for Morocco," *Military Affairs* 41 (December 1977): 176–182.

21. Purton, *A History of the Late Medieval Siege,* 405.

22. C. J. Rogers, "The Artillery and Artillery Fortress Revolutions Revisited," in *Artillerie et Fortification 1200–1600,* ed. N. Prouteau et al. (Rennes, 2011), 78; and J. Gommans, "Warhorse and Gunpowder in India *c* 1000–1850," in *War in the Early Modern World,* ed. J. Black (London, 1999), 113.

23. S. Pepper, "Sword and Spade: Military Construction in Renaissance Italy," *Construction History* 16 (2000): 14.

24. J. F. Guilmartin, *Gunpowder and Galleys: Changing Technology and Mediterranean Warfare at Sea in the Sixteenth Century* (Cambridge, 1974).

25. R. D. Smith, *Rewriting the History of Gunpowder* (Nykobing, Denmark, 2010).

26. B. S. Hall, "The Corning of Gunpowder and the Development of Firearms in the Renaissance," in *Gunpowder,* ed. B. J. Buchanan (Bath, 1996), 93–94.

27. J. Sephton, *Sovereign of the Seas. The Seventeenth-Century Warship* (Stroud, UK, 2011), 110.

28. B. J. Buchanan, ed., *Gunpowder, Explosives and the State. A Technological History* (Farnham, UK, 2006); and D. Cressy, *Saltpeter: The Mother of Gunpowder* (Oxford, 2013).

29. T. May, *The Mongol Conquests in World History* (London, 2012).

30. S. Gordon, *Marathas, Marauders and State Formation in Eighteenth-Century India* (Oxford, 1994), 188.

31. L. Kaba, "Archers, Musketeers and Mosquitoes: The Moroccan Invasion of the Sudan and the Songhay Resistance, 1591–1612," *Journal of African History* 22 (1981): 457–475.

32. J. Alm, *European Crossbows: A Survey,* ed. G. M. Wilson (Leeds, 1994).

33. C. J. Rogers, "The Development of the Longbow in Late Medieval England and 'Technological Determinism,'" *Journal of Medieval History* 37 (2011): 340.

34. B. S. Hall, *Weapons and Warfare in Renaissance Europe* (Baltimore, 1997).

35. T. Esper, "The Replacement of the Longbow by Firearms in the English Army," *Technology and Culture* 6 (1965): 382–389; and G. Phillips, "Longbow and Hackbutt, Weapons Technology and Technology Transfer in Early Modern England," *Technology and Culture* 40 (1999): 576–593.

36. K. DeVries, "Gunpowder Weapons at the Siege of Constantinople, 1453," in *War, Army and Society in the Eastern Mediterranean, 7th–16th Centuries* ed. Y. Lev (Leiden, 1996); and M. Philippides and W. K. Kanack, *The Siege and the Fall of Constantinople in 1453* (Farnham, UK, 2011).

37. C. Heywood, *Writing Ottoman History* (Aldershot, UK, 2002), no continuous pagination, section 16, pp. 5, 12.

38. Kritovoulus, *History of Mehmed the Conqueror,* trans. C. T. Riggs (Princeton, N.J., 1954), 171; and R. Irwin, "Gunpowder and Firearms in the Mamluk Sultanate Reconsidered," in *The Mamluks in Egyptian and Syrian Politics and Society,* ed. M. Winter and A. Levanoni (Leiden, 2004), 124, 134.

39. J. E. Woods, *The Aqquyunlu, Clan, Confederation, Empire: A Study in 15th/9th Century Turko-Iranian Politics* (Minneapolis, 1976), 132–144.

40. Irwin, "Gunpowder and Firearms," 136–138.

41. H. Inalcik and R. Murphey, eds., *The History of Mehmed the Conqueror by Tursun Beg* (Minneapolis, 1978), 62.

42. G. Phillips, *The Anglo-Scots War 1513–1550: A Military History* (Woodbridge, UK, 1999).

43. J. Raymond, "Henry VIII and the English Military Establishment," *Archives* 28 (2003): 112.

44. N. Machiavelli, *The Art of War,* trans. E. Farneworth (Indianapolis, 1965), 47–51.

45. M. C. Fissel, *English Warfare, 1511–1642* (London, 2001), 285; F. Gilbert, "Machiavelli: The Renaissance in the Art of War," in *Makers of Modern Strategy: From Machiavelli to the Nuclear Age,* ed. P. Paret (Princeton, N.J., 1986), 11–31; D. A. Neill, "Ancestral Voices: The Influence of the Ancients on the Military Thought of the Seventeenth and Eighteenth Centuries," *Journal of Military History* 62 (1998): 487–520; and B. Heuser, "Denial of Change: The Military Revolution as Seen by Contemporaries." I would like to thank Beatrice Heuser for letting me read this unpublished paper.

46. L. A. DiMarco, *War Horse: A History of the Military Horse and Rider* (Yardley, Pa., 2007).

47. L. King, ed., *Memoirs of . . . Babur,* vol. 2 (Oxford, 1921), 186–187.

48. G. Robinson, "Equine Battering Rams? A Reassessment of Cavalry Charges in the English Civil War," *Journal of Military History* 75 (2011): 719–731.

49. T. May, *The Mongol Art of War: Chinggis Khan and the Mongol Military System* (Yardley, Pa., 2007).

50. R. I. Frost, *The Northern Wars, 1558–1721* (London, 2000), 310–312; and W. Majewski, "The Polish Art of War in the Sixteenth and Seventeenth Centuries," in *A Republic of Nobles: Studies in Polish History to 1864,* ed. J. K. Fedorowicz (Cambridge, 1982), 179–197.

51. O. van Nimwegen, *The Dutch Army and the Military Revolutions 1588–1688* (Woodbridge, UK, 2010).

52. J. A. Lynn, "Forging the Western Army in Seventeenth-Century France" in *The Dynamic of Military Revolution, 1300–2050,* ed. M. Knox and W. Murray (Cambridge, 2001), 39–40, and *Giant of the Grand Siècle: The French Army, 1610–1715* (Cambridge, 1997), 476.

53. A. Balisch, "Infantry Battlefield Tactics in the Seventeenth and Eighteenth Centuries on the European and Turkish Theatres of War: The Austrian Response to Different Conditions," *Studies in History and Politics* 3 (1983–1984): 44. For the longevity of the bayonet, J. Stone, "The Point of the Bayonet," *Technology and Culture,* 53 (2012), pp. 885–908.

54. H. Kleinschmidt, "Using the Gun: Manual Drill and the Proliferation of Portable Firearms," *Journal of Military History* 63 (1999): 601–629.

55. D. B. Ralston, *Importing the European Army: The Introduction of European Military Techniques and Institutions into the Extra-European World, 1600–1914* (Chicago, 1990); J. Waley-Cohen, "China and Western Technology in the Late Eighteenth Century,"

American Historical Review 98 (1993): 1531–1532; and S. Shaw, "The Origins of Ottoman Military Reform: The *Nizam-I Cedid* Army of Sultan Selim III," *Journal of Modern History* 37 (1965): 291–295.

56. A. B. Pernal and D. F. Essar, eds., *A Description of Ukraine,* by Guillaume Le Vasseur (Cambridge, Mass., 1993).

57. F. Willmoth, *Sir Jonas Moore: Practical Mathematics and Restoration Science* (Woodbridge, UK, 1993).

58. I would like to thank Brian Davies for letting me read a prepublication copy of "Military Engineers and the Rise of Imperial Russia."

59. I. Boavbida, M. H. Pennec, and M. J. Ramos, *Pedro Páez's "History of Ethiopia," 1622,* vol. 2 (London, 2011), 327. See also 331.

60. J. Ostwald, *Vauban under Siege: Engineering Efficiency and Martial Vigor in the War of the Spanish Succession* (Leiden, 2007).

61. S. Bull, *The Furie of the Ordnance: Artillery in the English Civil War* (Woodbridge, UK, 2008).

62. See also, e.g., Jacob de Gheyn, *Wapenhandelinghe van roers, musquetten ende spiessen* (Amsterdam, 1608); and Adam van Breen, *Le Maniement d'armes de Nassau* (The Hague, 1618).

63. A. Pettegree, "Centre and Periphery in the European Book World," *Transactions of the Royal Historical Society* 6th ser., 18 (2008): 101–128.

64. K. W. Swope, "Crouching Tigers, Secret Weapons: Military Technology Employed during the Sino-Japanese-Korean War, 1592–1598," *Journal of Military History* 69 (2005): 37.

65. S. Morillo, "Guns and Government: A Comparative Study of Europe and Japan," *Journal of World History* 6 (1995): 105–106.

3. FIREPOWER, STEAMSHIPS, RAILWAYS, TELEGRAPHS, RADIO

The epigraph is from Burgoyne, BL. Add. 41410 fol. 2.

1. S. T. Ross, *From Flintlock to Rifle: Infantry Tactics, 1740–1866,* 2nd ed. (London, 1996).

2. For the value of breech-loading rifles, A. R. McGinnis, "When Courage Was Not Enough: Plains Indians at War with the United States Army," *Journal of Military History* 76 (2012): 459–460. For a warning against an exaggeration of the role of firearms, J. J. Guy, "A Note on Firearms in the Zulu Kingdom with Special Reference to the Anglo-Zulu War, 1879," *Journal of African History* 12 (1971): 557–570; and H. Bailes, "Technology and Imperialism: A Case Study of the Victorian Army in Africa," *Victorian Studies* 24 (1980): 83–104.

3. R. Jonas, *The Battle of Adwa: African Victory in the Age of Empire* (Cambridge, Mass., 2011), 150.

4. G. Phillips, "Military Morality Transformed: Weapons and Soldiers on the Nineteenth-Century Battlefield," *Journal of Interdisciplinary History* 41 (2011): 565–590.

5. G. Wawro, "An 'Army of Pigs': The Technical, Social, and Political Bases of Austrian Shock Tactics, 1859–1866," *Journal of Military History* 59 (1995): 411–433.

6. M. J. Bastable, "From Breechloaders to Monster Guns: Sir William Armstrong and the Invention of Modern Artillery, 1854–1880," *Technology and Culture* 33 (1992): 213–247.

7. R. M. Ripperger, "The Development of French Artillery for the Offensive, 1890–1914," *Journal of Military History* 59 (1995): 599–618.

8. M. Epkenhans, "Military-Industrial Relations in Imperial Germany, 1870–1914," *War in History* 10 (2003): 1–26.

9. R. Chickering, "Introduction: A Tale of Two Tales: Grand Narratives of War in the Age of Revolution," in *War in an Age of Revolution, 1775–1815*, ed. R. Chickering and S. Förster (Cambridge, 2010), 3–4.

10. D. Bell, *The Idea of Greater Britain: Empire and the Future of World Order, 1860–1900* (Princeton, N.J., 2007), 80.

11. J. H. Pryor, ed., *Logistics of Warfare in the Age of the Crusades* (Farnham, UK, 2006).

12. A. Roland, *Underwater Warfare in the Age of Sail* (Bloomington, Ind., 1978).

13. F. Winter, *The First Golden Age of Rockets: Congreve and Hale Rockets of the Nineteenth Century* (Washington, D.C., 1991).

14. J. L. Busch, *Steam Coffin: Captain Moses Rogers and the Steamship "Savannah" Break the Barrier* (New Canaan, Conn., 2010).

15. E. A. M. Laing, "The Introduction of Paddle Frigates into the Royal Navy," *Mariner's Mirror* 66 (1980): 221–229.

16. B. Greenhill and A. Gifford, *Steam, Politics and Patronage: The Transformation of the Royal Navy, 1815–54* (London, 1994); and A. D. Lambert, "Responding to the Nineteenth Century: The Royal Navy and the Introduction of the Screw Propeller," *History of Technology* 21 (1999): 1–28, esp. 25.

17. Fulton to William, Lord Grenville, British Prime Minister, September 2, 1806, BL. Add. 71593 fol. 134.

18. Y. Park, *Admiral Yi Sun-shin and His Turtleboat Armada* (Seoul, 1973).

19. A. Lambert, "'I Will Not Have a War with France.' Deterrence, Diplomacy and Mid-Victorian Politics," in *HMS Warrior: 150th Anniversary*, ed. A. P. Baines (Portsmouth, UK, 2011), 19–34.

20. J. P. Baxter, *The Introduction of the Ironclad Warship* (Cambridge, Mass., 1933).

21. J. W. Kipp, "The Russian Navy and the Problem of Technological Transfer," in *Russia's Great Reforms, 1855–1881*, ed. B. Eklof et al. (Bloomington, Ind., 1994), 129.

22. H. Holzer and T. Milligan, eds., *The Battle of Hampton Roads* (New York, 2006); and D. A. Mindell, *Iron Coffin: War, Technology, and Experience Aboard the USS Monitor*, 2nd ed. (Baltimore, 2012).

23. Lord Lyons, envoy in Washington, to John, Earl Russell, Foreign Secretary, April 13, 1863, April 25, 1864, NA. FO. 5/881 fols. 165–166, 5/948 fols. 119–120; and H. J. Fuller, "'This Country Now Occupies the Vantage Ground': Understanding John Ericsson's Monitors and the American Union's War against British Naval Superiority," *American Neptune* 62 (2002): 91–111, and *Clad in Iron: The American Civil War and the Challenge of British Naval Power* (Westport, Conn., 2008), 282.

24. C. I. Hamilton, *The Anglo-French Naval Rivalry, 1840–1870* (Oxford, 1993); and A. Lambert, "Politics, Technology and Policy-Making, 1859–1865: Palmerston, Gladstone and the Management of the Ironclad Naval Race," *Northern Mariner* 8 (1998): 9–38.

25. *Manchester Courier*, March 29, 1862. For a comparison of the *Monitor* with the British *Warrior*, cf. April 5, 1862.

26. This section benefits greatly from the advice of Howard Fuller and takes a different view to that of J. F. Beeler, *British Naval Policy in the Gladstone-Disraeli Era, 1866–*

1880 (Stanford, Calif., 1997), 199–200; and W. H. Roberts, *Civil War Ironclads: The U.S. Navy and Industrial Mobilization* (Annapolis, Md., 2002). On the weakness of American guns, report in April 1865, NA. FO. 5/1017 fol. 226.

27. Captain James Goodenough to Lyons, April 9, 1864, NA. FO. 5/948 fol. 136. See also Lyons to Russell, April 25, 1864, ibid. fol. 120.

28. M. S. Seligmann, "New Weapons for New Targets: Sir John Fisher, the Threat from Germany, and the Building of HMS *Dreadnought* and HMS *Invincible*, 1902–1907," *International History Review* 30 (2008): 325.

29. M. A. Smith, *Engineering Security: The Corps of Engineers and Third System Defense Policy, 1815–1861* (Tuscaloosa, Ala., 2009).

30. T. J. Crick, *Ramparts of Empire: The Fortifications of Sir William Jervois, Royal Engineer, 1821–1897* (Exeter, 2012), 52–84.

31. W. H. Thiesen, *Industrializing American Shipbuilding: The Transformation of Ship Design and Construction, 1820–1920* (Gainesville, Fla., 2006).

32. E. Gray, *Nineteenth Century Torpedoes and Their Inventors* (Annapolis, Md., 2004).

33. A. Røksund, *The Jeune École: The Strategy of the Weak* (Leiden, 2007).

34. J. Roberts, *The Battleship "Dreadnought,"* 2nd ed. (London, 2006); E. Grove, "The Battleship Is Dead: Long Live the Battleship: HMS *Dreadnought* and the Limits of Technological Innovation," *Mariner's Mirror* 93, no. 4 (2007): 415–427; N. Friedman, *Naval Firepower: Battleship Guns and Gunnery in the Dreadnought Era* (Annapolis, Md., 2008); and R. J. Blyth, A. Lambert, and J. Rüger, eds., *The "Dreadnought" and the Edwardian Age* (Aldershot, UK, 2011).

35. D. Howse, *Radar at Sea: The Royal Navy in World War 2* (Basingstoke, UK, 1993), 123–124.

36. A. Lambert, *The Crimean War: British Grand Strategy against Russia, 1853–56,* 2nd ed. (Farnham, UK, 2011), 349–350.

37. F. Patrikeeff and H. Shukman, *Railways and the Russo-Japanese War: Transporting War* (Abingdon, UK, 2009).

38. F. C. Schneid, "A Well-Coordinated Affair: Franco-Piedmontese War Planning in 1859," *Journal of Military History* 76 (2012): 395–425.

39. H. Mackinder, "The Geographical Pivot of History," *Geographical Journal* 23 (1904): 421–437.

40. Graham to Raglan, January 10, 1854, BL. Add. 79696 fol. 87.

41. For a valuable cautious note, A. D. Harvey, "Was the Civil War the First Modern War?" *History* (2012): 272–280.

42. E. Hagerman, "Field Transportation and Strategic Mobility in the Union Armies," *Civil War History* 34 (1988): 171.

43. NMM. Milne papers 124/2.

44. R. C. Black, *The Railroads of the Confederacy* (Chapel Hill, N.C., 1998).

45. E. A. Pratt, *The Rise of Rail-Power in War and Conquest, 1833–1914* (Philadelphia, 1916); and D. Showalter, *Railroads and Rifles: Soldiers. Technology and the Unification of Germany* (Hamden, Conn., 1975).

46. Regarding Russia, *Trewman's Exeter Flying-Post,* December 20, 1882.

47. B. A. Elleman and S. Kotkin, *Manchurian Railways and the Opening of China: An International History* (Armonk, N.Y., 2010).

48. T. G. Otte and K. Neilson, eds., *Railways and International Politics: Paths of Empire, 1848–1945* (London, 2006).

49. R. Beal and R. Macleod, *Prairie Fire: The North-West Rebellion of 1885* (Edmonton, 1984).

50. I. J. Kerr, *Building the Railways of the Raj, 1850–1900* (Oxford, 1995).

51. D. Stevenson, "War by Timetable? The Railway Race before 1914," *Past and Present* 162 (1999): 163–194.

52. R. Dunn, *Narrow Gauge to No Man's Land: U.S. Army 60 cm Gauge Railways of the First World War in France* (Los Altos, Calif., 2009).

53. S. Willis, *Fighting at Sea in the Eighteenth Century: The Art of Sailing Warfare* (Woodbridge, UK, 2008).

54. James Craggs, Secretary of State, to John, 2nd Earl of Stair, envoy in Paris, April 2, 9, 16, 1719, NA. SP. 104/30.

55. J. Langins, "The École Polytechnique and the French Revolution: Merit, Militarisation, and Mathematics," *Llull* 13 (1990): 91–105; and K. Alder, *Engineering the Revolution: Arms and Enlightenment in France, 1763–1815* (Princeton, N.J., 1997).

56. G. J. Holzmann and B. Pehrson, *The Early History of Data Networks* (Washington, D.C., 1995), 52–64.

57. J. Gleick, *The Information: A History, a Theory, a Flood* (London, 2011), 19–21, 140–161.

58. T. Standage, *The Victorian Internet: The Remarkable Story of the Telegraph and the Nineteenth-Century's On-Line Pioneers* (London, 1998).

59. G. Cookson, *The Cable: The Wire That Changed the World* (Stroud, UK, 2003); and D. P. Nickles, *Under the Wire: How the Telegraph Changed Diplomacy* (Cambridge, Mass., 2003).

60. C. Bright, *Imperial Telegraphic Communication* (London, 1911); P. M. Kennedy, "Imperial Cable Communications and Strategy, 1879–1914," *English Historical Review* 86 (1971): 728–752; and D. R. Headrick, *The Invisible Weapon: Telecommunications and International Politics, 1851–1945* (New York, 1991).

61. J. R. Winkler, *Nexus: Strategic Communications and American Security in World War I* (Cambridge, Mass., 2008).

62. A. Anduaga, *Wireless and Empire: Geopolitics, Radio Industry and Ionosphere in the British Empire, 1918–1939* (New York, 2009).

63. K. Kotani, *Japanese Intelligence in World War II* (Oxford, 2009).

64. J. B. A. Bailey, *Field Artillery and Firepower*, 2nd ed. (Annapolis, Md., 2004).

65. Schneid, "A Well-Coordinated Affair."

66. A. M. Bell, *Mosquito Soldiers: Malaria, Yellow Fever, and the Course of the American Civil War* (Baton Rouge, La., 2010).

4. THE INTERNAL COMBUSTION ENGINE

1. M. S. Seligmann, "A View from Berlin: Colonel Frederick Trench and the Development of British Perceptions of German Aggressive Intent, 1906–1910," *Journal of Strategic Studies* 23 (2000): 131.

2. BL. Add. 49703 fols. 128–129.

3. T. Pidgeon, *The Tank at Flers* (Cobham, UK, 1995).

4. D. T. Zabecki, *The German 1918 Offensives: A Case Study in the Operational Level of War* (Abingdon, UK, 2006).

5. AWM. 3 DRL 6643, 5/27, pp. 1–3.

6. D. J. Childs, *A Peripheral Weapon? The Production and Employment of British Tanks in the First World War* (Westport, Conn., 1998).

7. Chetwode to Montgomery-Massingberd, September 6, 1921, LH. MM. 8/22; and W. Ryan, "The Influence of the Imperial Frontier on British Doctrines of Mechanised Warfare," *Albion* 15 (1983): 123–142.

8. G. Phillips, "Douglas Haig and the Development of Twentieth-Century Cavalry," *Archives* 28 (2003): 160.

9. J. E. Alvarez, "Tank Warfare during the Rif Rebellion," *Armor* 106 (1997): 26–28.

10. LH. MM. 9/5/7, quotes pp. 9–10, 21. For the situation in the United States, G. F. Hofmann, *Through Mobility We Conquer: The Mechanization of U.S. Cavalry* (Lexington, Ky., 2006); and R. S. Cameron, *Mobility, Shock, and Firepower: The Emergence of the U.S. Army's Armor Branch, 1917–1945* (Fort McNair, Washington D.C., 2008). For Britain, J. P. Harris, *Men, Ideas, and Tanks: British Military Thought and Armored Forces, 1903– 1939* (Manchester, 1995).

11. LH. Milne papers, Box 3, quote p. 3.

12. S. H. Newton, ed., *Panzer Operations: The Eastern Front Memoir of General Raus, 1941–1945* (Cambridge, Mass., 2003).

13. For examples, D. Stahel, *Kiev 1941: Hitler's Battle for Supremacy in the East* (Cambridge, 2012), 74, 162–163, 227, 296, 326.

14. T. Andrade, *Lost Colony: The Untold Story of China's First Great Victory over the West* (Princeton, N.J., 2011), 326.

15. R. Ellenblum, *Crusader Castles and Modern Histories* (Cambridge, 2007).

16. G. Patton, "The Effect of Weapons on War," *Infantry Journal* 37, no. 5 (November 1930).

17. S. G. Fritz, *Ostkrieg: Hitler's War of Extermination in the East* (Lexington, Ky., 2011), 114–115.

18. LH. Alanbrooke papers 6/2/37.

19. O'Connor to Major-General Allan Adair, July 24, 1944, LH. O'Connor papers, 5/3/22.

20. C. J. McInnes, *Men, Machines and the Emergence of Modern Warfare, 1914–1945* (Camberley, UK, 1992), 39.

21. *Executive Sessions of the Senate Foreign Relations Committee*, vol. 11, 1959 (Washington, D.C., 1982), 125.

22. Z. Levey, *Israel and the Western Powers, 1952–1960* (Chapel Hill, N.C., 1997).

23. M. Uhl, "Storming on to Paris: The 1961 *Buria* Exercise and the Planned Solution to the Berlin Crisis," in *War Plans and Alliances in the Cold War: Threat Perceptions East and West*, ed. V. Mastny, S. G. Holtsmark, and A. Wenger (London, 2006), 46–71.

24. I have benefited greatly from the advice of Anthony Saunders in the section on tanks.

25. R. Osgood, *Limited War: The Challenge to American Strategy* (Chicago, 1957).

26. I. Trauschweizer, *The Cold War U.S. Army: Building Deterrence for Limited War* (Lawrence, Kans., 2008).

27. S. Bronfeld, "Fighting Outnumbered: The Impact of the Yom Kippur War on the U.S. Army," *Journal of Military History* 71 (2007): 477–478.

28. J. L. Young, "The Heights of Ineptitude: The Syrian Army's Assault on the Golan Heights," *Journal of Military History* 74 (2010): 852–870.

29. D. Andrade, *America's Last Vietnam Battle: Halting Hanoi's 1972 Eastern Offensive* (Lawrence, Kans., 2001).

30. *Daily Telegraph*, December 8, 2011.

31. Minutes by the General Staff, September 1919, NA. CAB. 24/89 fol. 11.

32. NA. WO. 33/2764 p. 257.

33. Young, "The Heights of Ineptitude," 864.

34. W. M. Donnelly, *Transforming an Army at War: Designing the Modular Force, 1991–2005* (Washington, D.C., 2007), 19–25.

35. M. Bowden, *Black Hawk Down: A Story of Modern War* (New York, 1999).

36. R. J. Reardon and J. A. Charlston, *From Transformation to Combat: The First Stryker Brigade at War* (Washington, D.C., 2007), 70.

37. R. L. DiNardo, *Mechanized Juggernaut or Military Anachronism? Horses and the German Army of World War II* (Westport, Conn., 1991).

38. M. R. Finlay, *Growing American Rubber: Strategic Plants and the Politics of National Security* (New Brunswick, N.J., 2009).

39. K. D. Gott, *Breaking the Mold: Tanks in the Cities* (Fort Leavenworth, Kans., 2006).

40. J. Bahadur, *The Pirates of Somalia: Inside Their Hidden World* (New York, 2011); and M. N. Murphy, *Somalia: The New Barbary? Piracy and Islam in the Horn of Africa* (London, 2011).

5. A NEW SPHERE

The epigraph is from NA. CAB. 24/250 fol. 119.

1. The best recent guide is provided by J. A. Olsen, ed., *A History of Air Warfare* (Washington, D.C., 2010).

2. NA. WO. 106/6/87.

3. Hamilton to Sir William Nicholson, January 2, 1909, LH. Hamilton papers 4/2/7; and A. Gollin, *No Longer an Island: Britain and the Wright Brothers, 1902–1909* (London, 1984).

4. W. F. Trimble, *Hero of the Air: Glenn Curtiss and the Birth of Naval Aviation* (Annapolis, Md., 2010); and P. E. Coletta, *Admiral A. Fiske and the American Navy* (Lawrence, Kans., 1980).

5. A. Gollin, *The Impact of Air Power on the British People and Their Government, 1909–1914* (London, 1989); and H. Driver, *The Birth of Military Aviation: Britain, 1903–1914* (Woodbridge, UK, 1997).

6. M. Paris, "The First Air Wars—North Africa and the Balkans, 1911–13," *Journal of Contemporary History* 26 (1991): 97–109.

7. H. Herwig, *The Battle of the Marne* (New York, 2009).

8. Callwell to General Sir William Birdwood, March 31, 1915, AWM, 3 DRL/3376, 11/4.

9. N. Grundy, *W. L. Wyllie, R.A.: The Portsmouth Years* (Portsmouth, UK, 1996).

10. D. Juniper, "Gothas over London," *Royal United Services Institute Journal* 148, no. 4 (2003): 74–80.

11. L. Kennett, *The First Air War, 1914–1918* (New York, 1991); J. H. Morrow, *The Great War in the Air: Military Aviation from 1909 to 1921* (Washington, D.C., 1993); M. Cooper, *The Birth of Independent Air Power* (London, 1986); G. K. Williams, *Biplanes and Bombsights: British Bombing in World War I* (Maxwell Air Force Base, Ala., 1999); and R. Martel, *French Strategic and Tactical Bombardment Forces of World War I*, ed. S. Suddaby (Lanham, Md., 2007).

12. M. Clodfelter, *Beneficial Bombing: The Progressive Foundations of American Air Power, 1917–1945* (Lincoln, Neb., 2010).

13. M. Paris, "The Rise of the Airmen: The Origins of Air Force Elitism, c. 1890–1918," *Journal of Contemporary History* 28 (1993): 123–141.

14. G. R. Perras and K. E. Kellner, "'A Perfectly Logical and Sensible Thing': Billy Mitchell Advocates a Canadian-American Aerial Alliance against Japan," *Journal of Military History* 72 (2008): 786.

15. J. I. Holwitt, "Reappraising the Interwar U.S. Navy," *Journal of Military History* 76 (2012): 199.

16. M. Paris, "Air Power and Imperial Defence 1880–1919," *Journal of Contemporary History* 24 (1989): 209–225.

17. J. Lewis, *Racing Ace: The Fights and Flights of Samuel "Kink" Kinkead* (Barnsley, UK, 2011), 104–108.

18. A. M. Roe, *Waging War in Waziristan: The British Struggle in the Land of Bin Laden, 1849–1947* (Lawrence, Kans., 2010), and "'Pink's War'—Applying the Principles of Air Control to Waziristan, 1925," *Air Power Review* 13, no. 3 (Autumn/Winter 2010): 97–117.

19. M. Darlow and B. Bray, *Ibn Saud* (London, 2010), 283.

20. Military Report on Mesopotamia (Iraq), Area 1 (Northern Jazirah), 1922, NA. WO. 33/2758, p. 39. See also note by the General Staff on British Military Liabilities, June 9, 1920, NA. CAB. 24/107 fol. 255.

21. D. Omissi, *Air Power and Colonial Control: The Royal Air Force 1919–1939* (Manchester, UK, 1990).

22. L. B. Poullada, *Reform and Rebellion in Afghanistan, 1919–1929* (Ithaca, N.Y., 1973).

23. The Bayerische Flugzeugwerke was renamed Messerschmitt AG in 1938 when Willy Messerschmidt acquired the company, but the air-frames were all marked Bf rather than Me.

24. Chiefs of Staff Sub-Committee, Annual Review, November 9, 1933, NA. CAB/24/244 fol. 138.

25. Report by G. H. Thompson, October 13, 1937, NA. CAB/24/271 fol. 303.

26. Chiefs of Staff Sub-Committee, "Appreciation of the Situation in the Event of War against Germany," September 14, 1938, NA. CAB/24/278 p. 356.

27. U. Bialer, *The Shadow of the Bomber: The Fear of Air Attack and British Politics, 1932–1939* (London, 1980).

28. J. Gleick, *The Information: A History, a Theory, a Flood* (London, 2011), 187, 237–239.

29. F. Krome, ed., *Fighting the Future War: An Anthology of Science Fiction War Stories, 1914–1945* (New York, 2011), 176–183.

30. J. P. Duffy, *Target: America: Hitler's Plan to Attack the United States* (Westport, Conn., 2004).

31. J. S. Corum, *Wolfram von Richtofen: Master of the German Air War* (Lawrence, Kans., 2008).

32. P. Addison and J. A. Crang, eds., *The Burning Blue: A New History of the Battle of Britain* (London, 2000); and R. J. Overy, *The Battle* (London, 2002).

33. A. Harvey, "The Battle of Britain in 1940 and 'Big Week' in 1944: A Comparative Perspective," *Air Power History* 59, no. 1 (Spring 2012): 35.

34. A. J. Cumming, *The Royal Navy and the Battle of Britain* (Annapolis, Md., 2010).

35. D. Tyrett, "Communications Intelligence and the Battle of the Atlantic, 1943–1945," *Archives* 22, no. 98 (April 1995): 59.

36. D. V. Smith, *Carrier Battles: Command Decision in Harm's Way* (Annapolis, Md., 2006).

37. Strategic review for regional commanders, August 16, 1941, AWM, 3DRL/6643, 1/27.

38. J. F. C. Fuller, *The Second World War 1939–1945: A Strategical and Tactical History* (Cambridge, Mass., 1993), 401.

39. I have benefited greatly from the advice of Anthony Saunders.

40. R. J. Overy, *The Air War 1939–1945* (London, 1987); S. L. McFarland and W. P. Newton, *To Command the Sky: The Battle for Air Superiority, 1942–4* (Washington, D.C., 1991); H. Boog, ed., *The Conduct of the Air War in the Second World War: An International Comparison* (New York, 1992); N. Gregor, "A *Schicksalsgemeinschaft?* Allied Bombing, Civilian Morale, and Social Dissolution in Nuremberg, 1942–1945," *Historical Journal* 43 (2000): 1051–1070; and E. Hammel, *The Road to Big Week: the Struggle for Daylight Air Supremacy over Western Europe: July 1942—February 1944* (Pacifica, Calif., 2009).

41. I. Gooderson, *Air Power at the Battlefront: Allied Close Air Support in Europe, 1943–1945* (London, 1998).

42. R. A. Slayton, *Master of the Air: William Tunner and the Success of Military Airlift* (Tuscaloosa, Ala., 2010); and J. D. Plating, *The Hump: America's Strategy for Keeping China in World War II* (College Station, Tex., 2011).

43. T. Downing, *Spies in the Sky: The Secret Battle for Aerial Intelligence during World War II* (London, 2011), 332.

44. K. P. Wervell, *Blankets of Fire: U.S. Bombers over Japan during World War II* (Washington, D.C., 1996); and H. S. Wolk, *Cataclysm: General Hap Arnold and the Defeat of Japan* (Denton, Tex., 2010).

45. D. J. Hanle, *Near Miss: The Army Air Forces' Guided Bomb Program in World War II* (Lanham, Md., 2007).

46. I. Kershaw, *The End: Hitler's Germany, 1944–45* (London, 2011), 269, 299.

47. S. M. Pavelec, *The Jet Race and the Second World War* (Westport, Conn., 2007).

48. M. Balous, J. Rajlich, and M. Velek, *Messerschmitt Me 262* (Prague, 1995).

49. Z. Shen and D. Li, *After Leaning to One Side: China and Its Allies in the Cold War* (Washington, D.C., 2011), 76.

50. C. C. Crane, *American Air Power Strategy in Korea, 1950–1953* (Lawrence, Kans., 2000); X. Zhang, *Red Wings over the Yalu: China, the Soviet Union, and the Air War in Korea* (College Station, Tex., 2002); A. R. Millett, *The War for Korea, 1950–1951: They Came from the North* (Lawrence, Kans., 2010); and R. B. Bruce, "Tethered Eagle: Lt. Gen. James A. Van Fleet and the Quest for Military Victory in the Korean War, April–June 1951," *Army History* 82 (Winter 2012):14, 17.

51. D. J. Mrozek, *Air Power and the Ground War in Vietnam: Ideas and Actions* (Maxwell Air Force Base, Ala., 1988); M. Clodfelter, *The Limits of Airpower: The American Bombing of North Vietnam* (New York, 1989); W. Thompson, *To Hanoi and Back: The U.S. Air Force and North Vietnam, 1966–1973* (Washington, D.C., 2000); and S. W. Wilson, "Taking Clodfelter One Step Further: Mass Surprise, Concentration and the Failure of Operation Rolling Thunder," *Air Power History* 48 (2001): 40–47.

52. M. L. Pribbenow, "The 'Ology War: Technology and Ideology in the Vietnamese Defense of Hanoi, 1967," *Journal of Military History* 67 (2003): 175–200.

53. S. Stanton, *The First Cav in Vietnam: Anatomy of a Division* (Novato, Calif., 1999).

54. M. B. Oren, *Six Days of War: June 1967 and the Making of the Modern Middle East* (Oxford, 2002).

55. Z. Schiff and E. Ya'ari, *Israel's Lebanon War* (London, 1984).

56. A. Cordesman, "Preliminary 'Lessons' of the Israeli-Hizbullah War," *Military Power Review* 2 (2006): 33–52.

57. J. Haslam, *Russia's Cold War* (New Haven, Conn., 2011), 271.

58. J. A. Olsen, *Strategic Air Power in Desert Storm* (London, 2003).

59. B. S. Lambeth, *NATO's Air War for Kosovo: A Strategic and Operational Assessment* (Santa Monica, Calif., 2001).

60. S. Biddle, *Afghanistan and the Future of Warfare* (Carlisle, Pa., 2002).

61. E. B. Westermann, "The Limits of Soviet Airpower: The Failure of Military Coercion in Afghanistan, 1979–1989," *Journal of Conflict Studies* 19 (1999): 39–71.

62. G. Torpy, "Counter-Insurgency: Echoes from the Past," *Royal United Services Institute Journal* 152, no. 5 (October 2007): 22.

63. J. Stephenson, *The 1994 Zapatista Rebellion in Southern Mexico, an Analysis and Assessment* (Camberley, UK, 1995), 17–18.

64. S. I. Schwartz, ed., *Atomic Audit: The Costs and Consequences of U.S. Nuclear Weapons since 1940* (Washington, D.C., 1998), 58; and R. Rhodes, *The Making of the Atomic Bomb* (New York, 1988).

65. P. A. Ndiaye, *Nylon and Bombs: DuPont and the March of Modern America* (Baltimore, 2007).

66. M. Walker, *German National Socialism and the Quest for Nuclear Power, 1939–1945* (New York, 1989); P. Henshall, *The Nuclear Axis: Germany, Japan, and the Atomic Bomb Race, 1939–1945* (Stroud, UK, 2001); and J. Cornwell, *Hitler's Scientists: Science, War and the Devil's Pact* (London, 2004).

67. K. P. Werrell, *Blankets of Fire: U.S. Bombers over Japan during World War II* (Washington, D.C., 1996).

68. Major-General William Penney, Director of Intelligence, HQ Supreme Allied Commander S.E. Asia, to Major-General John Sinclair, Director of Military Intelligence, British War Office, May 2, 1945, LH. Penney papers 5/1.

69. B. J. Bernstein, "Truman and the A-Bomb," *Journal of Military History* 62 (1998): 547–570; and D. McCullough, *Truman* (New York, 1992), 458.

70. W. D. Miscamble, *The Most Controversial Decision: Truman, the Atomic Bombs, and the Defeat of Japan* (Cambridge, 2011).

71. D. M. Giangreco, *Hell to Pay: Operation DOWNFALL and the Invasion of Japan, 1945–1947* (Annapolis, Md., 2009).

72. S. J. Maddock, *Nuclear Apartheid: The Quest for American Atomic Supremacy from World War II to the Present* (Chapel Hill, N.C., 2010).

73. *Foreign Relations of the United States 1946*, vol. 1 (Washington, D.C., 1972), 1198–1199.

74. G. Herken, *The Winning Weapon: The Atomic Bomb in the Cold War, 1945–1950* (New York, 1990); H. R. Borowski, *A Hollow Threat: Strategic Air Power and Containment before Korea* (Westport, Conn., 1982); and G. H. Quester, *Nuclear Monopoly* (New Brunswick, N.J., 2000).

75. British Chancery in Washington to American Department, Foreign Office, August 2, 1950, NA. FO. 37/81655.

76. C. C. Crane, "To Avert Impending Disaster: American Military Plans to Use Atomic Weapons during the Korean War," *Journal of Strategic Studies* 23 (2000): 2–88.

77. C. J. Bright, *Continental Defense in the Eisenhower Era: Nuclear Antiaircraft Arms and the Cold War* (New York, 2010).

78. W. S. Borgiasz, *The Strategic Air Command: Evolution and Consolidation of Nuclear Forces 1945–55* (New York, 1996); S. Dockrill, *Eisenhower's New-Look National Se-*

curity Policy, 1953–61 (Basingstoke, UK, 1996); and D. A. Carter, "Eisenhower versus the Generals," *Journal of Military History* 71 (2007): 1169–1199.

79. M. Farish, *The Contours of America's Cold War* (Minneapolis, 2010).

80. R. Jervis, *The Meaning of the Nuclear Revolution: Statecraft and the Prospect of Armageddon* (Ithaca, N.Y., 1989).

81. B. C. Hacker, *American Military Technology: The Life Story of a Technology* (Baltimore, 2006).

82. B. P. Greene, *Eisenhower, Science Advice, and the Nuclear Test-Ban Debate, 1945–1963* (Palo Alto, Calif., 2007).

83. A. Norberg and J. O'Neill, *Transforming Computer Technology: Information Processing for the Pentagon, 1962–1986* (Baltimore, 1996); and A. Roland and P. Shiman, *Strategic Computing: DARPA and the Quest for Machine Intelligence, 1983–1993* (Cambridge, Mass., 2000).

84. D. Kahn, *The Reader of Gentlemen's Mail: Herbert O. Yardley and the Birth of American Codebreaking* (New Haven, Conn., 2004).

85. S. Larington, *Moving Targets: Elliott-Automation and the Dawn of the Computer Age in Britain, 1947–67* (London, 2011).

86. C. S. Gray, "The Nuclear Age and the Cold War," in *The Practice of Strategy: From Alexander the Great to the Present*, ed. J. A. Olsen and C. S. Gray (Oxford, 2011), 254.

87. K. P. Werrell, *Death from the Heavens: A History of Strategic Bombing* (Annapolis, Md., 2009).

88. *Executive Sessions of the Senate Foreign Relations Committee*, vol. 12, 1960 (Washington, D.C., 1982), 7.

89. D. L. Snead, *The Gaither Committee, Eisenhower and the Cold War* (Columbus, Ohio, 1999).

90. B. Heuser, *NATO, Britain, France and the FRG: Nuclear Strategies and Forces for Europe, 1949–2000* (Basingstoke, UK, 1997).

91. L. V. Scott, *Macmillan, Kennedy and the Cuban Missile Crisis: Political, Military and Intelligence Aspects* (Basingstoke, UK, 1999).

92. T. Greenwood, *Making the MIRV: A Study in Defense Decision Making* (Cambridge, Mass., 1975); and D. K. Stumpf, *Titan II: A History of a Cold War Missile Program* (Fayetteville, S.C., 2000).

93. R. Rhodes, *Dark Sun: The Making of the Hydrogen Bomb* (New York, 1995).

94. D. E. Hoffman, *The Dead Hand: Reagan, Gorbachev and the Untold Story of the Cold War Arms Race* (London, 2011).

95. J. Haslam, *Russia's Cold War* (New Haven, Conn., 2011), 353–354.

96. The best introduction to the entire period is provided by M. Leffler and O. A. Westad, eds., *Cambridge History of the Cold War* (Cambridge, 2010).

97. O. Coté, "The Trident and the Triad: Collecting the D-5 Dividend," *International Security* 16 (1991): 117–145.

98. D. Chang, *Nuclear Showdown: North Korea Takes on the World* (London, 2007).

99. I. Shields and J. Spencer, "An Unmanned Future for Naval Aviation: UAV Carriers," *RUSI Journal* 156, no. 6 (December 2012): 48–54.

100. W. J. Boyne, *How the Helicopter Changed Modern Warfare* (Gretna, La., 2011).

101. P. W. Singer, "Robots at War: The New Battlefield," in *The Changing Character of War,* ed. H. Strachan and S. Scheipers (Oxford, 2011), 337; and "The Year of the

Drone: An Analysis of Drone Strikes in Pakistan, 2004–2011," http://counterterrorism .newamerica.net/drones.

102. D. J. Dean, *The Air Force Role in Low-Intensity Conflict* (Maxwell Air Force Base, Ala., 1986); and J. Hayward, ed., *Air Power, Insurgency and the "War on Terror"* (Cranwell, UK, 2009).

103. R. M. Basrur, *South Asia's Cold War* (London, 2008).

104. J. Mueller, *Atomic Obsession: Nuclear Alarmism from Hiroshima to Al Qaeda* (Oxford, 2011).

105. T. Yoshihara and J. R. Holmes, *Red Star over the Pacific: China's Rise and the Challenge to U.S. Maritime Strategy* (Annapolis, Md., 2010); F. K. Chang, "China's Naval Rise and the South China Sea: An Operational Assessment," *Orbis* 56 (Winter 2012): 23–24; and A. S. Erickson, A. M. Denmark, and G. Collins, "Beijing's 'Starter Carrier' and Future Steps," *Naval War College Review* 65 (2012): 26–27.

106. R. C. Rubel, "The Future of Aircraft Carriers," *Naval War College Review* 64, no. 4 (Autumn 2011): 19–26.

107. D. W. Barno, N. Bensahel, and T. Sharp, *Hard Choices: Responsible Defense in an Age of Austerity* (Washington, D.C., 2011).

6. REVOLUTION, TRANSFORMATION, AND THE PRESENT

1. S. Pinker, *The Better Angels of Our Nature: The Decline of Violence in History and Its Causes* (London, 2011).

2. P. Porter, *Military Orientalism: Eastern War through Western Eyes* (London, 2009).

3. R. R. Leonhard, *The Art of Maneuver: Maneuver-Warfare Theory and AirLand Battle* (Novato, Calif., 1991); and L. Freedman, *The Revolution in Strategic Affairs* (Oxford, 1998).

4. C. Coker, *The Warrior Ethos: Military Culture and the War on Terror* (London, 2007).

5. N. Galay, "The Soviet Approach to the Modern Military Revolution," in *The Military-Technical Revolution: Its Impact on Strategy and Foreign Policy,* ed. J. Erickson (London, 1966), 20–34.

6. A. R. Lewis, "The American Culture of War in the Age of Artificial Limited War," in *Warfare and Culture in World History,* ed. W. E. Lee (New York, 2011), 195; and C. S. Gray, *Weapons for Strategic Effect: How Important Is Technology?* (Maxwell Air Force Base, Ala., 2001), 35. Gray struck a skeptical note.

7. C. S. Gray, "Technology as a Dynamic of Defence Transformation," *Defence Studies* 6 (2006): 33.

8. C. Pursell, introduction to *A Companion to American Technology,* ed. C. Pursell (Oxford, 2005), 1.

9. B. Berkowitz, *The New Face of War: How War Will Be Fought in the 21st Century* (New York, 2003).

10. B. M. Linn, *The Echo of Battle—The Army's Way of War* (Cambridge, Mass., 2007).

11. T. G. Mahnken and J. R. FitzSimonds, *The Limits of Transformation: Officer Attitudes toward the Revolution in Military Affairs* (Newport, R.I., 2003), 111.

12. W. J. Astore, "Loving the German War Machine: America's Infatuation with *Blitzkrieg,* Warfighters and Militarism," in *Arms and the Man: Military History Essays in Honor of Dennis Showalter,* ed. M. S. Neiberg (Leiden, 2011), 14–17, 29.

13. S. Biddle, "Victory Misunderstood: What the Gulf War Tells Us about the Future of Conflict," *International Security* 21 (1996): 139–179.

14. T. G. Mahnken, *Technology and the American Way of War since 1945* (New York, 2008), 198.

15. J. R. Blaker, *Transforming Military Force: The Legacy of Arthur Cebrowski and Network-Centric Warfare* (Westport, Conn., 2007).

16. J. J. McGrath, *Crossing the Line of Departure: Battle Command on the Move—A Historical Perspective* (Fort Leavenworth, Kans., 2006), 225.

17. P. K. Van Riper and F. G. Hoffman, "Pursuing the Real RMA: Exploiting Knowledge-Based Warfare," *National Security Studies Quarterly* 4, no. 3 (Summer 1998): 1–19.

18. B. Owens, *Lifting the Fog of War* (New York, 2000).

19. G. Adams and G. Ben-Ari, *Transforming European Militaries: Coalition Operations and the Technology Gap* (London, 2006).

20. A. J. Bacevich, *The New American Militarism—How Americans Are Seduced by War* (Oxford, 2006); and T. Ricks, *Fiasco: The American Military Adventure in Iraq* (New York, 2006).

21. F. Zakaria, *The Post-American World* (London, 2008).

22. R. D. Fisher, *China's Military Modernization: Building for Regional and Global Reach* (Westport, Conn., 2008).

23. Q. Liang and W. Xiangsui, *Unrestricted Warfare: Assumptions on War and Tactics in an Age of Globalization* (Beijing, 1999); and P. Guangqian and Y. Youzhi, eds., *The Science of Military Strategy* (Beijing, 2005).

24. J. Bailey, *The First World War and the Birth of the Modern Style of Warfare* (Camberley, UK, 1996), 33.

25. C. J. Rogers, *Essays on Medieval Military History: Strategy, Military Revolutions and the Hundred Years War* (Farnham, UK 2010); and M. C. Prestwich, "The Gunpowder Revolution, 1300–1500," in *The Medieval World at War*, ed. M. Bennett (London, 2009), 183–203. For a non-firepower revolution, B. S. and D. S. Bachrach, "Saxon Military Revolution, 912–973? Myth and Reality," *Early Medieval History* 15 (2007): 186–222. For the value of history, P. O. Hundley, *Past Revolutions, Future Transformations: What Can the History of Revolutions in Military Affairs Tell Us about Transforming the U.S. Military?* (Santa Monica, Calif., 1999); and C. S. Gray, *Strategy for Chaos: Revolutions in Military Affairs and the Evidence of History* (London, 2003).

26. T. Benbow, *The Magic Bullet? Understanding the Revolution in Military Affairs* (London, 2004).

27. K. L. Shimko, *The Iraq Wars and America's Military Revolution* (Cambridge, 2010), esp. 21–25.

28. J. Hayward, ed., *Air Power, Insurgency and the "War on Terror"* (Cranwell, UK, 2009).

29. D. Marston and C. Malkasian, eds., *Counterinsurgency in Modern Warfare* (London, 2008).

30. S. Bronfeld, "Fighting Outnumbered: The Impact of the Yom Kippur War on the U.S. Army," *Journal of Military History* 71 (2007): 465–498.

31. D. N. Livingstone, *Putting Science in Its Place: Geographies of Scientific Knowledge* (Chicago, 2003).

32. K. Lieber, *War and the Engineers: The Primacy of Politics over Technology* (Ithaca, N.Y., 2008).

7. INTO THE FUTURE

1. E. Rhodes, "Do Bureaucratic Politics Matter? Some Disconfirming Findings from the Case of the US Navy," *World Politics* 47 (1994): 34.

2. For a warning of the need not to focus on asymmetric threats, S. Haines, "The Real Strategic Environment," *Royal United Services Institute Journal* 152, no. 5 (October 2007): 16.

3. Development, Concepts and Doctrine Centre (UK), *Global Strategic Trends—Out to 2040* (Shrivenham, UK, 2010), 145.

4. M. Howard, "The Transformation of Strategy," *Royal United Services Institute Journal,* 156, no. 4 (September 2011): 15–16.

5. A. J. Echevarria, *Fourth-Generation Warfare and Other Myths* (Carlisle, Pa., 2005).

6. J. Record, *Beating Goliath: Why Insurgencies Win* (Dulles, Va., 2007).

7. D. Edgerton, *The Shock of the Old: Technology and Global History since 1900* (Oxford, 2007).

8. Development, Concepts and Doctrine Centre (UK), *Global Strategic Trends,* 21.

9. R. C. Rubel, "The Navy's Changing Force Paradigm," *Naval War College Review* 62, no. 2 (2009): 18–19, 22.

10. A. Davies, "Up Periscope: The Expansion of Submarine Capabilities in the Asia-Pacific Region," *Royal United Services Institute Journal,* 152, no. 5 (October 2007): 65.

11. K. Schake, "Margin Call: How to Cut a Trillion from Defense," *Orbis* 56 (Winter 2012): 12–13.

12. R. Johnson, "The Army in India and Responses to Low-Intensity Conflict, 1936–1946," *Journal of the Society for Army Historical Research* 89 (2011): 174.

13. M. R. Smith, *Harpers Ferry Armory and the New Technology: The Challenge of Change* (Ithaca, N.Y., 1977).

CONCLUSIONS

The epigraph is from LH. Fuller papers, 4/6/24/2.

1. J. Tucci, "Warfare in the Ancient World," *Journal of Military History* 74 (2010): 886.

2. E. Wauters, "'Like Salt in a Fire . . .' Two Local Eyewitness Accounts of the Battle of Oudenarde," in *1708: Oudenarde and Lille,* ed. D. Money (Cambridge, 2008), 42.

3. G. Robinson, "Equine Battering Rams? A Reassessment of Cavalry Charges in the English Civil War," *Journal of Military History* 75 (2011): 719–731.

4. R. A. Fox, *Archaeology, History, and Custer's Last Battle: The Little Big Horn Reexamined* (Norman, Okla., 1993); J. Schofield, W. G. Johnson, and C. M. Beck, eds., *Matériel Culture: The Archaeology of Twentieth Century Conflict* (London, 2002); D. Scott, L. Babits, and C. Haecker, eds., *Fields of Conflict: Battlefield Archaeology from the Roman Empire to the Korean War* (Westport, Conn., 2007); and E. H. Cline and A. Sutter, "Battlefield Archaeology at Armageddon: Cartridge Cases and the 1948 Battle for Megiddo, Israel," *Journal of Military History* 75 (2011): 159–190.

5. For a recent example, T. E. Hanon, *Combat Ready? The Eighth U.S. Army on the Eve of the Korean War* (College Station, Tex., 2010).

6. D. Redford, *The Submarine: A Cultural History from the Great War to Nuclear Combat* (London, 2010).

7. I have benefited greatly from discussing this issue with Anthony Saunders.

8. A. Giustozzi, *Koran, Kalashnikov and Laptop: The Neo-Taliban Insurgency in Afghanistan* (London, 2007).

9. P. Bobbitt, *Terror and Consent: The Wars for the Twenty-First Century* (London, 2008).

10. G. C. Peden, *Arms, Economics, and British Strategy: From Dreadnoughts to Hydrogen Bombs* (Cambridge, 2007).

11. S. Biddle, *Military Power: Explaining Victory and Defeat in Modern Battle* (Princeton, N.J., 2004).

12. J. Black, *War and the Cultural Turn* (London, 2011).

POSTSCRIPT

1. U.S. Department of Defense, *Sustaining U.S. Global Leadership: Priorities for 21st Century Defense* (Washington, D.C., 2012).

Selected Further Reading

Bailey, J. *The First World War and the Birth of the Modern Style of Warfare.* 1996.

Black, J. *Beyond the Military Revolution: War in the Seventeenth-Century World.* 2011.

———. *The Great War and the Making of the Modern World.* 2011.

Brodie, B., and F. M. Brodie. *From Crossbow to H-Bomb: The Evolution of the Weapons and Tactics of Warfare.* 1973.

Buchanan, B. J., ed. *Gunpowder, Explosives and the State: A Technological History.* 2006.

Buckley, J. *Air Power in the Age of Total War.* 1999.

Cardwell, D. *Wheels, Clocks, and Rockets: A History of Technology.* 1995.

Cipolla, C. *Guns, Sails and Empires: Technological Innovation and the Early Phases of European Expansion 1400–1700.* 1965.

Creveld, M. van. *Technology and War: From 2000 BC.* 1989.

Donnelly, W. M. *Transforming an Army at War: Designing the Modular Force, 1991–2005.* 2007.

Dupuy, T. N. *The Evolution of Weapons and Warfare.* 1984.

Echevarria, A. *Fourth-Generation Warfare and Other Myths.* 2005.

France, J. *Perilous Glory: The Rise of Western Military Power.* 2011.

Freedman, L. *The Revolution in Strategic Affairs.* 1998.

Fuller, H. J. *Clad in Iron: The American Civil War and the Challenge of British Naval Power.* 2008.

Gat, A. *British Armor Theory and the Rise of the Panzer Arm: Revising the Revisionists.* 2000.

Glete, J. *Navies and Nations: Warships, Navies and State Building in Europe and America, 1500–1860.* 1993.

Gordon, A. *The Rules of the Game: Jutland and British Naval Command.* 1996.

Groot, G. de. *The Bomb: A Life.* 2004.

Guilmartin, J. F. *Gunpowder and Galleys: Changing Technology and Mediterranean Warfare at Sea in the Sixteenth Century.* 1974.

Hacker, B. C. *American Military Technology: The Life Story of a Technology.* 2007.

Hartcup, G. *The Silent Revolution: Development of Conventional Weapons 1945–85.* 1993.

Headrick, D. R. *Technology: A World History.* 2009.

———. *The Tools of Empire: Technology and European Imperialism in the Nineteenth Century.* 1981.

Holloway, D. *Stalin and the Bomb.* 1994.

Johnson, D. E. *Fast Tanks and Heavy Bombers: Innovation in the U.S. Army, 1917–1945.* 1998.

Kennett, L. *The First Air War, 1914–1918.* 1991.

———. *A History of Strategic Bombing.* 1982.

Lambert, N. *Sir John Fisher's Naval Revolution.* 1999.

Leonhard, R. R. *The Art of Maneuver: Maneuver-Warfare Theory and AirLand Battle.* 1991.

Lieber, K. *War and the Engineers: The Primacy of Politics over Technology.* 2008.

Lonsdale, D. *The Nature of War in the Information Age.* 2004.

Lorge, P. A. *The Asian Military Revolution: From Gunpowder to the Bomb.* 2008.

Macgregor, D. A. *Transformation under Fire: Revolutionizing How America Fights.* 2003.

Macksey, K. *Technology in War: The Impact of Science on Weapon Development and Modern Battle.* 1986.

Mahnken, T. G. *Technology and the American Way of War since 1945.* 2008.

McBridge, W. M. *Technological Change and the United States Navy, 1865–1945.* 2000.

McClelland, J. E., and H. Dorn *Science and Technology in World History.* 1999.

McNeill, W. H. *The Pursuit of Power: Technology, Armed Force, and Society since A.D. 1000.* 1982.

Millett, A., and W. Murray, eds. *Military Effectiveness: The Interwar Period.* 1988.

Omissi, D. *Air Power and Colonial Control: The Royal Air Force 1919–1939.* 1990.

Pryor, J. H. *Geography, Technology and War: Studies in the Maritime History of the Mediterranean, 649–1571.* 1988.

Rogers, C. J., ed. *The Oxford Encyclopedia of Medieval Warfare and Military Technology.* 2010.

Scales, R. H. *Yellow Smoke: The Future of Land Warfare for America's Military.* 2003.

Shrader, C. R. *The First Helicopter War: Logistics and Mobility in Algeria, 1954–1962.* 1999.

Sondhaus, L. *Naval Warfare, 1815–1914.* 2000.

———. *Navies in Modern World History.* 2004.

Sumida, J. T. *In Defense of Naval Supremacy: Finance, Technology, and British Naval Policy, 1899–1914.* 1989.

Winton, H. R., and D. R. Mets, eds. *The Challenge of Change: Military Institutions and New Realities, 1914–1941.* 2000.

Wright, P. *Tank: Progress of a Monstrous War Machine.* 2002.

Index

JEREMY BLACK is Professor of History at the University of Exeter. His books include *Fighting for America: The Struggle for Mastery in North America, 1519–1871* (IUP, 2011) and *War and the Cultural Turn*. Black received the Samuel Eliot Morison Prize from the Society for Military History in 2008.